TORTURE, TERROR, A

SCHOOL OF ORIENTAL AND AFRICAN STUDIES
University of London

Please return this book on or before the last date shown

Long loans and One Week loans may be renewed up to 10 times
Short loans & CD's cannot be renewed
Fines are charged on all overdue items

Online: http://lib.soas.ac.uk/patroninfo
Phone: 020 7898 4197 (answerphone)

Torture, Terror, and Trade-Offs

Philosophy for the White House

JEREMY WALDRON

OXFORD

UNIVERSITY PRESS

OXFORD

UNIVERSITY PRESS

Great Clarendon Street, Oxford OX2 6DP

Oxford University Press is a department of the University of Oxford.
It furthers the University's objective of excellence in research, scholarship,
and education by publishing worldwide in

Oxford   New York

Auckland Cape Town Dar es Salaam Hong Kong Karachi
Kuala Lumpur Madrid Melbourne Mexico City Nairobi
New Delhi Shanghai Taipei Toronto

With offices in

Argentina Austria Brazil Chile Czech Republic France Greece
Guatemala Hungary Italy Japan Poland Portugal Singapore
South Korea Switzerland Thailand Turkey Ukraine Vietnam

Oxford is a registered trade mark of Oxford University Press
in the UK and in certain other countries

Published in the United States
by Oxford University Press Inc., New York

First published 2010
First published in paperback 2012

British Library Cataloguing-in-Publication Data

Data available

Library of Congress Cataloging-in-Publication Data
Waldron, Jeremy.
 Torture, terror, and trade-offs : philosophy for the White House /
 Jeremy Waldron.
   p. cm.
 ISBN 978–0–19–958504–5
 1. War on Terrorism, 2001–2009. 2. Terrorism—United States—
 Prevention. 3. Torture—United States. I. Title.
 HV6432.W35 2010
 363.325′160973—dc22   2010010489

Typeset by Newgen Imaging Systems (P) Ltd., Chennai, India
Printed and bound by
CPI Group (UK) Ltd, Croydon, CR0 4YY

ISBN 978–0–19–958504–5 (hbk)
        978–0–19–965202–0 (pbk)

1 3 5 7 9 10 8 6 4 2

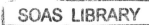

For Sam
to remember how important this is

Acknowledgments

With three exceptions, the papers collected here have been previously published. (One of them (Chapter 9) is being published more or less at the same time as this volume.) I am grateful to the editors of the journals and volumes concerned for permission to include them here. There has been some slight modification of text and footnotes, to update the arguments and the citations. Thanks are due as follows:

Chapter 2. 'Security and Liberty: The Image of Balance,' *Journal of Political Philosophy*, 11 (2003), 191.

Chapter 3. 'Terrorism and the Uses of Terror,' *The Journal of Ethics*, 8 (2004), 5.

Chapter 5. 'Safety and Security,' *Nebraska Law Review*, 85 (2006), 454.

Chapter 6. 'Security as a Basic Right (after 9/11)' in Charles Beitz and Robert Goodin (eds), *Global Basic Rights* (Oxford University Press, 2009), 207.

Chapter 7. 'Torture and Positive Law: Jurisprudence for the White House,' *Columbia Law Review*, 105 (2005), 1681.

Chapter 8. 'What Can Christian Teaching Add to the Debate about Torture?' *Theology Today*, 63 (2006), 330.

Chapter 9. 'Cruel, Inhuman, and Degrading Treatment: The Words Themselves,' forthcoming in *Canadian Journal of Law and Jurisprudence* (2010).

Chapter 10. 'The Rule of International Law,' *Harvard Journal of Law & Public Policy*, 30 (2006), 15.

Many of them, in various versions, have been presented at workshops and as public lectures in various places around the world, and I have been the beneficiary of the comments of innumerable colleagues and friends. I would like to express my particular gratitude to the following, whose comments and support have been especially helpful: Jose Alvarez, Victor Austin, Akeel Bilgrami, Eric Cave, Jean Cohen, William Dailey, Meir Dan-Cohen, Jules Coleman, Ronald Dworkin, Harold Edgar, Sian Elias, Jon Elster, Richard Fallon, the late Tom Franck, Charles Fried, David Garland, Conor Gearty, Jack Goldsmith, David Golove, Robert Goodin, Kent Greenawalt, Karen Greenberg, David Gushee, Moshe Halbertal, Bob Hargrave, Les Holborow, Stephen Holmes, Scott

Horton, Kirstin Howard, Grant Huscroft, Sam Issacharoff, Sanford Kadish, George Kateb, Benedict Kingsbury, Chris Kutz, Jacob Levy, David Lieberman, Deborah Livingston, Robin Lovin, David Luban, Campbell McLachlan, Jeff McMahan, Stephen Macedo, John Manning, Andrew Meade, Tamar Meisels, Frank Michelman, Martha Minow, Michael Moore, Glyn Morgan, Alan Musgrave, Tom Nagel, Gerald Neuman, Mary-Ellen O'Connell, Matthew Palmer, Stephen Perry, Richard Pildes, Susan Poser, Richard Posner, Eric Rakowski, Joseph Raz, Richard Revesz, Maritza Ryan, Samuel Scheffler, David Schmidtz, Henry Shue, Jerome Skolnick, William Storrar, the late Gwen Taylor, Dennis Thompson, Sam Waldron, Neil Walker, Joseph Weiler, and Melissa Williams. Alex Flach has been a fine editor at OUP. As always, I owe more than I can say to Carol Sanger, companion in these dark times, bearer of love and good cheer.

Contents

1

Introduction

Things changed on September 11, 2001. But despite what some people said, not everything changed.

Americans' understanding of the worst that terrorists could do to us certainly changed, as did the long experience of continental invulnerability against outside attack enjoyed by the American people since the last days of the war of 1812. (There had been terrorist attacks in the continental United States before, but they were homegrown terrorists—like Timothy McVeigh—with domestic grievances. And apart from some Japanese balloon-borne incendiaries in 1944–5, there had been no foreign attack on the American mainland since 1814. There was war certainly, from 1861–5, but it had the character of a massive internal rebellion.) But after September 11, things were different. We needed to change security arrangements for public buildings and our practices of search and scrutiny for passengers boarding airplanes; we strengthened the cockpit doors on our airliners; we began keeping better track of visitors to our shores; and we changed some of the arrangements for securing our ports against the importation of dangerous goods, including radiological bombs and weapons of mass destruction. (Many people believe that these arrangements need further strengthening still.)

We realized, too, that we could not stand by and let a country like Afghanistan become a safe haven for terror training camps and Al Qaeda operations, and we are still living with the consequences of that decision in the military operations that continue in that country (at the cost so far, at the time of writing, of more than 900 Americans killed and thousands seriously wounded).[1] There was an all-out effort to identify and apprehend terrorist operatives, particularly those associated with Al Qaeda, to find out as much as we could about the operation, to eavesdrop on anything that might remotely be considered a communication

---

[1] This was written in mid-November 2009. (The numbers here do not include the toll of the war in Iraq.)

between Al Qaeda operatives and fellow travelers, to disrupt their financing, and to interdict their operations. We refocused much of our foreign policy and almost all of our domestic security policy on anti-terrorism concerns and we pushed hard to ensure that as many other countries in the world as possible took the events of 9/11 and the sense of foreboding generated by those events as seriously as we did. Much of this represented a departure from our previous practices, lax and unfo-cused as they were. Those practices had to change after 9/11.

But some things did not change. Terrorist acts of the sort that we saw on September 11, 2001 were prohibited by law and condemned as wrong and murderous by morality on September 10 just as they were on September 12. Considered as acts of war, they were deliberate and egre-gious violations of the laws and customs of armed conflict. Considered as crimes—which they were—they were acts of mass murder. The moral-ity of terrorism didn't change on September 11. The spectacle did and many more people thought more about terrorism after the 9/11 events or condemned it more vehemently. Some of this thinking meant that people became both more precise, but also at the margins less confident, about the exact meaning of 'terrorism' and its distinction from other military doctrines and other kinds of crime. There has been a fruitful discussion of all that, to which Chapter 3 of this volume is a contribu-tion: what is morally or legally distinctive about terrorism? What distin-guishes it from other forms of murder or other forms of armed attack?

With a very few exceptions, this renewed focus on the concept of ter-rorism has not led to any revision in our evaluation of it, except perhaps at the margins where opinions may differ as to whether it is appropriate to use the term to cover such things as revolutionary armed struggle, partisan insurgency, unexpected attacks on armed forces (in barracks, for example), and the use of weapons of mass destruction against civilian populations by well-established states.[2] But the 9/11 attacks were right in the center, not at the margins, of the idea of terrorism. And so far as the core of the concept is concerned, the basis for condemning terrorism has remained constant: as I explain at the beginning of Chapter 4, ter-rorists make a military doctrine out of murdering civilians with the hope of exploiting to political and military advantage the terror and trauma likely to be occasioned by such a brazen violation of the laws of armed

---

[2] For a useful review and assessment of possible justifications for terrorism, see Saul 'Defending "Terrorism": Justifications and Excuses for Terrorism in International Criminal Law.' Saul notes, quite rightly, that the more encompassing the definition of 'terrorism,' the greater the chance that it may include some actions that seem justifiable.

conflict. That is why terrorism is always wrong, and that didn't change on September 11, 2001.

But other things stayed the same too, things whose constancy disconcerted those who were trying to prevent a repetition of the 9/11 attacks. There are certain things that a community may do to protect itself. But there are certain things that it may not do, even when they are thought to be necessary, and the list of these remained roughly the same. For example, though it was appropriate for the United States and its allies to apprehend, detain, and interrogate large numbers of terrorist suspects around the world, it would not have been appropriate—it would have been legally and constitutionally forbidden—to simply 'round up' American residents of Muslim faith or Arab extraction and concentrate them in camps, in order to sort out at leisure who was a suspect and who wasn't.[3] The laws prohibiting this did not change, and it was not something that anyone tried to do.

Other things remained unlawful, although they happened. The laws relating to torture did not change after 9/11. Torture remained absolutely forbidden by international law (by treaties that the United States has signed and ratified)[4] and domestic legislation (by a statute that Congress enacted in 1994).[5] The legal prohibition on torture was then and is now unequivocal and unconditional: there is no provision in law for the occurrence of traumatic events like those of 9/11 (or the prospect of their repetition) to make a difference to the legal status of deliberately inflicting severe mental or physical pain in the course of interrogation. In some bodies of human rights law, the prohibition on torture is made absolute in a very literal sense: the provision which permits some derogation from human rights in times of 'public emergency which threatens the life of the nation' is said explicitly not to apply under any circumstances to torture or the prohibition on inhuman and degrading treatment.[6] In other bodies of law, such as the U.S. Anti-Torture statute,

[3] This was the scenario envisaged in a movie made a year or two before 9/11, *The Siege* (20th Century Fox, 1998), directed by Edward Zwick starring Denzel Washington, Annette Bening, and Bruce Willis.

[4] See International Convention on Civil and Political Rights (ICCPR), Article 7; and Convention against Torture and Other Cruel, Inhuman or Degrading Treatment or Punishment.

[5] USC Title 18, Part I, Chapter 113C—Torture (§§ 2340–2340B).

[6] See, e.g. ICCPR Article 4: '(1) In time of public emergency which threatens the life of the nation and the existence of which is officially proclaimed, the States Parties to the present Covenant may take measures derogating from their obligations under the present Covenant to the extent strictly required by the exigencies of the situation, provided that such measures are not inconsistent with their other obligations under international law

there is no such explicit doctrine, because there is no arrangement for derogation of any provisions; the absoluteness of the rule against torture is simply inferred directly from its categorical imposition. No provision is made by legislation for any emergency exception and speculative attempts to exploit the criminal law doctrines of justification or necessity—e.g. by officials in the Justice Department's Office of Legal Counsel[7]—have usually met with skepticism from human rights lawyers. In the wake of 9/11, many of us assumed that the prohibitions on these practices would stand.[8]

Not only was there no change in the unlawfulness of torture after 9/11, even in the face of what seemed like an enhanced prospect of more destructive terrorist attacks and a pressing need for information to pre-empt them, but I believe there was no change in its moral status either. Torture was and remains a moral as well as a legal abomination. I did not say nearly enough about its moral wrongness in the article on torture that became Chapter 7 of this volume,[9] so let me try to say something here.

and do not involve discrimination solely on the ground of race, colour, sex, language, religion or social origin. (2) No derogation from article [ ] . . . 7 . . . may be made under this provision.'

[7] See Bybee, 'Standards of Conduct for Interrogation under 18 U.S.C. 2340–2340A,' in Greenberg and Dratel (eds), *The Torture Papers*, pp. 207–9. The obvious argument against the availability of a necessity defense is the law's insistence on the absolute nature of the prohibition. As Meisels points out ('Torture and the Problem of Dirty Hands', *Canadian Journal of Law and Jurisprudence*, 21 (2008) 149 at 167–8), the 'Convention [a]gainst Torture explicitly states that: "No exceptional circumstances whatsoever, whether a state of war, internal political instability or any other public emergency may be invoked as a justification of torture." And this should almost certainly be taken to apply to any necessity defense as well.'

[8] In July 2002, a Committee of Ministers of the Council of Europe (the organization responsible for the European Convention on Human Rights) adopted a set of guidelines for the fight against terror that included a reaffirmation of the absolute prohibition of torture. See *Guidelines on Human Rights and the Fight Against Terrorism* available at <http://www.coe.int/T/E/human_rights/h-inf(2002)8eng.pdf>. 'The use of torture or of inhuman or degrading treatment or punishment is absolutely prohibited, in all circumstances, and in particular during the arrest, questioning and detention of a person suspected of . . . terrorist activities, irrespective of the nature of the acts that the person is suspected of . . . ' For this reference I am grateful to Levinson, ' "Precommitment" and "Postcommitment": The Ban on Torture in the Wake of September 11,' at 2013–17.

[9] Though I claimed in that article that torture is morally forbidden in all circumstances, I did not really make the case for a moral absolute. I was concerned in that article to deepen our sense of a *legal absolute*, to take seriously what it means for something to be utterly forbidden by law, not just in the sense of there being a text forbidding it but in the deeper sense of its comprehensive incompatibility with the kind of legal order that we are familiar with.

Torture, like terrorism, instrumentalizes the pain and terror of human beings; it involves the deliberate, studied, and sustained imposition of pain to the point of agony on a person who is utterly vulnerable, prostrate before his interrogator, and it aims to use that agony to shatter and mutilate the subject's will, twisting it against itself and using it for the purposes of the torturer.[10] Before 9/11, it was widely thought that our experience in mid-century of the worst that could be done in these regards to a human being by a state would warn us away from ever again approaching the boundaries of these practices. It was thought, too, that our knowledge of what the regimes were like that continued to use torture after 1945 would only intensify this warning. Such states establish themselves on *a wholly different basis* than states that are determined to uphold the dignity of their subjects. They rule on a basis of fear and brutality, and that increasingly affects the way they carry out *all* the functions entrusted to them. Quite apart from its intrinsic wickedness, torture metastasizes; it infects all aspects of a state's operation.[11] At best, even when there is some assurance that the application of torture will be confined to outsiders and pariahs, its limitation (and whatever health, safety, and moral well-being can accrue to the regime that uses it) depends on a distinction between *us* and *them*. Such a distinction— between what we may do or countenance doing to each other and what we may do or countenance doing to outsiders—is itself something dangerous and terrifying in its broader implications for governance. All this was true and well-known before September 11, 2001, and it remained true after 9/11, even if many people tried to push out of their minds this knowledge of the true character of torture and its effects, in the interests of making themselves or their loved ones more safe.

Around 2003–4, I became acutely aware that I was in a minority on this matter, if not among ordinary Americans then certainly among my colleagues in moral philosophy and jurisprudence.[12] Once it became

---

[10] This account of torture's wrongness draws on Sussman, 'What's Wrong with Torture?' and on an unpublished lecture by Charles Fried delivered at Columbia Law School in March 2009. I am grateful also to Mary-Ellen O'Connell and Henry Shue for discussion of these terrible themes.

[11] The best account of this remains Shue, 'Torture.' See also Shklar, 'Liberalism of Fear' and Margalit, *The Decent Society*.

[12] The article on which Chapter 7 is based was written in the summer of 2004. It was a grim time, and other people who were trying to bring to light the facts about the use of torture had a much grimmer time than I did. The poetry of Wordsworth (*Prelude*, Book 10, pp. 373–83) seemed apt in those dark days: 'Most melancholy at that time, O friend, | Were my day-thoughts, my dreams were miserable; | Through months, through years, long after the last beat | Of those atrocities (I speak bare truth, | As if to

apparent that the government was using or contemplating the use of torture (or attempting to conceal or equivocate about the use of torture), in order to extract information about terrorist organizations and possible future terrorist attacks, there should have been an outpouring of condemnation. One would have expected a brave, honorable, and God-fearing citizenry to have said: 'Even if such interrogations make us safer, we do not want security that is tainted in this way by the abomination of torture.'[13] In fact there was a great deal of enthusiasm for torture,[14] and such condemnation as there was seemed to be half-hearted and heavily qualified. Prominent legal scholars, even people usually committed to civil liberties, spoke openly of the possibility of issuing 'torture warrants' to enable the imposition of severe pain in interrogation to take place under judicial supervision.[15] The churches were largely silent (at least until 2006):[16] nobody talked of excommunicating advocates for torture in the way that the Roman Catholic church talks routinely these days about excommunicating advocates for abortion. As for the philosophers, it seemed to them that our morality did not have the resources to rule out torture in every circumstance, and it became routine in discussions of this matter to always *begin* by emphasizing that *of course* in anything like a 'ticking bomb' situation, torture would be the appropriate, if not the morally requisite, recourse. In these discussions, reference to the horror of torture was unavailing; it would be parried by reference to the greater horrors that might be averted by the use of torture, horrors reformulated, if need be—with all the versatility associated with such casuistry—as horrors *of* torture averted *by* torture; all of which was supposed to yield the conclusion that we simply *couldn't* regard torture

thee alone in private talk) | I scarcely had one night of quiet sleep, | Such ghastly visions had I of despair, | And tyranny, and implements of death, | And long orations which in dreams I pleaded | Before unjust tribunals, with a voice | Laboring, a brain confounded, and a sense | Of treachery and desertion in the place | The holiest that I knew of—my own soul.'

[13] See Shue, 'Preemption, Prevention, and Predation.' See also the discussion in Chapter 8, below, at p. 270.

[14] See, e.g. Charles Krauthammer, 'The Truth about Torture: It's Time to Be Honest about Doing Terrible Things,' *The Weekly Standard*, December 5, 2005.

[15] See Dershowitz, *Shouting Fire: Civil Liberties in a Turbulent Age*, pp. 470–7 and *Why Terrorism Works*, pp. 132–63.

[16] No doubt these things take a while to percolate through the ecclesiastical imagination. It was *more than three years* after the first credible allegations emerged, that some church folk got together to form a National Religious Campaign against Torture; and some have been ostracized within their church hierarchies for this stand. I discuss this at greater length in Chapter 8.

as out-of-the-question in *all* circumstances.[17] That conclusion given, the philosophers could proceed to a discussion of real-world cases—at Bagram airbase or Guantánamo Bay—confident in a sense that whatever moral prohibition applied to torture was certainly not absolute.[18]

The Bush Administration always denied that it ordered or countenanced the use of torture against detainees in the 'war on terror.' That denial is probably disingenuous, depending at the very least on a tendentious classification of the near-drowning technique called 'waterboarding' as something other than torture. What is beyond doubt is that brutal and degrading techniques were used repeatedly—ranging from psychological attacks on the subjects' religious practices and sense of sexual modesty, through techniques such as sleep deprivation, solitary confinement in darkness with rodents and insects, stress positions, the use of heat and cold, and auditory assault by constant noise, all the way to direct physical assaults like severe beatings (in some cases detainees were beaten to death), repeated waterboardings, and assaults using animals.[19] Protests against the use of these techniques came much more consistently from military officials (particularly from military lawyers) than from clergymen or moral philosophers.[20] Moral philosophers for their part seemed perfectly willing to complement their approval of torture for extreme hypothetical cases with a more reckless approval of coercive techniques short of 'torture' (on the definitions they used) for real-life cases. A case in point is a piece published in 2004 by Jean Bethke Elshtain, Laura Spelman Rockefeller Professor of Social and Political Ethics at the University of Chicago Divinity School.[21] Elshtain frankly acknowledges that she hadn't thought critically about torture before the events of September 11, but now that those events have occurred, she withdraws what had previously been her pre-critical view that the prohibition on torture could never be overridden.[22] More ominously, she argued that the use of 'torture lite' or 'torture 2'—'forms of coercion

---

[17] Cf. the more abstract and honorable discussion of this kind of case in McMahon, 'The Paradox of Deontology' and Scheffler, 'Agent-Centered Restrictions, Rationality, and the Virtues.'

[18] Others have written about the dangers of conducting serious moral inquiry in this way: see Shue, 'Torture,' Luban, 'Liberalism, Torture, and the Ticking Bomb,' and Scheppele, 'Hypothetical Torture in the War on Terrorism.'

[19] The use of these techniques is documented in any number of sources including Mayer, *The Dark Side* and Danner, *Torture and Truth.*

[20] For the military lawyers' response, see Mayer, *The Dark Side*, pp. 213–37.

[21] Elshtain, 'Reflection on the Problem of "Dirty Hands."'

[22] Ibid., 77 and 83.

that involve "moderate physical pressure," and do no lasting physical damage'—might 'with regret be used.'[23] She said that a refusal to approve the use of these techniques is 'a form of moral laziness,' 'a moralistic code-fetishism,' or 'a legalistic version of pietistic rigorism in which one's own moral purity is ranked above other goods.'[24]

I guess I am familiar enough with my own piety and laziness (not to mention my fetishes) not to quibble with this characterization, but I wish Professor Elshtain had grappled just a little more forthrightly with the issue. She could have done so in two respects. The first would have been to acknowledge explicitly and in detail the form that these 'torture lite' or 'torture 2' techniques actually take in the real world of interrogation of terrorist suspects by U.S. agents. It is one thing to talk blandly about 'forms of psychological pressure.' It is another thing for a Professor of Divinity to approve the use of techniques that involve, for example, female interrogators straddling a Muslim subject in a lap-dancing mode, and smearing him with what appeared to be menstrual blood in the hope that if he was prevented from cleaning himself later he would feel unclean and unable to pray and that, hopefully, this would break his heart and make him more amenable to interrogation.[25] It is one thing to talk, as Elshtain does, about 'moderate physical pressure.' It is another thing to hear what this actually involved in Bagram or Guantánamo, like this from an un-named FBI agent:

On a couple of occasions, I entered interview rooms to find a detainee chained hand and foot in a fetal position to the floor, with no chair, food or water. Most times they had urinated or defecated on themselves, and had been left there for 18–24 hours or more…When I asked the M.P.'s what was going on, I was told that interrogators from the day prior had ordered this treatment, and the detainee was not to be moved. On another occasion…the detainee was almost unconscious on the floor, with a pile of hair next to him. He had apparently been literally pulling his own hair out throughout the night.[26]

---

[23] Ibid., 85–7, citing also Bowden, 'The Dark Art of Interrogation,' for a very general characterization of the relevant techniques.

[24] Elshtain, 'Reflection on the Problem of "Dirty Hands," ' 86–8.

[25] This was not an instance of the kind of out-of-control abuse by National Guard reservists that happened at Abu Ghraib; this was in the course of a well-organized interrogation at Guantánamo Bay. See Saar and Novak, *Inside the Wire: A Military Intelligence Soldier's Eyewitness Account of Life at Guantanamo*, pp. 225–8. See also the discussion of this sort of religious abuse in Chapter 8, below.

[26] Quoted by Mark Danner in 'We are all Torturers Now,' *New York Times*, January 6, 2005.

I make no apology for the horror of these details. The horror is part of what these techniques instrumentalize, part of their alleged effectiveness, and part surely of what any honest evaluation of the likely effects of approving 'coercive techniques short of torture' should involve. I do not believe that there is anything particularly honest or courageous about approving such techniques in general terms, but declining to lower oneself to the distasteful details that, for issues like this, lie close to the heart of the matter.

The other respect in which Professor Elshtain's account could have been more thoughtful would have involved acknowledgement of and reflection upon the other terms that the law has reserved for characterizing (and prohibiting) 'techniques short of torture.' International law prohibits cruel, inhuman, and degrading treatment, and outrages upon personal dignity, even when these forms of treatment do not amount to torture.[27] These are not flip terms like 'torture lite,' and they don't just mean 'techniques short of torture.' In the prohibitions in which we find them, they are terms that convey the importance of certain standards such as basic humanity and elementary dignity. The prohibition on inhuman treatment does not just counsel us to treat detainees 'humanely' (though that is also a requirement of the Geneva Conventions). It also requires us to reflect on 'inhuman-ness.'[28] Treatment properly described as 'inhuman' is treatment so harsh or so insensitive to the needs and rhythms of human life (the need to sleep, the need to urinate or defecate) or to human vulnerability (to pain or noise or stress) that it would be wrong and unreasonable to expect any human to endure it. I wish Professor Elshtain in the vaunted honesty of her essay had been willing to reflect a little on the application of this predicate 'inhuman,' with this meaning, to the techniques whose use she approved and explain whether she was comfortable about assaults on detainees that could properly be described as 'inhuman' even if they couldn't properly be described as 'torture.' I am not talking now about legal application as such, but about the missed opportunity to engage in the sort of reflection that terms like these invite. Similarly with 'degrading treatment.' When she counseled the use of techniques that fell short of torture, did Professor Elshtain have in mind that they would be techniques properly described as 'degrading'? We know that some of the

---

[27] ICCP, Article 7 and Geneva Conventions, Common Article 3.
[28] For a beginning of such reflection on the meaning of 'cruel,' 'inhuman,' and 'degrading,' see Chapter 9, below.

techniques were intended to humiliate subjects or deny them anything remotely resembling the elementary dignity of physical self-presentation. We know that some of these techniques—like torture itself—are calculated to induce regression to an infantile state or the complete domination of one's agency and consciousness by physical needs. Degradation is wrong and prohibited in these contexts because it fails to accord to people the minimal dignity associated with human personhood, the dignity that distinguishes men from animals or adults from infants. I wish the endorsement of 'torture lite' by Professor Elshtain had been associated with some reflection on the meaning of this standard, and had been accompanied either by a justification for ignoring it or by an account of how, in the real world, we might prevent 'physical coercion short of torture' from crossing the boundary into the use of human degradation as a means to our ends.

I have gone on at length about Jean Elshtain's essay because it is a fine illustration of the sort of discussion of torture and related practices that became standard among moral philosophers after September 11. As I said, I believe that the wrongness of torture was constant before and after the terrorist attacks. I don't really think philosophers like Elshtain believe that there was a change in moral reality after September 11, 2001: what they say is that September 11 afforded an opportunity to those who had previously been unthinking absolutists to focus more thoughtfully on what—they would say—turned out to have been the in-principle permissibility of torture for extreme cases even before the atrocities in New York and Washington. Torture, they would say, had always been permissible for certain cases and it was always a mistake to think otherwise. All that happened on September 11 is that we got a more vivid sense of what those cases might be.

I think people said the same sort of thing about rights in general. Some of us believe that rights are like 'trumps' over considerations of general utility or that they are side-constraints on the pursuit of the general good.[29] If these formulations mean anything, they mean that rights should have a certain resilience against campaigns for greater security, even when the exigencies of the pursuit of security change (as they did change after September 11). A commitment to rights means that we are willing to forego the increments in safety and convenience that might accrue from infringing certain liberties or basic guarantees.

---

[29] For these formulations, see Dworkin, *Taking Rights Seriously*, pp. xi and 190 ff. and Nozick, *Anarchy, State, and Utopia*, p. 28 ff.

Otherwise—on this view—we show that we weren't really committed to regarding those civil liberties and protections as rights at all.

Of course it does not follow that rights are impervious against all changes in circumstances. A very great increase in the danger associated with certain rights or in the costs associated with respecting civil liberties may in some cases warrant a rethinking of the traditional formulations. The terrorists who attacked New York and Washington on September 11, 2001 took advantage of the liberties we enjoy and some of those liberties may need to be curtailed if others, following their example, are not also to take advantage of them with similar or even more terrible results. I explored this question in Chapter 2, which was written in 2002; I think of this essay as being quite crucial for the chapters that follow because it attempts to mark out some dimensions of care that we need to take seriously when we think about rights in a post-9/11 era. I have already mentioned one of them: the fact that the rethinking of some rights might be warranted does not mean that other rights, traditionally regarded by law as absolute in the sense of non-derogable, should also be made vulnerable to such rethinking. We should not rule out in advance the idea that there are certain absolute legal and moral constraints on the way we fight terrorism. Some rights were designated long ago as absolutes precisely because of the temptation to rethink them or relativize them in times of panic, insecurity, and anger.

A second point is that we need to be very careful about talk of balancing in this regard—balancing liberty against security, for example. Such talk has a treacherous logic.[30] It beckons us in with easy cases—the trivial amount of freedom restricted when we are made to take our shoes off at the security checkpoint before we board an airplane is the price of an assurance that we will not be blown up by any imitators of Richard Reid. But it is also a logic that has been used to justify unwarranted spying, mass detentions, incarceration without trial, and abusive interrogation. In each case, we are told, some things that were formerly regarded as civil liberties have to be given up in the interests of security. But after a while we start to wonder what security can possibly mean, when so much of

---

[30] Much of this paragraph and the paragraphs that follow are adapted from Waldron, 'Is this Torture Necessary?' (reviewing Cole and Lobel, *Less Safe, Less Free: Why America Is Losing the War on Terror*). That review was intended as a tribute to David Cole, who, very early on in the discussion of these matters, distinguished himself by refusing to accept the bromide that we were all giving up some of our freedom in order to make all of us more safe. At the end of 2002, Cole published a short piece in the *Boston Review* entitled 'Their Liberties, Our Security,' which traced not just the unequal impact but the discriminatory intent of many of the liberty-affecting measures imposed after 9/11.

what people have struggled to secure in this country—the Constitution, basic human rights, and the Rule of Law—seems to be going out the window. I don't mean to be glib with the pun on 'security.' The topic is actually a difficult one as we navigate between a concept of security tied too tightly to physical safety and a concept of security embracing so much of what we value overall—so much of what we want to be 'secure' in the possession of—that it does not help us parse the trade-offs that may be necessary between the various goods that we are trying to secure. I pursue this matter in Chapter 4, which is devoted to an analysis of the complex meaning of 'security.'

I said the logic of balancing is treacherous. When logic betrays us, we have to retrace our steps—sometimes in a fussy and pedantic sort of way. So let us think carefully about the trade-off between liberty and security.

One crucial distinction is between intra-personal trade-offs and inter-personal trade-offs. The simplest case of an intra-personal trade-off is this. I accept the burden of a legal requirement to wear a seatbelt, restricting my freedom to sit in my car as I like, because I am convinced that this will make me safer, less liable to injury or death in the event of an accident. If we all do this, then each of us is safer though each of us is a little less free. We can think of it as a straightforward trade-off, once we understand what happens to human bodies in an automobile in a collision. It's like buying more potatoes (safety) and less meat (liberty), when we find that the price of meat has gone up. Another similar case, slightly less straightforward, is when we all accept a restriction on liberty not because our own actions pose a threat to our own safety, but because it is possible that some of us may pose a threat to the others and we don't know who. This is the logic of the airport security system; and it too seems to make innocuous sense. We all accept certain restrictions in the expectation that we will all enjoy greater security. Again, the trade-offs are intra-personal: each of us bears the cost and each of us reaps the benefits.

Quite different, however, is the *inter*-personal case, in which we sacrifice not our own liberty, but the liberty of a few people in our midst in order that the rest of us may be (or at least feel) more safe. A passenger notices some Muslim men praying before boarding an aircraft. She makes a fuss and the Muslims are removed from the flight. A little bit of liberty is lost, and perhaps a little bit of security is gained. But the person who gains the security is not the person who lost the liberty. This is utterly unlike the intra-personal trade-offs. It is a different game—a game of majorities and minorities—and the moral issues it gives rise to are much more serious.

It is different but of course it's not unusual. For there are winners and losers all the time in politics: a new highway benefits some restaurant owners at the expense of others whose establishments languish boarded-up along the route of the old road. But the stakes are much higher in the liberty–security trade-off. For what are traded off there are not just economic interests or mundane freedoms, like the freedom to sit without a seatbelt. Often what is traded off is something that was previously regarded as a right. Members of a minority are detained without trial, or spied upon, or beaten or humiliated during an interrogation, and all to make the rest of us more secure. This is troubling because rights are supposed to represent guarantees given to individuals and minorities about the outer limits of the sacrifices that might reasonably be required of them in others' interests. They are supposed to *restrict* trade-offs of some people's liberty and well-being for the sake of others'. They are not supposed to be traded off themselves.

It seemed to me enormously important to remember this and to remember too that this was not just a matter of trading some people's liberty for our security. Sometimes the security—indeed the safety—of outsiders or perceived outsiders was traded off as well. On July 22, 2005, a Brazilian electrician, Jean Charles de Menezes, was shot dead by police officers in Stockwell tube station on the London Underground. Those who shot him said they thought he looked and acted like one of the terrorist suspects they were watching in anticipation of a possible repetition of the attacks in London earlier that month. But Mr Menezes was not a terrorist; he was an entirely innocent and legal resident of the United Kingdom, and he was at the time doing nothing that justified firing on him. He was made radically less safe as a result of Britain's anti-terrorist measures, which included instructions to police to use deadly force to prevent perceived terrorist activity.

The same can be said about those who have been tortured and beaten—as I said earlier, in some cases beaten to death—by American security forces. The infliction of pain during interrogation renders a person not just less free—though he has to be made unfree (held down) in order to be tortured—but less secure in a very straightforward sense. The security that we all crave is security against violent attack, but that is exactly what many people lose when they are imprisoned in

Guantánamo Bay or in 'black' U.S. prisons in Eastern Europe, or when they are 'rendered' by U.S. agents to countries like Syria for torture by foreign authorities.[31] Their security is sacrificed, allegedly in order to make the rest of us more safe.

People like Maher Arar and hundreds of others who have been abused by our interrogators are not more secure from terror as a result of the Bush administration's security strategy. On the contrary, they are terrorized by us: their terror has been instrumentalized by officials of our government supposedly for our benefit. We may be more secure as a result, but it is a shameful thing to know that our safety has been purchased at their expense on the back of a waterboard or at the end of a frayed electrical cable.

Many of us thought that the idea of justifying such trade-offs in a simple consequentialist framework had been discredited in moral philosophy years ago. Robert Nozick had reminded us in 1974 of our liberal commitment to 'the inviolability of other persons.' He asked:

[W]hy may not one violate persons for the greater social good? Individually, we each sometimes choose to undergo some pain or sacrifice for a greater benefit or to avoid a greater harm: we go to the dentist to avoid worse suffering later; we do some unpleasant work for its results; some persons diet to improve their health or looks; some save money to support themselves when they are older. In each case, some cost is borne for the sake of the greater overall good. Why not, similarly, hold that some persons have to bear some costs that benefit other persons more, for the sake of the overall social good?

His reply was stark:

But there is no social entity with a good that undergoes some sacrifice for its own good. There are only individual people, different individual people, with their own individual lives. Using one of these people for the benefit of others,

---

[31] Consider the story of Maher Arar, a Canadian engineer, innocent of any involvement in terrorism. In September 2002, Arar was apprehended at JFK Airport while changing planes for Montreal. He was held for two weeks in Brooklyn while U.S. officials investigated charges that he had ties to Al Qaeda. Then, while his lawyer was lied to about his whereabouts, Arar was flown on a U.S. government–chartered jet to Jordan and driven to Syria, imprisoned there for a year in a grave-like cell, and tortured by Syrian authorities (for several days beaten for hours with a frayed electrical cable). The former U.S. Attorney-General Alberto Gonzales said that there were assurances from Syria that Arar would not be tortured. But this is very odd. We do not trust the Syrians' word on anything else and had the administration wanted to ensure that Arar's deportation would not result in his torture, they could have sent him to Canada, whose passport he held and where he resided as a citizen. The only conceivable reason for sending Arar to Syria was so that he would be tortured, and tortured in circumstances where no legal recourse was possible.

uses him and benefits the others. Nothing more. What happens is that something is done to him for the sake of others. Talk of an overall social good covers this up. (Intentionally?) To use a person in this way does not sufficiently respect and take account of the fact that he is a separate person, that his is the only life he has.[32]

Whatever philosophical differences there were between Nozick and his Harvard colleague, John Rawls, they were eclipsed by their consensus on this basic point: consequentialist trade-offs of one person's welfare, or liberty for the sake of others, fail 'to take seriously the plurality and distinctness of individuals.' That was the basis on which political philosophy was revived in the 1970s, and yet in the debate about anti-terrorist measures I often found that people wrote insouciantly about interpersonal trade-offs in a maximizing framework.[33] It was as though no progress had been made in distinguishing consideration of one person's trade-off among various goods that he or she enjoyed, on the one hand, and the pressing issues of justice raised when there was a proposal to trade off one person's well-being for the greater good of others.

One final thing whose constancy was called into question after 2001 was our attitude to international law. The sources of international law and the basis of its applicability remained the same before and after 9/11 and, as we have seen, many of its provisions ought to have had an urgent bearing on the choices that were made in the 'war on terror.' Those who were alarmed by reports of abusive interrogations in 2002–3 cited international conventions of one sort or another, and were shocked to find that these were held largely in contempt by many of their colleagues and sizeable sections of the population. The situation was exacerbated in 2003 with American fury at the insistence of some of its traditional allies on a legalistic approach to determining the appropriateness of military action against Iran. Suddenly there were scores of books and law journal articles questioning the status of international law and calling for America to think again about what had previously been its strong commitment to international legal institutions.[34]

There is not nearly enough on this issue in the present collection. I have included one brief paper about the Rule of Law in international law, which was written for a Federalist Society student symposium at

[32] Nozick, *Anarchy, State, and Utopia*, pp. 32–3.

[33] See, e.g. the remarks on aggregate maximization in Posner and Vermeule, *Terror in the Balance*, pp. 29–30.

[34] See, for example, McGinnis and Soman, 'Should International Law be Part of our Law?' and Goldsmith and Posner, *The Limits of International Law*.

Columbia Law School in 2006 in which the late Thomas Franck and I attempted to vindicate the demands of international law against Jeremy Rabkin and John McGinnis. It is a halting and inadequate start; clearly much more is needed.[35]

*   *   *

Things changed on September 11, 2001, and in the years following, the reputation of the United States in the world took a nose-dive. The United States was regarded as a 'torture state,' a repeated violator of human rights and international humanitarian law; some of its military bases were described by jurists elsewhere as 'legal black holes'; and it was seen as something like a rogue state, contemptuous in its actions and attitudes towards international law and the established opinions of mankind. Things changed again on November 4, 2008 with the election of Senator Barack Obama as President of the United States and on January 21, 2009, with his inauguration and the end of the Bush Administration. It seemed like an era of new hope, with Obama's pledge to close the detention facility at Guantánamo Bay and his initiation of an honest discussion of torture, marked by a clear acknowledgement at his 100 Days Press Conference, 'I believe that waterboarding was torture. And I think that the—and, whatever legal rationales were used, it was a mistake.'[36] Preparing this volume for publication, I had the interesting pleasure of changing many of the verb-tenses in Chapters 7 and 8 in particular from present to past tense, to mark the end of a shameful period.

But not everything changed, and not as quickly as many of us wanted. Almost a year after his election, detainees still languish at the Guantánamo Bay facility, not for any desire or policy of the President but because it has turned out to be much more difficult to relocate them. Many cannot be repatriated for fear that they will face reprisals and even worse torture at home than they faced while in American custody. Some cannot be released because we are afraid that our own abuses have radicalized them, making them hate Americans even more than they did before they were detained. If the detention facility is closed, many of the

---

[35] For an indication of what that 'more' might be, see Mary Ellen O'Connell, *The Power and Purpose of International Law* (Oxford University Press, 2008).

[36] See the following websites: <http://www.reuters.com/article/idUSN29465634> and <http://www.whitehouse.gov/the_press_office/News-Conference-by-the-President -4/29/2009/>.

most dangerous terrorist suspects will have to be detained in the United States, and a number of local communities near secure federal prisons have said that they are too frightened to countenance the presence of terrorist suspects in their vicinity. At the time of writing (November 2009), there are plans to put some of the suspects on trial in federal court in New York City. This too has proved controversial, though it is a welcome return to the criminal justice model, to address the mass murders that took place on September 11—a welcome move away from the 'act of war' approach which landed us in such difficulties (labeling those who conspired to hijack airplanes as 'unlawful combatants,' and grudgingly allowing them hearings before 'military commissions').[37] It remains to be seen what effect the maltreatment of these detainees will have on their trial for conspiracy to murder. It may not be the most important of the pragmatic arguments against torture, but it is a significant argument against it that, for some putative short-term gain in information, it can play serious havoc with our ability to deal justly and properly with a terrorist conspirator once his informational value has been exhausted.

There is the further question of what the Obama administration should do about the misdeeds of its predecessors—the official authorization of abusive and unlawful interrogations, the maltreatment and in some cases the murder of prisoners, the egregious and repeated violations of standards set by international human rights, international humanitarian law, U.S. constitutional requirements, U.S. statutes, and military discipline, and the attempt by civilian lawyers in the administration to deliberately distort the framework of law that is supposed to govern these matters. Those who participated in unlawful interrogations must accept responsibility; their guilt is in no way diminished by the greater and additional culpability of their superiors. And the culpability of their civilian superiors, reaching up into the highest levels of the Bush administration, is heavy indeed. Former officials like David Addington, Jay Bybee, George W. Bush, Dick Cheney, Alberto Gonzalez, Jim Haynes, Donald Rumsfeld, and John Yoo should be regarded as, at the very least, under suspicion of having engaged in conspiracy to torture and conspiracy to violate applicable U.S. laws. Whether it is appropriate to contemplate prosecutions against these suspects is another question.

---

[37] On October 4, 2001, The *London Review of Books* published 29 very short comments by various contributors, entitled '11 September.' I looked back recently at my contribution, written in haste for that issue, and was glad to see that, like several of my fellow authors (Thomas Powers and David Runciman, for example) I criticized as ill-advised the characterization of the 9/11 attacks as acts of war.

Attorney-General Eric Holder is conducting an investigation, as he is required to do by international law.[38] And other agencies, such as the Office of Professional Responsibility, are investigating the work done in the Department of Defense and in the Justice Department's Office of Legal Counsel in connection with the infamous 'torture memos.' There is some enthusiasm elsewhere in the world for trials to be conducted outside the United States along the lines of the *Pinochet* case in England in 2000[39] or along the lines of a recently completed hearing in Italy, in which 23 former CIA agents were sentenced *in absentia* to eight years' imprisonment for the kidnapping and rendition (from Aviano airbase in Italy) to Egypt of a Muslim cleric suspected of recruiting militants for Iraq.[40] Hopefully this will make some of the officials under suspicion for conspiracy to torture at Guantánamo and elsewhere think twice before they book their foreign holidays.

In the end the decision to prosecute any of the Bush administration officials is a matter of political judgment. I do not mean that it should be determined by partisan political advantage, but by considerations about the state of the republic and whether it can bear the cost and divisiveness of hearings and trials on this matter. For what it is worth, I see this as a most difficult decision. On the one hand, one has to consider the likely intensification of the already bitter and potentially violent divisions in the polity should action of this kind be undertaken by President Obama and the Attorney-General. On the other hand, it would be a pity if the sort of thing that went on in the Office of Legal Counsel, the Office of the Vice President, and the Pentagon in 2002–7 came to be regarded by future administrations and their appointed officials as privileged and invulnerable, so that no one need worry now or in the future about

---

[38] Article 12 of the Convention Against Torture, which the United States has signed and ratified, requires each signatory state party to 'ensure that its competent authorities proceed to a prompt and impartial investigation, wherever there is reasonable ground to believe that an act of torture has been committed in any territory under its jurisdiction.'

[39] See *R v. Bow St Metropolitan Stipendiary Magistrate, ex parte Pinochet* (No. 3), [2000] 1 A.C. 147, 198 (H.L. 1999), stating that '[t]he jus cogens nature of the international crime of torture justifies states in taking universal jurisdiction over torture wherever committed'. See also *Demjanjuk v. Petrovsky*, 776 F.2d 571, 582 (6th Cir. 1985), noting 'the general recognition since [1945] that there is a jurisdiction over some types of crimes which extends beyond the territorial limits of any nation,' and *Filártiga v. Peña-Irala*, 630 F.2d 876, 890 (2d Cir. 1980), stating that 'the torturer has become—like the pirate and slave trader before him—*hostis humani generis*, an enemy of all mankind.'

[40] See Manuela D'Alessandro and Daniel Flynn, 'Italy convicts former CIA agents in rendition trial,' *Reuters*, November 4, 2009, at <http://www.reuters.com/article/topNews/idUSTRE5A33QB20091104>.

either torturing detainees, or approving such torture, or legally certifying it, or needlessly muddying the framework of applicable law. Though it cannot continue, the present uncertainty has advantages of its own, and any decision not to prosecute should be presented to the public as a delicate upshot of judgment, rather than as an indication that prosecutions are and always were out of the question. A decision not to proceed further against Addington et al. will be disappointing to many. Some may say that it is bound to undermine the standing of the laws that, arguably, were broken. But that invests too much hope in the dramatics of criminal trials. Law has a presence and a resilience that goes beyond simple models of enforcement. In the case of the laws against torture and cruel, inhuman, and degrading punishment, the most important fact about their presence is the incorporation of those laws into the mentality and habits of those called to public political or military service. It is not something that depends wholly on fear of prosecution; often it is a matter of professionalism and honor. That is what it looked like we lost in 2002–5; but I believe it is something we can get back, by our experience of having stepped into that abyss and our relief as a nation at being taken seriously in the world when we say, yet again, that this is not someplace we want to go.

The essays in this volume were written mostly in the period 2002–7. Chapter 7, the long chapter on torture, was published originally with the subtitle 'Jurisprudence for the White House.' I have chosen a variation of that subtitle for the whole collection, because I think the considerations set out in these essays are of enduring importance. We should not expect the threat of terrorist attack to evaporate, nor the need for precautions against attack whether large or small. And if precautions continue to be necessary, then vigilance is also needed to ensure that the precautions we take are regulated by moral, legal, and constitutional constraints. It would be arrogant to regard the positions taken in these essays as the final word on these constraints. There are other opinions around and they are certain to make themselves heard. Still, it is important to bear witness to certain considerations that, as events have shown, are always in danger of getting lost in the rage that afflicts a country when its citizens come under attack: the inviolability of the individual, the complexity of security, the abomination of torture, the importance of humanity and dignity in our response to terrorism, and above all the integrity of law.

2

Security and Liberty:
The Image of Balance

There seemed to be general acceptance in the wake of the terrorist attacks of September 11, 2001 that some adjustment in our scheme of civil liberties was inevitable. This was in part the product of political defeatism: the state is always looking to limit liberty, and a terrorist emergency provides a fine opportunity because people become more than usually deferential to the demands of their rulers in these circumstances and more than usually fearful that if they criticize the proposed adjustments they will be reproached for being insufficiently patriotic or realistic.[1]

---

[1] I said in the original version of this chapter that this was inevitable, in part, because there was little likelihood that reductions in civil liberties would be opposed by the courts. Even in countries like the United States with strong judicial review, the courts have usually been very reluctant to oppose reductions in civil liberties in times of war or war-like emergency. This makes it something of a mystery why legal scholars continue to defend the counter-majoritarian power of the judiciary on the ground that this power is necessary in order to prevent panic-stricken attacks on basic rights by popular majorities. Those who make that argument know perfectly well that the judiciary is not immune from popular panic or from popular enthusiasm for attacks on minorities. They know perfectly well that in times of emergency the judiciary usually proves itself (in the words of Lord Atkin's lonely dissent in *Liversidge v. Anderson* [1942] A.C. 206) 'more executive minded than the executive.' Ronald Dworkin, one of the strongest defenders of American-style judicial review, acknowledged this point in 2002 in 'The Threat to Patriotism':

> People's respect for human and civil rights is very often fragile when they are frightened, and Americans are very frightened. The country has done even worse by those rights in the past, moreover. It suspended the most basic civil rights in the Civil War, punished people for criticizing the military draft in World War I, interned Japanese-American citizens in detention camps in World War II, and after that war, encouraged a Red Scare that destroyed the lives of many of its citizens because their political opinions were unpopular. Much of this was unconstitutional, but the Supreme Court tolerated almost all of it. We are ashamed now of what we did then: we count the Court's past tolerance of anti-sedition laws, internments, and McCarthyism as among the worst stains on its record.

Laurence Tribe said something similar a few months earlier in 'Trial by Fury':

> Historically, the judiciary has been so deferential to the executive in wartime as to provide virtually no meaningful check.... [I]t would be a terrible mistake for those

Political realism aside, there was also a sense that some curtailments of liberty might be *appropriate* in the wake of the terrorist attacks, and that it might be unreasonable to insist on the same restrictions on state action after September 11 as we insisted on before September 11.[2] A common suggestion invited us to think about this in terms of the idea of *balance*. According to this suggestion, it is always necessary—even in normal circumstances—to balance liberty against security. We always have to strike a balance between the individual's liberty to do as he pleases and society's need for protection against the harm that may accrue from some of the things it might please an individual to do. The former, surely, cannot be comprehensive even under the most favorable circumstances—nobody argues for anarchy—and the latter has to be given some weight in determining how much liberty people should have. So there is always a balance to be struck. And—the suggestion continues—that balance is bound to change (and it is appropriate that it should change) as the threat to security becomes graver or more imminent. The balance that is appropriate in time of peace is not the same as the balance that is appropriate in time of war. And even in the grey area of 'the war on terror,' the balance must be struck differently depending on the magnitude of the terrorist threat. One newspaper columnist, Nicholas Kristoff, put it this way:

[T]errorist incidents in the 1970s (such as at the Munich Olympics) had maximum death tolls of about a dozen; attacks in the 1980s and 1990s raised the scale (as in the Air India and Pan Am 103 bombings) to the hundreds; 9/11 lifted the toll into the thousands; and terrorists are now nosing around weapons of mass destruction that could kill hundreds of thousands. As risks change, we who care about civil liberties need to realign balances between security and freedom. It is a wrenching, odious task, but we liberals need to learn from 9/11 just as much as the FBI does.[3]

This is the proposition I want to examine: a change in the scale and nature of the harms that threaten us explains and justifies a change in

---

who worry about civil rights and liberties to pin too much hope on the judiciary in times of crisis.... In this regard, the current Court is no different from its predecessors, all of whom—when confronting the 'blood-swollen god' of war—nearly always deferred to the president in trading liberty for security.

According to Professor Tribe—in the same article—there seemed to be a much greater prospect that Congress would be a check on an overreaching executive in this sort of crisis than that the Supreme Court would be.

  [2] See also Meisels, *The Trouble with Terror*, p. 82.
  [3] Nicholas Kristoff, 'Liberal Reality Check: We Must Look Anew At Freedom vs. Security,' *Pittsburgh Post-Gazette* June 3, 2002, p. A9.

our scheme of civil liberties; and that process is best understood in terms of 'striking a new balance between liberty and security.'

1. The Image of Balance

The idea of striking a new balance can be interpreted more or less literally. 'Balance' has connotations of quantity and precision, as when we balance a set of accounts or when we determine which of two quantities of metal has greater weight. When we talk of striking a new balance, we seem to be suggesting that various quantitative observations and calculations have been carried out, and that they help explain and justify the new position we have taken.

But lawyers—of all people—are well aware that talk of balancing is often just cover, and that the rhetoric of precision is empty. A judge wrestling with a difficult problem might try to give an appearance of objective assessment as though he were watching a needle on a scale or scrutinizing columns of figures; he might *say* he is 'balancing' one set of considerations against another. But we know that he is just waiting for a decision one way or the other to strike him.[4] He may *say* he has figured out that there is more 'weight' on one side. But all that is really going on is that he has just *opted* for that side. He decided; and saying that he discerned greater weight on one side rather than the other is just another way of saying 'He decided.' So, on this account, 'striking a new balance between liberty and security,' means nothing more than 'taking up a new position on the issue.' It would not be (as it pretends to be) a way of describing the process of reaching this decision nor would it be a justification for the new position one adopts. Now I am not saying that this is actually what happens when people use the language of 'balance' to characterize changes in our attitude to civil liberties in a terrorist emergency. But it may be; and after 30 years of Critical Legal Studies' suspicion of 'balancing tests,' there is no excuse for overlooking the possibility.

We are supposed to be told something by the proposition that a balance that was previously satisfactory now requires readjustment. Something has changed, and that's what the balancer has noticed. But this too can be read in various ways. Sometimes public talk about striking a new balance between civil liberties and security does not indicate very much more than that people believe that *there is now something new*

---

[4] Cf. Kennedy, 'Form and Substance in Adjudication,' 1776.

to be said on the security side. The idea is that in the enduring debate about civil liberties, there are things that are said typically by civil libertarians and things that are said typically by the partisans of state power and security. After September 11, there were lots of new things for the partisans of state power and security to say. As a political matter, these new interventions in the debate were more likely to be listened to and less likely to be answered effectively in the new atmosphere that the events of September 11 created than they were in the old atmosphere. But again this tells us nothing about justification; only about dialectical effect. (Some interventions may silence opposition to a proposal even though they offer the proposition little support in a logical sense.) If 'striking a new balance' refers only to a change in the political dynamics—what works now as political rhetoric—then it doesn't help us very much with the proposition that an adjustment in our civil liberties is appropriate.

So my question is this. Is there anything more precise to the idea of 'striking a new balance' than this? Can the metaphor of balance actually help explain or justify the changes that people adduce it to support? Does it provide a useful framework on which various proposals about civil liberties can be evaluated?

2. Degrees of Liberty

Here is one possibility. We know that liberty is in some respects a matter of more or less. For example: I can range more or less widely without restrictions on my travel; or I may be permitted to come closer to or be kept back from important public sites or important public officials; or I may be permitted in my speech to push further or not so far into the realm of the obscene or the subversive. With regard to some areas of liberty, then, we may be able to make at least ordinal comparisons between different quantities of liberty L_x and L_y (for example, between one person's liberty and another's, or between my liberty one day and my liberty the following day).[5] And security may be conceived quantitatively, too, in terms of the extent of risk (R) faced by a person (where

---

[5] Note, however, that quantitative computations of liberty present enormous difficulties, many of them connected to the problem of the individuation of actions. For a discussion, see Steiner, 'How Free? Computing Personal Liberty' and also Steiner, *An Essay on Rights*, pp. 42–54.

R = magnitude of harm times the probability of its occurrence): we might say that a person is less secure the greater R is with regard to that person. With this primitive apparatus,[6] we might then be able to express the idea of the security cost to a person A of another person B having a certain amount of liberty. The security cost to A of B's having a higher amount of liberty L_y rather than a lower amount L_x is the difference between two risks, the higher risk (let's call it R_n) to A from B's having the greater liberty (L_y) and the lower risk (R_m) to A of B's having the lesser liberty (L_x).[7]

Now, if we assume (for the sake of argument) that the balance between security and liberty was exactly right on September 10, 2001, then maybe what happened the following day was that we became aware (or it became the case) that the risks of ceding a given amount of liberty were greater than we thought. Even on September 10, we knew that any amount of liberty carried with it a certain risk of harm. But we were prepared to accept a certain risk—say, R_n rather than a lower risk R_m—because any attempt to secure R_m would mean giving up something we valued at least as much as that extra security, namely a certain degree of liberty: on September 10, we thought that to secure R_m we would have to diminish individual liberty from L_y to L_x; and we were not prepared to do that. However even on September 10 we were not prepared to cede a greater degree of liberty than L_y—say L_z—because we knew that that would carry a risk of harm greater than R_n. And we were not prepared to accept a greater risk than R_n. But now it turns out (in light of the events of September 11) that the cost of L_y (which we *were* prepared to concede) is much greater than we thought—say, R_o rather than R_n. Since we were not prepared on September 10 to give up any degree of liberty that would pose a risk greater than R_n, consistency indicates that now we are going to have to settle for an amount of liberty much less than L_y—say, L_x—on September 12. That I think is what the case for 'striking a new balance' is often supposed to amount to. We have an idea of the maximum risk we are prepared to bear as a result of people's liberty, and accordingly we adjust their liberties downwards when it appears that the risk associated with a given quantum of liberty is greater than we thought (or greater than it used to be).

---

[6] See Chapter 5, below, for what I hope is a much less primitive account of security.

[7] In this argument, the ordinal relation between amounts of liberty is expressed crudely as follows: $L_x < L_y < L_z$. And the ordinal relation between magnitudes of risk (which is the inverse of security) may be expressed crudely as: $R_m < R_n < R_o$.

Of course it is possible that we could make the adjustment in the other direction. Instead of beginning with an idea of the maximum risk, R_n, that we were prepared to bear as a result of people's liberty, we might begin with an idea of the minimum liberty, L_y, we were prepared to accept. The recalculation after September 11 would then require us not to accept less liberty but to brave a higher risk for the sake of the liberty we cherish. The appropriate changes in public policy, then, would be calls to greater courage, rather than diminutions of liberty.

Most probably we work at the matter from both ends, and perhaps this is where talk of 'balance' really comes into its own. Our liberties are not untouched. There has been a downward adjustment, to help address some of the graver risks. But even with the adjustments in civil liberties that have been put in place (and are likely to be put in place) since September 11, no one feels as secure as before: so everyone has to be a little braver for the sake of the modicum of liberty that is left.

3. Objections to the Balancing Approach

Readers may think all this is over-fussy. Surely everyone knows what we mean when we talk about the balance between liberty and security—we talk about it all the time—and surely it is obvious that some adjustment has to be made after it becomes evident that terrorists can take advantage of our traditional liberties to commit murder on such a scale and evade detection. Does it really need to be spelled out with this sort of algebra? I think in fact we do need to be at least as anal as my analysis in section 1 was; we need to subject the balancing rhetoric to the most careful analytic scrutiny. This is for several reasons:

(i) *Objections to consequentialism.* Talk of balance—particularly talk of changes in the balance as circumstances and consequences change—may not be appropriate in the realm of civil liberties. Civil liberties are associated with rights, and rights-discourse is often resolutely anti-consequentialist. Maybe this imperviousness to consequences is something that rights-theorists need to reconsider. But that does not mean they should automatically buy into the sort of common-or-garden consequentialism involved in the argument set out in section 1.

(ii) *Difficulties with distribution.* Though we may talk of balancing our liberties against our security, we need to pay some attention to the fact that the real diminution in liberty may affect some people more than others. So, as well as the objection to consequentialism, justice requires that we pay special attention to the distributive character of the changes that are proposed and to the possibility that the change involves, in effect, a proposal to trade off the liberties of a few against the security of the majority.

(iii) *Unintended effects.* When liberty is conceived as *negative* liberty, a reduction in liberty is achieved by enhancing the power of the state. This is done so that the enhanced power can be used to combat terrorism. But it would be naïve to assume that this is the only thing that enhanced power can be used for. We need to consider the possibility that diminishing liberty might also diminish security against the state, even as it enhances security against terrorism.

(iv) *Real versus symbolic consequences.* Though talk of adjusting the balance sounds like hard-headed consequentialism, it often turns out that those who advocate it have no idea what difference it will actually make to the terrorist threat. Accordingly we must subject these balancing arguments to special scrutiny to see how far they are based on fair estimates of actual consequences and how far they are rooted in the felt need for reprisal, or the comforts of purely symbolic action.

I will discuss these concerns, one by one, in more detail in sections 4 through 7 of this chapter and I will try to show how they might apply to various issues of civil liberties.

As we pursue that discussion, we will need to bear in mind that the class of civil liberties at stake here is not necessarily a homogenous class of rights, principles, or guarantees. The term 'civil liberties' is used to represent a variety of concerns about the impact of governmental powers upon individual freedom. Because the issue of a change in the 'balance' between civil liberties and security plays out slightly differently for different kinds of concern, let me briefly set out some distinctions.

(a) In its most straightforward meaning, the phrase 'civil liberties' refers to certain freedoms understood as actions that individuals might wish to perform, which (it is thought) the state should not restrict. Free speech, religious freedom, and freedom of travel fall into this category.

(b) We also use the phrase 'civil liberties' sometimes to refer to more diffuse concerns about government power, concerns that are not necessarily driven by any sense of a privileged type of action which individuals should be left free to perform. For example, the government's ability to eavesdrop electronically on telephone conversations or e-mail is a civil liberties concern, even though the 'liberty' in question—sometimes referred to as 'privacy'—does not amount to very much more than the condition of not being subjected to this scrutiny.

(c) Sometimes 'civil liberties' refers to procedural rights and powers which we think individuals should have when the state detains them or brings charges against them or plans to punish them. These are rights like the right not to be detained without trial, the right to a fair trial process, the right to counsel, etc.

(d) 'Civil liberties' is also used to refer to certain protections individuals are supposed to have against certain abuses that might be inflicted on them—for example, beatings, degrading treatment, and torture.[8]

This short list is by no means complete. A comprehensive account would also say something about (e) the rights associated with democracy and civic participation. Fortunately these rights were not an issue in the post-9/11 period. So for the rest of the chapter, I will focus mainly on (a), (b), (c), and (d), and consider how the concerns I have outlined—(i) through (iv)—apply to them.

4. Is Balancing Appropriate for Civil Liberties?

The first point—point (i)—is that we need a clear idea of what the balancing argument is supposed to be, so that we can determine whether it is even an appropriate tool to use with regard to civil liberties. The argument given in section 2 assumes that an increase in risk is a *pro tanto* reason for diminishing liberty; maybe not a conclusive reason, but a reason that should count none the less. The argument assumes that the introduction of a new set of considerations (along the lines of 'Now we have to worry about terrorism') or the perception that old reasons have greater weight ('Terrorists are more deadly than they used to be')

---

[8] In Chapter 5, I shall argue that strictly speaking this is more a concern about (individual) security than a concern about civil liberties. A person who fears torture fears violence and harm just like a person who fears terrorist attack. See p. 145 below.

adds something to one side of the balance of reasons that apply to the issue of liberty. It assumes that even though there are good reasons for protecting civil liberties, civil liberties must give way if the reasons in their favor remain the same while something is added to the reasons on the other side. But this may be misleading; for in certain contexts, it is not always appropriate to relate reasons to one another in this simple additive way.

Consider—as an analogy—the reasons associated with promise-keeping. If I have already promised to meet with a student to discuss his paper at 12.30 p.m., then I may not accept an invitation to lunch with a colleague at that time. There are good reasons not to inconvenience my student or disappoint his expectations, and those reasons outweigh the reasons associated with lunch. So far so good. But then what if I find out that it is going to be a *really delicious lunch* (which I didn't know when I conceded that the obligation to the student 'outweighed' the lunch invitation)? Does the introduction of this new factor change the balance? Not at all. The attractions of lunch and the importance of meeting my student are not to be weighed against one another, once the promise has been given. The existence of the promise provides a reason for not acting on considerations like the quality of the lunch; it provides what Joseph Raz has called an 'exclusionary reason.'[9] Since the existence of the promise is supposed to exclude certain kinds of reasons for failing to meet my student, then changes in the weight or character of the latter reasons should not make any difference at all.

Maybe something analogous is true of civil liberties. Maybe—like promises—they too are not supposed to be sensitive to changes on the scale of social costs. Certainly some have thought so. Civil liberties are often regarded as rights, and the idea of 'rights as trumps'[10]—which many have found appealing, at least at the level of rhetoric—is precisely the idea that rights are not to be regarded as vulnerable to routine changes in the calculus of social utility.

Or consider a slightly different account—the proposition that civil liberties are best conceived as Nozickian side-constraints.[11] Perhaps the rule that the government must not imprison anybody it does not propose to charge with an offense is best understood on the model of the rule in chess that one may not move one's king into check. It would be

---

[9] Raz, *Practical Reason and Norms*, p. 37 ff.
[10] See Dworkin, *Taking Rights Seriously*, pp. xi and 190 ff.
[11] Nozick, *Anarchy, State, and Utopia*, p. 28 ff.

like a side-constraint on the pursuit of one's goals, not something which is supposed to make the pursuit of one's goals more efficient overall. If this account were accepted, then the notion of a change in the payoffs from detention without trial (greater security etc.) would be quite irrelevant, just as the change in payoff from moving one's king into check—'Just this once, it would really make a difference to my game' or 'Can't you see that my king is under quite extraordinary pressure?'—is irrelevant to the attitude it is proper to take towards that rule. (Or consider John Rawls's argument about the lexical priority accorded to the principle of basic liberties: if security falls into the domain of the principle governing social and economic goods, then a trade-off of liberty against security is simply ruled out.)[12]

None of this is conclusive against the balancing approach. 'Rights as trumps' is so far just another piece of imagery to put against 'striking a new balance.' And we must not be seduced by our technical familiarity with the idea of rights as side-constraints or with the idea of lexical priority into thinking that these philosophical ideas can be applied unproblematically to civil liberties. On the contrary, there is much in our tradition of civil liberties thinking which cannot be modelled in this way. We all know that existing legal guarantees of civil liberties are hedged around either with explicit provisos to the effect that they may be limited 'in the interests of national security, territorial integrity or public safety,'[13] or with implicit doctrines to the effect that the rights must be adapted to circumstances, the constitution is not a suicide pact, etc.[14] And how far these should be regarded as pure political compromises to get the state to offer any guarantees at all, or how far they should be

[12] See Rawls, *A Theory of Justice*, pp. 36–40 (lexical priority) and 214–20 (priority of liberty).

[13] See, e.g. European Convention for the Protection of Human Rights and Fundamental Freedoms, Article 10(2): 'The exercise of these freedoms, since it carries with it duties and responsibilities, may be subject to such formalities, conditions, restrictions or penalties as are prescribed by law and are necessary in a democratic society, in the interests of national security, territorial integrity or public safety, for the prevention of disorder or crime, for the protection of health or morals, for the protection of the reputation or rights of others, for preventing the disclosure of information received in confidence, or for maintaining the authority and impartiality of the judiciary.'

[14] See *McCulloch v. Maryland* 17 U.S. (4 Wheat.) 316, 415 (1819): The Constitution is 'intended to endure for ages to come, and consequently, to be adapted to the various crises of human affairs'; *Terminiello v. City of Chicago*, 337 U.S. 1, 37 (1949) (Jackson, J., dissenting) ('There is danger that...[the Court] will convert the constitutional Bill of Rights into a suicide pact'), and *Kennedy v. Mendoza-Martinez*, 372 U.S. 144, 160 (1963) ('[W]hile the Constitution protects against invasions of individual rights, it is not a suicide pact').

regarded as reasonable features of a well-thought-through theory of civil liberties, is an open question.

Even apart from outright opposition to the trumping idea and the other models of special priority, there are various things that the proponents of 'striking a new balance' can say in response to the concerns about consequentialism that I have raised in this section.

They may say, first, that it is important to distinguish between two questions: (1) How is a given right defined? (2) Once defined, what sort of priority does it have over other goals and values? Even if the answer to question (2) is quite stringent—trumps, side-constraints, lexical priority, etc.—that is, even if balancing is precluded at that stage, still the idea of a balance may enter into the way we answer question (1).[15]

At the beginning of section 2, I said that liberty could be a matter of more or less. For example, I am free to move around the country but I am not free (unless invited) to come within touching distance of the President; and I could be made a little less free than that by being required to stand back, say, a hundred yards from the President. Where that boundary is drawn—from a few feet to a hundred yards—is surely a matter that requires consideration of consequences; it will be drawn differently in a republic with handguns than in a republic where the weapon of choice for assassination is the stiletto. So we may say civil liberties are not even defined until some balancing exercise is undertaken. And all that was happening in a post-September 11 world was that our understanding of civil liberties was being made responsive to changes in the very factors that enter routinely into its definition. The balance did not affect the priority we accord to liberty: it affected only our discussion of what the appropriate liberty was.

Admittedly this line is easier to take for those freedoms, like freedom of movement, that have no intrinsic definition and are obviously a matter of degree than for those—like free speech and freedom of religion—whose definition may be given in large part by the nature of the

---

[15] An analogy, to illustrate this response: Robert Nozick believed that property rights were to be treated as side-constraints and not balanced or traded-off against other socioeconomic interests. But what property a person had, how much property a given appropriation gave rise to, and what property rights in general should look like—all this, he thought, was something that could be determined only by addressing the relation between the interests of the putative property-holder and the interests of others who might be affected by his acquisition or possession. (Hence the importance of what Nozick referred to as 'the Lockean proviso' in determining what rights we have; see Nozick, *Anarchy, State, and Utopia*, p. 175 ff.) So the idea of balance is not exactly ruled out by the idea of rights as side-constraints; it just enters into our discussion of rights at an earlier stage.

fundamental interest they embody. It will be quite implausible to say, for example, that ordinary political criticism doesn't count as 'speech' in a time of crisis though it may count as speech in a time of peace.

Secondly, it should be noted that most of the philosophical theories which oppose routine trade-offs between rights and consequences nevertheless toy with the idea of some sort of 'out' to avoid *ruat caelum* absolutism. Robert Nozick's caveat is typical: 'The question of whether these side constraints are absolute, or whether they may be violated in order to avoid catastrophic moral horror, and if the latter, what the resulting structure might look like, is one I hope largely to avoid.'[16]

It may be thought that the events of September 11 do constitute exactly that—catastrophic moral horror—and that the occurrence of such horror should trigger whatever qualifications we are prepared to impose on our rights-absolutism. But it is important to notice that the *occurrence* of catastrophic horror is not the issue; the issue is whether the abrogation of rights is a plausible means of avoiding it. I shall say more about this in section 7. For now, it is sufficient to point out that the balancing argument is supposed to turn on what we can achieve by diminishing liberty; it is not supposed to turn on the sheer fact of horror at what has happened nor of our fear at what might happen. Fear is only half a reason for modifying civil liberties: the other and indispensable half is a well-informed belief that the modification will actually make a difference to the prospect that we fear.

When Ronald Dworkin gave his version of the *ruat caelum* qualification—'Someone who claims that citizens have a right against the Government need not go so far as to say that the State is *never* justified in overriding that right'[17]—he suggested that the state may override a given right when this is necessary to protect the rights of others. This is a very common move in popular discussion of these matters. Someone worries aloud about changes in civil liberties and the rights of suspects and people respond: 'Well, what about the rights of those who might get blown up by terrorists?' Rights versus rights is a different ball-game from rights versus social utility. If security is a matter of rights, then rights are at stake on both sides of the equation, and it might seem that there is no violation of the trumping principle or of the idea of lexical priority when some adjustment is made to the balance.

---

[16] Nozick, *Anarchy, State, and Utopia*, p. 30 n. See also the discussion in Chapter 7, below, at pp. 216–17.

[17] Dworkin, *Taking Rights Seriously*, p. 191.

This business of conflicts of rights is a terribly difficult area—which moral philosophers are only just beginning to grapple with.[18] There are some who insist very strongly on distinctions between acts and omissions, and on structures of agent-relativity, that would make it quite wrong to posit an equivalence between a government violating someone's civil liberties and a government failing to save someone's life (because it refused to violate civil liberties).[19] Failing to do what is necessary to save P's life (because this would actively violate Q's rights) is not a way of disrespecting P; the responsibility rests with those—the terrorists— who kill P, not with the government that refuses to violate rights in order to stop them. Others, however, find the stringency of this approach unacceptable, either because they take a more consequentialist view of rights to begin with,[20] or because they accept that people do actually have certain rights to positive goods from their government—like the good of protection from attack—rights which simply cannot be handled in the manner indicated in the previous sentence. But even those who find the acts/omissions and agent-relativity approach unacceptable are still nervous about treating the infringement of a right simply as a bad consequence to be minimized on the model of the utilitarian calculus. At the very least, they want conflicts of rights to be dealt with in a way that is sensitive to issues about the distribution of infringements. (Some argue, for example, that we should trade off rights-infringements against one another using a maximin model rather than a utilitarian model.)[21] Rights-talk is about respect for individuals, one by one; and these philosophers figure that if we abandon that distributive concern—which I will discuss in more detail in the following section—then we forfeit our entitlement to say that we are balancing conflicts of rights as opposed to simply maximizing the satisfaction of underlying interests.

It is not my intention to get very much further into this discussion. I only wanted to show the depth, the complexity, and the philosophically controversial character of the issues that open up when we start talking about balancing rights against interests that are included under the heading of 'security' (whether we describe those too as rights or not). There's no philosophical consensus on any of these issues. But I think it is fair to say that even if there are very few who believe that rights

---

[18] See Kamm, 'Conflicts of Rights' and Waldron, 'Rights in Conflict.'
[19] Nozick, *Anarchy, State, and Utopia* would take this line. And Kamm does too in 'Conflicts of Rights.'
[20] See Sen, 'Rights and Agency,' esp. pp. 191–6.   [21] Ibid., p. 193.

should be utterly impervious to very large changes in social costs, there is almost nobody (who believes in rights) who thinks that they should be adjusted in every case where it appears that some other right-bearer has something to gain from the adjustment. Almost everyone believes that adjustments in rights require structured arguments for their justification—arguments that pay attention to the special character of rights, to the ordered priorities of moral theory, and to the intricacies of various possible relations between one person's rights and another's.

So this should put us on warning that a peremptory use of the balancing idea—something has been added to one tray of the scale, so the balance must now be struck differently—will not do. If security outweighed liberty on September 12 in a way it did not outweigh it on September 10, then there must be complicated reasons (rather than simple consequentialist reasons) why that is so, reasons that are not necessarily captured in the straightforward additive connotations of the balancing idea used in the argument in section 2.

5. Distributive Issues

My second concern is this: in order to evaluate the argument we are going to have to ask some tough questions about the distribution of the various changes envisaged in liberty and security. It is tempting to read the argument set out in section 2 in terms of a diminution in liberty for everyone—everyone's liberty is reduced from L_y to L_x—in order to secure the same amount of security for everyone. But it often doesn't work out that way.

The perpetrators of the September 11 attacks were foreigners, members of a foreign organization; and the government has taken that as grounds for drawing some quite sharp distinctions in the 2001 USA Patriot Act between the protections accorded to the civil liberties of Americans and those accorded to others who are legally in the United States. Section 214, for example, alters existing legislation concerning wire-tapping so that 'investigation of a United States person is not conducted solely upon the basis of activities protected by the first amendment to the Constitution.' (The class of 'United States persons' includes American citizens and legally admitted permanent residents; it does not include non-resident aliens legally present in the United States.) More importantly perhaps, the perpetrators of the September 11 attacks were not just non-residents but also members of a fairly visible ethnic group: and their actions mean that everyone (whether a United States person or not) who looks or dresses or speaks in any way like them is likely to face much greater levels of suspicion. Most of the changes in civil liberties were aimed specifically at suspected perpetrators or accomplices or persons who might be thought to have information about past or future terrorist actions, and most Americans assumed that persons in these categories would look quite different from themselves.

True—as a legalistic matter, the changes in civil liberties may have been formulated innocuously enough—'Anyone who is officially suspected of doing A or knowing B will have his or her liberty reduced from L_y to L_x'—and the 'anyone' term seems universalizable. However, we have to avoid a certain childish formalism in the claim that civil liberties are diminished equally for everyone. As Ronald Dworkin pointed out:

None of the administration's decisions and proposals will affect more than a tiny number of American citizens: almost none of us will be indefinitely detained for minor violations or offenses, or have our houses searched without our knowledge, or find ourselves brought before military tribunals on grave charges carrying the death penalty. Most of us pay almost nothing in personal freedom when such measures are used against those the President suspects of terrorism.[22]

So perhaps the balance we ought to be talking about is not so much a balance between one thing we all like (liberty) and another thing we all like (security). It is more like the balance that is sometimes referred to when we say we should balance the interests of a dissident individual or minority against the interests of the community as a whole.

Ronald Dworkin has argued in a number of places that there is some confusion in the idea of a balance of interests as between the individual and the community: 'The interests of each individual are already balanced into the interests of the community as a whole, and the idea of a further balance, between their separate interests and the results of the first balance, is itself therefore mysterious.'[23] But confusion is not the problem. There are in fact two ways of parsing the idea of a balance between the interests of an individual and the interests of the community in the present context, neither of them reassuring.

---

[22] See Dworkin, 'The Threat to Patriotism.' See also Dworkin's more general discussion of the proposition that '[i]t is never true, at any time, that all members of a society are equally likely to be accused of any particular crime,' in his essay 'Principle, Policy, Procedure,' p. 87.

[23] Dworkin, 'Principle, Policy, Procedure,' p. 73.

The first is that talk of balancing the interests of the individual against the interests of the community may be a way of indicating that 'the individual' in question is not really thought of as a member of the community at all: he is an alien, a foreigner, and so his interests have not already been counted in 'the interests of the community.' Alternatively, if we say that his interests are already counted in the interests of the community—e.g. because he too is more secure from being blown up, as a result of what we do to the liberties of suspicious characters (like him)—we may mean to indicate that a balance must be struck between (1) what justice requires in the way of respect for his interests and (2) what would best promote the aggregate interests—his included—calculated in a way that is indifferent to justice.

This second account is quite complicated, so let me explain a little further. We know that 'the interest of the community' is often calculated in a way that sidelines issues of justice and distribution: utilitarians do this all the time.[24] To take a very crude example: suppose that a choice between two policies (I and II) offers the following payoffs to three individuals:

	I	II
A	20	30
B	20	30
C	20	10

Plainly policy II best promotes the interests of the community (comprising A, B, and C) in an aggregate sense: the total payoff is higher and so is the average. But someone who believes this may also acknowledge that the outcome of policy I is fairer; and let's assume for the sake of argument that they are right. Now, since fairness is concerned particularly with what happens to individuals (rather than to arithmetical totals), and since A and B are both better off as individuals under the less fair policy, a concern about fairness and about the issue of sacrificing fairness to aggregate utility is likely to focus particularly on C. It would not be surprising if this concern were *abbreviated* as a concern about the balance between C's interests and the aggregate interests of the community, even though C's interests are actually counted in the aggregate interests of the community. Another way of putting it would be to say that the real issue is the relation

---

[24] See the discussion in Rawls, *A Theory of Justice*, pp. 19–22.

between a concern for justice, on the one hand, and the prospect of gains to some (or to the aggregate) from ignoring justice, on the other.

Talk of 'balance', here, is not (as Dworkin thought) mysterious. It is all too clear, and it is obviously insidious. Although it sounds all very moderate, the implication is that we should have *some* concern for justice, but not too much: a proper sense of balance requires us to give up on justice when the costs of pursuing it (to those who would benefit from injustice) become too high. Now, A and B might not think this in the choice between policy I and policy II above: there the cost to them of justice is not very great. But if we imagine that a new set of policy choices presents itself (say, on September 11), which greatly increases what A and B have to lose from sticking with justice—

	III	IV
A	10	30
B	10	30
C	10	5

—then we might be tempted to talk about 'adjusting the balance' between justice and utility. After all, it is one thing to require A and B each to give up 10 units of goodies for the sake of justice in the choice between I and II; it is quite another thing—and the afficionado of balance may say it is quite unreasonable—to expect them to give up twice that in the choice between III and IV.

I have put all this very provocatively—with what I hope is an ill-concealed sneer of outrage at the idea of 'striking a new balance' between the demands of justice, on the one hand, and what most members of a society could get for themselves if they were allowed to arrange their society unjustly, on the other. But the outrage doesn't matter at this stage. All I am trying to establish in this section is the need for care with the idea of balancing. If security gains for most people are being balanced against liberty losses for a few, then we need to pay attention to the few/most dimension of the balance, not just the liberty/security dimension. Given that the few/most dimension presents an issue of justice, it is by no means clear—I think it is clearly false—that simply adding something to the 'most' side of the balance is sufficient by itself to justify taking something away from the side of the 'few.'

In response, it may be said that the analysis in this section has neglected the point that those few whose civil liberties are particularly affected are terrorists or persons suspected of participation or complicity in terrorism. No one believes that criminals should have the same rights as the rest of us, and even those who are suspected but not convicted of criminal activity have lesser rights even in ordinary times: they may be held pending trial, or required to post bond, surrender their passports, etc. The point may be accepted, but the issue is whether we should now make some additional downward adjustments to the scheme that already puts criminal suspects in a special position of more restricted liberty. The civil liberties in category (c) define the procedures and protections that are offered to those suspected of ordinary crimes, from the trivial to the heinous. Is there a good reason for changing these, in the light of the events of September 11?

In the *New York Review of Books* essay to which I have already referred, Ronald Dworkin noted a temptation to think that the extraordinary gravity of the crimes that were committed on September 11 (or that terrorists are presently conspiring to commit) is itself a reason for diminishing the protections afforded to those who are charged with those offenses. But, as he said, that makes no sense: 'If they are innocent, the injustice of convicting and punishing them is at least as great as the injustice in convicting some other innocent person for a less serious crime.'[25] The 'civil liberties' in category (c) are oriented in large part towards preventing such injustice, and the case for respecting them increases rather than diminishes, the greater the crime that the suspect stands accused of.

Can it not also be said, though, that the greater the crime the greater the dangers of a wrongful acquittal? It's not true in all cases, but it may be true with terrorists. Michael Dorf put the point this way:

The traditional way we balance these things is with the maxim, 'It's better that 10 guilty men go free than one innocent man be in jail.' I think people are a little nervous about applying that maxim where the 10 guilty men who are going to go free could have biological weapons.[26]

[25] Dworkin, 'The Threat to Patriotism.'
[26] As quoted in Pam Belluck, 'Hue and Murmur over Curbed Rights,' *New York Times*, November 17, 2001, at p. B8. A similar point was later made by Laurence Tribe:

The old adage that it is better to free 100 guilty men than to imprison one innocent describes a calculus that our Constitution—which is no suicide pact—does not impose on government when the 100 who are freed belong to terrorist cells that slaughter innocent civilians, and may well have access to chemical, biological, or nuclear weapons.

Tribe, op. cit., cited also by Dworkin, 'The Threat to Patriotism.'

The implicit suggestion that the 1:10 ratio (or on some counts 1:100)[27] needs to be adjusted in the light of the greater damage that the 10 or the 100 may do sounds reasonable enough. But we must not give the impression that it is only a matter of striking a different balance between this one (innocent) suspect and these 10 (guilty) ones. That's not who the balance is between. We are not balancing the rights of the innocent against the rights of the guilty. We are balancing the interests in life or liberty of the one innocent man[28] against the security interests of those of the rest of us (non-suspects) that will be served if the 10 guilty men are convicted by the procedures that lead to the wrongful conviction of the innocent. The innocent man is being put to death or imprisoned, and his reputation drastically and wrongly besmirched, so that *we* may be safer. It may not be done intentionally, but the gist of the proposal is that it is something we are entitled to be reckless about. There was a way of taking care that it should not happen (or that it should happen less often)—that is what the civil liberties safeguards represent—but for our own benefit, we have decided to take less care.

James Fitzjames Stephen remarked, in connection with this business of trading off a certain number of guilty acquittals against innocent convictions, that '[e]verything depends on what the guilty men have been doing, and something depends on the way in which the innocent man came to be suspected.'[29] The first point is like Professor Dorf's. But Stephen's second point is relevant too. If the innocent persons who are sacrificed to security in this way are sacrificed because it was in the circumstances perfectly reasonable to suspect them of terrorist offenses (though, as it turned out, mistaken)—that is one thing. But if they were suspected in the first place because of appearance, ethnicity, or religion, and if the changes in the scheme of civil liberties facilitated suspicion on just that basis, and removed some of the safeguards that would prevent or mitigate this sort of suspicion—then, that is quite another thing. The injustice associated with the reckless conviction of one innocent man for the sake of the greater good becomes particularly acute—and the 'balancing' talk that underwrites it becomes particularly

---

[27] See Volokh, 'Aside: N Guilty Men,' for some discussion of the numbers cited in this saw.

[28] Actually not just his interest in life and liberty. A person who is punished knowing he is innocent bears a far graver cost—a moral injury in addition to the physical costs of punishment—than a person who receives the same punishment knowing he is guilty. For discussion, see Dworkin, 'Principle, Policy, Procedure,' p. 80 ff.

[29] Stephen, *A History of the Criminal Law of England*, Vol. I, p. 438, quoted by Menard, 'Ten Reasonable Men,' at 199.

objectionable—when it is associated with ethnic or religious prejudice. At that stage, our worrying has to go beyond the issue of individual costs and benefits and look to the moral corruption of the system as a whole.[30]

6. Suspecting the State

A third reason for taking care with balancing arguments, like the argument set out in section 2 of this chapter, is that one of the terms in the alleged balance—'liberty'—is a relational term, so that it has ramifications for both sides of the balance.

When liberty is understood (as it usually is) in a negative sense,[31] it is something that cannot be reduced without increasing something else, namely the powers and means and mechanisms that obstruct or punish the ability of individuals to do what they want. A reduction in liberty is necessarily an increase in the power of the state. Reducing liberty may prevent an action taking place which would otherwise pose a risk of harm, and so it may increase security to that extent. But it necessarily also increases the power of the state, and there is a corresponding risk that this enhanced power may also be used to cause harm or diminish liberty in other ways.

It is important not to lose sight of this possibility. The protection of civil liberties is not just a matter of cherishing certain freedoms (or certain levels of freedom) that we particularly value, i.e. certain actions we as individuals want to be allowed to perform or certain choices that we

---

[30] A system of civil liberties should not be just conceived as an array of individual benefits. It has aspects of a public good—and I believe there is a serious difference between having one's liberties secured in a system where the same liberties are scrupulously guaranteed to all (a system which resolutely turns its back on various forms of prejudice and discrimination) and having one's liberties secured as the artifact of a system that offers liberty to some but not others. This may make it less appropriate to describe the latter system as a scheme of *civil* liberties. I am grateful to Neil Walker of the European University Institute, for some conversations along these lines. Walker has also suggested that security should not necessarily be conceived just as an array of individual benefits. 'Public safety,' he says, 'is inexorably connected with the quality of our association with others.' (See Loader and Walker, 'Policing as a Public Good,' at 26.) If this is true, then there may be an internal connection between liberty and security which is not adequately captured in the metaphor of balance. It may follow from Professor Walker's analysis that, even though we are individually safer, our security may be degraded as a public good by degradation in our scheme of civil liberties. See also the discussion at pp.159–60 below.

[31] See Berlin, *Four Essays on Liberty*, p. 122 ff.

as individuals want to be permitted to make. That's partly what is going on in category (a) of the civil liberties concerns, mentioned in section 3. But it is also a matter of suspicion of power, an apprehension that power given to the state is seldom ever used only for the purposes for which it is given, but is always and endemically liable to abuse. Category (b) of our civil liberties concerns picks this up precisely. Whether there is a freedom at stake or not, there are certain powers which we have traditionally thought it better that the state should not have.

Another way of putting this is to say that a commitment to civil liberties is born in part of a 'liberalism of fear' (to use Judith Shklar's phrase).[32] It is not just a celebration of free individuality; it is an apprehension about what can be done to us using the overwhelming means of force available to the state. True, the events of September 11 have heightened our fear of the worst that can be done to us by individuals and groups other than the state. And an increase in the power of the state may be necessary to prevent or diminish the prospect of that horror. *But the existence of a threat from terrorist attack does not diminish the threat that liberals have traditionally feared from the state.* The former complements the latter; it does not diminish it, and it may enhance it. In this regard Shklar notes that the liberalism of fear owes a lot to the political philosophy of John Locke.[33] It will not do, said Locke, to justify strong unconstrained government, to point to the perils that it might protect us from: 'This is to think, that Men are so foolish, that they take care to avoid what Mischiefs may be done them by *Pole-Cats*, or *Foxes*, but are content, nay think it Safety, to be devoured by *Lions*.'[34] We have to worry that the very means given to the government to combat our enemies will be used by the government against *its* enemies—and although those two classes 'enemies of the people' and 'enemies of the state' overlap, they are not necessarily co-extensive.

Nowhere is this point clearer than in our apprehensions about the use of torture. We all hope and pray that our government will not have resort to this expedient, although there have been suggestions from hitherto respectable civil libertarians that it should do so.[35] There are official

---

[32] See Shklar, 'The Liberalism of Fear,' esp. p. 26 ff.

[33] Ibid., p. 30: 'What the liberalism of fear owes to Locke is also obvious: that the governments of this world with their overwhelming power to kill, maim, indoctrinate, and make war are not to be trusted unconditionally ("lions"), and that any confidence we might develop in their agents must rest firmly on deep suspicion.'

[34] Locke, *Two Treatises of Government*, II, §93.

[35] See Dershowitz, *Shouting Fire*, p. 477.

assurances that its use is out of the question,[36] though that has to be balanced against the depressing precedent of two of our closest allies in the war against terrorism—the United Kingdom and Israel—having resorted in recent memory to methods very close to torture in dealing with their own terrorist emergencies.[37] And even if we can count on the official assurances that torture will not be used (and to do so we would want a government that had been rather less mendacious than ours has been about its support for such practices by other regimes in the past), it is worth pondering why this expedient is unthinkable and what that should tell us about other areas where we are less reluctant to sacrifice civil liberties.

On the face of it, the prohibition against the use of torture should be exactly the sort of thing that gives way in the present atmosphere of adjusting the balance between liberty and security. What we are desperate for in the war against terrorism is information—who is planning what—and torture is supposed to be an effective way of securing information. Philosophy classes studying consequentialism thrive on hypotheticals involving scenarios of grotesque disproportion between the pain that a torturer might inflict on an informant and the pain that might be averted by timely use of the information extracted from him: a little bit of pain from the electrodes for him versus five hundred thousand people saved from nuclear incineration. But now the hypotheticals are beginning to look a little less fantastic. Alan Dershowitz asks: what if on September 11 law enforcement officials had 'arrested terrorists boarding one of the planes and learned that other planes, then airborne, were heading towards unknown occupied buildings'? Would they not have been justified in torturing the terrorists in their custody—just enough to get the information that would allow the target buildings to be evacuated?[38] How could anyone object to the use of torture if it were dedicated specifically to saving thousands of lives in a case like this?

The answer comes from Henry Shue: 'I can see no way to deny the permissibility of torture in a case *just like this*.'[39] But few cases are *just*

---

[36] Eric Schmitt, 'There Are Ways To Make Them Talk,' *The New York Times*, June 16, 2002 (Week in Review): 'Military officials say torture is not an option. But, they said, under the Geneva Conventions, anything short of torture is permissible to get a hardened Qaeda operative to spill a few scraps of information that could prevent terrorist attacks.'

[37] For Israel, see Julian Borger, 'Israeli Government Report Admits Systematic Torture of Palestinians,' *The Guardian*, Friday February 11, 2000. For the United Kingdom, see the ECHR decision in *Ireland v. United Kingdom*, Judgment of 18 January, 1978.

[38] Dershowitz, *Shouting Fire*, at p. 477.   [39] Shue, 'Torture,' at 141.

like this: few have the certainty of Dershowitz's formulation or the clean precision of the philosopher's hypothetical. Think of the background conditions that need to be assumed:

> The torture will not be conducted in the basement of a small-town jail in the provinces by local thugs popping pills; the prime minister and chief justice are being informed; and a priest and doctor are present. The victim will not be raped or forced to eat excrement and will not collapse with a heart attack or become deranged before talking; while avoiding irreparable damage, the antiseptic pain will carefully be increased only up to the point at which the necessary information is divulged, and the doctor will then immediately administer an antibiotic and a tranquillizer....Most important, such incidents do not continue to happen. There are not so many people with grievances against this government that torture is becoming necessary more often, and in the smaller cities, and for slightly lesser threats, and with a little less care, and so on.[40]

There is, as Shue notes, 'considerable evidence of all torture's metastatic tendency.'[41] In the last hundred years or so, it has shown itself not to be the sort of thing that can be kept under rational control. On the contrary—from a point near the beginning of the twentieth century in which it was thought it might disappear altogether, torture has returned and now flourishes on a colossal scale. What Judith Shklar calls the liberalism of fear is a response to this actuality—to the prospect that if we allow ourselves to be seduced into adjusting the balance in this regard, there is no telling what we will be letting ourselves in for.[42]

As I said, so long as there is no serious proposal to use it, the argument about torture is important mainly as an illustration of a more general misgiving, about the dangers of metastasis in regard to powers that had previously been withheld from government now being fearfully assigned to it. One troubling example is the power of detention without trial, and possibly without judicial review. It seems now that the United States has a policy of detaining even its own nationals indefinitely as 'enemy combatants,' not in order to charge them with anything but to find out what

---

[40] Ibid., 142.   [41] Ibid., 143.

[42] The formulations in this paragraph are adapted from Shklar, 'The Liberalism of Fear,' at p. 27: 'The most immediate memory is at present the history of the world since 1914. In Europe and North America torture had gradually been eliminated from the practices of government, and there was hope that it might eventually disappear everywhere. With the intelligence and loyalty requirements of the national warfare states that quickly developed with the outbreak of hostilities, torture returned and has flourished on a colossal scale ever since. We say "never again," but somewhere someone is being tortured right now, and acute fear has again become the most common form of social control.' See also the discussion at p. 187 below.

they know.[43] It is not hard to think of scenarios where detention without trial is justified. But it is hard to think of methods of ensuring that this power is not abused, that it does not get out of hand, and that detention does not turn into 'disappearance.' Once again, one's confidence would be greater if one were dealing with a government that had resolutely opposed all such abuses by its allies and client-states in the past. But we know, on the contrary, that in the recent past the United States has been complicit in abuses of the detention power in Latin America and elsewhere. There is a sort of magical thinking that we are supposed to forget all about such abuses when we evaluate, from a civil liberties perspective, what is being presently proposed: it is as though we are supposed to think that now, for the first time, remarkably, we have a government that can be trusted to tell the truth about its intentions. (Another, sadder way of putting this is to say that there are costs to the sort of mendacity that in the past U.S. government officials have routinely indulged in: such mendacity leaves no basis for trust when, later, trust may be desperately needed.)

Against all this, some will say that the threat from a more powerful state as a result of a reduction in civil liberties is nothing but an hysterical hypothesis, whereas the threat from terrorism is *real*. But this is exactly the sort of assertion we need to be careful with; in fact, as it stands, it is a fine example of the purely political use of the 'balance' idea mentioned at the end of section 1. In response we can say two things. First, no one but a fool thinks that the threat from the state is zero. Of course opinions about the magnitude of the threat may vary. But there is no reason to suppose that the introduction of a heightened threat from terrorist threat makes it *less* likely than it was (say on September 10) that the state will act oppressively. So if greater powers are given to the state, then the state has greater means to act oppressively, and unless we assume that the motivation to do so has somehow magically evaporated with the rise of the terrorist threat, we must assume that the net threat from the state goes up as the power accorded to the state increases. Secondly, even though the terrorist threat is very real, the hypothesis that an increase

---

[43] I infer this from the recent case of Jose Padilla, held for having talked about the possibility of detonating a radiological bomb in Washington D.C. See Benjamin Weiser with Dana Canedy, 'Traces of Terror: the Bomb Plot,' *The New York Times*, June 12, 2002, p. A24: 'Defense Secretary Donald H. Rumsfeld, speaking to reporters in Doha, Qatar, said the administration was, at least for now, far more interested in gleaning intelligence from Mr. Padilla to halt other terrorist acts than in bringing a prosecution. "We're not interested in trying him at this moment," Mr. Rumsfeld said, adding that the goal was to question him to gather information that might "protect the American people from future terrorist acts." '

in governmental power will diminish it is in many ways no less fanciful than the hypothesis that the government will abuse the extra power given to it. We must not confuse the means with the end. An enhanced ability to combat terrorism is not the same as an actual diminution in terrorist threat. This leads to the fourth of the grounds for caution that I mentioned in section 3.

7. Reality Check

The argument about balance is based on a consequentialist approach. We are supposed to consider civil liberties not just in and of themselves, but in terms of the consequences of their existence. If the consequence of a given degree of liberty is an enhanced level of risk, then we must take that into account when considering whether that degree of liberty should be maintained.

It is important to do these calculations honestly. The fact that a certain degree of liberty is associated in the public mind with a certain degree of risk is not itself a ground for diminishing the liberty given a concern for the risk. *We must be sure that the diminution of the liberty will in fact have the desired consequence*; or if the desired reduction in risk is only probable, not certain, then we must be as clear as we can about the probability. In particular, it is never enough for the government to show that reducing a given liberty is a necessary condition for combating terrorism effectively. It may be a necessary condition, and yet—because sufficient conditions are unavailable—the terrorist threat may continue unabated. There is an exact symmetry between the logic of this position and the logic of the apprehended threat from governmental tyranny: maybe the diminution of liberty that the state demands is a necessary condition for tyranny; but as supporters of the state will point out, it is not a sufficient condition for tyranny, and a non-hysterical approach to the matter will pay attention to the actual (not the fanciful) prospects for tyranny if this necessary condition is put in place. Well, similarly, the case for reducing liberty cannot consist simply in the fact that this is *necessary* for combating terrorism: the case must be based on the actual prospect that security will be enhanced if liberty is reduced. It may be said—quite reasonably—that we cannot know what the prospect is. Fair enough: then what has to be inferred is that we cannot know whether it is worth giving up this liberty, and thus we cannot legitimately talk with any confidence about an adjustment in the balance.

It is not that we know nothing about the effects of the change in our liberties. The immediate effects on suspects and dissidents are quite clear. It is the long-range effects for the sake of which these costs are imposed that are less clear. In fact, given the record of the bumbling incompetence and in-fighting of American intelligence and law-enforcement agencies wielding the already very considerable powers that they had in the weeks leading up to September 11, there is no particular reason to suppose that giving them more power will make them more effective in this desperately difficult task. But it might make them more effective in the somewhat easier task of acting oppressively towards vulnerable political dissidents at home.

Again, my intention is not to settle any argument with these considerations, but to insist on the importance of detailed scrutiny. The case for diminishing civil liberties is often presented as the hard-headed consequentialist alternative to the soft 'pious moralism' of theorists of rights. But those who are used to this sort of abuse know that it becomes most vehement when hard *consequentialist* questions are asked about enhancements of state power that turn out to be purely symbolic in relation to the threat they purport to be dealing with, and deadly dangerous in relation to liberty and justice on the domestic front. In fact I suspect that much of the popular pressure for a change in liberties is explained at the level of symbolism. When they are attacked people lash out, or they want their government to lash out and inflict reprisals on someone who might plausibly be regarded for the moment as an appropriate target. To put it a little more kindly, people want to feel that something is being done, in response to the attacks and in response to the continuing threat—preferably something violent (like the bombing of Afghanistan or the overthrow of the Taliban regime) or drastic like the setting up of new forms of detention camp or new types of tribunal. People are less interested in the effectiveness of these devices than in *the sense that something striking and unusual is being done*. No doubt the psychological reassurance that people derive from this has to be counted as a consequential gain from the loss of liberty. But whether it is the sort of gain that should count is another issue, and discussion of it would take us back to the first of the concerns I mentioned in this section.

The point can be illustrated with a consideration of due process issues. A reduction in due process guarantees may make it more likely that terrorist suspects will be convicted. And that, people will say, is surely a good thing. Is it? What reason is there to suppose that our security is enhanced by making the conviction and punishment of terrorist suspects more likely? We know that the conviction and punishment of an Al Qaeda fanatic, for example, will have no general deterrent effect; if anything, it will have the opposite effect—making it more rather than less likely that the country punishing the suspect is subject to terrorist attack. Of course, this is not a reason for *not* punishing the perpetrators of murderous attacks, but the reasons for punishing them are reasons of justice, not security (via general deterrence); and those reasons of justice may not be as separable from the scheme of civil liberties that are traded off against them as the image of striking a new balance might suggest. Maybe particular incapacitation is a means by which conviction might serve security, but for that it is especially important that we convict and punish the right people, and it may well be that limiting civil liberties in category (c) diminishes rather than enhances our assurance in this regard.

Once again undermining civil liberties—particularly the due process rights of terrorist suspects—may make us seem (at least to ourselves) more ferocious and vengeful in response to the atrocities of September 11. It is less clear that the psychological value we derive from adopting this posture is the sort of value for which procedural rights are appropriately sacrificed.

8. Conclusion

This chapter is neither conclusive nor itself particularly balanced or fair-minded. It does not embrace any particular policy or proposal. And it probably does not do justice to the policy changes that have been made and proposed for the sake of security. When it was written, it was intended mainly as a call for care and caution. We should be careful about giving up our civil liberties. We should be even more careful about giving up our commitment to the civil liberties of a minority, so that we can enjoy our liberties in greater security. We should be worried about the enhanced power of the state (and we should reject as magical thinking the idea that the risk from that power goes down as the risk from terrorism goes up). We should see the accusations of disloyalty which are used to slander those who raise these concerns for what they are: an attempt to distract us from careful public evaluation of these issues.[44]

---

[44] See Neil A. Lewis, 'The Senate Hearing; Ashcroft Defends Antiterror Plan—Says Criticism May Aid U.S. Foes,' *The New York Times*, December 7, 2001, p. A1: 'In forceful and unyielding testimony, Attorney-General John Ashcroft today defended the

And finally, if we are to remain receptive to the need to compromise our liberties, we must insist that those who talk the balancing-talk step up to the plate with some actual predictions about effectiveness. We should not give up our liberties, or anyone else's liberties, for the sake of purely symbolic gains in the war against terrorism.

administration's array of antiterrorism proposals and accused some of the program's critics of aiding terrorists by providing "ammunition to America's enemies." Emboldened by public opinion surveys showing that Americans overwhelmingly support the administration's initiatives against terrorism, Mr. Ashcroft told the Senate Judiciary Committee, "To those who scare peace-loving people with phantoms of lost liberty, my message is this: your tactics only aid terrorists." '

3

Terrorism and the Uses of Terror

This chapter is not a discussion of the morality of terrorism. It is not a discussion of whether violent means (like those that terrorists use) can ever be justified by noble ends (like those that terrorists sometimes invoke).[1] Terrorist attacks, like those of 9/11, are murderous atrocities and terrorists themselves, like torturers, pirates, and slavers might aptly be described as the enemies of mankind—*hostes humani generis*.[2] It is hard to imagine what could possibly justify terrorist actions and it is well to remember that they are forbidden by all the laws, customs, and usages of armed conflict recognized in the international community.[3] Instead, this chapter is oriented towards an understanding of what the means/end structures of terrorist action characteristically are. I don't think the structures are always as simple as formulations like 'the use of violence as a means' might suggest. Terrorists use violence in a particular way, aiming at certain kinds of intermediate results *en route* to their ultimate ends, and it is worth trying to elucidate that structure. Also, this chapter is not about the morality of our response to terrorism.[4] That is an admirable topic, but not one that I shall pursue in this chapter. (I say quite a lot about it in Chapter 2.) But I will pursue in this chapter some issues about various ways in which some of our responses to terrorist violence fit into the complex structure of the intentionality of terrorist action.

---

[1] For example, it is not like Honderich, *Violence for Equality* or *After the Terror*. See Meisels, *The Trouble with Terror*, p. 32 ff., for a good discussion of Honderich's approach.

[2] Cf. *Filártiga v. Peña-Irala*, 630 F.2d 876, 890 (2d Cir. 1980) ('[T]he torturer has become—like the pirate and slave trader before him—*hostis humani generis*, an enemy of all mankind').

[3] See also the discussion at the beginning of Chapter 4, below.

[4] For example, it is not like Hill, 'Making Exceptions without Abandoning the Principle.'

1. The Importance of Definitions

The issues I shall address are in large part definitional. Now, everyone acknowledges that it is difficult to agree on a definition of 'terrorism,'[5] and it may be thought that we should not waste time worrying about definitional issues. (Someone might say, 'Who cares how terrorism is defined? We know it when we see it, and we saw it on September 11.') Surely what matters is what we do about terrorism, not how we define it. I agree that it would be wrong to hold out much hope that philosophical inquiry might yield a canonical definition of the term, one that would be generally accepted. But definitional issues might still be important.

They are important, first, for the law, inasmuch as legislators often seek to distinguish terrorist crimes from other crimes like murder, arson, and piracy which exhibit similar criminality: it is worth inquiring as to whether such legislation is over- or under-inclusive so far as the point of drawing such distinctions is concerned. That necessarily involves an assessment of legislative definitions.

Second, there may be a counterpart for these legislative issues even in ordinary language. Many people have a sense that a special sort of moral outrage should be reserved for terrorist crimes, as distinguished from other homicides or acts of destruction. But our moral impulses, particularly under the impact of outrages that threaten to affect us, may not necessarily be reliable. So we put definitional pressure on our ability to articulate this sense that special outrage is appropriate for these offenses, just in order to see whether we can make coherent sense of this pattern of moral response. We ask: can terrorism of the sort that took place in the United States in September 2001 be distinguished in moral theory from the infliction of similar levels of destruction and causalities by acts of war, for example, or by preventable famine? We press on these points, not because what we want more than anything else is a clear and consistent definition; we press on them rather because asking hard questions, which sound like definitional questions, is a way of focusing steady moral inquiry.

Thirdly, and again in ordinary discourse, a definitional inquiry may be useful as a way of entering into some more general reflection on the phenomena we call terrorism. It need not be moral reflection. Terrorism is

---

[5] See Schmid, *Political Terrorism: A Research*, p. 110 and Dugard, 'International Terrorism: Some Problems of Definition,' at 67.

interesting (as well as appalling) as a phenomenon, and there is some virtue in trying to understand the structures of decision, action, and intentionality that it characteristically involves. Again, the point of undertaking such inquiry is not to *arrive* at a definition; the point is to ask hard questions, posed initially as questions about the way we use words, to focus a discussion of what we think is interesting and distinctive about this phenomenon. It is important to understand how this third characterization differs from the first two. Although it is true that we should not build a firewall between definitional issues and practical issues—our definition (or our definitional discussion) of terrorism should highlight aspects of it that are practically as well as empirically and theoretically interesting to us—still we should not assume that our only practical interest in understanding terrorism is to address moral questions about its justifiability or the justifiability of particular state or legal responses. People sometimes wonder whether it is possible to negotiate with terrorists or reach political accommodations with them. The mantra, heard so often—'You can't negotiate with terrorists'—is not always to be understood as a moral imperative ('You mustn't negotiate with terrorists; it just encourages them'). It may also be the product of a certain characterization of what terrorism is aiming at and how it proposes to achieve its aims; if so, we need to reflect on what the characteristic structure of terrorist strategy is. Of course, we may conclude that generalization is impossible, and that there is nothing to be gained by the sort of general reflection that, as I say, resembles definitional inquiry; but we cannot assume that in advance. Similarly people often talk about responding not just to terrorism but to the causes of terrorism; again this commits us to some sort of discussion of what terrorism is like, how it is characteristically motivated, and how those motivations fit with the structure of terrorist strategies. Again it is possible that abstract inquiry, which sounds like definitional inquiry, will be of some assistance to us in making progress on this front. At any rate, it is under this third heading that I see my discussion in the chapter that follows.

2. Terrorism and Coercion

Let us begin our inquiry by asking: is there a distinction between *terrorizing* someone and *coercing* or *intimidating* them?[6] If so, is it a necessary

---

[6] Some definitions may help here. According to the *Oxford English Dictionary* (on-line at <http://dictionary.oed.com/>) 'intimidate' means '[t]o render timid, inspire with fear; to overawe, cow; in modern use *esp.* to force to or deter from some action by threats

condition for an action or set of actions to be described as 'terrorism' that it aim at terrorizing people (perhaps in order to achieve some further end)? The United States Congress does not seem to think so. One of its recently legislated definitions defines 'terrorism' as:

activities that involve violent acts or acts dangerous to human life that are a violation of the criminal laws of the United States... [and] appear to be intended to intimidate or coerce a civilian population, to influence the policy of a government by intimidation or coercion; or to affect the conduct of a government by mass destruction, assassination, or kidnapping...[7]

There is no mention here of 'terror.' So if, as this definition appears to suggest, terrorism is any form of unlawful violent or dangerous act intended to intimidate or coerce governments or populations, then the link with 'terror' and 'terrorization' would seem to be contingent, perhaps just an artifact of etymology.[8] Terrorist acts might simply be acts aimed at imposing a cost on non-compliance with certain political demands, and they might be calculated to work through the victim's rational assessment of those costs (compared, for example, to the costs of compliance), rather through anything approaching the inducement of panic or terror. My point here is not just that something happens when you add the suffix '-ism' to 'terror'—moving perhaps from scattered acts of terror to a pattern or doctrine or theory of such acts.[9] It is rather that the 'terror' in 'terrorism' might be largely meaningless, so that maybe we should treat the term 'terrorism' as an unanalyzable whole.

I actually do not think we should accept this analysis, and in this chapter I shall argue that even if the connection between terrorism and terror is contingent, still we gain considerable insight into the

---

or violence.' It defines 'terrorize' as '[t]o fill or inspire with terror, reduce to a state of terror; *esp.* to coerce or deter by terror.' And it defines 'terror' as '[t]he state of being terrified or greatly frightened; intense fear, fright, or dread.' The same source defines 'coerce' as '[t]o constrain or restrain (a voluntary or moral agent) by the application of superior force, or by authority resting on force; to constrain to compliance or obedience by forcible means,' but philosophical usage tends to associate coercion in particular with the use of threats rather than force alone.

[7] U.S. Code, Title 18, section 2331. This is from the statutory definition of 'international terrorism.' There is another definition in 22 U.S.C. 2656f: '[T]he term "terrorism" means premeditated, politically motivated violence perpetrated against noncombatant targets by subnational groups or clandestine agents.'

[8] But other official definitions *have* made reference to terror. For example the 1937 Convention for the Prevention and Punishment of Terrorism categorized 'acts of terrorism' as 'criminal acts directed against a State and intended or calculated to create a state of terror in the minds of particular persons, a group of persons or the general public.' (See Dugard, 'International Terrorism,' at 68–9.)

[9] See the discussion in Hutchinson, 'The Concept of Revolutionary Terrorism,' at 383.

intentional structure of the phenomena that most of us describe as terrorism if we see that they assign an important role to psycho-social conditions rather like terror, even if they do not always amount to terror in the most literal sense of the word.

Here are a couple of initial clues that there might be more to the connection between terrorism and terror than meets the legislative eye. First, the legislative definition I mentioned already distinguishes terrorism in one particular way from common-or-garden coercion. In the classic case of coercion, the coercer threatens to perform an action which would impose costs on the victim (in the event of the victim's non-compliance with the coercer's demands). He says: 'Give me your wallet or I will shoot you.' But in the case of terrorism—at least as defined above—we are talking about a mode of coercion that already imposes at least some of the costs that the coercer is supposed to be threatening (or costs of the kind that the coercer is supposed to be threatening). The terrorist does not say: 'Comply with my demand or I will impose harm H.' Instead the terrorist first imposes harm H_1, and then he says: 'Comply with my demand or I will continue to impose harms (H_2, H_3,...) of the kind I have already imposed.' By imposing H_1 in advance, he demonstrates that he already has the ability and the will to impose harms of the kind he is threatening to impose in the event of non-compliance. But also, by imposing H_1 at the same time as (or before) he makes his demands, the terrorist already expects the recipient of his demands to be in something like a state of shock or injury from the initial demonstration of the terrorist's will and ability. A second point has to do with the likelihood that intimidation will succeed. As a contingent matter, we might observe that an action is unlikely to succeed in intimidating something as large as a whole civilian population (e.g. the population of a large city or country) unless it is also terrifying. So—even granted the legislative definition given above—any terrorist who knows his business will seek to terrorize his victim. These are not conclusive considerations. But they are, as I said, clues that there might be something to the connection between terror and terrorism, and that we would be wise not to dismiss it out of hand. These clues, I think, are worth following.

3. Terrifying Threats

Whether or not it is connected to the definition of 'terrorism,' it is worth asking: what is *terrorization*, and how does it differ from ordinary coercion? I will approach this question, in the first instance, by reference to a classic conundrum in the relation between ordinary coercion and negative freedom.

The classic definition of negative liberty is found in Isaiah Berlin's essay, 'Two Concepts of Liberty,' and it was Berlin, too, who elucidated the connection between negative liberty and coercion.

> To coerce a man is to deprive him of freedom—freedom from what? . . . I am normally said to be unfree to the degree to which no man or body of men interferes with my activity. Political liberty in this sense is simply the area within which a man can act unobstructed by others. If I am prevented by others from doing what I could otherwise do, I am to that degree unfree. . . . Coercion implies the deliberate interference of other human beings within the area in which I could otherwise act. You lack political liberty or freedom only if you are prevented from attaining a goal by human beings. Mere incapacity to attain a goal is not lack of political freedom.[10]

Now there are at least two different ways in which one person's action may count as deliberate interference with the free action of another. (1) One is by the application of physical force or restraint: P prevents Q from doing A, e.g. by physically restraining the bodily movements of Q that action A requires. This can be done retail—as when P grabs Q to stop Q doing some action in particular—or it can be done wholesale—as when P locks Q up in a tiny cell and thus prevents Q from doing all but a very small number of actions. (2) Or, secondly, P may interfere with Q's action by threatening Q with some harm if Q does A. Both cases count as coercion in ordinary language, even though they affect action in quite different ways. In case (1), the power of action of the victim is physically controlled by the coercer. In case (2), there may be no physical control, just the communication of a threat; in this case, the coercer's control consists in his ability to impose the cost that he threatens in the event of non-compliance, but the actions or the inactions that constitute compliance are still literally controlled by the victim. Q is the person who intentionally performs the act of taking his wallet out of his pocket and handing it to P after P has said 'Give me your wallet or I will shoot you.' The distinction is complicated—but not blurred—by the fact that in many cases P has to coerce Q in sense (1) in order to coerce Q in sense (2): unless the gunman can stop me running away, he can't make a credible threat to shoot me if I do not hand over my wallet. Often I have to

---

[10] Berlin, *Four Essays on Liberty,* at pp. 121–2.

be (physically) in his power before he can threaten me. But this is not true in all cases: some threats or some threat situations may not presuppose prior control of the movements of the victim. Also—another complicating factor—the content of the threat itself may (though it need not) involve the application of force. The penalty threatened in 'Give me your wallet or I'll break your arm' does involve the application of force; the penalty threatened in 'Give me your wallet or I'll tell your wife about the affair you've been having' does not. We may sum this up by saying that there are three—or perhaps four—stages to any coercive enterprise:

(i)   the coercer gets the victim in his power so that he can communicate the threat and impose the threatened harm if he has to; and

(ii) the coercer demonstrates the threat, by actually imposing harms of the kind that he is threatening; and

(iii) the coercer by making the threat affects the decision-making of the victim; or

(iv) if the victim defies him, the coercer actually inflicts the harm.

Stage (ii) need not be present in most coercive situations, but as we have seen it is present in most terrorist situations. Force, in the sense of actual physical restraint, *may* be involved in (i) but it need not be; it *may* be involved also in (ii) but it need not be; and, again, it *may* be involved in (iv), but it need not be. However our inquiry is primarily about (iii), i.e. about the actual character of the intimidation that, first, coercion in general and, secondly, terrorist coercion involves. (We want to ask whether stage (iii) necessarily involves terror or terrorization in the case of coercion by terrorists.)

Patently, if threats undermine freedom they do so in a way that is quite different from the way physical restraints—chains, prison walls, actual man-handling—undermine freedom. It is probably tiresome to invoke the classic Jack Benny routine, but it conveys an important reminder:

A man comes up with a gun and he says 'Your money or your life?' Complete silence from the victim. So the gunman says again 'Come on! Your money or your life?' Still no response. The guy with the gun is getting really mad, so he yells 'Are you deaf or something? I said 'Your money or your life?'' And the victim says 'I'm thinking! I'm thinking!'

It is an old joke, but it illustrates the point that when a threat is made, the coercer gives his victim a choice and asks him to make a decision. The victim can ponder the advantages and disadvantages of defying the threat ('Is life worth living anyway?'), add up the costs and benefits ('How much is my life insurance worth to my family, compared with what's in my wallet?'), and engage the ordinary apparatus of rational choice.[11] Indeed, since the response to coercion looks so much like ordinary rational choice—albeit choice from a rather abruptly curtailed choice-set—many theorists have found it difficult to distinguish coercion from other cases where P confers benefits or imposes harms on Q depending on whether Q does what P wants him to do: 'Lower your price or I'll take my business elsewhere,' 'Work for this paltry wage or I will not employ you.'[12]

Thomas Hobbes was so impressed by this point—about coercion's not precluding rational choice—that he argued in *Leviathan* that the gunman's threat does not diminish my freedom at all. Coercion may work through intimidation, that is, through inducing fear. But, as Hobbes insisted,

Feare and Liberty are consistent; as when a man throweth his goods into the Sea for feare the ship should sink, he doth it nevertheless very willingly, and may refuse to doe it if he will: It is therefore the action, of one that was free: so a man sometimes pays his debt, only for feare of Imprisonment, which because no body hindred him from detaining, was the action of a man at liberty. And generally all actions which men doe in Commonwealths, for feare of the law [are] actions, which the doers had liberty to omit.[13]

It is easy to dismiss this as an aberration in our philosophical tradition, but it was at any rate utterly central for Hobbes. As Andrzej Rapaczynski has noted, 'Fear, in [Hobbes's] theory of man is the most important motivating force of human action, and it is with the help of a man's fear of violent death that Hobbes explains most or even all of his

---

[11] But is it a real choice? Suppose I opt to give up my life; so I tell the gunman that and he shoots me. Now it is unlikely that he will then fastidiously leave my full wallet lying beside my body, saying 'A deal's a deal.' His threat is more properly rendered either as 'Your money, or your life *and* your money,' or as 'Either you must give me your wallet or I'll shoot you and take it myself.' Perhaps we should concentrate on cases that do involve a genuine choice, like 'Tell me the secret combination to the safe or I will break your arm.'

[12] See particularly Nozick, 'Coercion,' pp. 114–15. Nozick argues that whether a statement is a threat (and thus coercive) or an offer (and thus non-coercive) depends on how the carrying out of the statement in the event of non-compliance affects the otherwise normal and morally expected course of events as between P and Q. So, he says, 'one would expect that people will disagree about whether something is a threat or an offer because they disagree about what the normal and expected course of events is, which is to be used as a baseline in assessing whether something is a threat or an offer.'

[13] Hobbes, *Leviathan*, ch. 21, p. 146.

behaviour.'[14] Voluntary deliberation, according to Hobbes, is nothing but the weighing of fears against fears; without fear, human choice is empty and unmotivated. Even so, although he was committed to this position by his metaphysics, it was something Hobbes found embarrassing in his discussion of law. It was not particularly convenient for him to have to say that the laws of the civil sovereign—which threaten penalties in the event of non-compliance—leave his subjects as free as they were before (which is what he would have had to say if he followed this line consistently). If he had said that, he would not have been able to say things like '[l]iberties…depend on the silence of the Law.'[15] Like everyone else, Hobbes had to acknowledge that there is a common use of the word 'free' such that people faced with the threat of sanctions *are* less free than they were before. So he tried to fudge the issue:

But as men, for the attaining of peace, and conservation of themselves thereby, have made an Artificial Man, which we call a Common-wealth; so also have they made Artificial chains, called Civil Lawes, which they themselves, by mutual covenants, have fastened at one end, to the lips of that Man, or Assembly, to whom they have given the Soveraigne Power; and at the other end to their own Ears. These Bonds in their own nature but weak, may nevertheless be made to hold, by the danger, though not by the difficulty of breaking them. In relation to these Bonds only it is, that I am to speak now, of the Liberty of Subjects…[16]

Hobbes's position here is reputable only if he is taken to be saying that a penal law is sufficiently like a real impediment—like the actual use of restraining force, for example—to be treated as such for certain purposes. But given the emphasis he placed on fear as the motivation of almost all voluntary action, to assimilate it to an impediment, even metaphorically, does strain the fabric of his philosophy.

Fortunately, for the purposes of this chapter we are not required to solve Hobbes's difficulty. But it may lead us to reconsider the psychology of intimidation, along the following lines. On Hobbes's account, intimidation involves fear—fear of losing something we value (such as life, for example)—but it is just one fear (one source of aversion, as Hobbes would put it)[17] among many; and, as I said, on this model rational decision consists simply in calculating which fear, which prospective source of hurt, is greatest in a given situation. In particular the calculation

---

[14] Rapaczynski, *Nature and Politics*, p. 35.
[15] Hobbes, *Leviathan*, ch. 21, p. 152.   [16] Ibid., ch. 21, p. 147.
[17] Hobbes defines fear as 'Aversion, with opinion of hurt from the object,' ibid., ch. 6, p. 41.

requires us to think about probabilities: the probability of death, for example, if we do not comply with the threat, versus the enhanced probability of death (via the change in our relative position of power if the coercer gets his way) if we do comply. Can we assume, however, that a person under threat is always psychologically in a position to engage in this sort of calculation, this sort of rational thinking? Might there not be some threats which loom so large in the mind of the person to whom they are directed as to preclude or overwhelm the capacities of practical deliberation which, following Hobbes, we are assuming here?

Consider this example. In a famous bullion robbery that took place at Heathrow Airport some years ago, the robbers poured gasoline over a security guard and threatened to set him alight if he did not open the vault.[18] Now I guess the guard in this case *might* have made a rational choice, quickly calculating the expected utility of being burned alive versus the expected utility of the loss of the gold. He might have paused, asked for a pencil, and considered carefully the pain involved in each alternative, the probability associated with it, and so on and figured out, in a familiar way, which of the two alternatives presented to him, for him to choose among, would maximize his expected utility. *Or* his mental processes might have run along the following lines:

My God, I'm soaked in petrol. He's going to kill me. Shall I give him the combina—...He's got a lighter. He's going to set fire to me. Is it worth...—He's going to set fire to me. He's going to set fire to me! I'm going to burn!

That is, the guard might have tried to think rationally about the issue, but maybe every time he tried he would find his mind crowded and overwhelmed with the thought: 'I'm going to be set alight! I'm going to burn!' He might find it quite impossible to *deliberate* (in any recognizable sense of that word). I don't mean that as soon as he begins to calculate he finds straightaway that he attaches infinite value to life so that it quickly and evidently outweighs anything else at stake. I mean rather that, with this threat present to him, he is not in a psychological state to think clearly about the issue at all. The gasoline and the lighter held in front of him is a breaking point, so far as the normal activity of his deliberative faculties is concerned. The self-possession, the patience, the care, and the self-control that are essential to rational choice might desert him in these circumstances, leaving him in a state of panic.

---

[18] See Michael Horsnell, 'Noye Guilty of Brinks-Mat Bullion Plot,' *The Times* (London), July 24, 1986.

In a recent book, Jon Elster has suggested that we distinguish two ways of talking about fear:

On the one hand, talk about fear may simply refer to a certain complex of beliefs and desires. We believe that unless we do something to prevent it, X will happen. We don't want X to happen. Hence if it is not too costly or difficult, we try to prevent it....On the other hand, talk about fear may refer to the visceral emotional state, as when we believe ourselves to be in acute and imminent danger.[19]

In this second case, there is no guarantee that the emotional state (together with our beliefs) will direct us toward a prudent outcome. Flight, in panic, is no doubt directed away from the state of danger, but it may not be directed to a place of safety. We may, as Elster puts it, find ourselves 'fleeing from the fire into the frying pan.'[20] This captures the sort of distinction I have in mind, and it may be worth reserving the word 'terror,' in our discussion, for mental states that are roughly of this kind, mental states which are not (like common or garden preferences and fears) just inputs into rational choice, but work more or less to short-circuit deliberation in this panic-stricken way. And we might want to reserve the term 'terrorize' for forms of intimidation that work in this way, not just by changing the odds so that the victim rationally makes the choice desired by the intimidator, but by presenting 'alternatives' in a way that simply overwhelms rational deliberation.

There is a vivid description of the sort of mental state I have in mind in Hannah Arendt's book *The Origins of Totalitarianism*. She writes of 'the bestial, desperate terror which, when confronted by real, present horror, inexorably paralyzes everything that is not mere reaction,'[21] and she suggests that 'under conditions of total terror not even fear can any longer serve as an adviser of how to behave.'[22] A man threatened with torture may confess to something that carries an even worse penalty later, because the present prospect of the lash or the electrodes is so awful as to overwhelm any prospect of prudential deliberation about the future. Fear is no longer his *guide* to action; it is simply the basis of his recoiling from a certain stimulus. The threat that is offered—along with a vivid demonstration of the sanction—so panics those who are confronted with it that they respond immediately to avert it, without

---

[19] Elster, *Alchemies of the Mind*, p. 233.
[20] Ibid., p. 275. See also Loewenstein, 'Out of Control: Visceral Influences on Behavior.' I am grateful to my colleague Sam Issacharoff for suggesting these references.
[21] Arendt, *The Origins of Totalitarianism*, p. 441.   [22] Ibid., p. 467.

consideration of whether even more fearful consequences will accrue thereby. As a mark of respect for her analysis, I will call this *Arendtian terrorization*, and I will contrast it with what we may call (in acknowledgment of the joke I retold earlier) *Jack Benny-style coercion*, which leaves room and is intended to leave room for rational calculation on the part of the victim.

4. Terrorizing Governments and Terrorizing Populations

Now leaving aside the legislative definition, for a moment, is it a defining feature of terrorism as we ordinarily understand it that it involve terrorization, i.e. intimidation of the Arendtian kind? It is certainly true that some terrorists behave like the bullion robbers I mentioned a page or so ago, when they are setting up their operations or carrying them into effect. It is likely, for example, that the terrorists responsible for the September 11 attacks on New York and the Pentagon behaved somewhat like that to the flight attendants and pilots on board the aircraft they commandeered: they murdered some and then they threatened the others so viciously as to overwhelm their resistance. But that's a matter of terrorist tactics: it is what I called earlier a stage (i) issue. The further question—and for our purposes the one to focus on—is whether it is essential to our conception of someone as a terrorist that he seeks to do such things in order to terrorize the government or population that he is trying to intimidate. Is it the intention of the terrorist who commandeers an aircraft (using, perhaps, terrorization as his means to do *that*) to terrorize us with the destruction and carnage that results from his crashing it into a building?

One possible reason for answering this question in the negative is that terrorists often seek to intimidate *governments*, and governments may not be the sort of things that can be terrorized in the Arendtian sense. On the account I gave in the previous section, terrorization is what happens when a person's power of rational decision-making is overwhelmed with desperate panic induced by the actions and threats of another. But maybe effects of this sort are confined to face-to-face interactions, involving flesh-and-blood individuals with real human psychology; maybe nothing comparable can be achieved at the level of the artificial person of the state. Maybe the better characterization is that although terrorists do inflict and threaten terrible harm, they still rely—they have no choice but to rely—on some sort of rational calculation by the targeted government in response to the atrocities they perpetuate and the threats that they announce. We know that governments characteristically do respond to terrorist threats in what seems to be a classic rational choice mode: they hold out as long as possible, pursuant to a calculation that they stand to lose more by giving in than they would by the terrorists' carrying out their threats. Then in some cases, they eventually agree to meet the terrorists and discuss their demands, even while they are still realistically, if not explicitly, under the shadow of their threats. And some process of negotiation takes place and various bargains are struck. Even when governments refuse to negotiate (announcing as a matter of principle that 'You can't negotiate with terrorists'), it is plain that this is a political or moral strategy, rather than a panic-stricken failure of the capacities of deliberation and choice that would have to be used if negotiations were to take place. It looks then as though the intimidation practiced by terrorists is straight Jack Benny-style coercion, rather than Arendtian terrorization.

There are several reasons, though, for not resting content with this account. First of all, is it so clear that governments cannot be terrorized? Certainly particular officials may be terrorized, including ministers and heads of government, and their terror may amount to the government's terror for all practical purposes. We do sometimes talk of governments being terrified or paralyzed by fear, and I do not think it is always figurative. Secondly, although governments may respond in rational choice mode to terrorist outrages, calculating costs, benefits, and probabilities etc.,[23] the populations that such governments are sworn to protect may not. And the terrorist strategy may be to coerce the government (Jack Benny-style) by terrorizing the population (Arendt-style). Thirdly, the account given in the previous paragraph may exaggerate the extent to which terrorist groups are actually pursuing a means-end strategy. Some certainly are. They have a set of goals; they make demands in relation to those goals; and they make threats to coercively back up their demands. But some may not. Some may aim to inflict terror for its own sake, or because they think, allegedly on ethical grounds, that it is preferable that members of the victim-population should be in some mental state other than (say) the arrogant self-satisfied complacency which they normally

---

[23] I do not mean that they always respond rationally or well, but that they respond *like* someone seeking to weigh up costs and benefits etc., i.e. they respond in that mode.

exhibit. I shall consider this third possibility in section 6. But, for now, I would like to focus on the second point, the point about the terrorization of populations rather than governments.

The American legislative definition we were considering earlier implied that terrorists seek either to intimidate governments or (alternatively) to intimidate populations. Clearly there are ways of doing the first without doing the second. Suppose a country is ruled by an occupying force, and the inhabitants of the country form themselves into clandestine bands to assassinate the soldiers and officials of the occupying force, threatening explicitly or implicitly to continue the assassinations (which are indiscriminate among the soldiers and officials of the occupying force)[24] unless the force withdraws from their country. Ordinary inhabitants of the country may be largely unaffected by these actions. So any intimidation is intimidation of the occupying force directly and its own cadre of officials. No doubt, the occupying force will condemn and stigmatize these actions as terrorism. But mostly when *we* talk about terrorism, we mean to refer to cases where there is an attempt either to intimidate the population of a country, or to intimidate a government by intimidating the population. Now, even if governments are not capable of being directly terrorized (or even if that is not usually the terrorists' intention), still, it may be possible to terrorize populations. In these cases, then, it might not be out of place to suggest that terrorism works by terrorization: the terrorists terrorize the population in order to intimidate the government into doing something.

The idea of terrorizing whole populations is familiar to us from two recent examples, both involving actions by governments. (On some definitions of 'terrorism,' although states may sponsor terrorism by non-state actors, states or state officials acting in role can't themselves be terrorists. But no one denies that states can be terrorizers.) The first is the use of terror bombing by the British and American air forces during the Second World War, setting fire to large civilian conurbations—by mass conventional fire-bombing (in Hamburg, Dresden, Tokyo etc.) or by the use (in Hiroshima and Nagasaki) of nuclear weapons of mass destruction. As far as anyone understands, the aim of these campaigns was to strike such terror and despair into the civilian populations that were affected, that the governments responsible for those civilian

---

[24] I add this parenthesis because some would argue that a policy of targeted assassination, assassinating particular identified officials because of their particular position or power or importance, is different from terrorism.

populations would find it impossible to continue the war. The idea was that the horrific destruction and carnage wrought among civilians— 100,000 dead in the Tokyo fire-bombings alone—would either lead the surviving civilians to pressure their governments to surrender, or in some other way coerce the government by breaking the will of the civilian populations.[25]

The second case of terrorization by a state is Hannah Arendt's example of the Nazi state's terrorization of the populations under its control.[26] The terms in which Arendt characterizes terror as applied to a whole population are interesting. The impact of state terror consists not merely in the atrocities it perpetrates nor in the impact it has on innocents or on dissidents who (we think) ought to have been protected or tolerated. It has to do—first—with the change produced in a social world which is no longer structured by calculable law and predictable exercises of force. Force is now used, and beatings, torture, incarceration, and death are imposed, without the remotest regard to guilt or innocence as these are juridically conceived (let alone as they might be conceived under laws that were just), even without regard to people's political positions or convictions, without regard to anything they may do, say, or think in opposing or supporting the regime. *Anything* might count as an occasion for the unleashing of state-controlled force against a person—apparently innocuous actions, ascriptive characteristics, trivial grudges or incidents of offense. And the aim of this is not to cow people into doing any one set of things rather than another; but just to produce a human population that is cowed (*tout court*). The population is kept deliberately unclear—to say the least!—about what actions will and what actions will not attract punishment; and this not because the regime has aims that it wants to keep secret from them, but because it wants to get them into the state that people get in when they have no idea from which direction and on what occasions the terrifying threat will come.[27] Independent action and initiative is paralyzed under people's experience of such conditions, which may be something aimed at for its own sake,

---

[25] See Hoyt, *Inferno: The Fire-Bombing of Japan* and Sebald, *On the Natural History of Destruction.*

[26] There's a slight complexity here because Arendt denies that the Nazis organized *a state* in the proper juridical sense. (See Arendt, *Origins of Totalitarianism,* pp. 392–419— the section entitled 'The So-called Totalitarian State.') But the Nazis certainly had a ruling apparatus, which held itself out to the world as a government, and which exercised control through terror over whole populations.

[27] It's a little like Thomas Hobbes's definition of 'terror'—'Feare, without apprehension of why or what' (Hobbes, *Leviathan,* ch. 6, p. 42).

or aimed at for the sake of unleashing something in a population other than the exercise of individual agency. (Hannah Arendt's own account of the overall purpose of terror in a totalitarian society is that it aims to change human agency and consciousness *en masse* in a way that makes it possible for what the terrorizer believes is 'the force of nature or of history to race freely through mankind, unhindered by any spontaneous human action.')[28]

The second sort of effect of pervasive terrorization by a state or state-like agency is social.[29] It damages and undermines the possibility of certain sorts of social interaction, and in particular the possibility of conversation among the citizens to discuss, criticize, and evaluate what is going on. This is partly a product of the use of secret police and informers in the practice of state terrorism. Not only do the citizens not have notice of laws which define the occasions for penalization, but they never know when they are talking to an official—in disguise—who might report something they have said or done as a ground for sanctions. By destroying—through this radical and panic-stricken mistrust—the opportunities for both public deliberation and private conversation, the terrorizing regime effects a radical isolation of individuals from one another, leaving what were once citizens as helpless, terrified, isolated animals.[30] Given her views in moral psychology, Arendt believes that the end-result of this is destruction of the human capacity for moral thought, which she believes cannot really take place as a Thoreau-like exercise of solitary conscience under these conditions.[31]

Now Arendt's example is of course an example of a state's terrorization (or terrorization by something like a state) of its own population—a sort of 'reign of terror.' But presumably something like the effect she observed in Nazi Germany might also work as the strategy of one state against another. As I said a moment ago, the aim of sustained campaigns of terror-bombing might be not just to induce great fear, but to make it eventually impossible for the citizens of the target state to continue to be mobilized in that state's war effort. Disoriented, paralyzed by pervasive fear, rendered helpless, inarticulate, and unthinking by the terror

---

[28] Arendt, *Origins of Totalitarianism*, p. 465.

[29] For a good account, see chs 1–2 of Villa, *Politics, Philosophy, Terror.*

[30] Arendt, *Origins of Totalitarianism*, pp. 437–59 and 474–9.

[31] The way in which even solitary thought models itself on articulate dialogue is key to Arendt's position here. See Arendt, *The Life of the Mind*, p. 185 ff. So her suggestion is that the comprehensive extirpation of the possibility of real dialogue is bound to have effects on the ability of individuals to think morally by themselves.

raining daily from the skies, the population may become like a panic-stricken herd of animals running hither and yon in a vain quest for safety and security, incapable of following the instructions of their rulers, even instructions intended to enhance their security. When the Japanese government failed to respond with sufficient alacrity to the destruction of Hiroshima and the United States threatened to continue using weapons of mass destruction, it must have been something like this—not just destruction and carnage *per se*—that they were aiming at.[32]

In these ways, then, the terrorization of a population may be a means which an intimidator aims at in order to coerce a government. The intimidator need not presuppose that the government itself is rendered helpless with terror: it may have been no part of the Hiroshima/Nagasaki strategy, for example, to have that effect. On the contrary, President Truman surely hoped that the Japanese government would have revised its response (to the ultimatum that was issued at Potsdam) rationally after the atomic bombings. Nevertheless the idea I am pursuing is that a government might be coerced by the loss of something it values very highly—indeed, something indispensable for its status as government—namely the ability to command and mobilize a large civilian population. By rendering or threatening to render the population mindless with terror, the intimidator deprives the target regime of something it needs, a population capable of rational choice. One might even say that it deprives the target regime of an object of Jack Benny-style coercion: with a terror-stricken population, the target government can no longer exercise the ordinary coercion essential to ordinary government.

5. Undermining Legitimacy and Morale

It is one thing to do all this with the United States Air Force; it is another thing to do it with the puny resources and mostly inconsiderable weapons that those we call terrorists have at their disposal. Can those we ordinarily call terrorists—say, the Irish Republican Army in the 1970s and 80s, the Palestinian suicide bombers active in the second *intifada*, the terrorists of Al Qaeda[33]—hope to achieve anything similar in the way of

---

[32] U.S. President Truman's threat after Hiroshima was as follows: 'If they do not now accept our terms they may expect a rain of ruin from the air, the like of which has never been seen on this earth.' ('Address to the Nation,' August 6, 1945.)

[33] For convenience, I shall call such groups 'ordinary terrorists,' not to minimize the wickedness of their activities, but to distinguish them from terrorizing states (i.e. states

terrorization, as a means of accomplishing their aims? (Remember that these are groups trying to intimidate some of the most powerful and lethal armed organizations in history—the British, Israeli, and American states.)

The answer is probably 'no,' at least while ordinary terrorists do not have access to the weapons of mass destruction that states like Britain, Israel, and the United States have in their armory. Still, there may be analogues to the terrorization we have been discussing in the strategies and capacities of these terrorist groups. That is, there may be a level of abstraction at which the terrorization we discussed in section 4 reveals something in common with the impact that ordinary terrorists can reasonably expect to have. We have considered one such abstraction already: *both kinds of entity seek to coerce or intimidate.* But I believe we can come up with something a little richer than this—an abstract description of the way in which terrorists seek to coerce or intimidate which is remarkably like the terrorization sometimes practiced by states. What I have in mind is something along the following lines:

Terrorism is not just simple coercion. It looks to the possibility of creating a certain psycho-social condition, R, in a population that is radically at odds with the range of psycho-social states $\{N_1, N_2, \ldots N_n\}$ that the government wants or needs or can tolerate in its subject population. The terrorist group performs various actions—explosions, killings etc.—which tend to put the population or large sections of it into condition R. The terrorist group does this with the aim of giving the government a taste of what it would be like to have its subject population in condition R. And it threatens to continue such actions, with similar effects, until the government yields to its demands.

In this account, R might be a state of terror, as we have been describing it. Or R might be something else—something short of the kind of 'bestial desperate panic' that Hannah Arendt described, but nevertheless a state or condition that governments cannot afford to let their populations fall into or languish in for long.

For example, one noticeable effect of the September 11, 2001 terrorist attacks in the United States was a short-term collapse (and the exacerbation of a longer term downturn) in economic activity. The Dow Jones index lost 7.1 per cent of its value in the first day of trading after September 11 and continued to fall in the week that followed. Another example is the collapse of the tourist trade in Israel—a decline

that use terror, whether in war or in peace, with effects that are orders of magnitude greater than the effects achieved by the IRA, the suicide bombers, Al Qaeda, etc.).

of 50 per cent or more—in the wake of suicide bombings in 2002–3. These economic effects may be attributable to widespread fear that outrages of the sort that have already occurred are likely to continue—that is, they are symptoms of general insecurity. But beyond that they are also the result of people's apprehensions about the effects of the pervasive occasioned by the individual outrages. Fear itself is a reasonable object of fear, especially when the fear that is feared is widespread in a society and impacts all sorts of other activities. Even if frequent terrorist incidents do not occur, the fear that they might occur can radically undermine the morale of a society, if the society relies for a large part of its prosperity on a cheerful bullish mentality among consumers and investors. If the government is thought to be in some sense responsible for economic morale, then the government will be in principle coerce-able with the threat of actions that are likely to have this effect. (Or so the terrorists may reckon.)

The collapse of economic morale is a very mild example of the sort of value for R that I am interested in. But the proliferation of insecurity may go well beyond that, in the direction of a pervasive disruption of the routines and fabric of ordinary life. In a society like the United States, we go cheerfully about most of our business in public places—like shopping malls, restaurants, schools, colleges, churches, sports fields, and cinemas—with minimal attention to security issues. Imagine the extent, though, to which that would change if America were to experience explosions in these places at the rate of (say) one or two a month, each causing the sort of casualties that recent suicide bombings have caused in Israel,[34] each publicized as a national tragedy with the full panoply of CNN coverage etc. We need not surmise that this would result literally in *terror* of the sort discussed in section 4 in order to see that even the taking of reasonable precautions by large numbers of people in the wake of such experience would radically alter the way that life is lived in this country. We have had a taste of it with the enhancement of security at airports, but we have to imagine that similar precautions are introduced into *all* public spaces in which people gather by the scores or hundred: malls, soccer fields, schools, movie theaters, etc. People would be afraid, but my point now is not the quality of the fear. My point is that even what seemed like a merely prudent response to this fear on the part of hundreds of millions of pusillanimous Americans would lead

---

[34] This chapter was written in the first half of 2003, a period in which Israel suffered at least 11 suicide bombings, killing at least 80 people.

to the emergence of a new sort of ethos governing choices about going out *versus* staying home, an attenuation of large-scale social interaction, and a marked degradation in the practices of mass consumer society that depend on secure large-scale social interaction, and in the cheerful spirit of security that permeates such a society and on which its prosperity depends. None of this could possibly be regarded as acceptable from the point of view of a government; even if it had no particular affection for the aspects of civil society that would be affected and degraded in this way, the government's economic responsibilities and its general status as the organization responsible for the very high level of personal safety that in untroubled times we take for granted, would make this a catastrophe for the state.[35]

My point is not to speculate that this would definitely happen. Everything would depend on circumstances, frequency, and the extent of other distractions. Maybe we would all soldier on, putting our children on school buses, going to the mall, catching movies, eating in McDonald's, etc., with just a few extra security guards. But it is not unimaginable that there would be a catastrophic disruption in the routines of everyday life. And it is part of the logic of terrorism, I think, that it aims or threatens to bring about something like this, and expects to use its ability to bring it about as a point of leverage with the government.

6. Means and Ends

In the discussion so far, I have assumed that terrorism involves a means–end strategy, and that the *term* 'terrorism' describes certain activity on the basis of the sort of means that it uses, and leaves open the description of the cause which such means are calculated to advance.

Distinctions between means and ends are quite important in our reflections on terrorism. For example, I think greater attention to the means/end distinction would help put to rest the old adage that 'one man's terrorist is another man's freedom fighter.' I actually do not think

---

[35] Note that I am not here attempting to explain what is *wrong* with terrorism. If that were our aim, we would surely focus more on the deaths, injuries, and destruction wrought by the terrorists in the atrocities they perpetrate, and less on the role that the fear occasioned by such deaths, injuries, and destruction plays in the overall logic of terrorist coercion. But this chapter is devoted to a discussion of the latter, following the legislative suggestion—see text accompanying n. 7—that it is *the type of coercion or intimidation that they practice* that distinguishes terrorists from other murderers and arsonists etc.

this adage indicates any definitional difficulty at all, once we recognize that actors and modes of action may be described in many ways, and that it is preposterous to think that of any two descriptions of the same actor or the same mode of action we have to choose just one. Modes of action may be described in terms of their means or in terms of their ends ('One man's garbage collector *[means]* is another man's disease-preventer *[end]*,' 'One man's carpenter *[means]* is another man's house-builder *[end]*'). Moreover one of these descriptions may have negative connotations, while the other is positive or neutral ('One man's bureaucrat *[negative]* is another man's protector of the environment *[positive]*,' or 'One man's clergyman *[neutral or positive]* is another man's purveyor of superstition *[negative]*'). An individual can be *both* a freedom-fighter *[end, described positively]* and a terrorist *[means, described negatively]* if he uses terroristic means in his struggle for freedom; or he can be one or the other or neither of these things. We might privilege one of these descriptions over the other to express the view that terroristic means are always wrong, no matter what end they are aiming at, or our view that the fight for freedom is always worthwhile no matter what means are deployed. But most of us hold a view that is more complicated—and more uneasy—than that.

The characterization of people as terrorists is best understood as a characterization of them primarily in terms of the means that they use. I think it would be a mistake to try to define terrorists in terms of their characteristic ends, because those ends are many and varied and they are often capable (at least in principle) of being pursued also using non-terroristic means. (Indeed it is part of our condemnation of terrorists that the ends they pursue, if they are legitimate, ought to be pursued using non-violent methods.)[36]

But is the means-end structure of terrorism always some version of the means–end structure of coercion? In a case of classic coercion, P wants Q to do A: Q's doing A is P's end. P tries to bring that about by threatening

[36] My colleague Jose Alvarez has suggested that a definition of terrorism in terms of its characteristic aims may be fruitful if it identifies aims (or kinds of aim) that cannot be pursued using ordinary non-violent political means. For example: the modern world tries to put the boundaries and the basic legitimacy of most existing states beyond political question. Except in rare instances, political means are not defined for seeking revision of boundaries or revocations of basic legitimacy. So political groups which pursue these ends are driven to adopt extraordinary means. This insight is not incompatible with a primarily means-based approach to the definition of terrorism, and if it is borne out in a large number of instances of terrorism, it would have the advantage of helping to explain the terrorist's choice of means.

Q that if Q does not do A, then P will inflict harm H: the threat of H is P's means to his end. Now, I noted at the beginning of this chapter that terrorism may be distinguished from this model by the fact that the terrorist characteristically also gives Q a taste of H: he doesn't just make a threat, he carries it out in part, in order to show that he has the will and ability to keep imposing H in the event of non-compliance by Q. This is element (ii) in the schema we set out in section 3.

But now I want to consider the possibility that element (ii), which is characteristic of terrorism, is not necessarily part of a coercive strategy at all. What else might it be? A number of possibilities suggest themselves, each of which suggests a non-coercive model of terrorist action (in the simple demand-plus-threat sense of coercion). I think it is important to understand this array of non-coercive possibilities, for they may help us to see that while some terrorist violence is intended to coerce or intimidate, this is not the only point that terrorists may have for the violence they use. As I set out these possibilities, I hope readers will bear in mind that describing some terrorism as non-coercive is not intended to mitigate or excuse it. The condemnation of the murderous violence remains constant, but our moral, political, and legal responses to it may be enriched—if that is the right word—with a more sophisticated understanding of how violence and its effects (terror or some similar state R) fit into the diverse strategies of terrorism.

(1) The terrorist act might simply be an incident of warfare—as one American official described it, part of 'a new pattern of low technology and inexpensive warfare against the West and its friends.'[37] To say this is not to legitimize it as an act of war, nor is it to confuse terrorist action with the use of terrorizing coercion as an act of war (along the lines of the Allied terror-bombing campaigns we discussed earlier). Right now, I am considering the possibility that terrorist atrocities may be regarded simply as acts of war and as no more *coercive* in structure or intent than firing a mortar in battle.

(2) The terrorist act might be intended as punishment or retaliation for some real or imagined offense, and not calculated to achieve anything beyond that. Moreover, the offense that is being punished need not be conceived as defiance of a coercive threat: it may just be something wrong that P thinks Q has done and that Q deserves to be punished for. I am sure many Al Qaeda operatives approach their murderous assignments in this spirit: the United States is a great satanic wrongdoer

---

[37] Whitehead, 'Terrorism—the Challenge and the Response,' 215–16.

and it simply deserves retribution. Retribution need not be intended to affect (let alone coerce or intimidate) the subsequent conduct of the victim; this, after all, is what distinguishes retributive from consequentialist characterizations of punishment.

(3) As Frantz Fanon speculated, violent action might be viewed as a form of therapy for the perpetrator, particularly where the perpetrator has suffered for long time in the ignominy and humiliation of some oppressive form of subordination.[38] Thus Fanon writes things like the following:

> [T]o shoot down a European is to kill two birds with one stone, to destroy an oppressor and the man he oppresses, at the same time: there remain a dead man, and a free man. . . . At the level of individuals, violence is a cleansing force. It frees the native from his inferiority complex and from his despair and inaction, it makes him fearless and restores his self-respect.[39]

It is not clear though whether we should regard this as a distinct structure of action or as a collateral feature of action already structured in some other way. By that I mean, a terrorist act may perhaps be therapeutic in Fanon's sense only by virtue of being an act of war, or retaliation, or part of a structure of coercion, etc.

(4) The terrorist act might be intended simply to attract publicity to the cause of those who perpetrate the atrocity, without any ulterior coercive intent. In other words, an act of terrorism may be an example of what Kropotkin called 'the propaganda of the deed,'[40] or, as one commentator described it,

> a crime for the sake of publicity. When a bomb explodes, people take notice; the event attracts more attention than a thousand speeches or pictures. If the terror is sustained, more and more people will become interested, wondering why the atrocities occurred and whether the cause seems plausible. Hence . . . the perpetrators only intend to harm their victims incidentally. The principal object is the public, whose consciousness will be aroused by the outrage.[41]

This logic of murder and arson as publicity stunts may well belie the appearance of randomness sometimes associated with terrorism. In the popular imagination, the terrorist chooses his victims randomly from among the broad class of innocents or non-combatants. Certainly the

---

[38] See Fanon, *The Wretched of the Earth.*　　[39] Ibid., pp. 94 and 122.

[40] See Kropotkin, *Paroles d'un Révolte*, p. 286, cited in Novotne, 'Random Bombing of Public Places,' 225.

[41] Rapoport, 'Fear and Trembling: Terrorism in Three Religious Traditions,' at 660.

class of victims is perceived as 'extra-normal,' in relation to what people regard as the legitimate or ordinary casualties of war.[42] But the reality may be that the terrorists carefully calibrate their choice of victims in order to gain maximum publicity. (And actually the same may be true even of terrorism that conforms to the coercive model set out in section 5. As Edward Mickolus argues, '[r]ather than "deliberately choosing victims at random," terrorists attempt to give the impression that their targeting is random, when it is in fact chosen to have symbolic value...and designed to create the climate of fear that is an integral part of the terrorist strategy.')[43]

The idea behind (4) is that the publicity attracted by an atrocity (and perhaps also by the state of mind R that the atrocity generates) is itself a strategic asset for the terrorist groups, which it can use for all sorts of purposes, not just for the narrow range of intimidatory purposes that the American legislative definition seems to presuppose. It may be used to win recruits, or to put an issue on the political agenda, or to attract international attention to some situation which the terrorist manages to associate with the campaign. A few explosions may be worth a million leaflets in bringing the grievances or aspirations of a marginalized group to popular attention, and making them a talking point in mainstream politics. Of course these purposes sometimes backfire, and people lose sympathy with a cause that is being promoted by these methods. But it would be unwise to think this was necessarily or always the case. Often conversation which proceeds explicitly on the basis that a worthy end cannot justify terrorist means, nevertheless involves its participants in discussion about the end—and that itself may be a major achievement for a previously obscure political group.

(5) Connected with the publicity stunt characterization is the idea that terrorist acts might be intended as acts of expression, to send a message of some sort to the targeted population or to the world at large. I guess if we take 'send a message' broadly enough, then there is an expressive element in almost all of the strategies we are discussing. Certainly, if terrorism is intended as straightforward intimidation, there has to be a message conveyed, namely, the implicit demand and threat. Also we can say that there is some sort of message conveyed in (4), the propaganda of the deed—'Here we are, and we have these grievances'—and in (3), the therapeutic approach—'We are no longer passive.' The punitive

[42] Ross and Gurr, 'Why Terrorism Subsides,' 407.
[43] Mickolus, 'Terrorists, Governments, and Numbers,' 56.

approach in (2) may have an expressive element, inasmuch as punishment involves denunciation, and it may also express some proposition about proportionality. And as we proceed, readers will be able to construct for themselves the expressive possibilities inherent in strategies (6) and (7). But I mention the expressive strategy separately in order to emphasize that strategies (1)–(4) and (6)–(7) should not be reduced to whatever element of expression they contain. For even if a message is sent in each and every one of these strategies, it is a different message, and the strategies may make sense also quite apart from whatever message is being sent.

The messages that may be sent via the medium of terrorist activity can be quite complicated. If the terrorist activity is intended as punishment for some real or imagined offense, it can be used to send a message about proportionality: 'What you did is as bad as *this*.' Or, if it is intended as an act of war, it can be used to send a message about who should and who should not be regarded as innocent combatants: some Palestinian terrorist factions have intended their distinction between attacking settlers and attacking civilians in Israel proper to be read in this way. Also we must not assume that the targeted population is the primary audience. Sometimes terrorist acts are intended to send a message to more moderate factions of the enterprise to which the terrorists think of themselves as belonging or to those who claim to speak for them: 'Don't go too far—or, you have already gone too far—in your negotiations and concessions.' Needless to say the potential for interference, misreading, and acoustic separation in this medium is enormous, and each side to the conflict may have an interest in misrepresenting the message even if they fully understand it.

(6) The sixth possibility is one that I alluded to earlier in section 4. Terrorism may aim at the inculcation of terror or of some similar psycho-social state R in a population for *ethical* reasons, either for its own sake, or in order to bring about some sort of further ethical transformation in the mentality or attitudes of the targeted population.

Now, I want to say at the outset that I find it both a difficult and a delicate task to characterize this particular form of terrorist strategy. For many of us, the idea of *ethical terrorism* is a contradiction in terms, especially when (as here) the 'ethical' does not even refer to the noble goals of liberation, national independence, freedom from oppression, etc. that 'freedom-fighters' are often thought to be aiming at. And in the version under consideration here it seems a particularly offensive oxymoron, since what is being suggested is that there might be some ethical value in the terror, panic, or demoralization, *as such*, which are the natural responses to terrorist atrocities. But by calling it ethical, I mean only to categorize the strategy, not endorse it.

The idea, as I understand it, is this. The populations of prosperous countries are often perceived to languish in complacency and self-satisfied indifference to what happens in less prosperous parts of the world: their mentality is inauthentic and irresponsible, they give little thought to the predicament of anyone other than themselves and their fellow-countrymen. Their mental state—call it N_1—is offensively inappropriate to the reality of the world in which they live, but of which they seem blithely and viciously unaware. This is the first element in this model of 'ethical' terrorism—a critique of the mentality of the target population. The critique can be very general—a general critique of culture, if you like, of the sort put about by the Frankfurt school[44]—or it may have to do with some specific situation relative to the population of a specific country. Suppose state X is oppressing some other society Y. The people of X may be in a state of mind that neglects or fails to comprehend the oppression being practiced in their name, because their government behaves scrupulously towards its own citizens while ruling brutally in its colonies or in other territories abroad. In a case like this, the offensive mental condition of the people of X—call it N_2—consists in the fact that they have no idea what it is like to be a member of Y, under the brutal heel of X. So—the terrorist reckons—these mental states, N_1 and/or N_2, ought to be changed. Perhaps N_2 ought to be changed as part of a wider strategy to end the oppression or occupation. Or perhaps it is thought that these mental states ought to be changed simply because they are *ethically inappropriate* to the world or to the circumstances in which the relevant society finds itself. It would be good, the terrorist reckons, for Americans to become less arrogant and complacent; or it would be good for the British or the Israeli citizenry to experience the fear and insecurity that their subject populations have to live with every day. And so the terrorist considers various means by which this could be accomplished—public education and leaflets, for example—and he concludes that there might be nothing so effective as a few atrocities—bombings, murders, spectacular acts of destruction—calculated to generate widespread terror, panic, or some other of the psycho-social states R that we spoke about earlier. The reason for

---

[44] See, e.g. Marcuse, *One-Dimensional Man*.

doing that, on this model, is not the reason we developed in section 5, *viz.* that the threat of bringing about and sustaining R gives the terrorist group some sort of leverage with the targeted government. It is rather that R represents an improvement over N_1 or N_2; it is an improvement in and of itself, or it is an improvement because of the more sober and responsible reorientation of social attitudes that R may lead to in the long run.

To illustrate the latter possibility, I can cite a comparatively innocuous analogy, from Jean-Jacques Rousseau's educational treatise, *Émile*. Here is how Rousseau imagines that a child might be taught respect for the principle of property:

The child, living in the country, will have gotten some idea of field work... He will not have seen the gardener at work more than two times—sowing, planting, and growing vegetables—before he will want to garden himself.... I will not oppose his desire; on the contrary, I shall approve of his plan, share his taste, and work with him.... I shall be his under-gardener, and dig the ground for him till his arms are strong enough to do it. He will take possession of it by planting a bean, and this is surely a more sacred possession, and one more worthy of respect, than that of Nuñes Balboa, who took possession of South America in the name of the King of Spain by planting his banner on the coast of the Southern Sea. We come to water the beans every day, we watch them coming up with the greatest delight. I increase this delight by saying, Those belong to you. To explain what that word 'belong' means, I show him how he has given his time, his labour, and his trouble, his very self to it; that in this ground there is something of himself which he can claim against anyone else, just as he could withdraw his arm from the hand of another man who wanted to hold it against his will.

One fine day he hurries up with his watering-can in his hand. What a sad scene! All the beans are pulled up, the soil is dug over, you can scarcely find the place. Ah, what has become of my labour, my work, the beloved fruits of my care and sweat? Who has stolen my property? Who has taken my beans? The young heart revolts; the first feeling of injustice brings its sorrow and bitterness. Tears come in torrents; the devastated child fills the air with sobs and cries. I share his sorrow and anger; we look around us, we make inquiries. At last we discover that the gardener did it. We send for him.

But we are greatly mistaken. The gardener, hearing our complaint, begins to complain louder than we: What, gentlemen, was it you who wrecked my work? I had sown some Maltese melons; the seed was given me as something quite precious and which I meant to give you as a treat when they were ripe. But you have planted your miserable beans and destroyed my melons, which were coming up so nicely and which I cannot replace. You have done me an irreparable wrong, and you have deprived yourselves of the pleasure of eating some exquisite melons.[45]

It is a sorry tale, and it may appear to be a heartless strategy for moral education: why should the child's ethical development require the infliction of this sort of traumatic disappointment? But evidently Rousseau believed that unless a child was given some such devastating shock as this, he would not grow up with the appropriate respect for others' rights (nor even with an appropriate understanding of his own).[46] The child's complacent pride in his little vegetable plot is the analogue of N_1 and his distress when he finds that his plants have been torn up is the analogue of R; Rousseau hopes that, properly handled, R will lead not to general and permanent disorientation but to an ethically improved attitude which involves an appropriate respect for other's rights and therefore an ethically more appropriate sense of the child's own rights.

Now, there are also of course massive disanalogies. The tutor and the gardener do not conspire to blow anything up or to actually injure the child. (But they do destroy something the child cherished as his own and they do set out to traumatize him.) Moreover, to the extent that we sympathize with the Rousseauian strategy, it may be because we credit the gardener's complaint that the child was actually encroaching on the gardener's legitimate rights, and so all the gardener was doing was asserting and exercising those rights (which is not all that our 'ethical' terrorists are doing). Still, the point of the analogy from *Émile* is just to illustrate something about the structure of this form of terrorist intention, and to distinguish it in aim and strategy from the coercive model that tends to dominate our thinking.

Of course, our 'ethical' terrorist, if he is realistic, may have doubts about whether the eventual redemption of the targeted population is really possible. If he does not believe that it is, then he may abandon the ethical strategy altogether, or he may figure that *nevertheless* the mentality that his activity induces, R, is still preferable to N_1 or N_2. That is, he may figure that even though it is traumatizing and distressing for those who experience it (and even though it is achieved through atrocity and murder), R is better from an ethical point of view as a permanent state of mind than the complacency and moral torpor that previously characterized the target population.

---

[45] Rousseau, *Émile, or On Education*, Bk II, paras 289–93.
[46] For discussion, see Nichols, 'Rousseau's Novel Education in the *Émile*,' 539.

(7) Finally, in this list of non-coercive strategies associated with terrorism, we must include the approach that seeks, through atrocity and fear, to make the targeted state 'show its true colors' and engage in acts of political repression that will discredit it in the eyes of its subjects or the international community, and undercut its reputation as a paragon of freedom and a respecter of rights.[47]

Under heading (6) I mentioned the possibility that a state, X, oppressing another society, Y, may act scrupulously towards its own citizens while acting brutally towards the members of Y. Political theorists have speculated that in the long run it is difficult to hold this line, and that brutal practices associated for example with colonialism tend eventually to come home to roost and infect the domestic system of law and order upheld by the imperial power.[48] Whether or not this is inevitable, the terrorist strategy may be to expedite it, either to drive home a message to ordinary members of the population of X, or perhaps also—but this is more far-fetched—to precipitate a revolutionary situation in X.

A strategy of this kind raises interesting conundrums about the appropriate response to terrorism. For one thing, it indicates the futility of the slogan one sometimes hears: 'We must never give the terrorists what they want.' Since what the terrorists often want is precisely things that flow from our acting more prudently or more robustly to protect the security of the targeted population, the cost of complying with this slogan would be to go on exactly as before, as though no greater vigilance were needed or as though prudence did not dictate any particular response. For another thing, it perhaps reinforces the point that attention to the Rule of Law and to civil liberties is at least as important in responding to

---

[47] This was particularly effective in Britain and the United States after the events of September 11, 2001. Britain moved explicitly to derogate from its human rights obligations under the European Convention of Human Rights, so that it could detain international terrorists indefinitely without trial. (See Tomkins, 'Legislating against Terror,' 106.) And in the American response, the U.S. government acted decisively against constitutionalism and the Rule of Law by setting up military tribunals to try terrorist suspects on capital crimes and camps for the indefinite detention, interrogation, and torture of the Al Qaeda and Taliban members it holds captive. (See, e.g. Duncan Campbell, 'US interrogators turn to "torture lite,"' *The Guardian* (London), January 25, 2003 and Andrew Gumbel, 'US "is using torture techniques" to interrogate top al-Qa'ida prisoners,' *The Independent* (London), December 27, 2002. For an early U.S. response to these rumors, see Dana Priest and Barton Gellman, 'U.S. Decries Abuse but Defends Interrogations; "Stress and Duress" Tactics Used on Terrorism Suspects Held in Secret Overseas Facilities,' *Washington Post*, December 26, 2002.) This chapter was written in 2003; since then the extent of the U.S. involvement in torture has become much more widely known: see particularly the discussion in Chapter 7, below.
[48] See, e.g. Arendt, *Origins of Totalitarianism*, pp. 243–9.

a terrorist threat as it is in peacetime: the point here is that any deroga-
tions from the Rule of Law and civil liberties in response to terrorism are
not just costly in themselves but are likely to be seized on by the terrorists or by those who support them as further evidence that the society
under threat is one that deserves to be attacked.

7. Conclusion

As I said at the outset, defining terrorism is difficult, and except for legal
purposes it is probably not an enterprise worth undertaking, at least not
for its own sake. This is particularly so if a proposed definition is supposed to be answerable to ordinary language, because ordinary usage is
of course permeated and distorted by the effects of the emotive or value-
loading of the word. For most people, certainly for most politicians, the
word 'terrorist' is a word of the most severe condemnation. To describe
someone as a terrorist is to put him beyond the pale of political interaction. To describe an action as terrorism is to condemn it, with the severity appropriate to the condemnation of murderous atrocity: it is a mode
of condemnation people are reluctant to assign, for example, to acts of
war by the armed forces of their own nation, even those that result in
civilian deaths. Because the term carries this tremendous (negative) evaluative or emotive weight, people have an incentive to ensure that, if possible, it is applied to their dangerous political adversaries or to persons or
programs that they disagree with strenuously on other grounds. This is
an example of the familiar business of 'persuasive definition': when the
usage of a word has both a descriptive and an emotive component, there
may be some advantage in decoupling the two and, while holding the
emotive component constant, applying the word to a new category of
items in virtue of a new set of descriptive features.[49] Equally, if the term
has these negative connotations, there is inevitably some advantage to
resisting its application to one's friends or to actions and programs that
one approves of, even when they clearly appear to satisfy the descriptive criteria normally associated with the term.[50] A proposed definition

[49] Stevenson, 'Persuasive Definitions,' 331.
[50] There are other difficulties too. An emotively or rhetorically powerful term tends
to be extended, by metonymy, to almost anything that can be associated with a person or
group once some act or opinion of theirs can plausibly be condemned as terrorism. My
favorite example is the condemnation of the theory of natural rights as 'terrorist language'
because it was espoused by French Revolutionaries associated with the terror in France

of terrorism is liable then to all sorts of rebuttals and counter-examples which represent nothing more solid than the vagaries of a particularly inflamed form of political discourse. Linguistic intuitions are entangled with political prejudices, and the returns accruing to any debate about whether states can be terrorists, or whether terrorist attacks necessarily target the innocent, or whether there is such a thing as eco-terrorism, are bound to diminish very quickly.

The discussion in this chapter is not intended as the basis for a definition. As I tried to make clear at the outset, my strategy is to use questions that sound like definitional questions to open up lines of inquiry and reflection on the subject of terrorism that may be worthwhile in other ways. This is particularly true of my observations about coercion and terror. On the one hand, I wanted to argue that the strategies associated with terrorist action are not necessarily coercive; that is they don't necessarily have the structure of demand-plus-threat. Some instances do have this structure; but in other cases the use of terrorist violence is associated with military or retributive or therapeutic or publicity-seeking or expressive or ethical strategies or strategies simply designed to discredit the targeted state.

I have proceeded on the basis that all terrorism involves violence, but I have tried to stay away from the vexed question of whether it has to be violence directed at the innocent or at civilians or at non-combatants.[51] I am not sure that anything is gained by stipulation or definition in this area: it is enough to note that modern terrorism often attacks civilians in a way that distinguishes it from the normal rules and constraints of war, and that it is worth pondering what the point of that might be (as well as whether there is the remotest possibility of ever justifying it). I speculated that in many cases, as the term suggests, the point is to create a state of *terror* in a society, or some psychological state, R, resembling terror, and that it is worth trying to understand how the creation of R fits into the various kinds of strategy we have been considering. But obviously it would be a mistake to argue that the intention to create R is a necessary aspect of terrorism, and it would be an even greater mistake to suppose that any activity which promotes R has to be regarded as terrorism for that reason alone. Coming to understand terrorism is a piecemeal and

in 1793–4. As a matter of interest, this phrase comes hot on the heels of Jeremy Bentham's famous characterization of 'natural and imprescriptable rights' as 'nonsense upon stilts' in Bentham, 'Anarchical Fallacies,' p. 53.

[51] But see Chapter 4 below.

multi-faceted enterprise, and it almost certainly involves shifting our attention among classes of cases, each of which may be regarded as 'core' or central for various purposes. I hope I have contributed something to the richness of our understanding—if only by moving us away from very simple models that stress simply the violence or the coercive uses to which violence might be put. And if, as seems likely, that makes the goal of an agreed definition of 'terrorism' recede even further into the distance I don't think that should be regarded as a cost at all. The point is not to define terrorism but to understand it (so we can figure out, in a reasonably sophisticated way, what to do about it).

4

Civilians, Terrorism, and
Deadly Serious Conventions

On the morning of September 11, 2001, members of the terrorist organization Al Qaeda commandeered four American airplanes with civilian passengers. They flew two of them into the twin towers of the World Trade Center in Lower Manhattan, murdering around 2,800 people—more than 200 passengers and crew aboard the airplanes, almost 2,200 men and women working in the World Trade Center, and more than 400 of the police and firefighters who responded to the emergency.

Why do we call these 'murders'? Why not 'casualties of war'? We regard ourselves as engaged in a war against terrorism and apparently the Al Qaeda organization publicly declared itself to be in a state of war with the United States long before September 11.[1] I can imagine someone arguing that if *war* is what we have going on here, then we should use other terms to describe these killings—terms that are more appropriate to killings in time of war.

The immediate answer to this challenge is that the infliction of these 2,800 deaths took place in clear and deliberate violation of the laws and customs of armed conflict. The laws and customs of armed conflict distinguish killings that are in some sense privileged as acts of war from those that are not so privileged.[2] They require us to follow a principle of distinction, to make distinctions. The principle enshrined in the law at the moment is what I shall call the *traditional* principle of distinction: I shall also use the phrase 'the rule about civilians.' It privileges the killing of combatants on either side, but it prohibits direct attacks on non-combatants, i.e. on civilians. The basic legal principles are set out in Articles 48 and 51 of the First Protocol to the Geneva Conventions.[3] As

---

[1] See <http://www.pbs.org/newshour/terrorism/international/fatwa_1998.html>.

[2] The term 'privileged' is used in its Hohfeldian sense.

[3] Article 48: 'Basic rule: In order to ensure respect for and protection of the civilian population and civilian objects, the Parties to the conflict shall at all times distinguish between the civilian population and combatants and between civilian objects and military objectives

treaties, the Geneva Conventions only bind the states that have signed and ratified them.[4] But the principle of civilian immunity is also a principle of customary international law. In addition Article 8(2)(b) and (e) of the Rome Statute of the International Criminal Court makes it a crime for any organization or individual to intentionally direct attacks against the civilian population as such.[5]

Apart from the special provisions of war crimes legislation, killings that are not privileged as acts of war are to be assessed in the usual way as culpable homicides—mostly as murders, that is, unlawful intentional killings. The 9/11 killings were of that kind, the Al Qaeda actions being deliberately aimed at civilians in exactly the way that the laws and customs of armed conflict prohibit. That is why the September 11 attacks were wrong. (But 'wrong' is too mild a word: they were murderous atrocities.) And that is why terrorism in general is wrong, in all cases and in all circumstances, because terrorism is an approach to armed conflict that involves little else besides attacks of this kind.[6] The military doctrine of terrorism is to create fear and panic in a population by murdering large numbers of civilians in circumstances where they are going about their ordinary business with little thought that they will be made targets of armed attack because they believe they are protected both by the laws of war and by the ordinary laws concerning homicide. The laws and customs of armed conflict prohibit this. But the military doctrine of terrorism holds the laws and customs of armed conflict in contempt, at least so far as the terrorists' own actions and strategies are concerned.

In what follows, I would like to explore the grounds and presuppositions of this judgment. In particular I want to discuss the moral

and accordingly shall direct their operations only against military objectives.' Article 51: '1. The civilian population and individual civilians shall enjoy general protection against dangers arising from military operations. To give effect to this protection, the following rules, which are additional to other applicable rules of international law, shall be observed in all circumstances. 2. The civilian population as such, as well as individual civilians, shall not be the object of attack. Acts or threats of violence the primary purpose of which is to spread terror among the civilian population are prohibited. 3. Civilians shall enjoy the protection afforded by this Section, unless and for such time as they take a direct part in hostilities.'

[4] See also the observation of Alston, *Report of the Special Rapporteur on Extrajudicial, Summary or Arbitrary Executions: Mission to Israel and Lebanon*, at p. 7 (§ 19): 'Although Hezbollah, a non-State actor, cannot become a party to these human rights treaties, it remains subject to the demand of the international community, first expressed in the Universal Declaration of Human Rights, that every organ of society respect and promote human rights' (on file with author).

[5] ICC Statute, Article 8(2)(b)(i)–(ii) and (e)(i), available at <http://untreaty.un.org/cod/icc/statute/romefra.htm>.

[6] See also the discussion in Meisels, *The Trouble with Terror*, pp. 24–5.

significance of the positive laws, conventions, and customs that make terrorist attacks illicit. Some theorists maintain that the laws and customs of armed conflict are conventional in character, rather than representing any deep moral insight. They could be otherwise; we can imagine them otherwise; they have been otherwise in other times and places. So, we have to ask: is the infringement of the laws and customs of armed conflict a matter of any greater significance than a breach of local convention? Is its wrongness not relative to the contingencies of time and place where these conventions happen to flourish? If so, why do we judge these actions so vehemently, using terms of moral condemnation normally reserved for violations of the most serious moral absolutes?

I should say at once that I think there are convincing answers to these questions. I believe that the language of murder that I used in the opening paragraphs of this chapter *is* appropriate. (I did not use it as a sneaky academic's *oratio obliqua,* intending eventually to discredit it or attribute it to someone else.) Though I want to subject the judgments with which I began to some scrutiny, my aim is to understand them, not deconstruct or criticize them. Indeed one of my purposes in this chapter is to defend the view that terrorism is murder against philosophers who argue that the blanket prohibition on attacking civilians is unjustified, irrational, or obsolete.[7]

1. McMahan on Civilian Immunity

A recent paper by Jeff McMahan provides a useful point of departure for our discussion. In 'The Ethics of Killing in War,'[8] McMahan argues that there is no moral justification for any blanket prohibition on intentionally attacking civilians. He thinks one could make a moral case for saying that certain civilians are properly liable to intentional attack— for example, civilians who share responsibility for an unjust war. This is because he believes that 'it is moral responsibility for an unjust threat

---

[7] This chapter does not explore the distinction between lawful and unlawful combatants (distinguished in terms of status and appearance, rather than actions). For a convincing argument to the effect that the distinction between lawful and unlawful combatants serves the distinction between combatants and non-combatants, see Meisels, *The Trouble with Terror*, p. 91 ff.

[8] McMahan, 'The Ethics of Killing in War,' 693.

that is the principal basis of liability to [be the target] of defensive (or preservative) force.'

The requirement of distinction should then hold that combatants must discriminate between those who are morally responsible for an unjust threat, or for a grievance that provides a just cause [for war], and those who are not. It should state that while it is permissible to attack the former, it is not permissible intentionally to attack the latter...[9]

It would follow, on McMahan's approach, that soldiers who are not themselves engaged in an unjust war—soldiers who are resisting unjust aggression, for example—are not legitimate targets; and civilians who *are* responsible for unjust aggression *may* be legitimate targets of deadly force. I know that McMahan does not think that any of the 9/11 casualties fall into the latter category. But on his view, the wrongness of killing them is not simply a function of their being civilians; we have to also figure out whether they had any responsibility for the unjust aggression that Al Qaeda claimed it was responding to.

In some contexts this might make an important difference. McMahan believes, for example, that the American capitalists who persuaded the Eisenhower administration to organize a coup in Guatemala in the 1950s so that they could get back some land that had been nationalized would have been legitimate targets for Guatemalan forces resisting American aggression.[10] Not that McMahan is arguing against the very idea of a principle of distinction. He insists that his argument does not challenge the principle 'in its most generic formulation, which is simply that combatants must discriminate between legitimate and illegitimate targets. Rather, it challenges the assumption that the distinction between legitimate and illegitimate targets coincides with that between combatants and noncombatants.'[11] McMahan thinks that we need to complicate the categories we use by introducing categories of guilty and innocent civilians and justified and non-justified combatants, and adjusting our sense of the appropriate distinctions accordingly.[12]

I hope McMahan will forgive me if I add that many terrorists hold a similar view. For example, some Al Qaeda officials argue that the rule about civilians is wrong inasmuch as it protects the people who, in a

---

[9] Ibid., 722–3.   [10] Ibid., 725–6.   [11] Ibid., 718.
[12] For an example of what a more complex taxonomy would look like, see Honderich, *After the Terror*, p. 159, distinguishing non-combatants, unengaged combatants, half-innocents, clear innocents, etc.

democracy, vote for and pay for wars of aggression.[13] It is impossible to know whether this is said sincerely or in good faith; one rather thinks it is not. On the other hand, some intellectual apologists for terrorism have said something similar: they say that the real criminals, imperialist politicians in the West and those who support them, should not be given the benefit of outmoded laws of war designed mainly to protect their own interests. I do not say this in order to discredit McMahan's critique by association. For reasons I will discuss in section 3, he opposes and condemns violations of the existing laws and customs of armed conflict. I mention the use of similar arguments by terrorists and their apologists only to show that this is a real-life dispute, not a made-up philosopher's dilemma.

2. Distinguishing the Legal and the 'Deep Moral' Issue

It is not McMahan's intention to justify terrorist attacks. But he is anxious that we should think complex moral thoughts rather than simple-minded ones in our condemnation of them. He is surely right about that. What I want to do in this chapter is to bring that complex thinking to bear also on our understanding of what it is for conduct in this area to be governed by positive law.

In particular I want to consider the suggestion that violations of the rule about civilians are not exactly wrong in the way that murder is wrong, but wrong more as a technical matter, rather like the violation of a convention. Another similar suggestion is that violations of the rule about civilians are wrong in the sense of *mala prohibita*, not wrong in the sense of *mala in se*—wrong because they are prohibited, not prohibited because they are wrong.[14] I shall argue that even if the killing of civilians is categorized as a breach of convention or as *malum prohibitum*, that does not diminish the seriousness of these violations. I shall argue also that a move from the moral simplicities of *mala in se* to the complexities of conventional rules does not necessarily correspond to a move from deontological prohibitions to consequentialist assessment. In certain circumstances, the violation of a convention or of a merely technical rule may be absolutely forbidden from a moral point of view.

---

[13] See Holmes, *The Matador's Cape*, p. 52, citing interview with Osama bin Laden.
[14] For this distinction, see Blackstone, *Commentaries*, Vol. I, Introduction, sect. 2.

In addition, there is the complexity associated with the distinction between idealized moral thinking and the sort of assessments that are appropriate for embodiment in law. That this distinction might be important is suggested by some remarks McMahan makes at the end of his article. McMahan observes that although he takes himself to have mounted a successful moral attack on the rule about civilians, it is probably a good idea for the laws of war to continue to prohibit intentional attacks on civilians (any civilians).

[T]he account I have developed of the deep morality of war is not an account of the laws of war. The formulation of the laws of war is a wholly different task, one that I have not attempted and that has to be carried out with a view to the consequences of the adoption and enforcement of the laws or conventions. It is, indeed, entirely clear that the laws of war must diverge significantly from the deep morality of war as I have presented it.[15]

For example, although McMahan organizes his deep moral account around the principle of responsibility, he believes that the laws of war are oriented to different values: '[T]he laws of war are conventions established to mitigate the savagery of war.'[16] McMahan emphasizes that when we move from what he calls the deep morality of warfare to these conventions, we are still in the realm of the moral.

It is in everyone's interests that such conventions be recognized and obeyed.... Given that general adherence to certain conventions is better for everyone, all have a moral reason to recognize and abide by these conventions. For it is rational for each side in a conflict to adhere to them only if the other side does. Thus if one side breaches the understanding that the conventions will be followed, it may cease to be rational or morally required for the other side to persist in its adherence to them. A valuable device for limiting the violence will thereby be lost, and that will be worse for all.[17]

This claim, that the rule about civilians is best understood as a valuable convention, is quite common in the literature.[18] One of its best-known proponents is George Mavrodes.[19] Non-combatant immunity, says Mavrodes, is best thought of in relation to 'a convention which substitutes for warfare a certain form of limited combat.'[20] We could substitute single combat for warfare, but it is unlikely that that convention

---

[15] McMahan, 'The Ethics of Killing in War,' 730.   [16] Ibid.
[17] Ibid., 730.
[18] See also the discussion in Meisels, *The Trouble with Terror*, p. 119.
[19] Mavrodes, 'Conventions and the Morality of War.'   [20] Ibid., 127.

will be viable. So we substitute limited fighting among designated participants—large numbers of participants, but not as large as the number that would be involved in total warfare between all the members of rival communities. Mavrodes observes that the convention we have may actually be inferior to some other viable and morally less disreputable convention. But he denies that this means that we now have a duty to follow the improved convention that we imagine. '[T]he results of acting in conformity with a preferable convention which is not widely observed may be much worse than the results of acting in conformity with a less desirable convention which is widely observed.'[21]

Still, neither thinker believes that the importance of following existing and observed conventions renders moral critique redundant. If a case could in fact be made for single combat as an alternative, then Mavrodes reckons we would have a 'moral obligation to promote its adoption.'[22] And McMahan's view is that we should establish laws and conventions for war that are 'best suited to get combatants on both sides to conform their action as closely as possible to the constraints imposed by the deep morality of war.' He believes the moral arguments he has given can provide a basis 'for the reevaluation of the rules we have inherited.'[23] He acknowledges, in some suggestive passages at the end of his article, that it might be 'dangerous to tamper with rules that already command a high degree of allegiance.' 'The stakes,' he says, 'are too high to allow for much experimentation with alternatives.'[24] He acknowledges too that the conventional rules, though defective from a strictly moral-philosophy point of view, 'may be well suited to the regulation of the conduct of war in conditions in which there are few institutional constraints, so that the restraining effects have to come from the content of the rules rather than from institutions in which the rules might be embedded.'[25] McMahan says:

It is possible that the rules of *jus in bello* coincide rather closely with the laws that would be optimal for regulating conduct in battle. These rules have evolved

---

[21] Idem.   [22] Idem.   [23] McMahan, 'The Ethics of Killing in War,' 731.

[24] Ibid. McMahan even wonders whether it might not be appropriate to suppress his and others' moral criticisms: 'Suppose…that…if combatants are to be sufficiently motivated to obey certain rules in the conduct of war, they will have to believe that those rules really do constitute the deep morality of war. If it is imperative to get them to respect certain conventions, must we present the conventions as the deep morality of war and suppress the genuine deeper principles? Must the morality of war be self-effacing in this way? I confess that I do not know what to say about this…' (Ibid., 732).

[25] Ibid., 731.

over many centuries and have been refined, tested, and adapted to the experience of war as the nature of war has itself evolved.[26]

This is all extremely interesting, and it attests to the seriousness with which McMahan regards the laws and customs of armed conflict even as he undertakes a deep moral critique of one of their leading principles. I shall not say very much more about that critique in this essay, but I will try to explore the reasons that should lead—and I think mostly do lead—McMahan and other moral philosophers to take the positive law of the matter very seriously.

3. Is the Moral Question Prior to the Legal?

Some philosophers think that concentrating on the legal question—the laws and customs of armed conflict—is a red herring.[27] Of course, the actions of Al Qaeda and other terrorist groups are legally wrong they will say; but legal wrongness leaves open the question of moral wrongness and it is moral wrongness we should be interested in. I agree that the issue of the sheer illegality of terrorism is not what people want to talk about. It is too easy: no one doubts that the terror attacks were illegal. The moral question is much more to the philosopher's taste: is terrorism ever morally permissible or morally justified? But in answering it we should take into account all the circumstances of the actions under consideration and the relation of the actions to existing positive law is one of those circumstances. I can imagine someone responding that the law's view of terrorism can be one of the circumstances attending an act of terrorism only if the law has formed a view of terrorism, and to do so the law must already have addressed the question of the rightness or wrongness of terrorism. And necessarily—so this response may continue—it must have addressed *that* question apart from the legal issue. The moral issue seems to be prior and inescapable.

But I do not accept that this is necessarily the order of priority, for all sorts of reasons. First: law often colonizes an area of normative inquiry first, before serious moral inquiry as we know it begins. Often we learn how to moralize by learning how to ask and answer legalistic questions: I strongly believe that law is a school of moral philosophy. Historically, this has been particularly true of the laws and customs of armed conflict.

---

[26] Ibid.   [27] See, e.g. Honderich, *After the Terror*, pp. 94 and 104.

In this area, people were asking what it was lawful to do long before they were asking—in any refined sense—what it was right and wrong to do. We know that the modern law of war commenced in the spirit of 'natural law' inquiry and, although it is tempting to say that natural law inquiry was just high-level moralizing (in a vaguely Catholic mode), that is an impression that cannot survive acquaintance with the actual natural law reasoning of early pioneering figures such as Gentili and Grotius.[28]

Secondly, even the most moralistic of philosophers will acknowledge that there are some matters that need to be settled by law even though they cannot be settled by moralizing. There are, for example, coordination problems that need to be solved: the rule of the road, the nature of the currency, and so on. As I have mentioned several times, many theorists of the laws and customs of armed conflict believe that some of its leading principles—including the rule about civilians—are best understood in this light. They may be wrong—or, as I shall argue in section 7, they may be only half-right. But still the suggestion needs to be taken seriously. If we accept it, then we do need to consider what the moral significance is of these essentially legalistic solutions.

Thirdly, even with the best will in the world on all sides, we are unlikely to find moral reasoning on these matters converging on moral consensus (let alone a consensus that all can regard as objective moral truth). I don't mean to sound skeptical; I mean simply to indicate that what John Rawls called 'the burdens of judgment' have particular application in this area.[29] The area under study in this chapter is the area of inter-communal conflict and violence. To the extent that things can go very badly without the settlement that law alone makes possible and to the extent that law can provide settlement even in the absence of consensus about what McMahan calls the 'deep morality' of war—to that extent, a cavalier or dismissive attitude towards the moral significance of law is not acceptable.

These last two points suggest that the existence and operation of law in an area like this must itself be regarded as a morally important institution. Its importance as an institution may vary from context to context: it is a matter of what law can do in a given area of human conduct, of what it can contribute, of what goods it can promote, and what evils it can avert or mitigate (discounted of course by the improbability of

---

[28] See Gentili, *On the Law of War*, Bk I, ch. 1, p. 8 and Grotius, *The Rights of War and Peace*, pp. 42–50. See also Waldron, 'Ius Gentium: A Defense of Gentili's Equation of the Law of Nations and the Law of Nature.'

[29] Rawls, *Political Liberalism*, pp. 54–8.

its having the effect that it aims to have or that it is valued for). In the area of armed conflict, law—mainly international law and international humanitarian law—has both modest and ambitious aims. Since 1945 international law has sought, with only moderate success, to suppress armed conflict between nations altogether. More modestly, international humanitarian law seeks to mitigate the horrors of warfare when armed conflict takes place. This is an extremely important aim. So long as it remains possible that law can succeed in this aim, we must always be prepared to give great weight to its moral importance.

How the moral importance of law figures in our calculations also depends on the extent to which our actions—or the actions of those we are assessing—have an impact on the viability of law in this area and the likelihood of its succeeding in its aims. In some areas of human life, law is so robust and funded so well with the resources and the means of coercion, that we need not consider the impact of our actions on it. (We can afford to be preoccupied with its impact on us.) This was not always so. When Socrates imagined the Laws asking him:

Can you deny that by this act which you are contemplating you intend, so far as you have the power, to destroy us, the Laws, and the whole State as well? Do you imagine that a city can continue to exist and not be turned upside down, if the legal judgments which are pronounced in it have no force but are nullified and destroyed by private persons?[30]

he was asking about the impact of defiance by citizens of sentences handed down in routine criminal cases. Lacking any extensive means of coercion, the Athenian laws relied largely on self-application as the primary mode of their administration. That is no longer so much the case: we make coercive arrangements for citizens to serve their sentences rather than asking them to carry out those sentences themselves.

Unlike modern criminal law, however, the laws of war rely immensely on self-application. There are sporadic *post facto* prosecutions for war crimes, and these may become more common with the institution of the International Criminal Court. But for the immediate application of the rules protecting civilians, we rely on the discipline and military doctrines of the world's armed forces. We know that in the recent past, these prohibitions were seriously violated, even amongst the most civilized and best organized armed forces: the use of fire-bombing and weapons of mass destruction against civilian areas in Germany and Japan

---

[30] Plato, *The Crito*, p. 86.

by the United Kingdom and the United States are appalling examples. Thankfully, the nations that perpetrated these atrocities do not seem to have repudiated the principle of distinction altogether. Since 1945 they have reaffirmed it in their practice (to a certain extent), in their international commitments, and in their military doctrine. But the events of 1943–5 showed how fragile the law in this area is. Doubtless there will always be violations, even when doctrine is firm. But the growth of international terrorism represents the emergence of armed groups that repudiate the laws restricting the waging of armed conflict not just at the level of individual incidents but as a matter of doctrine. It remains to be seen what the broader impact of this will be. But it is not hard to see how we could adapt the Laws' characterization of the Socrates escape plan in the *Crito* to the actions and doctrines of these terrorist organizations:

Can you deny that by these actions which you are contemplating you intend, so far as you have the power, to destroy the laws and customs of armed conflict? Do you imagine that a regime of international humanitarian law can continue to exist and not be turned upside down, if its leading principles are nullified and destroyed by armed groups such as yours?

Terrorists have organized a whole way of fighting around the repudiation of the laws and customs of armed conflict; they have adopted institutionally and doctrinally the principle of acting as though the viability of this body of law did not matter. Since the body of law in question is both fragile and important, this is a staggeringly irresponsible course to have embarked on.

4. Disagreement and Compromise

I turn now to consider the formal character of law in this area. How should we think about the existing laws and customs of armed conflict? McMahan and Mavrodes suggest that the rule about civilians is better understood as a convention than as a legal rule aiming directly to capture the force and content of some moral principle. They may be half right, as I will argue in section 6. But I worry that their path to this conclusion is suspect.

The path goes something like this.[31] Professor X begins reflecting on the very idea of a principle of distinction in warfare. He asks what such

---

[31] What follows is a bit of a caricature, intended to make a point.

a principle might possibly be based on. He comes up with the idea of *innocence*: many of those who are most vulnerable to attack are innocent of the crimes that the attackers take themselves to be resisting or punishing. So he considers that a good approach to distinction in warfare might be organized around the idea of guilt or innocence—around what McMahan calls the principle of responsibility. But then Professor X examines the principle of distinction that we actually have in international humanitarian law (the rule about civilians) and he sees that it doesn't correspond to the innocence approach. True, it protects some innocents like very young children. But it also protects some guilty people, like civilian politicians and influential citizens who voted and argued for unjust aggression. And in other cases it renders innocents liable to attack, like young conscripts under orders who are not in any moral sense 'guilty' of their superiors' crimes against peace. Faced with this mismatch, Professor X considers whether to dismiss the rule about civilians altogether, pending its replacement by one organized more consistently around the idea of innocence. But he balks at this; the prospect of leaving armed conflict unregulated in the meantime does not appeal to him. So he concludes that the rule about civilians must be justified in the meantime on grounds other than its inherent merits. He concludes that the rule must have the moral status of a convention. It does not reflect any moral truth in itself. (If it did, Professor X reckons it would reflect his moral principles.) But it still may have the significance of a convention solving a coordination problem.

Now, of course X is not the only moral philosopher reflecting on these matters and following a path like this. Professor Y has also been reflecting on the idea of a principle of distinction in warfare. Professor Y thinks it ought to be organized around the idea of self-defense: a person is permitted to try to kill those, but only those, who are trying to kill him or who pose a deadly threat to himself and others. He recognizes that some of these may be innocent in the moral sense; he accepts the idea of innocent threats; but he reflects that one is entitled to kill even an innocent threat in self-defense. The trouble is that Professor Y's approach does not match the existing legal rule about civilians either: that rule permits one to bombard members of the catering corps if they are in uniform, but not a college of civilians doing the science that will make deadlier weapons available for use against us. So Professor Y goes through ruminations analogous to those that Professor X went through. If the rule about civilians deserves our support, it does so not on the merits, but perhaps as a convention.

I hope it is clear why X's or Y's path to the convention conclusion may be unsafe. The rule that each of them describes as a convention may in fact represent a victory for moral factions in the lawmaking community who do not share Professor X's ideas (or Professor Y's ideas). X may describe as a convention what is in fact a victory for Y's moral ideas and vice versa.

An even more likely account is that the existing law represents not a decisive victory for any one side—for as we have seen neither Professor X nor Professor Y regards it as such—but a compromise between people like X and people like Y and perhaps others besides. The compromises may look ragged and unsatisfactory from a moral point of view. But like the outcome of a vote, they may still have fairness-based process-based claims on us. So *a compromise* or *a moral position that we oppose* are two alternatives to the convention hypothesis.

I believe there is a lot in the compromise characterization. The traditional principle of distinction has elements in it that make moral sense. It certainly tries to protect a large category of individuals whose innocence is indisputable. It also gives those who are engaged in actual fighting the right to protect their lives against those who are trying to kill them. By trying to do these two things together, it ends up being both over- and under-inclusive in both regards, and that is a mark of legal compromise. Much positive law has this character. I stressed earlier the Hobbesian point that law has to do its work and secure its allegiance among people who disagree about moral priorities. Sometimes it does so in a morally coherent way, by opting exclusively for one set of priorities through a fair political process. More often however the strategy is to take on board as much as possible from each contesting moral position even if the result looks incoherent from a theoretical point of view. Some jurists deplore this.[32] I think they are wrong to do so. Be that as it may, the compromise hypothesis arguably provides a better explanation of what some regard as the moral arbitrariness of the rule about civilians than the convention hypothesis.

5. Technicality

In addition we also need to take account of considerations of legal technicality and implementation which may make a positive norm, any

---

[32] See, e.g. the discussion of 'legislative integrity' in Dworkin, *Law's Empire*, pp. 167–84.

positive norm, look odd by the standards of moral philosophers. There are several points to consider here.

First, the relevant laws have to be administered among people who almost certainly disagree about justice and guilt in relation to the armed conflict in question. It may be difficult to administer norms using words like 'just' and 'guilty' in their traditional moral senses, or to impose tests about whose application there is likely to be irresolvable disagreement. McMahan acknowledges this.

Perhaps most obviously, the fact that most combatants believe that their cause is just means that the laws of war must be neutral between just combatants and unjust combatants, as the traditional theory insists that the requirements of *jus in bello* are.[33]

The laws *in bello* have to use simple categories like the distinction between members of the organized military and civilians even though these categories are certainly over- and under-inclusive by moral standards. But the moral standards by which we judge them to be so could not possibly be administered effectively in these circumstances of dissensus. But this does not show that norms *in bello* that we do administer are just conventions. Instead they may be approximations to the moral truth—the closest we can feasibly get in the circumstances of disagreement.

Perhaps the laws *ad bellum* can afford to use criteria whose application is more controversial; perhaps they have to. But in their modern form even they strive to avoid the difficulty we are discussing by orienting themselves not to disputable questions of justice but either to authoritative political determinations (e.g. UN Security Council determinations) or to circumstances that are thought to be patent and indisputable (like the imminence of attack). The 1967 war in the Middle East and the American invasion of Iraq in 2003 show that we have not wholly succeeded in this: the import of an array of Security Council resolutions can be a matter of dispute and the imminence of attack, justifying a resort to self-defense without authorization, can be a contested matter of judgment. So we do get some irresolvable disagreement over *ius ad bellum*, which makes the administration of these norms quite difficult. Imagine the havoc that would result if the administration of the norms *in bello* were as contestable as this; that might well be the price of making the norms morally more refined.

---

[33] McMahan, 'The Ethics of Killing in War,' 730.

A second feature of legal administrability has to do with the reasonableness of the burdens that the laws and customs of armed conflict lay upon combatants. The laws of war (especially *ius in bello*) are to be administered not only in circumstances of moral disagreement, but in circumstances of panic, anger, and great danger. The moral burdens they impose have to be shouldered by those whose lives may be imminently at risk as a result of compliance. With regard to some of the laws of war, we just accept this: for example, we say that prisoners are not to be executed, even if that is the only way for their captors to avoid defeat and death. But too much of this, and the laws of war become utopian and impossible to enforce—especially to the extent that they rely on self-administration by the forces concerned. What is true of danger is also true of anger. We impose certain absolute prohibitions that have to stand up to and curb the worst excesses of the anger and mutual hostility that combat involves: for example, in no circumstances may a military unit proceed on the basis that no quarter is to be offered to its opponents. So sometimes the laws of war defy anger, just as in some respects they defy fear. But again a delicate balance must be struck; for the most part the laws of war must work around the emotions like fear and danger that the circumstances of warfare impose, rather than assuming they do not (because they morally should not) exist.

Moreover, we should not assume that this is a balance that can be arrived at in the philosopher's armchair. The rules have to emerge from the experience of war itself. This is the basis of one of McMahan's concessions to the existing laws (whose deep morality he deprecates):

It is possible that the rules of *jus in bello* coincide rather closely with the laws that would be optimal for regulating conduct in battle. These rules have evolved over many centuries and have been refined, tested, and adapted to the experience of war as the nature of war has itself evolved.[34]

Thirdly, laws designed to govern conduct in the fog of war cannot take account of every detail that a deep moral theory will take account of. Much of *ius in bello* is self-administered by individual soldiers and their unit commanders. A refined moral principle might require of our combatants a delicate inquiry of the guilt and moral status of every person or unit fired upon. But that would be utterly unworkable. Even if it is crude by moral standards, some criterion such as the wearing of

---

[34] Ibid., 731.

uniforms has to be used instead. No doubt these criteria are conventional in character. They place what may seem to a philosopher undue emphasis on trivialities like uniforms, or insignia, and the open (visible) carrying of weapons, and they denounce, again with what must seem like un-called-for vehemence, the perfidious use of flags and signage of various sorts. But these conventional criteria are indispensable for the administration of any norm like the rule about civilians in the circumstances where they have to prevail.

Fourthly, apart from reasonableness and administrability there are simply the technical aspects of positivization. Positive law is never just an application of natural law or of moral ideas; it involves specification, or as the natural lawyers called it *determinatio*. Moral ideas do not initially present themselves in law-like form, if what we mean by law-like is something that can really work like a law. But real-life laws are complex bodies of articulate doctrine and ordered criteria, organized in ways that most moral philosophers can barely comprehend.[35] The layman sometimes complains that cases in law are won or lost on 'technicalities.' But lawmaking is largely a technical matter, with all sorts of devices that look counter-intuitive to the sensitive conscience but which are required to ensure administrability (e.g. in the particular and themselves highly regulated circumstances of a court), to take into account other moral needs that may be relevant to administration (procedural fairness, for example), and to allow a given norm to take its place in a coherent and complex *corpus juris*.

There is a sense in which these technical elements are conventional rather than directly moral. But that does not necessarily make the rules themselves into conventions. The technical aspects of positivization would have to apply even if the legal norm in question purported to be just an embodiment of a moral norm. So even in the case of rules which undoubtedly are not conventions—e.g. the rule against killing—John Finnis observes that 'it is the business of the draftsman to specify, precisely, into which of these costumes and relationships an act of killing-under-such-and-such-a-circumstance fits. That is why "*No one may kill...*" is legally so defective a formulation.'[36] Details have to be settled; rules of evidence, presumptions and burdens of proof laid down; bright lines drawn; operationalized criteria established; and so on.

---

[35] The best modern account of this is Finnis, *Natural Law and Natural Rights*, ch. 10.
[36] Ibid., p. 283.

6. The Idea of a 'Convention'

So far, my intention in this chapter has not been to show that the 'mere convention' hypothesis is completely wrong as an account of the rule against killing civilians. Instead I have tried to show how it may be layered with other elements that provide an alternative or additional explanation why the rule might seem unsatisfactory from a moral point of view. But now I want to confront the 'convention' suggestion more directly.

The word 'convention' can mean many things; it has a technical sense in philosophy—corresponding roughly to what are known as 'Lewis-conventions,' and it has a number of looser senses, some but not all of which are quite unrelated to the technical sense. One meaning, which we can put aside at this point, is the sense used in the phrase 'Geneva Convention,' referring to a multi-lateral agreement, negotiated internationally and binding on a party by virtue of its consent expressed through signature and ratification. As we have already seen, the Geneva Conventions themselves are hugely important as sources of the modern principles of international law that protect civilians in wartime. But that is not the sense of convention I am about to discuss. The Geneva Conventions contain certain rules that are definitely not conventional in the sense I am about to discuss: the rule against torture, for example, in Common Article 3.

Another much looser sense of 'convention' is that which contrasts the *conventional* with the *natural*. There is a version of this in David Hume's contrast between virtues that are natural and virtues that arise out of human artifice or contrivance.[37] Hume argues that justice and respect for property are artificial virtues.[38] Based on our understanding of the advantages that accrue from certain arrangements—such as mutual respect for one another's possessions—we respond to actions and situations in terms of an artificial and often quite complex classification; as such our response is quite different from the responses generated by our natural and unreconstructed passions. The contrivance here need not take the character of a deliberate agreement. Instead, the origin of an

---

[37] Hume, *A Treatise of Human Nature*, pp. 474 and 477.
[38] Hume acknowledges that in a sense of course the products of human judgment and understanding are as 'natural' as our immediately given sentiments: they arise in complex ways from our nature; see ibid., pp. 474 and 484.

artificial virtue may be found in a convention which Hume understands as the upshot of what is often a tacit sense of common interest:

> I observe, that it will be for my interest to leave another in the possession of his goods, provided he will act in the same manner with regard to me. He is sensible of a like interest in the regulation of his conduct. When this common sense of interest is mutually express'd, and is known to both, it produces a suitable resolution and behaviour. And this may properly enough be call'd a convention or agreement betwixt us, tho' without the interposition of a promise; since the actions of each of us have a reference to those of the other, and are perform'd upon the supposition, that something is to be perform'd on the other part.... In like manner are languages gradually establish'd by human conventions without any promise.[39]

We must be careful, however, not to run together the two notions of artifice and coordination in Hume's account. Some of the virtues that Hume calls artificial do not have the coordinative character that we see in the examples he gives here (property and language). The virtues associated with government—such as loyalty or allegiance—fall into this category, as do the virtues regarding modesty and chastity.[40] This is an important point because some theorists who recognize the artificial character of our traditional principle of distinction have sometimes felt obliged—wrongly, in my view—to represent it as something like a common-interest solution to a coordination problem.

The best-known philosophical explication of conventions is that of David Lewis.[41] Lewis is interested in conventions that solve coordination problems among two or more agents. In a simple two-person coordination problem, each of two persons faces two options and each person's choice between these options must be made independently of the other's. If two agents each face two choices there are four possible pairs of choices. There is no conflict of interest, but there are two pairs of choices either of which would be regarded by the players as advantageous and two pairs of choices either of which would be regarded by the players as disadvantageous. Two cars approach each other from opposite directions on a narrow road: each driver could move either to his own left or to his own right. If each of them moves to his own left, they can pass each other unobstructed and if each of them moves to his own

---

[39] Ibid., p. 490.
[40] See Hume's passage on 'Of the source of allegiance,' ibid., p. 539 ff. and his passage on 'Of chastity and modesty,' ibid., p. 570 ff.
[41] See David Lewis, *Convention* (1986).

right, they can pass each other unobstructed. But if one of them moves to his own left and the other moves to his own right, then there will be a collision or at best an impasse. When situations of this kind tend to recur, a convention can be helpful. A convention in Lewis's sense is a regularity of behavior which, if observed by both parties, tends to solve such coordination problems. In America we drive on the right. We could all drive on the left as they do in Britain. That would be an equally good rule if everyone was prepared to follow it. But we have our own settled convention in the United States; and no sensible person drives on the left around here. The convention means that, whenever these situations occur, each of us approaches them with the same expectations about the other's likely choice. This enables us to find our way through these situations with little or no difficulty.

Lewis offers a useful general definition of a convention, along the following lines.[42] (What follows is not exactly Lewis's formulation, but a simplified version of it.)

A regularity R in the behavior of members of a population P when they are agents in a recurrent situation S is a convention if and only if it is true that, and it is common knowledge in P that, in almost any instance of S among members of P, (1) almost everyone conforms to R; (2) almost everyone expects almost everyone else to conform to R; (3) almost everyone has approximately the same preference regarding all possible combinations of actions; (4) almost everyone prefers that any other person conform to R on condition that almost everyone conform to R; (5) almost everyone would prefer that any other person conform to a different regularity R′ on condition that almost everyone conform to R′ (where R and R′ indicate alternative incompatible actions in S).

The rule of the road obviously satisfies this definition: S is the situation where two drivers approach one another from opposite directions; in America, R is 'Bear to one's own right' and R′ is 'Bear to one's own left.' Each of us prefers that the others follow the same regularity that we are following ourselves; it does not particularly matter whether we follow R′ or R; but since R has become established among us, that is the convention we follow.

It is not hard to see how someone might think the rule about civilians might be an instance of R in this schema, where S is the recurrent situation of armed conflict. Recall that McMahan suggested that this convention exists to mitigate the horrors of war.[43] Each member of the

---

[42] Ibid., p. 78.　　　　[43] McMahan, 'The Ethics of Killing in War,' 730.

international community prefers that the horrors of war be mitigated. R is one way of mitigating the horrors of war. It limits the class of those who are liable to be attacked or killed to those who are members of armed forces in uniform. But there are other ways of limiting the class of those who are liable to be attacked or killed: we could have a rule that no women and children are to be targeted, for example (call this R'). But if most of other nations are following R rather than R', then each nation has an interest in following R, the traditional principle. So it is a convention. The reason for following it is not anything about the merits of R that would differentiate it from R': the reason for following it is that most others are following it and most others expect others (including ourselves) to follow it.

If the rule about civilians is to be understood as a Lewis-convention, then some important consequences would follow. First, it would seem to follow that if other armies are not abiding by the rule about civilians, it makes no sense for my army to abide by that rule. That would be like me driving on the left in Britain after everyone has for some reason started driving on the right.[44] Secondly, it seems to make the rule about civilians highly contingent on the interests of the warring parties. Even if each side has an interest in mitigating the horrors of war, it may not be the case that that interest always trumps other interests that a nation or army might have. Or it might be trumped by an interest in mitigating the horrors of war in some other way: in 1945 the United States reckoned that the deliberate killing of hundreds of thousands of civilians in Hiroshima and Nagasaki would be a better way of mitigating the horrors of the final stages of the Second World War than continued combat which observed the traditional principle of distinction.

In these ways, the Lewis account[45] seems to undermine the idea of the rule about civilians as a moral absolute. It shows that in certain circumstances, it makes sense to violate it, and it gives no other account of the rule that would stand against this. Of course, theorists differ in the tone in which they point this out. Some think it is an advantage of the Lewis account that it has these consequences. Others think that these points indicate that the Lewis account must be wrong. I am in the latter camp. I think the Lewis account is defective as an explication of the rule

---

[44] See Mavrodes, 'Conventions and the Morality of War,' 86–7.

[45] My phrase 'the Lewis account' just means an explication of the rule about civilians as a Lewis-convention. I know of no evidence that the late David Lewis thought the rule about civilians was a Lewis-convention.

about civilians. If the rule about civilians is a convention, it must be a convention in a looser sense than this. Let me explain why.

Lewis-conventions have two notable features. The first concerns the coincidence of interests: it is better for all concerned if all or most of the others follow some rule; and if all or most of the others follow R, it is better for oneself to follow R. I call this the *convergence of interest* feature. The second notable feature of Lewis-conventions has to do with the relation between R and R'. They are arbitrary alternatives in the sense that any differences between them pale in comparison to the importance of following one of them or the other as opposed to no such regularity. I call this the *arbitrary alternative* feature. Lewis's conception requires the presence of both features.

I think it is at least arguable that the rule about civilians and its alternatives satisfy the arbitrary alternative feature; I shall talk more about that in a moment. But I don't think it satisfies the convergence of interest feature. When two groups are locked in armed conflict, it is easy to imagine that any one of them would most prefer that the other observe R while it does not. Following R, after all, is costly. What could be better from a selfish point of view than that the other side bear the costs of refraining from attacking one's own civilians, while one wages indiscriminate warfare oneself? In a classic game of coordination, it makes no sense to violate the regularity that one expects others to conform to. But in the situation of war it often does. I believe terrorist groups often operate with this in mind. They complain when *they* are not accorded the benefit of the rules of armed conflict; but they routinely violate these rules themselves. Their actions are wrong; but they are not unintelligible in the way that 'defecting' in a coordination game would be unintelligible.[46]

More important: it can make sense for one side to continue to follow the rule about civilians even when the other side does not. This is because the rationale of the rule is partly (on both sides) altruistic rather than self-interested. One follows the rule out of concern for the civilians in question, civilians on the other side as well as civilians on one's own side.[47] The rationale usually given for the rule—mitigating the horrors

---

[46] True, if X violates R, it might expect retaliation. Or X might expect that the other side will not long continue observing R once it becomes clear that X is not following it. And these features of reciprocity and retaliation may lead X back to conformity. But these are secondary matters and by themselves they do not establish the sort of essential coordinative background that Lewis-conventions seem to presuppose.

[47] Maybe one has greater concern for the latter. But refraining from attacking the other side's civilians need not be merely a strategy for protecting one's own civilians. See also the discussion in Margalit and Walzer, 'Israel: Civilians and Combatants.'

of warfare—recognizes this. My refraining from targeting civilians obviously mitigates the horrors of warfare even if others do target them. I do not mean to suggest that Lewis-conventions cannot operate in a context of altruism. There may be cases of altruistic coordination, where it makes no sense for me to play my part in a given altruistic scheme unless others are also playing theirs.[48] But the rule about not targeting civilians is not like that.[49]

For these reasons, I don't think the rule about civilians can usefully be regarded as a Lewis-convention in the strict sense. It lacks the crucial element of interdependence of interests (even taking moral interests into account).

Is there perhaps a looser sense of interdependence that applies to the rule about civilians? I can imagine someone saying that observing the rule is something of a handicap to a warring army, and that it cannot be expected to labor under this handicap unless the opposing army does so too. The handicap need not be equal on both sides, but there may nevertheless be a sense of its being *unfair* for one party to wage unrestrained warfare while the other party observes the legal constraints. In this sense—a very loose sense of interdependence indeed—we may not expect a principle of distinction to survive unless it tends to be followed by both sides in most conflicts.[50]

What about the *arbitrary alternative* feature? There the Lewis account is more suggestive. Various alternatives to the rule about civilians are imaginable. Jeff McMahan seems to be imagining one alternative. And others can be imagined. In the past, some Palestinian terrorist organizations have proclaimed their adherence to an alternative principle of distinction which forbids the targeting of Israeli citizens living within Israel's pre-1967 borders, but permits the targeting of settlers within the

[48] Derek Parfit said something about this in *Reason and Persons*, p. 95 ff. See also the fine account of coordination for the common good in Finnis, *Natural Law and Natural Rights*, ch. 7.

[49] So I think McMahan is mistaken when he writes ('The Ethics of Killing in War,' at 730) that it is rational for each side in a conflict to adhere to the rules of war only if the other side does: '[I]f one side breaches the understanding that the conventions will be followed, it may cease to be rational or morally required for the other side to persist in its adherence to them.'

[50] Statman, 'Targeted Killing,' 196, associates interdependence with the 'moral' force of the convention: '[T]he moral force of this convention is contingent on its being followed by all sides. Hence if one side violates the convention, the other is no longer committed to adhering to it.' But the moral force may consist just in the good that accrues from any side—either side—following the rule, irrespective of what others do. For a further discussion, see Meisels, *The Trouble with Terror*, p. 119 ff.

Occupied Territories. Or in Northern Ireland during the troubles there, nationalist groups said they would target civilians involved in supplying goods and services to the police and the military but not civilians (even members of the opposing community) who were unconnected with the security forces. We know that the rule about civilians has varied over time. It used to be the practice to put the civilian inhabitants of a besieged city as well as its military defenders to the sword when a siege was successful. We no longer allow this. But the element of historical relativity might seem to suggest we are dealing with something conventional.

Can we therefore proceed with a looser sense of convention which, though it lacks the *convergence of interest* feature, is characterized by the artificiality associated with the *arbitrary alternatives* idea? I am not sure whether it is possible entirely to separate the two features. Andrei Marmor has outlined an understanding of convention that seems to be dominated by the idea of *arbitrary alternatives*.[51]

A rule, R, is conventional, if and only if all the following conditions obtain: 1. There is a group of people, a community, P, that normally follow R in circumstances C. 2. There is a main, or primary, reason (or a combination of reasons), call it A, for members of P to follow R in circumstances C. 3. There is at least one other potential rule, [R'], that if members of P had actually followed in circumstances C, then A would have been a sufficient reason for members of P to follow [R'] instead of R in circumstances C.[52]

Marmor's feature 2 replaces the interdependence of interest with the idea of a shared reason. But there is still an element of interdependence in Marmor's account of arbitrariness:

Arbitrariness is an essential, defining feature, of conventional rules. This is actually a twofold condition. First, a rule is arbitrary if it has a conceivable alternative. If a rule does not have an alternative that could have been followed instead without a significant loss in its function or purpose, then it is not a convention. Basic moral norms, for instance, are not conventions; properly defined and qualified, they do not admit of alternatives (in the sense defined above).... Second, the reason for following a rule that is a convention depends on the fact that others follow it too.... The reason for following a convention partly depends on the fact that it happens to be the rule that people in the relevant community actually follow. Had they followed an alternative rule, the same reason, A, would have applied to the alternative rule, namely, the one that people actually follow.[53]

---

[51] See Marmor, 'Deep Conventions,' 500.
[52] I have changed Marmor's algebra slightly so that it coincides with Lewis's.
[53] Marmor, 'Deep Conventions,' at 590–1.

In the absence of convergence of interest, what could explain this interdependence? One possibility is that if war is to be limited at all, it has to be limited by rules laid down and accepted by all or most members of the international community in advance of a given conflict. The rules must be a common juridical resource, on the shelf, waiting for conflicts as they arise. If the rules are not settled in advance, it will be too late once conflict breaks out. So perhaps we can explain Marmor's condition 3, *viz.*

There is at least one other potential rule, [R'], that if members of P had actually followed in circumstances C, then A would have been a sufficient reason for members of P to follow [R'] instead of R in circumstances C

by saying that, had R' instead of R been agreed and available on the shelf (as it were) in advance of this conflict (or any given conflict), then R' would have been the rule the parties followed to promote reason A (if they were to follow any such rule at all).

But then the sense of arbitrariness becomes quite weak. R's being on the shelf rather than R' may be evidence of moral progress. For example, maybe we think our approach to the killing of civilians is superior to the usages of siege warfare. Or to take another example: Grotius observes that the permissibility of killing prisoners used to be taken for granted at least in certain circumstances, but that now civilized countries no longer follow that rule.[54] We may still say that, had the earlier rule still been on the shelf, *that* is the one we would have followed. But this does not show that the two rules are *arbitrary* alternatives. Rather the continued presence of the earlier rule as our only juridical resource for dealing with this sort of situation would indicate that there hadn't been the moral progress necessary to get to a better rule.

In section 4, I raised the issue of moral controversy. For example: there is a dispute between Jeff McMahan and others about what is the best principle of distinction. Traditionalists defend what I have called the rule about civilians; McMahan proposes a better rule (based on his 'principle of responsibility'). But McMahan understands the danger of an unresolved controversy among combatants about which is the appropriate rule to follow: if *both* rules are (so to speak) on the shelf, there is a danger that no rule will be followed, because neither of them will seem to combatants in the heat of incipient battle to be *the* rule to follow. So McMahan acknowledges that, for the time being at least, it is better if

---

[54] Grotius, *The Rights of War and Peace*, Bk III, ch. vii, p. 1364.

all combatants follow the traditional rule. But this does not mean he regards them as arbitrary alternatives. His acknowledgment is like the position of a player in a 'Battle of the Sexes' game.[55] (Husband and wife want to go out one evening; he prefers to go to the opera and she prefers to go to the ballet; but most of all they want to go out together rather than each to his or her favorite entertainment alone.)[56]

7. Deadly Serious Conventions

I implied at the beginning of this chapter that I was less interested in refuting the thesis that the traditional principle of distinction is a convention, than in showing that its conventional character (or whatever conventional character it has) should not be thought of as diminishing its moral importance. I imagined someone asking, 'What is the big deal about killing civilians if the rule prohibiting it is just a convention or an artificial technical device?' As it stands the question is corrupt and irresponsible. But there is a serious issue to be faced: if we accept that the rule about civilians has important conventional elements as well as technical elements that are bound to distinguish it from familiar moral norms, how should we think about the seriousness of violating it?

The first thing that needs to be said is that even if the choice of a conventional rule is arbitrary, the point of having a convention may not be. Take the example of the rule of the road. Nothing seems more trivial than the choice of driving on the left or driving on the right. But if we do not coordinate on one or the other then the result is chaos and paralysis at best and very likely carnage. The underlying goal won't be served at all unless we choose—and stick with—a convention. And the key point is that the reason for having a convention generates a reason for observing it. In many instances a violation of the rule will result in death and mayhem. This is an arbitrary convention; but it is a *deadly serious* arbitrary convention.[57] If the rule about civilians is a convention, it is a

---

[55] There is an excellent account in Hampton, *Hobbes and the Social Contract Tradition*, pp. 150–61.

[56] Marmor sees this when he observes (Marmor, 'Deep Conventions,' at 590) that 'arbitrariness…should not be confused with indifference….[C]ondition [3] does not entail that people who follow the convention ought to be indifferent as to the choice between R and R'. The rule is arbitrary, in the requisite sense, even if people do have a reason to prefer one over the other, but only as long as the reason to prefer one of the rules is not stronger than the reason to follow the rule that is actually followed by others.'

[57] See also Finnis, *Natural Law and Natural Rights*, p. 232.

convention of this kind. It is a deadly serious convention: serious in its responsiveness to an important underlying reason, namely the mitigation of the savageries of war, and deadly serious in the consequences of this violation.

Of some conventions, it is true that individual violations may have little deleterious impact on the convention. My grammatical errors, for example, do not undermine the language. But it does not follow that violations are harmless. My driving on the right in Britain is still incredibly dangerous even though it is unlikely to rock the prevailing convention. For some cases, however, violations may also undermine the convention or the public good that the convention aims to secure. I think this is true of the rule about civilians. As well as the sheer diminution of carnage, the rule seeks to establish as a collective good some sort of atmosphere of moral restraint even amid the horrors of war. One of the things that is wrong with deliberate violations of civilian immunity—and certainly (to return to our original subject) one of the things that is wrong with terrorism—is that it makes the securing of this collective good much more vulnerable to collapse. Violations here are not like individual contributions to pollution: a drop in the ocean, so to speak, making little discernable difference. Quite the contrary, sustained violations as a matter of policy by powerful entities may bring us quickly and closely to the tipping-point where the convention simply collapses. We should remember that, despite the large numbers of people actually engaged in combat, the numbers of individual states and armed organizations with military doctrines is quite small (numbered in the hundreds, not the millions).[58] Also, the knock-on effects of perceived violations, especially if these seem like acts of policy, are likely to be extensive. (Terrorism amplifies and aims to amplify the knock-on effects of violations, so that particular incidents are accompanied by a more general diminution of confidence.) Because of what is at stake for any group in armed conflict, because of the problem of the costs of compliance, because of the temptations of positional advantage and the fear of being taken advantage of, any sense that others are securing an advantage in armed conflict by violating these norms is likely to lead to others' violating them as well.

Any convention can stand a certain amount of defection and still survive; but the amount that it can stand and still survive may be quite

---

[58] I don't just mean the numbers with regard to any given war, but even the numbers in regard to wars in general.

limited.[59] In the case of the laws of war, the environment in which they operate is such that they are inevitably close to this threshold most of the time. They are observed imperfectly at best and sometimes not at all. Sustained violations therefore, or the development and implementation of doctrines that hold the laws of war in contempt, stand a good chance of adding so much to the number of violations that the convention has to reckon with anyway, that they will contribute significantly to the failure of the entire enterprise.

8. Murder

I have left the most important point till last, and it will help us finally think about conventions in a way that explains and justifies the opening paragraph of this chapter. The artificial laws of war (to the extent that they are artifices) including the conventional principle of distinction between soldiers and civilians (to the extent that it is a convention) do their work not just against a background of danger, destruction, and death, but against a background of *murder*.

The norm we are considering—the rule about civilians—may be artificial and conventional, but it does not prohibit things that apart from its operation would be perfectly permissible. It is not like a set of parking regulations, introducing prohibition into an area where there was no prohibition before.[60] On the contrary, the conventional rule that prohibits attacks on civilians prohibits something that—apart from the laws of war—would already be a grave moral offense. The default position, apart from any convention, is that intentionally killing or attacking any human being is prohibited as murder. The laws of armed conflict provide an exception to that; they establish what we call in the trade a Hohfeldian privilege in relation to what is otherwise forbidden. And the rule about civilians is to be understood as a limitation on the scope of that privilege.

Absent the laws and customs of armed conflict, *all* killing in war would be murder.[61] (The default position is emphatically *not* that you

---

[59] Cf. the argument in Kraut, *Socrates and the State*, pp. 131–4.

[60] Cf. the account of the Bush Administration's approach to the Geneva Conventions in Chapter 7 below, pp. 196–8.

[61] Much of what we call 'collateral damage' would be murder too, for legally and morally the category of murder is not confined to intentional killings. (Absent the laws of war, blowing up a building to kill one person you intended to kill with the predictable effect

are allowed to kill anyone you like and that the rule about civilians has encroached upon *that*.) The situation is that the laws of war have drawn an artificial line withdrawing the prohibition on murder from a certain class of killings. The rule about civilians reflects the point that this withdrawal of the prohibition on murder from certain killings is a partial, not a wholesale withdrawal. In this regard, the position about *malum prohibitum* that has been toyed with from time to time in this chapter—sometimes attributed to others, sometimes entertained by me—is misleading. The basic premise of any adequate account has to be that the killing of civilians is always *malum in se*. The element of artifice or convention does not affect that.

Perhaps this argument is a little too quick. Most accounts of the background, i.e. of the basic moral rules which make killing wrong, provide various qualifications. The most notable one is for self-defense or defense of others, and perhaps even more generally for resisting and repelling unjust aggression. And we may want to see the conventional elements—like the rule against not killing civilians—as affecting *this part* of the background rather than as qualifying the rule against killing *per se*. On this account, if we take away the conventional element (or whatever the rule about civilian immunity is), we are left not with the bare rule against murder, but with a qualified rule against murder. The point is well taken. But we must not exaggerate the qualification. On the one hand, self-defense is a very strictly limited justification for homicide, both legally and morally. It certainly does not entitle a person to kill anyone if that would contribute to their defense of themselves or others; only the most imminent deadly threats may be answered in this way. And on the other hand, the rule about civilians also has some such qualification built into it: a civilian aiming a rifle may be killed.[62] So even if we accept that the moral background—the default position—is complicated in this way, an account of the rule about civilians will reflect this complexity. And still the conclusion I have been arguing for in this

that other persons you didn't intend to kill would die as a result would clearly constitute the murder of the latter group. It is a pernicious fallacy of philosophers to think that the Doctrine of Double Effect makes some killings like this permissible. Most legal systems punish as murder reckless killings of this kind.) The laws of war modify that situation by permitting the intended killing (if it is of an enemy combatant) and of sometimes permitting the unintended killing if it is necessary for and proportionate to the securing of a legitimate military objective. But if those conditions (necessity and proportionality) fail, the unintentional killing remains murderous or (at best) a serious form of culpable homicide such as manslaughter.

[62] See, e.g. Article 51(3) of the First Protocol to the Geneva Conventions.

section will follow: the deliberate killing of civilians, even when it seems to be a military necessity, is murder. It is murder, not on account of the operation of the rule about civilians, but on account of the limit that this rule represents so far as the artificial privilege of killing combatants is concerned.

Notice, too, that a plausible account of the complexity of the background will certainly not yield anything like an entitlement to kill those who are responsible for unjust aggression or other forms of injustice. Someone who wanted to pursue McMahan's suggestion might try to take this line and say that the rule about civilians artificially limits that, by prohibiting (perhaps for good reasons) what would otherwise be the justified killing of the guilty. But it will not work. There is no general moral permission to kill those who are guilty of injustice.

The immediate upshot of this is to vindicate the position taken at the beginning of this chapter. The September 11 killings were murders, and they were murders in a quite straightforward sense. They were not justified as self-defense; and they could not have been justified on grounds that people working in the World Trade Center were complicit in the injustice of capitalism or American foreign policy. They were murders, pure and simple. This is not a special or artificial sense of 'murder.' The rule about civilians, conventional though it may be in certain respects, does not create a special or artificial sense of murder. Instead it reminds us of the severe limits placed upon the special artificial privileging of the killing of combatants in wartime.[63]

There are also some more consequences, some of them philosophically quite interesting. If some rule is a convention, it is tempting to think that it must be supported by consequentialist calculations—the good of setting up and having the convention—and that it may also be vulnerable to consequentialist considerations too, when the advantages of violating or abandoning it seem to outweigh the good consequences of having it. Or at best, it may seem that conventions are rather like

---

[63] This conclusion, by the way, applies not only to the deliberate killings of civilians by terrorists, but also to the deliberate killings of civilians by organized armed forces. The killings of civilians in Hiroshima and Nagasaki are murders in this straightforward sense. (I am not saying there is a moral equivalence between Hiroshima and the September 11 attacks; there plainly is not, though readers may disagree about the direction of the asymmetry; all I am saying is that they have this in common, that they both involved a large number of murders in the sense I have explained.) As for foreseen but unintended killings of civilians by armed forces, the points made above in n. 61 apply. Unless these are specifically justified by norms of necessity and proportionality, they too are culpable homicides and often murders in a straightforward sense.

rule-utilitarian or indirect-utilitarian norms in a two-level theory.[64] They may perhaps be insulated to a certain extent from direct conse- quentialist calculations, but in the long run they cannot and should not survive if their purposes could be promoted by other rules more effectively.

But now we see that even if this is true of some conventional rules, it is really not true of the rule about civilians. Several times throughout this chapter I have endorsed the view that the point of the rule is to miti- gate the horrors of warfare, and we have imagined various ways in which the rule might be undermined by that teleology: for example, maybe the horrors of war can be mitigated more decisively by the use of ter- ror weapons on large cities, to bring the war to a speedy end. But actu- ally that is a misleading account of the normative force of the rule. The normative force of the rule is deontological: 'Thou shalt not kill.' The wrongness of killing civilians is established independently of the goal of mitigating the horrors of warfare: killing civilians is murder.[65]

The goal of mitigating the horrors of warfare comes into play in the following way. For whatever reason, the law of nations has recognized the special character of warfare and privileged certain killings that would otherwise be murders. That, we all know, has the potential to generate a morally horrific situation: legally unregulated killing fields. To lessen the horror of *that*, we have insisted that any privileging of kill- ings in wartime is not to be comprehensive; it covers some killings but leaves others as murders. The choice as to which killings to privilege— the choice as to how large the residual area of murder should remain and how it should be delineated—all that is perhaps dominated by con- sequentialist considerations. It could hardly be organized deontologi- cally (at least not without pretending that we have certain deontological principles that in fact we don't have—such as McMahan's principle of responsibility: it is right to kill those who are responsible for aggression and injustice).

The difficulty, however, is that we really don't have a clear picture in moral or legal theory of what justifies the privileging of certain killings in wartime (at least not one which takes seriously what it is to privilege a killing that would otherwise be murder). We have worked too long with a model that assumes that the default position is that you can kill

---

[64] See, e.g. Hare, *Moral Thinking*, pp. 25–64.

[65] Of course it is possible that someone may have a utilitarian account of the wrong- ness of murder, in which case their principles are vulnerable all the way down to conse- quentialist calculations.

anyone you like in wartime and that people have to be argued out of *that* if civilians are to be given immunity. (And maybe that is the practical or political problem; but it is not the right perspective for moral theory.) We have worked so long with that model, that we have forgotten how to think clearly—and carefully and with appropriate moral severity—about the legitimate taking of human life in time of war. That should be the next issue for discussion; but unfortunately not in this volume.

5

Safety and Security

I. The Neglect of Security in Political Philosophy

When people talk, as they often do, about a trade-off between security and liberty—when they say (as many people said after September 11, 2001) that we need to adjust the balance between security and civil liberties[1]—what do they mean by *security*? Talk of a liberty/security balance has become so common that many view it as just an ambient feature of our political environment: '[I]t has become a part of the drinking water in this country that there has been a tradeoff of liberty for security,... that we have had to encroach upon civil liberty and trade some of that liberty we cherish for some of that security that we cherish even more.'[2] When we talk in this way, we often spend a certain amount of time discussing the definition of 'liberty' and the concept of civil liberties; we want to be clear under this heading, because we know it makes a difference to the trade-off what liberties in particular we have in mind. But we almost never address the question of what 'security' means. In fact when people talk in the literature or in court about 'the definition of security,' what they usually produce is some view about what security requires at a particular time (in the way of legal or political measures). They say nothing about the meaning of the concept itself.[3] Though we know that 'security' is a vague and ambiguous concept and though we

---

[1] We hear talk of a balance between security and liberty from all sides. We hear it from conservatives (e.g. *Free Societies Must Balance Security, Civil Liberties, Bush Says*, at <http://www.america.gov/st/washfile-english/2005/May/20050508152353521elootom 0.4186169.html> last visited January 13, 2010), from liberals (e.g. Cole, 'Enemy Aliens,' at 955: 'In the wake of September 11, we plainly need to rethink the balance between liberty and security'), and from almost everyone in between. See also Issacharoff and Pildes, 'Emergency Contexts without Emergency Powers,' at 298.

[2] Comey, *Fighting Terrorism and Preserving Civil Liberties*, at p. 403.

[3] Pozen, 'The Mosaic Theory, National Security, and the Freedom of Information Act,' at 63: '[T]he government has the advantage in FOIA appeals of controlling both the disputed information and... the definition of national security.'

should suspect that its vagueness is a source of danger when talk of trade-offs is in the air,[4] still there has been little or no attempt in the literature of legal and political theory to bring any sort of clarity to the concept.

When legal scholars write about liberty they can take advantage of an immense literature in political philosophy on the meaning of the term.[5] But it is shocking to discover how little attention has been paid to the topic of security by political philosophers. Historically, the two philosophers who have written most about security are Jeremy Bentham and Thomas Hobbes. In his book *The Theory of Legislation*, Bentham argued that 'the care of security' was 'the principal object of the Laws.'[6] What he meant by security, however, was legal constancy, certainty, and predictability so far as property rights were concerned, and it might be thought that this is of limited interest in our discussion of the liberty/security trade-off in the war on terrorism. In fact that is not the case; later in the chapter we will find some aspects of Bentham's analysis to be quite useful (even though it is not an analysis which has been picked up on by any modern discussant of security.)

If any thinker in the canon of political philosophy could serve as the focus of a modern discussion of security, surely it would be Thomas Hobbes. For Hobbes, as we all know, the whole point of the political enterprise is security. It is for the sake of security—security against each other, and security against outsiders—that we set up a sovereign.[7] It is the drive for security that leads us to give up our natural liberty and submit to the sovereign's commands.[8] It is the exigencies of security that determine the scale, the level, the duration, and the quality of

---

[4] In *United States v. United States District Court* 407 U.S. 297 (1972), at 320, the Supreme Court spoke of the 'inherent vagueness of the domestic security concept . . . and the temptation to utilize such surveillance to oversee political dissent.'

[5] The most famous starting point for the modern discussion is Berlin, *Four Essays on Liberty*. See also the essays collected in David Miller (ed.), *Liberty* for a sampling of this literature.

[6] Bentham, *Principles of the Civil Code*, p. 109.

[7] Hobbes, *On The Citizen*, pp. 77–8 (ch. 6): 'Men's security requires not only accord but also subjection of wills in matters essential to peace and defence; and . . . the nature of a commonwealth consists in that union or subjection. . . . [T]he security of individuals, and consequently the common peace, necessarily require that the right of using the sword to punish be transferred to some man or assembly; that man or that assembly therefore is necessarily understood to hold sovereign power in the commonwealth by right. . . . No greater power can be imagined.'

[8] See, e.g. Hobbes, *The Elements of Law*, p. 111 (ch. 20, sect. 5): 'The end for which one man giveth up, and relinquisheth to another, or others, the right of protecting and defending himself by his own power, is the security which he expecteth thereby, of protection and defence from those to whom he doth so relinquish it.'

organization that is requisite in the political realm.[9] Now, Hobbes was a great analyst of concepts.[10] Yet almost alone among the leading concepts of the political realm, security is not subjected by Hobbes to any extensive analysis. The closest he comes is in a passage from *The Elements of Law*, where he writes:

> a man may…account himself *in the estate of security*, when he can foresee no violence to be done unto him, from which the doer may not be deterred by the power of that sovereign, to whom they have every one subjected themselves; and without that security there is no reason for a man to deprive himself of his own advantages, and make himself a prey to others.[11]

Hobbes says surprisingly little beyond this about what 'security' actually means, and he is followed in that by his modern commentators, who as far as I can tell do not so much as list the concept in their indexes.

Maybe this is because security operates as a sort of *adjectival* value in Hobbes's account; maybe it is a mistake to look for treatments of it as an end in itself. Hobbes is interested in security of self-preservation, security of life and limb, security against violent death, security of 'living out the time, which Nature ordinarily alloweth men to live.'[12] Perhaps what I should be looking for in the index is safety, survival, or self-preservation, not security as such. And in fact there *is* some discussion in Hobbes's book *On the Citizen* of safety and the sovereign's obligations in respect of his subjects' safety. We are told that '[b]y safety one should

---

[9] See, e.g. Hobbes, *Leviathan*, p. 118 (ch. 17): '[I]f there be no Power erected, or not great enough for our security; every man will and may lawfully rely on his own strength and art, for caution against all other men.…Nor is it the joyning together of a small number of men, that gives them this security.… The Multitude sufficient to confide in for our Security, is not determined by any certain number, but by comparison with the Enemy we feare; and is then sufficient, when the odds of the Enemy is not of so visible and conspicuous moment, to determine the event of warre, as to move him to attempt.'

[10] Ibid., p. 28 (ch. 4): 'Seeing then that Truth consisteth in the right ordering of names in our affirmations, a man that seeketh precise Truth, had need to remember what every name he uses stands for; and to place it accordingly; or els he will find himselfe entangled in words, as a bird in lime-twiggs; the more he struggles, the more belimed.…So that in the right Definition of Names, lyes the first use of Speech; which is the Acquisition of Science: And in wrong, or no Definitions lyes the first abuse; from which proceed all false and senslesse Tenets…'

[11] Hobbes, *The Elements of Law*, at p. 111 (ch. 20, sect. 5). In the same chapter, at p. 112 (ch. 20, sect. 8), Hobbes also adds an external dimension: 'And forasmuch as they who are amongst themselves in security, by the means of this sword of justice that keeps them all in awe, are nevertheless in danger of enemies from without; if there be not some means found, to unite their strengths and natural forces in the resistance of such enemies, their peace amongst themselves is but in vain.'

[12] Hobbes, *Leviathan*, p. 91 (ch. 14).

understand not mere survival in any condition, but a happy life so far as that is possible,'[13] and we are told also that because the sovereign can operate only through general laws, 'he has done his duty if he has made every effort, to provide by sound measures for the welfare of as many of them as possible for as long as possible.'[14] Both points will be important in what follows.

Whatever hints Hobbes has given us have not been followed up in the political philosophy literature. 'Your search returned no results,' said JSTOR, when asked for articles in two prominent political philosophy journals—*Political Theory* and *Philosophy and Public Affairs*—with the word 'security' in the title. ('Liberty' or 'freedom' for the same domain gave me 70 results.)[15] With monographs, it is harder to quantify. In my library, I know that there are brief discussions of the concept of security in Henry Shue's book *Basic Rights* and in Robert Goodin's book *Political Theory and Public Policy* (Chicago, 1982).[16] Both will be discussed in what follows, but I will say now that these are mainly on the importance and priority to be accorded to security, not on its meaning. There is little or no discussion of security in the main texts of political philosophy.[17] The topic does not so much as rate a mention in Will Kymlicka's intro-ductory text[18] or in William Connolly's *Terms of Political Discourse*,[19] while in D.D. Raphael's text, discussion of security is limited to a brief discussion of the state's role in upholding rights.[20]

As for the spate of instant books that appeared in the years imme-diately following the terrorist outrages of September 11, 2001, there is constant reference to the liberty/security trade-off in almost all of these. But though the authors give us all sorts of recommendations and bright ideas about what is likely to promote or enhance security, they offer us little or nothing on what security means.[21]

---

[13] Hobbes, *On the Citizen*, p. 143 (ch. 13).   [14] Ibid.

[15] Search conducted March 3, 2006 at <http://www.jstor.org/search/ExpertSearch>.

[16] Shue, *Basic Rights*, pp. 20–2; Goodin, *Political Theory and Public Policy*, pp. 220–41. For further discussion of Shue's account, see Chapter 6, below.

[17] There is also some discussion of topics surrounding security and the obligations of the state in Nozick, *Anarchy, State, and Utopia*, pp. 54–146. But this is mostly entangled in a technical discussion of the legitimacy of a minimal libertarian state.

[18] Kymlicka, *Contemporary Political Philosophy*.

[19] Connolly, *The Terms of Political Discourse*.

[20] Raphael, *Problems of Political Philosophy*, pp. 46–9.

[21] A representative example is Heyman, *Terrorism, Freedom and Security*. Heyman devotes a final chapter to 'Values and Security' (ibid., pp. 158–79), which contains a sophisticated and helpful account of the trade-offs we face between security and demo-cratic liberties. But there is no discussion of the meaning of security.

I want to be clear about what I am looking for. There is an immense literature on *national security* and also on *collective security* in the theory and study of international relations. There are whole journals called *National Security Outlook* and *Journal of National Security Law and Policy* and innumerable articles with 'collective security' in the title.[22] But these concepts are not quite the same as the security I have in mind.

The idea of *collective security* operates at the wrong level; it concerns security as among the nations of the world (or various subsets of them) as determined by institutions, alliances, and the balance of power, whereas I am interested in security conceived as an attribute of individuals and populations. This is not to say that there may not be things to glean from the literature on collective security. The *collective* aspect itself is worth considering. What is striking in that discourse is that security is not understood as something most nations can pursue by and for themselves. It needs to be pursued by groups of nations either acting in concert or by sets of antagonists acting in ways that establish stable equilibria; or it needs to be pursued by the whole community of nations acting in concert. The very concept of security may not entail this—i.e. the need for concert or equilibrium may not be axiomatic. Very powerful countries may sometimes be in a position to pursue their own security unilaterally, by their own energy and resources in the international arena. Still, for most countries, most of the time, and even for the most powerful countries some of the time, the pursuit of national security is impossible except in the context of collective security as a structured good enjoyed multilaterally. I think that when we drop down a level from the international arena (where a couple of hundred nations jostle for security) to the interpersonal level (where millions of individuals jostle for safety in a particular political community), we should be open to the possibility that the notion of security appropriate at this level also needs to be considered as a collective rather than an individual good.

What about the concept of *national security*? Here the trouble is that the phrase 'national security' conveys ideas about *the integrity and power of the state itself* as an institutional apparatus and that is something which may or may not be related to ordinary citizens' being more secure.[23] I do

---

[22] See, e.g. Betts, 'Systems for Peace or Causes of War? Collective Security, Arms Control, and the New Europe' and Kelsen, 'Collective Security and Collective Self-Defense under the Charter of the United Nations.'

[23] There is an interesting discussion of the ambiguities of 'national security' in Wolfers, ' "National Security" as an Ambiguous Symbol.' See also Goodin, *Political Theory and Public Policy*, at p. 235.

not think that is the meaning of security that people have in mind when they say they are willing to trade off liberty against security. When it is said that liberty must be traded off for the sake of security, I think what is meant by 'security' is *people* being more secure rather than governmental institutions being powerful. Of course national security agencies are involved in the struggle to protect us against terrorism. But *their* security is valued for the sake of *our* security; the power of the national security apparatus is not valued as an end in itself. Maybe '*homeland* security' is a better term. '*Human* security' is another phrase in increasingly common use;[24] and it has the additional advantage of avoiding some of the residual national-security connotations of 'homeland security' in the United States.

In general, what I see is that although there is a massive literature on collective security and national security, it is not complemented by nor is it able to build upon or presuppose a similarly rich and copious theoretical literature on security as a compelling domestic political ideal. We philosophers write endlessly about the meaning of liberty; but we have devoted very little attention to the ideal on the other side of the balance—homeland security, human security, people's security—as a primary goal or function of the state. So long as our study remains unbalanced in that way, we can hardly reach an adequate view of the trade-off.

II. The Pure Safety Conception and its Shortcomings

In this chapter, I propose to begin remedying that situation. I shall attempt to analyze the concept of security, and tease out of that analysis some important issues that are relevant to clear thinking about the trade-offs we face between security and liberty.

---

[24] See Slaughter, 'Security, Solidarity, and Sovereignty,' at 623–4. See also Nanda, 'Preemptive and Preventive Use of Force, Collective Security, and Human Security,' at 10: 'Over the years, the concept of security—traditionally viewed as state security—has expanded to include human security as well as state security. As the Commission on Human Security articulated in 2003, the international community "urgently needs a new paradigm of security." The reason given by the Commission is that: "...The state remains the fundamental purveyor of security. Yet it often fails to fulfill its security obligations—and at times has even become a source of threat to its own people. That is why attention must now shift from the security of the state to the security of the people—to human security." '

Let us begin the analysis with a modest question: what is the relation between security and personal safety? I am safe to the extent that I am alive and unharmed. Is a population more secure simply by virtue of people being safer, i.e. simply in terms of a diminution in the prospect of their being killed or harmed? Or should we have in mind a richer notion of security involving elements of well-being other than survival, or a more structured notion (perhaps thinking of security as a certain kind of public good or as a good connoting a certain quality of relationship with others)?

It is surely tempting to associate the 'security' that we talk about—when we oppose liberty to security in assessing changes in our laws and practices since September 11, 2001—with the probability that any given one of us will be affected physically by a terrorist outrage. Nobody wants to be blown up. So security might be understood simply as a function of individual safety. We might say: *I* am more secure against terrorist attack when the probability of *my* being killed or harmed as a result of such attack goes down; and *we* are more secure when this is true *of many of us.* I shall call this *the pure safety conception.*

Though it is a very good starting point, I shall argue that we should not be satisfied with the pure safety conception. It is a radically stripped-down idea, and it is worth listing the issues it fails to raise and the concerns (commonly associated with the security side of the liberty/security balance) that it does not address. Seven issues seem important (though this is by no means an exhaustive list):

1. The pure safety conception offers no explanation of why we fear death or injury in some guises and not others—why we orient the notion of safety which we are using to form our conception of security towards *violent* death or injury and perhaps particularly towards violent death or injury at the hands (or as a result of the actions) of a particular sort of assailant, namely terrorists.
2. The focus of the pure safety conception is bodily survival and bodily integrity. But what about material loss, such as loss of property or economic value? Is a notion of security adequate if it does not take these into account?
3. The pure safety conception focuses on the objective facts of death and injury and the actual probabilities of their occurrence. It says nothing about the subjective aspect—fear, for example, considered not just as an emotional response to a diminution in actual safety, but as a mental state that is itself partly *constitutive* of insecurity.

4. Similarly, the pure safety conception does not adequately highlight the element of assurance or guarantee that the word 'security' connotes. I am secure not just because I happen to be safe, but because I am *sure* of not being killed or harmed.

5. The shortcoming referred to in point (4) also means that the pure safety conception does not alert us to the relation between security and the possession of other values that the element of assurance may relate to. It may be inappropriate to think of security as a good in its own right; it may be more sensible to think of it as a mode in which other goods are enjoyed. I enjoy my property securely or my health. I may enjoy certain liberties securely: I may enjoy security in the practice of my religion or the freedom to express my political views.

6. The pure safety conception focuses mainly on the individualized physical facts of death, injury, and loss rather than more diffuse harms to persons and people in general resulting from disruption of their way of life or the interruption of familiar routines. In that regard, it fails to capture the connection between the idea of security and the idea of social order, which by definition, is something enjoyed by many.

7. Finally, being a purely individual measure, the pure safety conception does not yet provide a basis for talking critically about the security of the whole community. It does not adequately confront aggregative or distributive issues. In setting out the pure safety conception I talked about safety as a probabilistic measure of death or injury for individual persons; the most I could say about security for a whole society is that *we* are more secure when the probability goes down for many of us. But this is very imprecise. We need to consider ways of talking about situations in which one person's security is purchased at the cost of another's; in these situations how are we to say whether the security of the whole society has gone up or down?

It is no part of my agenda in this chapter to denigrate or dismiss the pure safety conception, to argue that it is incoherent, or to propose that we replace it with some more amiable notion of communal solidarity. The hard Hobbesian link between security and survival is without doubt the core of the concept. Moreover, it is not unreasonable for people to be preoccupied with their personal safety, under the heading of 'security,' when they contemplate trade-offs between liberty and security in relation to the threat from terrorism. The threat from terrorism is deadly, not just disruptive. I will say it again: nobody wants to be blown up. The pure safety conception may be defective. But no attempt to remedy its defects can possibly be adequate if it cuts it adrift from the element of physical safety. When people are frightened, the issue of physical safety looms large, and it may be difficult to focus on those more sophisticated aspects of security as goals which are not immediately connected with this issue of the prospect of death, injury, or loss. At the same time, it is worth considering what a richer notion of security involves, if only to see how much we are panicked into losing when we become preoccupied with physical safety under the immediate pressure of events.

Let me add an important word of caution. In conversation about this, people say to me that a 'deepening' or a theoretical 'enrichment' of the notion of security is often a trick to try and sneak civil libertarian concerns into the other pan of the balance. We are supposed to be balancing liberty against security, they say, and we should not confuse matters with some fancy analysis that shows that security actually requires liberty. My friends are right: all such trickery should be resisted. On the other hand, we are not in a position to say that liberty and security are utterly independent values which can be weighed and balanced against each other until we have a clear and honest sense of what security involves. It is possible that analysis of these concepts will reveal some internal connections, in which case we will need to be much more careful in our talk about 'balance' and 'trade-offs.' We cannot rule that out, out of hand. Moreover, if there are important internal connections between the concepts, they are likely to cut both ways in the political debate. Partisans of security may need to face up to the fact that what most people (in this country) want to secure is not just life, but their American way of life, which has traditionally been associated with the enjoyment of certain liberties. But equally, partisans of civil liberties need to face up to the fact that what people want is *secure liberty*, not just liberty left open to abuse and attack. We should not be playing word-games. On the other hand we should not dismiss or ignore connections like these simply because they are likely to be misused politically by advocates on the Left or on the Right. I will return to this at the very end of the chapter.

Here is how I want to proceed. I want to consider adding to or enriching the pure safety conception in respect of its *depth* and in respect of its *breadth*. Depth looks to the enrichment of our notion of a person's security; breadth looks to the enrichment of our notion of a whole community's security. In addition we should think of ways in which the two dimensions are connected, for a sense of individual security is not easily separable from a sense of what an entire community has to lose when it is subject to attack.

Inasmuch as I deal with the two dimensions separately, I will address them as follows. Under the heading of *depth*, I will ask: how shallow is an account of individual security which focuses purely on safety? Are there aspects of people's apprehensions or their sense of what they have to lose that it fails to take into account? This raises issues (1) through (5) on my list. Should our estimation of security take into account, not just threats to life and limb, but also threats to material and economic well-being, the fear of such threats (whether substantiated or not), and the assurance that people crave as against such apprehensions? And should it take into account threats that come from agents other than terrorism— threats from hurricanes, for example, and other ways in which life and health are endangered? What about threats from the state—if not for citizens of this country then for citizens of other countries, where the very organization that is supposed to guarantee security is the main thing that many people fear? Those are our questions about depth, and I emphasize that what we face here are not just choices—'Let's *decide* to think about security this way or that'—but the exploration of reasons. The pressure to deepen our notion of personal security arises from the fact that many of the reasons that motivate the pure safety conception also seem to point us towards a deeper conception. On the other hand, if we are reluctant to extend our conception of security too far in any of these directions, we need to ask what the ground is of that reluctance? Is it that deepening of the concept would be politically embarrassing? Or are there genuine reasons for not budging from the pure safety conception's emphasis on life and limb?

Under the heading of breadth, I want to raise mainly issue (7) on my list, which invites us to pay attention to ways of talking about safety across the whole range of those who are supposed to be protected by our government's actions. We saw that Thomas Hobbes suggested that because a sovereign can operate only through general laws, 'he has done his duty if he has made every effort, to provide by sound measures for the welfare of as many of [his subjects] as possible for as long as possible.'[25] Is this satisfactory? Is security a majoritarian concept (like the greatest happiness of the greatest number)? Is Hobbes's reason—the generality of law—sufficient to convince us of that? Or should we think of security more as a basic right, to be guaranteed at least at a minimum

---

[25] Hobbes, *On the Citizen*, p. 143 (ch. 13).

level to everybody, or perhaps as a primary good, to be subject to principles of distributive justice?[26] There are hard questions to be faced here.
We need to explore the possibility that diminutions or enhancements in
security may be unevenly distributed, that the government may respond
to a threat to the security of some but not to a threat to the security of
others. Above all we need to say something abut the prospect that the
security of some is protected or enhanced only because the security of
others has been reduced (and reduced or even threatened by state activity not just by neglect). To address these possibilities, we may need to
add some *structure* to the pure safety conception, as it applies to a whole
community. To be sure, security is not another word for distributive justice. But if it is conceived as a good, then the question of how it is distributed—who enjoys it and who does not enjoy it—cannot be ignored.
So, under the heading of *breadth*, we will try to understand security for
a whole community as a *complex* function of individual safety—a function that pays attention to the means by which safety is assured and the
relational aspects of the distribution of safety so far as that is upheld in a
public order of a certain kind.

I shall begin the discussion with the issues of depth that I have identified. We need to know more about the nature and quality of the good
we are considering before we consider the way in which it is provided
and distributed. However, this strategy will prove difficult to sustain.
The two dimensions—depth and breadth—become quickly entangled.
When we start asking ourselves what a person's security consists in
beyond his personal safety, we are bound to consider the importance for
each person of certain *social* goods, and these may introduce an implicit
distributive dimension or a consideration of modes of public provision
that short-circuits any tidy separation of issues of depth and issues of
breadth. Equally when we talk—also under the heading of depth—
about the mode of assurance associated with each person's security, we
quickly find ourselves considering the idea of *mutual* assurance (the way
we help each other in society on these matters), and this too takes us
across the tidy border to distributive issues.

What I will do then, is divide the discussion of depth into two phases.
I will consider it first in Part III: there we will consider items (2) through
(5) on my list. That will be followed in Part IV by a discussion of

---

[26] For the basic rights approach, see Shue, *Basic Rights*, at pp. 20–2; see also the discussion in Chapter 6, below. For the idea of primary goods see Rawls, *A Theory of Justice*,
pp. 90–5.

breadth—i.e. of distributive issues and issues about the formal provision of security to the members of a society: here, as well as item (7) on the list, we will also address item (1), because the way in which distributive issues arise is often affected by who or what is seen as the threat to security. Then in Part V, we will return to issues of depth in the light of that discussion of breadth: this will involve some consideration of item (6) on the list—the importance for each of us of security for our whole way of life, which cannot so easily be separated from communal, distributive, and civil libertarian concerns.

III. Deepening the Pure Safety Conception

A. Economic loss and mode of life

Nobody wants to be blown up. People worry about the loss of their lives in relation to terrorist attacks. But they also worry about being injured or maimed; they worry about their bodily integrity, even if sheer survival is still their most important concern. Beyond this, what about damage to property—to homes, cars, and the things that people rely on for their ordinary activities? A plan for security that did not propose to protect property would be regarded by most of us as pretty impoverished. It is not just a matter of protecting it as material wealth; it is a matter of protecting the role that people's possessions play in their individual and family mode of life. By mode of life, I mean not just daily routines but also the reasonable aspirations people have for their lives, the trajectory of their lives, if you like. Each individual has and pursues a mode of living, a life plan (in a very informal sense), for him- or herself and his or her family members, and an awful lot of things play a part in that. People value and rightly demand the protection of all that under the heading of their security. I do not mean that people are entitled to an assurance of success. But they may well think themselves entitled, as an aspect of security, to protection for the assets they have accumulated for themselves and their families as part of a normal attempt to put an ordinary plan of life into action.

Once we start thinking along these lines, we see that an adequate (adequately deep) conception of security should aim to protect people's individual and familial modes of living themselves, and not just the life, health, and possessions that are necessary for it. A situation in which lives and property were safe from attack but one's mode of life was not (because a lot of time had to be spent cowering in sealed rooms), or a situation in which one's daily routines were safe and protected, but at the expense of the ordinary aspirations that most people have for the trajectory of their lives (pursuing a career, raising a family, seeking education, promotions, etc.)—neither of these would or should be regarded as a situation of security. The pure safety conception ignores factors like these; but a deeper notion of security will insist on taking them into account.

B. Security and fear

Each person wants not only protection for his or her life, health, possessions, and mode of living, but they also want not to be fearful about these things. (One meaning of the word 'security' connotes nothing but the absence of this fear: 'Freedom from care, anxiety or apprehension; a feeling of safety or freedom from or absence of danger.')[27] That the fear is not insignificant is indicated by the word 'terrorism' itself.[28] It is a mode of attack on people's lives which is calculated to generate an enormous amount of fear and anxiety, not to mention the anguish and horror that accompany the loss of life and limb associated with terror attacks. Diminishing the objective threat to life, health, possessions, and mode of living—diminishing the probability that they will be harmed or damaged—is one way of securing against this fear. On the other hand, we have to figure what to say about the extent to which the fear and terror associated with insecurity may be disproportionate to the actual likelihood of the events that frighten us.

It is common for cynics to remind people that their chance of death and injury due to road accidents, for example, is much greater than their chances of death or injury due to terrorist attacks, and it is sometimes suggested that people are irrational in not calling for precautions against the former in the same way that they call for precautions against the latter.[29] There is something to this point, but not much. Certainly incidents involving large numbers of deaths—such as in the World

---

[27] This is the third meaning given for 'security' in the online Oxford English Dictionary: <http://dictionary.oed.com/entrance.dtl> (accessed on March 24, 2006).

[28] See the discussion in Scheffler, 'Is Terrorism Morally Distinctive?' See also Chapter 3 above, at pp. 50–2 and 65–7.

[29] Elster, 'Fear, Terror, and Liberty,' 8–9, suggests that 350 excess deaths were caused after September 11, 2001, by Americans using their cars instead of flying to wherever they were going (citing Gigerenzer, 'Dread Risk, September 11, and Fatal Traffic Accidents').

Trade Center attacks or the crashing of a hijacked airplane—have a grip on the fearful imagination which is out of proportion to people's response to the same number of deaths spread out across thousands of ordinary accidents.[30] But actually, there is considerable rationality to the enhanced fear as a result of attacks such as those that took place on September 11, 2001. First, in the months that followed 9/11, nobody knew that there would be no repetition of these attacks on the same or even greater scale: were these isolated incidents or were we going to end up in a situation like that of modern Israel, in which—as it seemed at the time—terrorist outrages occurred weekly or monthly, with a constant drumbeat of death and injury?[31] It is as though a car accident suddenly involved a hundred or a thousand deaths, with no guarantee that accidents would not continue happening on that scale. Secondly, the risk of death or injury from terrorist threats is not an *alternative* to the threat of death or injury on the roads (as though we could choose one or the other). The threats are cumulative. Thirdly, it is just not true that we have taken no efforts to address carnage on a similar scale on the roads. An immense amount of effort has been devoted to making our roads safer and our driving safer, and the effort continues. There is probably a number of death-and-injury-accidents that will keep occurring despite our best efforts, though no one is complacent about that. The point about terrorist attacks on the U.S. mainland is that they represented a *new* kind of threat, and new restrictions were thought necessary to meet them (just as new restrictions were thought necessary with the advent of the automobile). People are understandably very frightened while we take the measure of this new threat. Fourthly, people are rightly worried about intentional threats, particularly intentional threats which seem to aim at targeting people in their ordinary peaceful activities (as opposed to the context of military conflict where intentional threats are expected). Partly this is because it is harder to guard against intentional threats: road accidents are not *trying* to test and to penetrate our defenses. And it is partly because—in a way that

---

[30] See, e.g. Feigenson et al., 'Perceptions of Terrorism and Disease Risk,' for the suggestion that this effect is quite localized depending on the vividness of recent experience in a given country. See generally for a discussion of illusions and faulty reasoning in regard to fear under conditions of uncertainty, Tversky, 'Assessing Uncertainty,' esp. 149–52.

[31] In the 59-month period since September 11, 2001, Israel has endured more than 98 suicide and other bombing outrages, resulting in 627 deaths and injuries to more than 3,463 people. (This was true as of June 4, 2006: see <http://www.mfa.gov.il/mfa/go.asp?MFAH0i5d0>. Since then, the extent of terrorist incidents in Israel has been greatly reduced.)

is not always easy to figure out—it is somehow intrinsically worse to face a prospect of deliberate attack than to face a prospect of accidental death.

Still, fears are not always rational; they do not always conform to the objective probabilities or follow them up or down in any orderly fashion. Inasmuch as the two diverge—inasmuch as fear of attack does not correspond exactly to probability of attack (e.g. with fear remaining high even when probability diminishes)—it may be thought that the reduction of fear ought to be regarded as an additional and independent element of security. In other words, fear is not just a response to something called insecurity; it is partly constitutive of insecurity. A given degree of fear may not be a rational response to a given probability of death or injury. But still we have to treat the fear as significant for security in its own right.[32] Fear itself is something to be dreaded inasmuch as it can have a psychologically debilitating effect.[33]

Regarding fear as in itself an aspect of insecurity gives rise to all sorts of dangers. Suppose Americans experience a level of fear of terrorist attack in 2006 that is rationally appropriate to the actual frequency of attack in (say) Israel but not to the actual frequency of attack in the United States. Should the American government respond to that insecurity with measures that would be appropriate to the Israeli situation, in the hope that this will allay Americans' fears to some extent? If we say 'No,' it sounds as if the government is not taking people's fear seriously; it is condescending to those who are afraid and telling them that it will respond only to rational fears, not to the debilitating fear that they actually experience. On the other hand, we need to remember that pandering to these exaggerated fears may also involve adverse effects on others. What if people's irrational fears will not be allayed unless we incarcerate all young Muslim men in our cities? Certainly there will be objections to doing this from the civil liberties side of the balance. But are we clear what to think about this from even the security side?

I can imagine someone responding that all this provides a good reason for keeping the discussion of security simple, for keeping it focused on objective facts about safety, tying it down (if need be) to the pure safety conception. If we try to enrich it with psychology, we get into these

---

[32] See Wolfers, ' "National Security" as an Ambiguous Symbol,' 485, for the suggestion that security has a subjective as well as an objective sense: '[S]ecurity in an objective sense, measures the absence of threat to acquired values, in a subjective sense, the absence of fear that such values will be attacked.'

[33] See also the discussion in Chapter 3, above, pp. 65–7.

terrible conundrums about what security requires in regard to irrational fears. I think this is a mistake. We should not define our concepts just to avoid hard questions. We did not begin with any guarantee that the concept of security was straightforward or morally unproblematic. Our task in analyzing the concept is to find out whether that is so. I think it is better to say upfront that there is an inherent reference to levels of subjective fear in our concept of security and that therefore the pursuit of security is fraught with moral difficulty, than to try sanitizing the concept and pretend that all its difficulties arise exogenously from competition with other values.

C. Security and assurance

Connected with the points I have made about fear are some points about the relation between security and assurance and our view of the future. Earlier I mentioned the work of the early nineteenth-century utilitarian theorist Jeremy Bentham. In his writings on civil law, Bentham invited us to 'consider that man is not like the animals, limited to the present...but...susceptible of pains and pleasures by anticipation; and that it is not enough to secure him from actual loss, but it is necessary also to guarantee him, as far as possible, against future loss.'[34] Expectation is crucial to human life, according to Bentham: 'It is hence that we have the power of forming a general plan of conduct; it is hence that the successive instants which compose the duration of life are not isolated and independent points, but become continuous parts of a whole.'[35] The need to secure expectations was the basis of Bentham's conception of property. He argued that if people do not have an assurance projected into the future that what they have they can hold, the enjoyment of property and the incentives that are supposed to derive from that enjoyment will simply evaporate. 'When insecurity reaches a certain point, the fear of losing prevents us from enjoying what we possess already. The care of preserving condemns us to a thousand sad and painful precautions, which yet are always liable to fail of their end.'[36] Bentham also recognized that in the field of property, expectation is entirely the work of law: 'I cannot count upon the enjoyment of that which I regard as mine, except through the promise of the law which guarantees it to me.'[37] Now, this sort of security faces a threat from law

---

[34] Bentham, *Principles of the Civil Code,* p. 110.   [35] Ibid., p. 111.
[36] Ibid., p. 116.   [37] Ibid., p. 112.

itself, if expectations are overturned with too-frequent legal change.[38] But there are external threats as well:

> Fraud and injustice secretly conspire to appropriate [labor's] fruits. Insolence and audacity think to ravish them by open force. Thus security is assailed on every side—ever threatened, never tranquil, it exists in the midst of alarms. The legislator needs a vigilance always sustained, a power always in action, to defend it against this crowd of indefatigable enemies.[39]

To sustain security, therefore, it is not enough that threats of this kind be repelled. There must be an *assurance* that they will be repelled, an assurance that people can count on and build upon in advance of the outcome of any particular attack.

Bentham made his points about property but analogous points might be made about safety. It is not enough that we turn out to be safe. We are not really secure unless we have an *assurance* of safety. We need that assurance because we want not only to *have* our lives and limbs but to *do* things with them, make plans and pursue long-term activities to which an assurance of safety is integral.[40] Our safety is not just an end in itself, but an indispensable platform or basis on which we will enjoy other values and activities. It cannot serve those other values unless it is assured. We may be thankful for our survival, but we cannot use our safety if survival is simply the fortuitous outcome of a long process of shivering terror.

D. Security and other goods

Should we therefore follow Bentham's lead and detach security from considerations of survival altogether? Bentham's property-owner, who

---

[38] Ibid., p. 113: 'As regards property, security consists in receiving no check, no shock, no derangement to the expectation founded on the laws, of enjoying such and such a portion of good. The legislator owes the greatest respect to this expectation which he has himself produced.'

[39] Ibid., p. 110.

[40] We might develop a similar point on the basis of Hobbes's claims about all the human goods that will be unattainable if there is no assurance against war and violent death. See Hobbes, *Leviathan*, p. 89 (ch. 13): 'In such condition, there is no place for Industry; because the fruit thereof is uncertain; and consequently no Culture of the Earth; no Navigation, nor use of the commodities that may be imported by Sea; no commodious Building; no Instruments of moving, and removing such things as require much force; no Knowledge of the face of the Earth; no account of Time; no Arts; no Letters; no Society; and which is worst of all, continuall feare, and danger of violent death; And the life of man, solitary, poore, nasty, brutish, and short.'

craves security of expectation so that he can give himself up to the cultivation of a field 'with the sure though distant hope of harvest,' does not
necessarily have his *survival* at stake (though of course in some cases his
subsistence may depend upon his plan for cultivation). What he wants
security *of* is the enjoyment of the fruits of his labor. Security is oriented
to enjoyment not to safety. Similarly a professor values his tenure, not
because it gives him security of life and limb; he may be perfectly able
to survive if he is fired. He wants security of tenure so that he can be
assured that his controversial writings will not endanger his scholarly
career. People want security, in this sense, for all sorts of things. Pursuing
this line of thought, we can see that security is not so much a good in
and of itself, but (as I said earlier) something 'adjectival'—a mode of
enjoying other goods, an underwriting of other values, a guarantor of
other things we care about.

Some of these goods might be liberties. We might think of ourselves
as secure (or insecure) in the privacy of our homes, secure (or insecure)
against arbitrary incarceration, secure (or insecure) in our religious freedom. A demand for civil liberties is often a demand for security in this
regard. Does this show that the connection between security and liberty is internal, so that talk of a balance or trade-off is inappropriate?
(Usually it is independent values that we balance and trade off against
one another.) I think that conclusion would be too hasty. There is certainly *a sense* of 'security' in which it refers to a mode of enjoying liberty
(and other goods), and *in that sense* it might be inappropriate to talk of a
liberty/security trade-off. But that does not mean there cannot be trade-
offs between liberty and security, in a sense of security that is tied more
closely to safety: security of life, limb, and property, security in relation
to one's ordinary expectations and way of life, security from fear that
might imperil one's enjoyment of all that. I will return to this at the end
of this chapter.

The point I am making is a delicate one. I do think we need to deepen
our notion of security so that it is not just a matter of probability of
bodily harm and I do think that any reasonable notion of security has to
indicate some degree of confidence or assurance in regard to the goods
it protects. But deepening the concept and paying attention to the element of assurance should not be a way of evacuating it of its distinctive
content. Those who want to persist with talk of a liberty/security trade-
off may be perfectly happy to talk, in more complicated terms, about
a trade-off between assurance (or security) of liberty and assurance (or
security) of safety, and we should not play word-games to obstruct this.

On the other hand, we have to remain open to the possibility that there are substantial—as opposed to purely verbal—internal connections between security (or security of safety) and liberty (or security of liberty). Henry Shue defends such a position in his book *Basic Rights*. He argues that security against the threat of attack is absolutely necessary for the enjoyment of any right:

> No one can fully enjoy any right that is supposedly protected by society if someone can credibly threaten him with murder, rape, or beating, etc. when he or she tries to enjoy the alleged right. Such threats to physical security are among the most serious and—in much of the world—the most widespread hindrances to the enjoyment of any right.... In the absence of physical security people are unable to use any other rights that society may be said to be protecting without being liable to encounter many of the worst dangers they would encounter if society were not protecting the rights.[41]

Note, however, that Shue is concentrating on security against threats actually targeted at the enjoyment of one's rights. It is a further question whether his argument goes through for security generally. Suppose I am insecure because of the danger of terrorist attack. Assuming that the terrorists simply intend to kill and wound a large number of people (perhaps including me) and do not really care either way about other rights enjoyed or exercised by the potential victims of their attacks. Is it still true that the enjoyment of rights is debilitated by insecurity in that sense? Perhaps, but the argument would be less direct than the argument Shue provides. The argument would be that security in this sense is a condition for rights inasmuch as I need to be able to concentrate on my rights-exercise and make plans etc. with my rights, and I cannot do this if I am distracted by terror.

If we accept anything like Shue's argument, then it looks as though defenders of rights should be hesitant to voice rights-based complaints against increases in security, since security is the *sine qua non* for the enjoyment of their rights. However, even if security is the necessary condition for the enjoyment of rights, it does not necessarily follow that that security should have absolute priority. For one thing, a necessary condition for X is worth supplying only if there is a practicable possibility of securing sufficient conditions for X; if there is no such possibility, then we should forget about the necessary conditions for X.[42] More

---

[41] Shue, *Basic Rights*, at p. 21. See also the discussion in Chapter 6.

[42] This can be illustrated with an analogy. A necessary condition for me to visit the moon is that I begin astronaut training right now. But even assuming that my visiting the

importantly, there is something perverse about giving absolute priority to security over rights if security is valued only for the sake of rights. Surely we do not want to devote all our resources and energy to a necessary condition for something we value, and nothing at all to the thing that we value. We need to find some balance between the conditions for securing a value and (perhaps sometimes precarious) enjoyment of the value itself.[43]

In any case, though Shue's point is no doubt important, it is probably a mistake to think of physical security only as a basic condition for the enjoyment and exercise of rights.[44] People value their safety and their physical survival in and of itself, and they will fight to preserve their lives long after it has become evident that for them a life of enjoyment and autonomy is unavailable. It may seem odd to some of us that life should be clung to apart from its quality, or that bodily integrity should be valued apart from the freedom to decide what to do with our bodies, but there it is: many people's values work in this way and an understanding of security should be sensitive to that.[45]

IV. The Distribution of Security

Having completed an initial deepening of the pure safety conception, I turn now to questions of breadth. The aim in this part of the chapter is to consider the application of the term 'security' to the conditions of life of a whole population as opposed to one individual. In what follows, I am going to assume everything that we have established in Part III. From now on when I talk about individual security, I will intend not just a reference to improbability of harm to life and limb, but protection of one's basic mode of life and economic values, as well as reasonable protection against fear and terror, and the presence of a positive assurance that these values will continue to be maintained into the future. What we now need to discuss is how to think about the application of

moon is highly desirable, the necessary condition for it is simply of no interest since *it is not going to happen.* See also the discussion at p. 44 above.

[43] See Goodin, *Political Theory and Public Policy*, at p. 233.

[44] Shue recognizes this when he says: '*Regardless of whether the enjoyment of physical security is also desirable for its own sake*, it is desirable as part of the enjoyment of every other right' (Shue, *Basic Rights*, at p. 21; my emphasis).

[45] For an interesting discussion of different ways of reckoning the value of life, see Dworkin, *Life's Dominion*, pp. 81–101 *et passim*.

that somewhat deeper notion of security across a whole population of millions or hundreds of millions of individuals. Only by doing this is it possible to think about security as a political goal, as opposed to an individual goal.

A. Breadth and distribution

When I introduced what I called 'the pure safety conception,' I observed that it barely moves beyond a Hobbesian individual measure. It provides no basis for thinking about *the security of the community* as opposed to the security of this or that individual (at a given time). The pure safety conception treats security as a probabilistic measure of death or injury for individual persons. The most I was willing to say in Part II about its application to the security of a whole society is that perhaps it can be said that *we* are more secure when the probability of death, injury, or loss goes down *for many of us*. That is both imprecise and unsatisfactory.

So we must turn now to questions of breadth. How do we think about the provision of security across a whole population? Survival and safety refer to individual life and limb; how do we move from there to talk of the security of a society as a whole? Readers will recall that our direct interest is not in what is called 'national security,' for that seems to refer to the integrity and power of the state apparatus. We are interested instead in what national security is *for*—namely, the security of the *people* of the nation. So our question is: how do we move from talk about one person's security to talk about the security of a population comprising (say) three hundred million people? Remember that security for each person is a matter of more or less and that our discussion of depth has indicated that this 'more or less' might have to be assessed across various dimensions. How are we to think about cases where some individuals could be made much more secure (in some dimensions) by making others somewhat less secure? What are the implications of such possibilities for our talk of the security of a whole population? When we talk about security for a whole population, are we implying anything about the distribution across that population of security as enjoyed by individuals? If we are, is that implication purely aggregative (as Hobbes suggests with his talk of 'sound measures for the welfare of as many of them as possible')? Or does it have an egalitarian component—for example 'equal protection'? Are we committed to maximizing security or paying attention to the equity of its enjoyment?

B. Policy and definition

In thinking about this, it is not always easy to distinguish questions of definition from questions of policy. As a matter of security policy, we might ask questions like the following: Should the government pay attention to the equality or inequality of the security enjoyed by individuals? Should it aim to see that the security of all its members is above a certain threshold, and regard itself as having failed if any significant number of people falls below that threshold? Or should it take its task to be purely additive—to make as many people as secure as possible, even if that means accepting the endangerment of some for the sake of the security of the greater number? Now, we might return answers to these policy questions, on various grounds, without any reference to the meaning of the word 'security' as applied to whole populations. We might think that analysis of meanings does not help us very much with these questions, or we may reject the idea of being dictated to in maters of policy by conceptual analysis.

Still, we should not rule out the possibility that as applied to whole populations, the word 'security' has a meaning which inclines towards one of these policy options and not the others. Many of the value-concepts of our political philosophy are structured to incorporate implicit distributive assumptions. In some cases this is obvious: when we consider whether a given society is *democratic*, we have no choice but to consider how the franchise is distributed among the members of the society. Democracy implies political equality, and it is simply not compatible with a situation in which the formal political power of some individuals is much greater than others. Similarly, when we consider whether a society enjoys the Rule of Law, we must pay attention to the distribution of access to legal services (at least in a formal sense) and to the generality of the laws' applicability across the whole array of citizens. In both cases, an understanding of the concept rules out certain approaches to the distribution of the goods that the concept protects. A society does not enjoy the Rule of Law by virtue of most people being treated as legal subjects with legal rights; it requires that they *all* be treated as legal subjects with legal rights. Similarly, a society does not enjoy democracy by virtue of most citizens having the vote; unless *all* adult citizens have the vote, the society is not a democracy. We ought to consider the possibility that security is like democracy and the Rule of Law in also being structured by some such implicit distributive assumption.

A further intimation along these lines comes by way of analogy with the liberty side of the liberty–security trade-off. We know that *liberty* may be differentially distributed.[46] But we know too that the very idea of liberty is associated with some firmly established views about what that distribution ought to be. Though liberty is mainly a good to the individuals who have it, there are strong principles in the liberal tradition about ensuring that each person's liberty is made compatible with an *equal* liberty assigned to everyone else. The systematic equalization of liberty or its maximization subject to an equality constraint—'the most extensive basic liberty for each compatible with a similar liberty for all,' in Rawls's formula—has been a powerful Kantian theme in the history of liberal thought.[47] Most liberals say that pure maximization of aggregate liberty or average liberty is out of the question: it would be quite wrong to try to secure greater liberty for some by restricting the liberty of others. To try that would be to act—absent some special explanation[48]—as though

[46] And we know also that the real impact on liberty of measures designed to enhance security may be differentially distributed. As I said in Chapter 2, most of the changes in civil liberties since September 11, 2001 are aimed specifically at suspected perpetrators or accomplices or persons who might be thought to have information about past or future terrorist actions, and most Americans imagine that persons in these categories will look quite different from themselves. In fact, if you leave aside increased searches at airports, then as Ronald Dworkin has argued (Dworkin, *The Threat to Patriotism*), '[n]one of the administration's [security] decisions and proposals will affect more than a tiny number of American citizens: almost none of us will be indefinitely detained for minor violations or offenses, or have our houses searched without our knowledge, or find ourselves brought before military tribunals on grave charges carrying the death penalty. Most of us pay almost nothing in personal freedom when such measures are used against those the President suspects of terrorism.'

[47] Kant, *The Metaphysics of Morals*, p. 24; Rawls, *A Theory of Justice*, p. 250; Dworkin, *Sovereign Virtue: The Theory and Practice of Equality*, p. 128. See also Berlin, *Four Essays on Liberty*, at pp. 124–7 for a slightly different formula, calling for the equalization of liberty subject to an individual adequacy constraint.

[48] One obvious area that requires more discussion is the special position, with regard to liberty, of those accused or suspected of crime. Plainly, there is some differentiation between the level of liberty thought appropriate for them and the level of equal liberty appropriate for members of the community generally. However, these differentiations are treated with great caution and organized in a way that is as closely commensurate with the principle of equal respect as possible. We do not think ourselves entitled to differentiate casually, simply because we think some of us will be better off if others' liberty is restricted. The principle of equal respect impacts in at least three ways on the appropriate manner in which suspects of serious crime or danger are treated: (i) it requires us to stay open to the possibility that they may be innocent; (ii) it constrains the means we use to determine guilt or innocence; and (iii) it constrains the way we deal with—including the way we punish—those who we are sure are attackers, criminals, or terrorists. Though, in each of these regards, there may well be an issue of lesser liberty, still the according of

the others were not worthy of respect, did not count in society, so far as the government was concerned. It is certainly never enough to say, for example, that the loss of liberty for these few is made up for by the greater liberty of all other individuals, or that liberty is better off on average, or that we are better off in some other dimension as a result of restricting some people's liberty. So strong is the association between the value of liberty and this principle for its appropriate distribution that the very word 'liberty' is sometimes used in a way that suggests that the distributive principle is incorporated into the concept. Any demand for liberty that is incompatible with this principle of equal liberty is seen sometimes as a demand for *license*, not liberty. So far as security is concerned, this is just an analogy; it does not tell us anything. But when the good being weighed against security has this distributive structure, we should not be surprised if security turns out to have a structure of this kind as well.

C. Maximization: the greatest security of the greatest number?

I guess we could treat the security of a whole society in a straightforwardly aggregative way, simply summing or averaging over individual safety to define a measure of security for society as a whole. That is, we might say that a whole community is less secure when the average probability of individual death, injury, or loss among the members of the community goes up. This aggregative approach would take account of the variations in the impacts of security measures on different individuals, and it would enable us to define something analogous to the economist's social welfare function—a social *security* function—that took all those disparate impacts into account. On the basis of this sort of conception of security, we would then be in a position to talk more precisely about trade-offs. Would this be satisfactory? Is this the way to arrive at an adequate conception of security for a whole society?[49]

---

lesser liberty to someone suspected of criminal activity, or even to someone convicted of it, is always to be done in a way that is compatible with underlying principles of respect. The traditional civil liberties add up to a system that is supposed to effect that compatibility. No doubt such systems require adjustment from time to time, to reflect the greater dangers that we face. But the adjustment must never lose touch with the underlying principles of respect in regard to suspects and convicts. We are not entitled to readjust the system of civil liberties simply to make ourselves safer. If we are concerned to make ourselves safer, any readjustment must be filtered through the medium of these principles.

[49] Can a pure aggregate or average measure of security be defended as a distributive principle, along the lines of John Harsanyi's response to Rawls's 'original position'

We saw earlier that Thomas Hobbes adopted something like a maximizing approach to security. The sovereign, he said, should provide for the security of as many people as possible for as long as possible, and this may be compatible with some people doing badly for the sake of the majority.[50] Whether or not this is the right position, it is certainly not supported by the argument that Hobbes provides for it. Hobbes's argument for this sort of maximization is that '[t]he sovereign as such provides for the citizens' safety only by means of laws, which are universal.'[51] In fact, Hobbes provides no argument for the position that the sovereign is not sometimes empowered to act directly on the basis of discretionary intervention; that is, he provides no argument against what John Locke would later call 'prerogative power.'[52] And anyway, if we confine ourselves to general laws, the fact is that general laws can be oriented either to the maximizing of security or to equal protection. Generality as such does not prejudge that issue.

There are all sorts of reasons for being hesitant about the maximizing approach. None of them is conclusive, but they should put us on alert to the likelihood that this approach is to be rejected as wrong-headed.

(i) The first set of reasons comprises general worries about this form of consequentialism. Over the last 30 years or so, moral philosophers have become convinced that there is something deeply wrong with the position that attempts to maximize important values without any attention to their distribution. This skepticism is particularly focused on utilitarianism, in the sense of maximizing welfare.[53] But it would not be surprising if it did not apply also to a utilitarianism of security.

argument?—i.e. the argument in John C. Harsanyi, 'Can the Maximin Principle Serve as a Basis for Morality?' to the effect that people in Rawls's 'Original Position' would choose average utility as their best bet for a society in which they did not know what place they would occupy. (See also Rawls, *A Theory of Justice*, p. 161 ff.) The answer is 'Probably not.' Harsanyi's argument depends on the notion that a distribution of security with the highest average offers the best bet for a person who does not know which place he will occupy in the society; the notion of a best bet for such a person makes most sense when people can think of themselves as repeat players (like a person choosing a strategy for a whole evening of poker) and least sense when people think of themselves as making a one-off bet; but the distribution of security, with its arguably mortal consequences, is perhaps the least plausible candidate for such a stochastic approach. Rawls's comment here is apposite: 'We must not be enticed by mathematically attractive assumptions into pretending that the contingencies of men's social positions and the asymmetries of their situations somehow even out in the end. Rather, we must choose our conception of justice fully recognizing that this is not and cannot be the case' (ibid., 17).

[50] Hobbes, *On the Citizen*, p. 143 (ch. 13).   [51] Idem.

[52] See Locke, *Two Treatises*, pp. 374–5 (II, §§159–60).

[53] For the modern consensus against this sort of maximizing consequentialism, see Rawls, *A Theory of Justice*, p. 27: 'Utilitarianism does not take seriously the distinction

(ii) Another reason for thinking that the distribution of deep-safety should not be governed by a principle of maximization, one reason for thinking that it should be governed by egalitarian principles similar to those with which we govern the distribution of liberty and constrained in similar ways, under the auspices of a richer notion of security, concerns the relationship between security and human rights. As we have seen, in *Basic Rights*, Henry Shue argues that physical security is an indispensable prerequisite for the enjoyment of any right: it is, in that sense, a *basic* right.[54] Since the general principle of the distribution of human rights is equality, it is not unreasonable to infer that the distribution of this very basic prerequisite to the enjoyment of human rights should be distributed on that basis as well.

(iii) Defenders of a security–liberty trade-off have to be able to respond adequately to the point that since civil liberties are rights and rights are trumps, civil liberties are not supposed to be traded off easily against other important goods. The best response to this point is for the defenders of security to say that rights are also at stake on their side of the balance: there is a right to life and a right to safety which we are balancing against rights to various liberties.[55] That is not implausible. But if security is going to be treated as a right, then it has to have the distributive structure of rights and the distributive structure of rights is egalitarian, not maximizing.

(iv) The maximizing approach does not even measure up as a description of our practice. Often we assign resources to the protection of some individual from an extraordinary threat to an extent that would make no sense if we were simply trying to maximize the overall amount of security in the population. The sustained campaign by British police and security forces to protect Salman Rushdie after the fatwa issued against his life in 1988 is a clear example. The resources assigned to Rushdie's protection involved enormous and sustained expense for many years, and there was no reason to suppose that making him more secure made anyone else more secure. Quite the contrary—cutting him loose and leaving him to his fate might well have reduced the danger to others, especially his

---

between persons.' See also Nozick, *Anarchy, State, and Utopia*, at pp. 32–3: '[T]here is no social entity with a good that undergoes some sacrifice for its own good. There are only individual people, different individual people, with their own individual lives. Using one of these people for the benefit of others, uses him and benefits the others. Nothing more.... Talk of an overall social good covers this up. (Intentionally?)'

[54] Shue, *Basic Rights*, pp. 20–2.

[55] See the discussion in Chapter 2, above, pp. 31–3.

police bodyguards. The only explanation is that the British authorities found it unacceptable that any one individual's security should suddenly be reduced—by external threats—to a level so far below the security of most other Britons. I am not saying that their aim was equality of security,[56] but it evidently involved qualifying a maximizing approach with the principle that no one's security should be allowed to drop drastically below a certain minimum level.

D. Does sheer survival trump distributive justice?

It may be thought that the area of security is one in which we should not pursue issues of distributive justice too fastidiously. Issues of security involve brutal questions of primal survival. In the last resort, people must be expected simply to do what they can to guarantee their own safety and that of their families in circumstances of imminent mortal threat. They cannot reasonably be expected to attend fastidiously to fine points of distributive equity under these circumstances. This point was made (about justice) by David Hume:

> Suppose a society to fall into such want of all common necessaries, that the utmost frugality and industry cannot preserve the greater number from perishing, and the whole from extreme misery; it will readily, I believe, be admitted, that the strict laws of justice are suspended, in such a pressing emergence, and give place to the stronger motives of necessity and self-preservation. Is it any crime, after a shipwreck, to seize whatever means or instrument of safety one can lay hold of, without regard to former limitations of property? Or if a city besieged were perishing with hunger; can we imagine, that men will see any means of preservation before them, and lose their lives, from a scrupulous regard to what, in other situations, would be the rules of equity and justice? The use and tendency of that virtue is to procure happiness and security, by preserving order in society: but where the society is ready to perish from extreme necessity, no greater evil can be dreaded from violence and injustice; and every man may now provide for himself by all the means, which prudence can dictate, or humanity permit.[57]

But this is not a convincing response in the present context, for two reasons. First, if it works at all, the Humean argument works only in the face of the most imminent, focused threat—*clear and present danger to*

---

[56] But see the discussion of an analogous case in Vlastos, 'Justice and Equality,' at pp. 49–50.
[57] Hume, *An Enquiry Concerning the Principles Of Morals*, at p. 186.

the individuals concerned. That is not what I am considering in this chapter. I am considering not how individuals should respond personally to an immediate threat to themselves or their families, but how the law and politics of a large organized community like this one should respond to a threat level that is elevated overall, but still quite small for each individual. Under these circumstances, it is not unreasonable to insist on some degree of distributive sensitivity.

Secondly, even in the circumstances to which it applies, Hume's argument is not a reason in favour of a maximizing approach. It is a reason for taking no interest in the social dimension of the matter at all. So it is no help for our discussion of security as a social or political ideal. Maybe from the point of view of a Hobbesian individual, egoistically obsessed with his own survival, there is no basis for thinking about the proper distribution of security for others.[58] I am interested in my survival and you are interested in yours; it is not clear on Hobbesian grounds why anyone should be interested either in equal protection or in the security of the majority, except to the extent that they personally benefit from the implementation of one or other of these distributive options. But if it is possible to take a point of view that transcends that of particular individuals, then there is a distributive question to be faced that is not trumped by the urgent impulsion of individual survival. I think Hobbes's sovereign necessarily must adopt such a perspective in order to figure out his duty, 'since governments were formed for peace, and peace is sought for safety' and 'a commonwealth is formed not for its own sake but for the sake of the citizens.'[59] It may be true, as I think, that Hobbes makes a mistake in thinking that the sovereign's duty is to maximize security; but it is not a mistake to assume that the sovereign must devote attention to the principle on which security is to be supplied to the citizens. The inherent urgency of security, the fact that it is a matter of life and death, does not show that this consideration of a principle for breadth is inappropriate. The sovereign is constrained by the fact that it exists to promote the safety of *all of us, in a given community*, not just of *me alone*.

---

[58] Hobbes, *On the Citizen*, p. 27 (ch. 1): '[E]very man is drawn to desire that which is Good for him, and to Avoid what is bad for him, and most of all the greatest of natural evils, which is death; this happens by a real necessity of nature, as powerful as that by which a stone falls downward.... Therefore the first foundation of natural Right is that each man protect his life and limbs as much as he can.... By natural law one is oneself the judge whether the means he is to use and the action he intends to take are necessary to the preservation of his life and limbs or not.'

[59] Ibid., p. 143 (ch. 13).

Maybe as a Hobbesian man, I am preoccupied with what the sovereign provides for *me*; but I know that *the state* cannot be preoccupied with this to the exclusion of all else. Even if *I* am entitled to act in certain circumstances as though the safety of others didn't matter as much as my safety does, the sovereign cannot act as if my safety mattered more than other people's safety (and I can't reasonably ask it to). I know that the sovereign must have in mind its impact on their safety too.

Another way of putting it is to say that even if security is a desperate issue of life and death from the individual's point of view, the individual has to recognize that there are limits on what he can expect the state to do for his security. Maybe the individual will fight tooth and nail, with little regard for others, to protect his life and that of his family. But he cannot expect *the state* to fight for him and his family *with little regard to others*. The state must have regard to all of those whose security it is bound to protect, and that necessarily qualifies what it can do for any one of us. So again, each of us must consider what the appropriate principle is—equal protection or a maximizing principle—for the state to supply security across the whole population. For only then will we be in a position to articulate reasonable and responsible demands (on the state) on our own behalf.

E. Security as a public good

Maybe there is another way of avoiding the distributive issue. It is possible that we might avoid some of these issues about aggregation and distribution, by treating security, insofar as it applies to a whole society, as a *public good*. If something is a public good, then by definition any member of the public gets the benefit of it and so the distributive question is put to rest. We need to proceed carefully with this suggestion, however, because the phrase 'public good' is used in a number of ways in political and economic theory. It is used to refer to (a) goods provided in a society as a matter of public responsibility; (b) goods whose enjoyment by and provision to individuals have certain distinctive features; and (c) goods enjoyed communally or collectively. Of these, (a) is a rather loose sense, and it will not be our concern here, though often it is said that goods are public in sense (a) on account of their being public in sense (b). Sense (c) we shall consider later in the discussion, in Part V of this chapter. At this stage, I shall focus on sense (b)—goods whose enjoyment by and provision to individuals have certain distinctive features.

The term 'public good' is used by economists in sense (b) to refer to goods whose provision and enjoyment have one or both of the following characteristics:

(b-i)   the good is *non-competitive*, in the sense that one person's enjoyment of it does not diminish the amount of it available for enjoyment by anyone else; and/or

(b-ii) the good is *non-excludable*, meaning that if it is made available to anyone in a given group (such as a whole society) it is necessarily made available to all members of that group.[60]

Publicness in either sense diminishes the importance of distributive issues raised in this section. Goods that are non-excludable are hard to guarantee to some but not others, and goods that are non-competitive do not really pose distributive issues at all; these are goods which we all enjoy without anyone's enjoyment having to be traded off against anyone else's.

In *The Logic of Collective Action*, Mancur Olson observed that security and national defense are public goods, at least in sense (b-ii):

The basic or most elementary goods and services provided by government, like defense and police protection, and the system of law and order generally, are such that they go to everyone or practically everyone in the nation. It would obviously not be feasible, if indeed it were possible, to deny the protection provided by the military services, the police, and the courts to those who did not voluntarily pay their share of the costs of government...[61]

The idea is that if the government provides a national defense to stop our enemies from attacking our homeland, then it provides it willy-nilly to all members of the nation. There is no way any particular person can be excluded from its benefits (say, for refusing to pay a specific fee or tax). You cannot sell tickets for national defense. We might say, too, that defense is a paradigm case of non-competitiveness: the benefit to any individual of being protected from invasion by the Russians is not reduced by anyone else's enjoyment of this good. We can neither exclude nor crowd others out of this benefit. Of course, the government might choose to provide this good for none of us or provide it for us all only at

---

[60] A lighthouse is a public good in senses (b-i) and (b-ii); an encrypted radio signal (whose content is enjoyable only by those who have paid for a key) is public in sense (b-i), but not sense (b-ii); and fresh air in a large sealed chamber is public in sense (b-ii), for those in the chamber, but not in sense (b-i).

[61] Olson, *The Logic of Collective Action*, p. 14.

an unacceptable level. And that in itself might be an issue of justice. But once it is provided, there do not seem to be any distributive issues with regard to its provision. Accordingly, on this line of thinking, we might be able to avoid the distributive issues about security which I said (at the beginning of this section) were raised under the heading of 'breadth.'

Unfortunately, the economist's characterization of security as a public good is a bit of a cheat. What we all enjoy—non-excludably and non-crowdably—in regard to national defense is the benefit of being a member of a nation that is not attacked by its enemies. This makes the good public more or less by definition. But it leaves it unclear whether security—in the sense of individuals' *safety* being actually secured against the threat posed by enemy attack—is provided equally and in the same way.

There are certainly elements of a public good, for example, in the state's anti-terrorist policy. If we assume that the terrorists attack large targets and that there are a small number of them, out of proportion to the number of their intended victims, then frustrating any one terrorist or any one terrorist cell may protect many people against large-scale and repeated attacks. When a cell is taken down, a large number of people benefit from the elimination of a threat to life and limb and the elimination of a source of fear; and the enjoyment of this good by some who would otherwise be threatened is not affected by the enjoyment of it by others.

One the other hand, it is evident that security is far from a perfect example of publicness. First, people may be differently situated with regard to a given threat. Some regions may be more vulnerable than others. This is true of classic wartime security: remember the British government sent children out of the main cities in the Second World War, figuring that this was something they could do to keep them more secure (safer) from air attack than others whose presence in the cities was required. And the same is true of security against internal threats. Some people may be forced into situations where they are more likely than others to be victims of terrorist attack (e.g. poor people in Israel who have no choice but to use buses).

Secondly, the authorities may attempt to secure members of the community against some threats and not others, or they may act for the sake of some people's safety and not others' and so people may benefit differentially from state action. Even under 'normal' circumstances, it is notorious that police treat certain minority neighborhoods as 'no-go' areas, entering them only to pursue fugitives or make arrests, but not to aid or enhance the safety of those who live there. If police or anti-terrorist resources are scarce, then people and communities may quarrel over them and their allocation will pose issues of distributive justice.[62]

Third, some of the actions by which the government provides security may in fact compromise the safety of some members of the population. When a government shoots on sight those it suspects of participation in terrorist attack, then people who match closely the profile of terrorist suspects may be much less secure against deadly attack than other members of the society (taking into account the prospect of deadly attack by the government as well as the prospect of deadly attack by terrorists).

For these reasons, it is a mistake to assume that, as a matter of fact, security is always provided equally, even-handedly, non-competitively, and non-excludably by the government. Later we shall consider whether security or any aspect of security can be regarded as a public good in the more diffuse sense of a communal good—sense (c) of those identified above. For the time being, however, it is a mistake to think that the notional designation of security as a public good solves or preempts any issue about distribution. We have no choice but to address the various ways in which security might be unevenly provided across a given population.

F. Diminishing the security of some to enhance the security of others

In the previous section I mentioned the possibility that some of the actions by which the government provides security may in fact compromise the safety of some members of the population. I now want to devote some time particularly to that possibility, because it brings issues of breadth and distribution acutely into focus. We are familiar with the idea that measures taken to increase security may impact adversely upon liberty; that, after all, is the starting point of our discussion. But we need

---

[62] At the time of writing (2005–6), there were serious disputes in the United States about the allocation of Homeland Security funding. See, e.g. Eric Lipton, 'Security Cuts for New York and Washington,' *New York Times*, June 1, 2006, p. 18: 'After vowing to steer a greater share of antiterrorism money to the highest-risk communities, Department of Homeland Security officials on Wednesday announced 2006 grants that slashed money for New York and Washington 40 percent, while other cities including Omaha and Louisville, Ky., got a surge of new dollars. The release of the 2006 urban area grants, which total $711 million, was immediately condemned by leaders in Washington and New York. "When you stop a terrorist, they have a map of New York City in their pocket," Mayor Michael R. Bloomberg of New York said. "They don't have a map of any of the other 46 or 45 places." '

to consider also the possible adverse impact *upon security* of measures intended to enhance security (or measures defended on the basis that they will enhance security).

Thus consider the measures that are commonly used against internal or quasi-internal enemies of the state, supposedly to secure the safety of citizens. Israel's response to terrorist activity by members of the Palestinian community is a good example. The Israeli measures include (or have included in the past): targeted assassination of those suspected as terrorist leaders; physical violence against those suspected of aiding terrorists; abusive interrogation sometimes amounting to torture of non-terrorists to obtain information about terrorists; detention, concentration, and incarceration without trial of some of those suspected as terrorists or terrorist accomplices; armed incursions into communities that are suspected of sheltering terrorists; detention, concentration, and incarceration without trial of those who constitute the communities in which it is thought terrorists can move and organize easily; and destruction of houses and property as collective punishments, or as deterrents, or to make certain communal areas more amenable to surveillance and incursion by the state.[63]

In all these cases, state action, motivated by a desire to enhance public safety, may also threaten the safety of certain members of the public. Suppose, for example, that the terrorist threat comes from a certain reasonably well-defined (geographically and/or ethnically well-defined) section of the community. Then members of that section of the community—innocent members as well—may be particularly vulnerable to actions of the kind listed above. In some cases, innocent people will be vulnerable to collateral damage intended to harm the guilty. In other cases, they will be vulnerable as the intended targets of actions motivated by a desire to raise the costs of terrorist activity or lower the costs of combating it. True, the innocent members of the section of the community in question may also benefit from any reduction in the threat posed by terrorists which results from these measures. But there is no guarantee that they faced the same threat as the rest of the public in the first place, nor is there any guarantee that they will receive the

---

[63] I say not saying that these measures are unjustified. Some may be; some may not; many are prohibited by relevant provisions of Israel and international humanitarian law. If we were to consider their justification, we would have to take into account (among other things) the threat to the existence of the state of Israel and the toll of death and injury from terrorist outrages referred to at n. 31, above. See Meisels, *The Trouble with Terror*, p. 90 ff for a discussion.

benefit of anti-terrorist measures to the same extent as other members of the public. And anyway, the enhanced threat to their safety as a result of the state's measures might well outweigh whatever enhancement of security they receive as a result.

I can anticipate that there will be challenges to this way of describing trade-offs between the security of some and the security of others. I want to consider and respond to three of them.

(i) We are supposed to be talking about the security of a community as a political goal for the state which is in charge of that community. But in our discussion in this section, we have focused on its relation to those who are arguably outsiders. Perhaps this makes the Israeli/Palestinian example a special case. It might have been better had we focused say on the situation in Northern Ireland in the 1970s to 1980s, where all the participants were citizens of the United Kingdom. However, just because of its difficulty, the Israeli example does highlight certain issues that need to be faced about whose security a state should concern itself with. Palestinians in the West Bank and Gaza Strip are not Israeli citizens. But all of them until recently were Israeli subjects—that is, they were subject to the power and authority of the Israeli state—and many of them still are. A case can be made that a state is required to concern itself with the security of all those who are in its territory (or any territory it occupies) and subject to its authority. Shortly we will see that there are important connections between security and state legitimacy, and legitimacy certainly relates to the way in which a state deals with its subjects not just to the way in which it deals with the subset of subjects it calls its citizens. International law supports this conclusion too. A state is responsible for the physical security of those it takes as prisoners, and it is responsible also for the physical security of the inhabitants of lands that it occupies (whether the occupation is lawful or unlawful).[64]

---

[64] For prisoners of war, see *Geneva Convention relative to the Treatment of Prisoners of War*, adopted on 12 August 1949, Articles 19 ('Prisoners of war shall be evacuated, as soon as possible after their capture, to camps situated in an area far enough from the combat zone for them to be out of danger') and 23 ('No prisoner of war may at any time be sent to or detained in areas where he may be exposed to the fire of the combat zone, nor may his presence be used to render certain points or areas immune from military operations. Prisoners of war shall have shelters against air bombardment and other hazards of war, to the same extent as the local civilian population'). For occupations, see Regulations respecting the Laws and Customs of War on Land, annexed to the Hague Convention (IV) of 18 October 1907, Article 43 ('The authority of the legitimate power having in fact passed into the hands of the occupant, the latter shall take all the measures in his power to restore, and ensure, as far as possible, public order and safety, while respecting, unless absolutely prevented, the laws in force in the country').

(ii) A second objection might protest against describing these actions taken by the state as actions threatening its subject's *security*. The conventional trade-off is between security and liberty, and it may be thought that we should file these costs of the struggle for security, suffered by those who are shot, beaten, or tortured, under the heading of liberty. Some of the costs borne by subject populations surely can be described in that way: restrictions on freedom of movement, detention, incarceration, and surveillance can all be understood as denials of freedom. But not all such costs can be understood as denials of freedom. Beatings and torture go directly to the issue of safety from violence, as do death and injuries suffered as collateral damage, or as a result of targeted assassination or forced incursions.[65] These are matters of safety and we have no choice but to factor them into whatever matrix of safety we are going to use to concoct our conception of security (as a matter of breadth). It is all too easy to think lazily about this. Consider torture, for example. The fact that torture is sometimes said to be justified for the sake of security does not mean it has to be regarded as an element of liberty in the great liberty–security trade-off. (Remember: we are regarding it as an open question whether the idea of a liberty–security trade-off might not to be too simplistic to capture the moral issues involved in the war against terrorism.) Similarly the fact that civil libertarians oppose torture does not mean that torture is in itself a diminution of liberty (though usually people's liberty has to be restricted in order to torture them); what it means is that civil libertarians defend a number of rights over and above liberty-rights. To be sure, liberty is an expansive category; but it is a mistake nevertheless to assume that every harm, or every imposition of death or pain, can be rendered as a threat to liberty for the purposes of an overly simplistic liberty–security categorization.[66]

(iii) Maybe you think that we should avoid this factoring in of threats from the state because these prospects of death or violence do not come at the hands of the right agent. After all, the security we want is security *against terrorists* not against death or injury as such (irrespective of

[65] Sometimes costs of the two kinds are bundled together: people are incarcerated (which is a loss of liberty) and then beaten or tortured (which is a loss of security). But we can still distinguish the various costs from one another, even when they are bundled together in this way.

[66] For a useful discussion along these lines of the analytic relation between liberty and harm, see Hart, 'Rawls on Liberty and its Priority,' at 547–8. See also Shue, *Basic Rights*, at pp. 187–8, for a criticism of the tendency to treat security as an aspect of liberty (rather than as something important for liberty).

its source). The state is not a terrorist organization; it is not the sort of entity we seek security against.

There is something to this point but not much. It is true that people do discriminate among different prospects of death; I mentioned this earlier as the first problem with the pure safety conception of security. We are all mortal and we all face illness, disease, and accidents of various sorts; and though we do our best to postpone death and fight illness and be vigilant against accidents, we do not think it is the function of the Department of Homeland Security to promote longevity as such, nor do we think that the success of anti-smoking or road safety measures should be factored into our reckoning of such an agency's effectiveness.[67] But the threats to safety involved in beatings, torture, collective punishment, collateral damage, and so on suffered at the hands of the state are much more like threats to safety from terrorism than like road accidents or cancer. They are violent and they are inflicted by human agency. I do not mean to argue for any sort of moral equivalence as between suicide bombings and military brutality or as between Hamas or Hezbollah and the Israeli state, or as between Al Qaeda and the present jailers at Guantánamo Bay. Moral equivalence is not the issue. My aim at the moment is just to consider which enhanced prospects of death, injury, or loss should be factored into our understanding of security—particularly for the purpose of figuring out how to approach the distributive question which envisages not a simple trade-off between liberty for all and security for all, but a trade-off of the liberty of a few for the sake of the enhanced security of some and the diminished security of others.

G. States, security, and political legitimacy

At this stage, it is worth pausing to remind ourselves why it is appropriate to consider threats to safety originating from the state when characterizing security as a basic value that states are required to promote. I said that states are not terrorist organizations. But we know that in a number of respects, this confident assertion needs to be qualified.

Some states—rogue states, for example—may fail and lapse into terrorist or quasi-terrorist organizations. There was concern that this might

---

[67] Philosophically these discriminations are something of a mystery: why does Hobbesian man fear violent death more than death as such? Mercifully they are not our subject here. It is interesting that in the United States, the Department of Homeland Security has responsibility not just for protection against terrorist threats, but also for protection against natural disasters like Hurricane Katrina.

be true of Iraq; it was certainly said to be true of Afghanistan prior to 2002. In figuring out whether this has happened, we will of course look at what the allegedly rogue state is doing so far as the security of outsiders is concerned. If it has become a promoter of international terrorism then we shall have to consider the threat that it poses to (say) Americans or Israelis. But it will also be appropriate to consider, in this connection, the threat that it poses to its own subjects. No doubt even a terrorist or quasi-terrorist state seeks the security of some of its members. But it may threaten the security of others, and most people believe that there is in this regard a (vaguely-defined) tipping-point in which we say that the entity in question no longer counts as a legitimate state. Conversely, we know that many organizations formerly condemned as terrorist can become legitimate states, by assuming powers of government and using those powers to promote security for all its subjects, rather than using terrorist powers to promote the insecurity of say the members of a colonial regime.[68] It will be impossible to chart this transition without essaying a sort of security calculus which can weigh the threat that the erstwhile terrorist organization poses to the security of some of the people in the territory against the protective functions it performs or which can weigh the threat that a rogue state poses to its subjects and balance that against the residual security functions that it still manages to discharge.

To go into this matter in slightly greater detail, think of two para-military organizations—say, the Irish Republican Army (IRA) and the Ulster Defence Force (UDF)—in a city like Belfast in the 1980s. These organizations aimed to inflict violence on each other's members and on members of each other's communities, the loyalist community and the nationalist community respectively. And they sought to protect members of their home communities against these attacks: the IRA undertook to protect members of the nationalist community against attacks by the UDF and vice versa. But the measures taken by the IRA included measures *against* members of the nationalist community, members suspected

---

[68] See Walker, 'Cyber-Terrorism,' at 657: 'The idea that "once a terrorist, always a terrorist" is belied by history, including the life stories of at least one Prime Minister of Israel (Begin), one President of Cyprus (Makarios), and one President of South Africa (Mandela).' See also Ron Walters, 'The Black Experience with Terrorism,' at 79: 'The first time I read the word "terrorist," it was in connection with the Mau Mau uprising in Kenya in the late 1950s. Jomo Kenyatta, associated with this group, which attempted to make Kenya ungovernable by the British, was referred to as a terrorist and was hunted down by the British colonial authorities and jailed as such.' For a good general discussion, see Elkins, *Imperial Reckoning: The Untold Story of Britain's Gulag in Kenya.*

of collaborating with the UDF, or even just suspected of giving insufficiently enthusiastic support to the IRA's campaign; it also included measures designed to deter collaboration or whip up enthusiasm and measures designed just to make IRA operations easier. Now, obviously, if we were wondering whether the security of members of the nationalist community was actually enhanced by the IRA's activities, we should have to take into account not just the benefit (to members of the relevant community) of measures taken by the IRA against the other paramilitary group, but also the effect (both beneficial and detrimental) of measures taken by the IRA against members of the very community it claims to be protecting.

I believe we ought to consider the actions taken by a government in exactly the same way. We ought to consider the positive effects of something that calls itself a government on the safety of the individuals in its territory and balance those against the negative effects of this entity on the safety of the individuals in its territory. Some individuals will be affected one way, some the other way, and some both ways. Only if we consider all these effects are we in a position to talk about the government's contribution to security generally for the people in the territory it controls. We still have not addressed the question of how to assess these individual effects for the purposes of arriving at an overall verdict on the entity's contribution to the security of the population under its control. My point at this stage is that we must assemble all the information that is available about its positive and negative effects on individual safety in order to begin that assessment

Once again, some readers will protest that it is wrong to reach this conclusion on the basis of an analogy between legitimate governments and paramilitary terrorist organizations like the IRA. But one of the things that makes the analogy between governments and paramilitary organizations inappropriate—when it *is* inappropriate—is that a legitimate government takes care in regard to security. A legitimate state takes care in regard to the safety of those in the territory it dominates, whereas an illegitimate regime is either careless of the safety of those who are at its mercy or solicitous of the safety of some of them but not of others. Legitimacy has to be earned, and I suspect that one important dimension in which it is earned is in regard to the pattern of impact of a regime's actions on the persons subject to its power. Assuming then that the impact of a government's actions on people's safety may be uneven and in some cases harmful, we need to ask whether it is possible to articulate any constraints on the extent of the unevenness, for the purposes of a conception of security that pays proper attention to this question of breadth. How uneven can the impact be while the government is still claiming credibly to promote *security* (as opposed to acknowledging that it promotes only the safety of a few favored clients or of a delimited class of people in a territory)?

H. Breadth and the logic of legitimacy

I think that if we pursue this connection between security and legitimacy, we might be able to make progress in our thinking about issues of breadth, so far as security is concerned. We might begin, very modestly, by saying that a regime counts as a legitimate government only if it has some positive impact on the safety of all of those it claims as its subjects. This is unlikely to be a sufficient condition of legitimacy, but it might be sufficient so far as safety is concerned. And perhaps the word 'security' is defined in a way that marks this point. No government is legitimate if it does not promote security, and we may say that the word 'security' captures the pattern of impact on safety that governments are supposed to have so far as that elementary legitimacy is concerned. The idea is that the government has an elementary obligation to promote security; if it fails in that obligation it undermines its legitimacy; and what security means in this context is (at the very least) some positive impact on the safety of all of its subjects.

On this account, a regime is illegitimate if there is some person or class of persons who would be better off without it (so far as their safety is concerned), irrespective of what the positive impact on others' safety might be. We might frame this account in two ways, either by insisting that a legitimate regime must bring each person's safety up to at least a certain level, or by insisting that the regime must make at least a substantial positive difference to each person's safety, even though the actual level of safety for each may vary according to background circumstances and baseline (i.e. how safe each might be in these circumstances absent any reasonable government).

This account will seem exasperating to a certain hard-headed pragmatic mentality. From this point of view, the person-by-person evaluations that the account requires are prissy and over-demanding. How can we ever be sure that there is not someone who is left out when 'everyone's' security is improved? How can we possibly leave political legitimacy for a nation of three hundred million souls at the mercy of a criterion as demanding as this?[69] As Hobbes reminded us, governments

---

[69] It might also be objected to the account we have given that it fails to leave room for two important options that should not be ruled out at the level of definition. The

have to design their security strategies in broad terms, taking account of the overall impact of what they do. They cannot be expected to undertake the detailed evaluations that this account requires, when they are addressing the safety of a quarter billion people. And the same is true of external assessments of legitimacy. Our distinction between legitimate and illegitimate governments—effective states and failed states or rogue states—in international law is very broad-brush, and it might be thought that a utilitarianism of safety captures it reasonably adequately.

However, although it is true that our assessments of legitimacy are rough-and-ready and may not be as fine-grained as a literal application of an egalitarianism of safety (SE) might require, but they are also not as fine-grained as a ubilitarianism of safety (SU), read literally, might require. The question is, when we deploy a rough-and-ready understanding of the security–legitimacy requirement, what is it a rough-and-ready version *of*? In at least some of the cases already discussed, it seems that we work with a rough-and-ready version of (SE) not (SU). For example, when we assess the legitimacy of regimes from the outside, we do not rest content with a rough showing that the safety of more people is advanced than harmed. We look also at the situation of minorities, and we often hold regimes illegitimate on account of their failings in regard to the safety of minorities—sometimes quite small minorities—irrespective of the benefits that accrue thereby to the safety of members of the (large) majority.

The most powerful argument in favor of option (SE) is based on the elementary logic of political legitimacy. The basic theory of political legitimacy is individualistic, not collective. Its starting point is the fact that political regimes make demands upon individuals one by one: I must pay my taxes and you must pay yours; I must obey each of the laws, for my part, and you must obey them for your part. (The government does not countenance my disobedience or my failure to pay on the ground that most others are complying!) If the individual challenges these demands, some response on behalf of the regime must be given *to him or to her*.[70] It will normally be along these lines: 'You are better off

first is that it may sometimes be necessary to destroy an individual who poses a threat to the security of others; the second is that it may be necessary, in certain circumstances, to require some to lay down their lives (e.g. in combat) for the sake of the security of others. But while it is true that we need a theory of security that does not preclude *a priori* either conscription or capital punishment, it is also the case that the logic of conscription and capital punishment presupposes that we are already in possession of a concept of security defining what these practices might be set up to defend.

[70] There is an excellent discussion of all this in the first chapter of Bernard Williams's (posthumous) book *In the Beginning was the Deed*, pp. 3–6.

in certain respects (e.g. safer) as a result of the existence and activities of the regime. That is why it is reasonable that we make these demands upon you.'

This logic is most vivid in the contractarian approach to political legitimacy. People enter society in order to provide greater security for themselves than they could get by their own efforts. 'No rational creature,' wrote John Locke, 'can be supposed to change his condition with an intention to be worse,'[71] and no one can be deemed willing to accept that his own security is properly neglected for that of others. Maybe this is not an argument for pure equality of security, but it is certainly an argument against the position that governments are entitled to neglect the security of some for the sake of the greater security of others or that they are entitled to impact negatively on the security of a few purely for the sake of the security of the majority.

We have ended a long discussion of breadth. The upshot is that the issue of breadth presents many difficulties when we consider the application of the term 'security' to a whole society or a population. Our discussion considered whether it is appropriate to take a maximizing approach to security (the greatest security of the greatest number) or whether it is appropriate to organize the pursuit of security as a political goal around some idea of *equal* protection or the attaining of at least a minimum security for everyone. Our discussion here has not been conclusive, though powerful arguments based on political legitimacy and also on the connection between security and rights have been adduced against the pure maximizing approach. What is clear, however, is that the distributive issues raised under this heading of breadth—Whose security is protected or enhanced? Whose security is neglected or diminished (perhaps for the sake of the security of others)?—cannot be ignored or finessed if security is to be treated as a political goal.

V. Breadth and Depth Together

So far we have considered security as an array of individual goods. From a social point of view, it is necessary for each of us to consider the relation between our own security and that of others; attention to my security may distract from attention to yours; or my security may be enhanced only at the expense of yours. These are the familiar problems

---

[71] Locke, *Two Treatises*, p. 353 (II, §131).

of competition, aggregation, and distribution that we dealt with in Part IV. So far, however, we have not explored any *positive* connections between one person's security and another's. We have not looked at ways in which one person's security may actually depend on that of another, or ways in which one person's security may be an ingredient in another person's security. This will be the topic of the second phase of our exploration of *depth* in relation to the concept of security. Because it involves a deepening of individual security by taking into account its positive relation to the security of others, our account at this stage will combine considerations of what we have been calling till now breadth and depth.

Earlier when I set out the various shortcomings in the pure safety conception, I mentioned the failure of that conception to give adequate accounts of the relation between security and fear, between security and assurance, and between security and the idea of social order. People don't just want to be safe—e.g. surviving, but terrified, in a sealed room. They want some system of mutual assurance of safety which allows them to deal with one another and go about their business—following familiar routines and exploring new possibilities. In section III(A), I talked about the *modes of life* of individuals and families and about the fears that they may have in relation to their modes of life and their need for assurance. Now we are going to explore some connections between that and wider issues of the social distribution of such assurance.

A. Fear and social identity

Given that each of us thinks of our safety not just momentarily but projected into the future, we may be concerned about what happens to others as prefiguring what may happen to us. This is a matter of anxiety and assurance. If something happens to another person, X, to diminish his safety (perhaps in order enhance my safety at time t_1), I cannot necessarily detach, from my sense of safety at t_1, the threat that what happened to X (for my sake) at t_1 may happen to me for someone else's sake at time t_2.

So far this is just algebra.[72] But you may say: in the real world, I often *can* have such an assurance based on my ethnicity. If I am white (or at

---

[72] But the algebra reminds us of the famous Martin Niemoller poem: 'When the Nazis came for the communists, I remained silent; I was not a communist. | When they locked up the social democrats, I remained silent; I was not a social democrat. | When they came for the trade unionists, I did not speak out; I was not a trade unionist. | When they came for the Jews, I did not speak out; I was not a Jew. | When they came for me, there

any rate if I do not look like an Arab), if I look, sound, and behave like a native-born American, there is little chance that I will suffer the impact of measures designed to combat terrorism. To the extent that this is so, then I can regard my security as independent of others' security. Even if my security is being upheld by diminishing the security of (say) Arab-Americans, there is no reason here for apprehension on my part, since there is little likelihood that the tables will be turned and people like me will be incarcerated or tortured to maintain the security of others. That may be so. But then this may already represent a cost to me in terms of political identity. Instead of now organizing my sense of security around my identity as an American, I have to retreat to some narrower (and in other contexts more invidious) sense of identity: I am secure on account of my identity as a white American or my identity as an American who does not look Arabic. That may be a cost to me: I now suffer this (as a result of terrorism or as a result of the state's response to terrorism), *viz.*, that I have to change the way I think about the connection between identity and security. And that may compromise something that an appropriately deep conception of security would be concerned about.

B. Security and the market

If a deeper notion of security is conceived as offering a platform on which we might securely enjoy other goods, exercise other rights, and participate in activities other than the mere avoidance of danger, then this has important consequences for our relations with others in society. If I am to participate and flourish in the order of everyday life, I will want to be able to deal with others, and in many of these dealings with others it will be important that they are as secure as I am. No doubt there are some exceptions to this: some people may flourish from dealing with others' insecurities: e.g. those who sell (and can raise the price of) bottled water, etc. But I suspect that for the most part, people's personal safety is a platform on which, hopefully, they can deal—in a market fashion or in some other sociable fashion—with others whose safety is equally assured. Others' willingness to produce the commodities that I need to purchase or to produce or consume using the commodities that I produce depends on their being undistracted by terror and anxiety about their personal safety.

---

was no one left to speak out.' The exact form and original source of this poem is a matter of controversy. For a useful survey, see <http://www.history.ucsb.edu/faculty/marcuse/niem.htm> (visited on June 4, 2006).

It was once said that 'the only thing we have to fear is fear itself.'[73] Most people acknowledge that widespread fear or widespread insecurity is something for them to fear even if they don't share the first-order fear or insecurity themselves. In a modern market economy the situation of any one actor is exquisitely sensitive to the climate of confidence generally. For example, one noticeable effect of the September 11 terrorist attacks in the United States was a short-term collapse (and the exacerbation of a longer-term downturn) in economic activity. The Dow Jones index lost 7.1 per cent of its value in the first day of trading after September 11 and continued to fall in the week that followed.[74] Another example is the collapse of the tourist trade in Israel—a decline of 50 per cent or more—in the wake of recent suicide bombings.[75] These economic effects may be attributable to widespread fear that outrages of the sort that have already occurred are likely to continue—that is, they are symptoms of general insecurity. But beyond that—and I think this is particularly true of the Dow Jones decline—they are also the result of feedback into the system of mutual confidence generally of people's apprehensions about the pervasiveness of the fear occasioned by the individual outrages. Even if frequent occurrences of this kind are not expected, still fear itself becomes something to be feared, particularly in a society like ours which relies for its prosperity on a cheerful bullish mentality among consumers and investors.

C. Our way of life

In Part III, I spoke of the importance to individuals and families of their mode of life. There is obviously a connection between individuals and

---

[73] Franklin Delano Roosevelt, *First Inaugural Address* (1933): 'So first of all let me assert my firm belief that the only thing we have to fear is fear itself—nameless, unreasoning, unjustified terror which paralyzes needed efforts to convert retreat into advance.'

[74] See Bill Barnhart, 'Markets Reopen, Plunge; Dow Drops 684 Points as Trading Resumes,' *Chicago Tribune*, September 17, 2001 (Final Markets Extra Edition), p. 1: 'The Dow Jones industrial average closed down more than 684 points, or more than 7 percent, closing below the 9000 mark at 8921, according to preliminary figures, on extraordinarily heavy New York Stock Exchange volume. That pushed the Dow to its lowest close since December 1998.' See also Stephen King, 'Latest Declines Already the Worst Since 1973 Crash,' *The Independent* (London), September 24, 2001, p. 17: 'The collapse in equity prices over the last few days has been extraordinary by any standards.'

[75] Daniel Ben-Tal, 'Booking our Brethren,' *The Jerusalem Post*, October 15, 2004, p. 5: 'Tourism to Israel peaked in 2000 when an unprecedented 2,672,000 foreign visitors entered the country. But, the beginning of the Al-Aqsa Intifada in September that year and the ensuing wave of terrorist attacks, decimated the local tourist market. Hotel stays by foreign tourists plummeted by 80% between October 2000 and October 2001.'

families valuing their own routines, their own mode of life, and their own reasonable aspirations for the trajectory of their lives (on the one hand) and (on the other hand) their valuing a whole way of life for the society. Usually people's mode of life is both an instance of and dependent upon the broader way of life that the members of society treasure in general. When we think about our own way of life, we relate it to the ways of life practised generally in the society, and even if our mentality is not conformist, still as social beings we look for some sort of congruence between what we are doing with our lives and what is being done with their lives by others around us. Many of the activities we pursue make no sense except as pursued in a wider social context. We have just seen that this is true for market activity, but it is true also for countless other activities in work, leisure, romance, and worship. We live together with others and even if we feel relatively secure, we cannot cut ourselves off from others' insecurities.

At the very least, we rely on the existence of something called 'public order'—securing the basic conditions of action and interaction in public places, parks, sidewalks, streets, and highways. But it is also much more than this. Our social actions make sense when we play roles in narratives that assign roles also to others—whether as co-workers, customers, neighbours, babysitters, teachers, team-members, and so on. The disruption of such narratives by danger or the fear of danger can leave us unsure of what to do or what our actions amount to. In a society like the United States, we go cheerfully about most of our business in public places—like shopping malls, restaurants, schools, colleges, churches, sports fields, and cinemas—with minimal attention to security issues. Imagine the extent, though, to which that would change if America were to experience explosions in these places at the rate of (say) one or two a month, each causing the sort of casualties that recent suicide bombings have caused in Israel, each publicized as a national tragedy with the full panoply of CNN coverage etc. Even ordinary prudence on the part of millions of individuals, responding to this—the taking of reasonable precautions in the wake of such experience—would radically alter the way that life is lived in this country. We have had a taste of it with the enhancement of security at airports, but we have to imagine that similar precautions are introduced into *all* public spaces in which people gather by the scores or hundreds: malls, soccer fields, schools, movie theatres, etc. People would be afraid, but my point right now is not the quality of the fear itself. My point is the likely emergence of a new sort of ethos governing choices about 'going out *versus* staying home,' an attenuation of large-scale social interaction, and a marked degradation in the collective practices and routines of our society. I guess it is possible that we would all soldier on, putting our children on school buses, going to the mall, catching movies, eating in McDonald's, etc., with just a few extra security guards. But it is not unimaginable that there would be a catastrophic disruption in the routines of everyday social life.

Of course, we have to be careful with this. Protecting security is not the same as protecting a way of life in (say) the spirit of those who talk about cultural rights—the preservation of traditions etc.[76] But there are some important analogies. Pervasive and society-wide disruption of the routines and fabric of ordinary life that we find after terrorist attack is quite like the longer-term cultural disruption that (say) indigenous peoples are said to experience as a result of colonial incursion and settlement.[77]

D. Legal and constitutional routines

The routines of ordinary life whose security we value are not just first-order routines, like shopping, schooling, and soccer; but also secondary routines that respond to what might be thought of as routine problems. There are fires, crimes, and accidents; there are threats from nature and sometimes threats from outsiders; there are disagreements about what ought to be done in response to these. Among our repertoire of mechanisms for dealing with danger, disorder, and dissensus, we have fire brigades, hospitals, and police forces; we have a legal system, courts, and prisons; we have FEMA and the national guard; we have our political system, at municipal, state, and federal levels; and we have our constitution, our fundamental rights, and our settled obligations under human rights law.

The existence and the effectiveness of these mechanisms is crucial to the assurance that security in normal times involves. Disruption of them may enhance our anxiety and undermine our security; and sometimes the appropriate response may be to strengthen them or transform them so that they become more effective against the dangers they are supposed to protect us from even at the cost of other values they are supposed to embody.

But these mechanisms are also valued in and of themselves as parts of our way of life and our social routines. As such, they are valued for the

---

[76] See, e.g. Kymlicka, *Liberalism, Community, and Culture*, pp. 135–7.
[77] Ibid., pp. 147–9.

way they reconcile the demands of security and other values. We like knowing that searches cannot be conducted without warrant, that those who are arrested must be mirandized, and are entitled to legal representation and an early hearing, and that there are limits on what can be done to people—not just to us, but to anyone—under the auspices of our crime control system. If these mechanisms are transformed in an emergency to make them more effective against threats then that transformation may itself be experienced as a disruption of the very way of life we say we are trying to protect. The detention and indefinite incarceration of citizens, the prison at Guantánamo Bay, changes or suggested changes in our legal system to permit cruel, inhuman, and degrading treatment during interrogation, and the widespread use of extraordinary means of surveillance and wire-tapping—these changes may be justified but they are without doubt transformative and disruptive of many people's expectations as to how their society and their legal system operates.

I am not sure how far we should factor this in to the concept of security. It is sometimes thought that terrorists aim to undermine our legal and constitutional arrangements by attacking us. They want to force the state that they are attacking to drop the pretence of legality and civil liberties and 'show its true colors' as a repressive entity.[78] But the fact that terrorists want to force a change in our legal and constitutional arrangements does not by itself show that such arrangements are part of our security, especially since the change they are trying to force is change by the state they are attacking, rather than change by their own terrorist actions. Clearly if we do regard our legal and constitutional routines as part of what we value under the heading of our security, then we undermine any simple talk of a trade-off between security and constitutional rights. I will address this issue in Part VI. On the other hand, there are costs in not regarding the integrity of these mechanisms (including the integrity of legal, constitutional, and human rights guarantees) as part of what people value under the heading of security, or as part of what they have to lose under the impact of terrorist attack. Since there is obviously some connection between security and our way of life, any such exclusion has to draw a rather artificial line, and it would not be satisfactory to draw that line simply for the sake of underwriting the simplicity of our ordinary talk about a security–liberty trade-off.

---

[78] See also Chapter 3, above, at pp. 76–7.

E. Security as a collective good

Very early in this chapter I mentioned the idea of *collective security*. I said that in the discourse of international power politics, security is not understood as something most nations can pursue by and for themselves. It needs to be pursued by groups of nations acting in ways that establish stable equilibria or it needs to be pursued by the whole community of nations acting in concert. I think that when we drop down a level from the international arena, we should be open to the possibility that the notion of security also needs to be understood as something we provide together. In one sense this is obvious: we rely on a collective mechanism for much of our actual protection. And we rely on a set of mutual restraints to maintain each other's security in everyday life. But in a richer sense, we also act together to secure the way of life and the patterns of interaction in which our security partly consists. After terrorist attacks, people often act cooperatively and publicly to show that they are determined to maintain their way of life, even in the face of great anxiety or great anger. When this sort of action takes place, it is a clear instance of the collective provision of security—of security being maintained by a whole community showing its determination not to degenerate into a disaggregated set of terrified individuals. It is an instance of a general point about the relation between security and mutual assurance. Security is something we provide for each other by enjoying together the social order of activity and interaction that defines our way of life and by acting in solidarity with one another to ensure that the benefit of this system is available to all.

I also mentioned earlier a number of different uses of the term 'public good.' As well as the technical economist's sense of the term—(b) a good enjoyed non-excludably and/or non-crowdably—I mentioned (c) the idea of a good enjoyed communally. Many goods that are public in the economist's sense are enjoyed individually: even when they are non-crowdable and non-excludable, they are still individual goods. So, for example, clean air is an individual good in the sense that its ultimate benefit is to the lungs and respirations of individuals one by one. But not all goods are enjoyed individually. Some goods are communal in the sense that their enjoyment by any one person depends on their enjoyment in common with him by others. Conviviality, at a party, is a clear example: others may include certain aspects of the good of language or culture.[79]

---

[79] See the discussion in Waldron, 'Can Communal Goods be Human Rights?' at pp. 354–9.

Many social institutions and the realization of many social aims and ideals are public goods in this sense; their enjoyment, non-excludably and non-crowdably, by many people at a time is not a contingent factor of the technicalities of their provision, but an essential part of their social existence.[80] The good of a tolerant society, a cultured society, or a society which exercises self-determination: these are all examples of communal or non-contingent public goods.[81]

Should we regard security as a public good in this sense? In a recent article on policing, Ian Loader and Neil Walker have made a suggestion to this effect.[82] They want to emphasize 'the irreducibly social nature of what policing offers to guarantee,'[83] and they say we should think of this not just in terms of individualized safety but in terms of a communal good. Citing my earlier work on communal goods, they refer to goods which are valuable for human society without their value being adequately characterizable in terms of their worth to any or all of the members of the society considered one by one.[84] They ask about policing and security: 'Is this a public good in this thicker, communal sense?' Their answer is 'unequivocally in the affirmative.'[85] And they argue that 'public safety is inexorably connected with the quality of our association with others' and that it 'depends upon the texture of social relations and the density of social bonds.'[86] Some of us might be safer, they say, under a regime of very aggressive policing, but 'our security [would be] degraded as a public good by distributive degradation in our scheme of civil liberties.'[87]

There is some plausibility to Loader and Walker's argument. Security is certainly connected with the public enjoyment of public order and we have seen that it involves aspects of our shared way of life. But it would be wrong to exaggerate the communal element or pretend that it exhausted the content of the concept. Much of my work in this chapter has sought to deepen and broaden what I called the pure safety conception of security. But I have said from the beginning that it is important for the concept of security to remain anchored in the physical safety of individual men and women. That anchoring is irreducible and nonnegotiable. I will say it one last time: nobody wants to be blown up, and security in the end is about elementary matters of harm and survival.

---

[80] See also Raz, *The Morality of Freedom*, pp. 198–9.
[81] For these examples, see ibid., pp. 198–209.
[82] Loader and Walker, 'Policing as a Public Good,' at 11.   [83] Idem.
[84] Ibid., 25, citing Waldron, 'Can Communal Goods be Human Rights?'
[85] Ibid., 26.   [86] Idem.   [87] Idem.

It may have communal aspects and it may be something that we provide jointly and mutually for one another in various ways, but most of the complications developed here have attempted to show that security is a complex and structured function of individual safety, not an amiable communal alternative to it.

VI. Complicating the Trade-Off

The analysis of security undertaken in this essay is done partly as an end in itself, to fill the disgraceful gap in political philosophy in the analytic treatment of the main goals, principles, and values of politics. Security is an enormously important goal. It is fundamental to our thinking about legitimacy. It is deceptively simple on the surface, but as we have seen it is quite complex underneath. And it is a matter of shame for political philosophy that it has not been subject to greater analytic attention. Conceptual analysis, at its best, is a collective enterprise; others see sometimes what we do not see or defects in our account that we have become insensitive to. This chapter is just a beginning and it is far from perfect. I hope that it will elicit some responses from others who are interested in this analytic project.

The task of establishing a clear understanding of security, sensitive to its conundrums and complexities, is particularly important in these troubled times, when security is constantly invoked as a reason for diminishing the extent of other values, such as liberty, or the application of other principles, such as other individual rights. If we face a trade-off between liberty (or civil liberties) and security, then it is as important to know what security is as it is to know what liberty is (or what civil liberties are), so we can see what is at stake on either side of the balance.

I have expressed doubts about the more simple-minded versions of the liberty–security trade-off elsewhere.[88] I did not undertake this study of security specifically to undermine this talk of trade-offs. But throughout this chapter, I have said we should be alert to the possibility that the relation between liberty and security is more complicated than at first appears.

One set of complications is that we are not talking about trade-offs among abstract homogenous values, but about values that may distributed unevenly across a population. We know already that this is true for

---

[88]   See Chapter 2 above.

liberty: even if liberty starts out being roughly equally distributed in the community, the changes that are envisaged as a result of the trade-off are not evenly spread changes in everyone's liberties, but a diminution in the liberties of some against the general background in which most citizens' liberties are unaffected. In this chapter, we have seen that it is also true for security. Some of the changes that are advocated and undertaken for the sake of security actually have uneven impact on that security; they protect the security of some while neglecting or actively undermining the security of others. To point this out, with regard to liberty and security, is not to deny that changes might need to be made, and that these changes might need to be justified for security's sake. But we must not think childishly about the changes. It is not a case of everyone giving up a few liberties so that everyone can be more secure. Some are making a slight sacrifice in liberty, others are making a very considerable sacrifice of liberty, and a few are actually losing their security, so that most can be more secure. If we plan on justifying this, we should not do so insouciantly using the discourse of a simple trade-off between liberty and security. Instead we should think in terms of a distributive matrix of liberty or civil liberties, uneven across different people or categories of people (e.g. majorities and minorities) facing a distributive matrix of security, uneven across different people or categories of people, again with majorities and minorities. And we should think about the prospect of various changes in the values arrayed in the two matrices. If we can begin thinking like that—thinking in terms of *whose* liberty, *whose* security is being enhanced or diminished—then we will have made some progress.[89]

As well as distributive issues, we need to think about the impact of our substantive analysis on the idea of a trade-off between liberty and security. The idea of a trade-off between liberty and security makes clearest sense if we think of liberty and security as separate values, logically independent of one another, and related in a sort of inverse way: the more liberty there is, the less security you are likely to get; the more security

---

[89] In conversations on these matters, I have found that those who think in economic and rational choice terms about trade-offs between two commodities—using indifference curves and so on—are enormously resistant to this point. Because they know how to diagram simple intrapersonal trade-offs (between, say, milk and oranges), they will tend to regard any situations that do not conform to that image as deviant or marginal. But the features that distinguish the trade-offs we face from the simple trade-offs diagrammed using indifference curves—features like considering the loss of liberty for some for the sake of an increase in security for others—are morally crucial and absolutely salient to the politics of the war on terror. The familiarity of economists and rational choice theorists with a certain sort of diagram is not an adequate reason for ignoring this.

you want, the more liberty you're going to have to give up in order to get it. But if we find that liberty and security are not logically independent and that there are important internal relations between them or if conceptual analysis indicates that they stand sometimes in a direct rather than in an inverse relation to one another, then talk of a trade-off will be complicated, if not undermined.

Some ways of making this point are more sophisticated than others. In a recent article Thomas Powers observes that 'the point of security is liberty,'[90] and he quotes Montesquieu as saying that '[p]olitical liberty consists in security or, at least, the opinion one has of one's security.'[91] Then he makes the following observation:

Every threat, from whatever source, is as much a threat to our liberty as to our security.... American democracy would be done a service if we would use exclusively either the language of security or the language of liberty. A debate, for example, over how to weigh the threat military tribunals pose to the liberties of war-crimes suspects against the threat terrorists pose to the liberties of citizens would be more clear-sighted than is our current division of these issues along liberty versus security lines. Similarly, sorting out the impact of new police powers under the USA PATRIOT Act in terms of security against terrorism on the one hand, and security against errors of state prosecution or police abuses on the other, would more accurately capture what is at stake. What we need is to reframe our discussion around the decidedly unglamorous task of balancing one threat to liberty against other threats to liberty, one threat to security against other threats to security. I do not wish to suggest that recasting the question in these terms will easily settle the many difficult choices that must be made in the war on terror, but it would permit us to face them more clearly and without fearing that we are being either unprincipled or soft-headed.[92]

The points that Powers makes are interesting and they recall earlier themes in our discussion. On the one hand, his proposal reminds us of a suggestion which we considered earlier that we might detach the term 'security' from its specific connection with safety and use it to refer to the assured possession and enjoyment of any value (including liberty).

On the other hand, his proposal reminds us of a suggestion which we rejected that threats to life and limb, or the infliction of harm and pain, can be reclassified as threats to liberty. We considered and rejected that with regard to the costs that are imposed on certain people when the state seeks to enhance security by killing or beating or torturing some of

[90] Powers, 'Can we be Secure and Free?' 3.
[91] Montesquieu, *The Spirit of the Laws*, p. 188 (Bk12, ch. 2).
[92] Powers, 'Can we be Secure and Free?' 22–3.

those subject to its authority. I think we should also reject it with regard to the damage that terrorists are seeking to inflict upon us. I suppose one could say that they intend to attack our liberties: 'They hate our freedoms' etc.[93] But it is a misleading way of talking if it is supposed to describe the direct and murderous intention they have against our lives and other aspects of our safety. The language of security, I have argued, is not reducible to safety, but it *is* firmly anchored to safety and we should not flinch from saying that this is what the terrorists are trying to attack and this is what we are trying to protect. For all its complexity the language of security is more apposite than the language of liberty here. By the same token, the language of liberty is sometimes more useful than the language of security to describe costs that are being imposed in the war against terrorism. Some of those costs are security-costs (as when some individual is beaten or tortured by agents of the state), but many of them are liberty-costs. Those who are incarcerated at Guantánamo Bay have suffered a drastic loss of liberty, and the same is true of some U.S. citizens, like Yaser Esam Hamdi.[94] Their liberty has been radically diminished to make us more secure against murderous attack. No amount of word-play—provocative though it may be in Powers' article—can take away the fact that someone's liberty is being traded off against someone's security in these instances.

At the beginning of this chapter (and again towards the end), we considered whether security should be taken to comprise people's individual, familial, and social way of life. President Bush said that our way of life is certainly a target for terrorism: 'These terrorists kill not merely to end lives, but to disrupt and end a way of life.'[95] While Bush's statement in itself does not mean that the maintenance of our way of life is comprised in our security, it is pretty clear that security would be impoverished without taking this aspect into account. In the course of that discussion we considered whether in this regard security might be thought to comprise some reference to aspects of our civil liberties. Certainly our way of life consists in part in our constitutional traditions and the path-

---

[93] *Transcript of President Bush's Address* [to Joint Session of Congress, September 20, 2001], *Washington Post*, September 21, 2001, p. A24: 'Americans are asking, "Why do they hate us?" They hate what they see right here in this chamber: a democratically elected government. Their leaders are self-appointed. They hate our freedoms: our freedom of religion, our freedom of speech, our freedom to vote and assemble and disagree with each other.'

[94] See *Hamdi v. Rumsfeld*, 542 U.S. 507 (2004).

[95] George W. Bush, Address to Joint Session of Congress (September 20, 2001), in *Washington Post*, September 21, 2001, at p. A24.

ways of our legal system. But again: we need to be very careful with this. Instead of saying that we have identified an overlap between security and liberty, we might say that the partisans of security just like the partisans of liberty identify important aspects of our way of life that they want to emphasize, but they emphasize them in different ways and in light of somewhat different concerns.

Our way of life is a common reservoir of values, common to both sides in this debate. The civil libertarians emphasize the liberties that matter to us, and certainly it is right to point out that those liberties require security for their meaningful exercise. The partisans of security point out that they are trying to protect our way of life (as well as our lives themselves) against attack, and certainly it is right to point out that you cannot do that if you treat our liberties as unimportant. But still there is a genuine trade-off. Even if it is not a trade-off between one set of values and another quite distinct set of values, it is a trade-off between the importance of protecting certain values in one way and the importance of vindicating certain values in another way.

VII. Conclusion

In this chapter, I have tried to complicate and enrich our sense of what security involves, and that has involved exploring some internal connections between security and liberty and between security and constitutional values. But I have tried to respect the idea of security as an important array of concerns that cannot be wished away or turned into something else. I have tried to preserve the core connection between security and safety, while noting the various ways in which that connection is not the whole story about security. And I have tried to do what the pure safety conception by itself cannot do: provide an account of security not just as an individual value but as an articulate social concern.

Analytic philosophers are fond of quoting Bishop Butler's aphorism: 'Everything is what it is and not another thing.'[96] And that may be said

---

[96] Butler, *Fifteen Sermons*, p. xxix. G.E. Moore used this aphorism as the motto for *Principia Ethica*, to express his position that even if goodness is consistently associated with some property like pleasantness, still that is a correlation rather than an identification: goodness and pleasantness remain distinct properties. Isaiah Berlin used a version of it in his discussion of liberty. See Berlin, *Four Essays on Liberty*, at p. 125: 'Everything is what it is: liberty is liberty, not equality or fairness or justice or culture, or human happiness or a quiet conscience.'

of security: security is what it distinctively is. It is not a site where we try to cram together a lot of other disparate values. But that does not relieve us from the task of analysis and from exploring connections with other values if there are any, connections which are important to the notion of security, connections whose suppression would misrepresent and impoverish the concept. The philosopher W.K. Frankena added a mischievous gloss to Butler's aphorism. He wrote: 'Everything is what it is and not another thing; unless of course, it is another thing, in which case that is what it is.'[97] That is how I believe we should think about security. We should keep faith with its distinctiveness as a political ideal, but not take that as a license for simple-mindedness about what it involves. Certainly, we should never take its distinctiveness as a reason for avoiding or denying aspects of security itself just because they are troubling to our strategies in the war on terror or just because they reproach or expose as inadequate some of what we propose to do to protect our people and their country.

[97] Frankena, 'The Naturalistic Fallacy,' 472.

6

Security as a Basic Right (after 9/11)

Should we give up any of our rights for the sake of security? The world is a dangerous place, more dangerous perhaps than it was when our human rights or constitutional rights were first defined. Many people think we would be safer if we were to abandon some of our rights or at least cut back on some of our more aggressive claims about the extent and importance of our civil liberties. Or maybe the trade-off should go in the other direction. Maybe we should be a little braver and risk a bit more in the way of security to uphold our precious rights. After all, security is not the be-all and end-all; our rights are what really matter. But this brave alternative will not work if it turns out that security is valuable not just for its own sake, but for the sake of our rights. What if the enjoyment of our rights is possible only when we are already secure against various forms of violent attack? If rights are worth nothing without security, then the brave alternative is misconceived.

I considered some of these issues in Chapter 2. But in that chapter I did not explicitly address the point that security might be a precondition for enjoying any rights at all. In this chapter, I want to consider that possibility. In doing so, I shall make use of an earlier analysis of the relation between security and rights, set out in Henry Shue's book, *Basic Rights*.

1. Basic Rights

Basic Rights makes a vivid and compelling case for regarding security and also subsistence as indispensable conditions for the enjoyment of human rights.[1] 'No one,' says Shue, 'can fully if it all enjoy any right if he or

---

[1] Shue, *Basic Rights: Subsistence, Affluence, and U.S. Foreign Policy*. Page references in parentheses in the text are to this work. (I use the 1980 edition rather than the second edition of *Basic Rights* published by Princeton University Press in 1996, because the latter does not include an important chapter on U.S. foreign policy, chapter 7 of the original edition).

she lacks the essentials for a reasonably healthy and active life' (p. 24). And the same, he says, is true of security: '[T]hreats to physical security are among the most serious and—in much of the world—the most widespread hindrances to the enjoyment of any right' (p. 21). Threats of violence and lack of subsistence are standard threats which anyone interested in any rights must be prepared to contend with. The abatement of these standard threats is part of the moral minimum; it represents everyone's minimum reasonable demand upon the rest of humanity (p. 19). No one can expect to be taken seriously in his juridical proclamations about rights, says Shue, if he is not prepared to commit himself to a concern for the security and for the subsistence that are presupposed by the enjoyment of the rights that he proclaims.

Much of the discussion of *Basic Rights* has focused on Shue's thesis as it concerns subsistence.[2] Less has been said about the security side of the argument. I believe there is a lot to learn from Shue's argument about security. But I also think that when it is considered in the light of recent events, Shue's argument may need to be clarified or rethought. Certainly when we compare what Shue said with very similar-sounding claims that have been made more recently, we may see the need to engage more critically with his argument about security.

Shue's claims about the indispensability of security for the enjoyment of human rights were made in 1980. Twenty-one years later, something happened in the United States which gave a different resonance to claims about the importance of security. After the terrorist attacks of September 11, 2001, it was commonly said that security needed much greater emphasis among our political values and that liberty needed to give way to security in the priorities of a modern democratic society. As one commentator observed,

it has become a part of the drinking water in this country that there has been a tradeoff of liberty for security, ... that we have had to encroach upon civil liberty and trade some of that liberty we cherish for some of that security that we cherish even more.[3]

Now, when complaints are made, in opposition to these suggestions— complaints that some of the trade-offs being proposed encroach not just on liberty in general but on certain basic liberties that are valued as human rights—what is said in response sounds remarkably similar to

---

[2] See, for example, Nickel and Hasse, 'Review of *Basic Rights*' and Smith, 'On Deriving Rights to Goods from Rights to Freedom.'
[3] Comey, 'Fighting Terrorism and Preserving Civil Liberties,' at 403.

Shue's thesis of 21 years earlier. You cannot set up human rights against security, it is said, because security is the precondition for the enjoyment of any rights. If we have to give up or cut back on some of our rights for the sake of security, we need to understand that that sacrifice is necessary in order to be able to enjoy any rights at all. I will refer to this in what follows as the 9/11 argument.

Sometimes the 9/11 argument is put forward disingenuously. There were many people in the Bush administration who responded opportunistically to the crisis of 2001 to limit civil liberties, enhance executive authority, and shake off the shackles of rights-based constraints without any real feeling that what these changes were ultimately about was providing an environment in which rights could flourish. They just wanted to enhance executive authority and the power of the national security apparatus. But many proponents of the 9/11 argument are perfectly sincere. They care about rights, but they say that if we want to continue as a free and rights-upholding society, we cannot ignore the security issue. Security is important for everything including rights. And, they say, we should not rule out the possibility that this greater attention to security might require substantial adjustment in our understanding of the rights we have.

As I have said, the 9/11 argument is reminiscent of Henry Shue's argument from 1980. But appearances are sometimes deceptive. Maybe what Shue was getting at is different from what the 9/11 argument is getting at. Indeed it is possible that Shue's argument might throw into relief—illuminate by contrast—some of the flaws and deficiencies in the 9/11 argument. After all, Shue is not generally regarded as a supporter of the modern security state. If anything, his work has been influential in the opposite direction: I refer particularly to his seminal article on torture.[4] It is possible, of course, that Shue might not want to distinguish his argument from the 9/11 argument. Or even if he wants to, it may be wrong to do this because the logic of his case may fit the 9/11 argument exactly. After all the case that is made in *Basic Rights* is not Shue's property to do with as he will; it purports to draw our attention to certain objectively important connections between security and the rest of our rights, and it is important to see how exactly those connections play out in the post-9/11 world, whatever Shue thinks or hopes.

There are two possible ways in which Shue's argument about security might be distinguished from the 9/11 argument. One way is to

---

[4] See Shue, 'Torture.' See also Shue, 'Preemption, Prevention, and Predation.'

distinguish the conceptions of security that are being used in these two arguments. The other is to look a little more closely at what Shue says (and what the 9/11 argument says) about the logic of the relation between security (however it is conceived) and other rights. I will consider the first of these possibilities in sections 2, 3, and 4 and the second in sections 5 and 6 of this chapter.

2. Security in Political Philosophy

Our pursuit of the first possibility is hampered by the sorry state of the discussion of security as a concept in political philosophy. Security has not been properly analyzed.[5] We know that the word is vague and ambiguous and that there is good reason to regard its vagueness as a source of danger when talk of trade-offs is in the air.[6] But few attempts have been made in the literature of legal and political theory to bring any sort of analytic clarity to the concept.[7]

Shue's account in *Basic Rights* is no exception. He provides little in the way of analysis of the concept of security. His use of the term is quite narrow. He talks of 'physical security' (p. 20) and says we have a right 'not to be subjected to murder, torture, mayhem, rape or assault' (p. 20). The only analytic points he makes are about the distinction between security and liberty and between a right to security and a right to life. On the first point, Shue is adamant that security is not just a matter of freedom. It is true that one can characterize security in terms of 'freedom from' beatings, torture, murder etc., but this idiom connotes only the absence of an evil, not freedom in any meaningful sense (p. 181–2n).[8] On the second point, despite the prominence of mortal threats in his account of security, Shue is reluctant to treat the right to security as simply part of the right to life (p. 186n). How one individuates rights is probably just a matter of pragmatics, but Shue finds it illuminating to deal separately with security and subsistence (which arguably could also be treated as part of the right to life) and their importance, respectively, for rights in general.

---

[5] See the discussion in Chapter 5, above, esp. at pp. 111–16.

[6] In *United States v. United States District Court* 407 U.S. 297 (1972), at 320, the Supreme Court spoke of the 'inherent vagueness of the domestic security concept . . . and the temptation to utilize such surveillance to oversee political dissent.'

[7] But see the discussion in Glyn Morgan, *The Idea of a European Superstate*, pp. 97–104.

[8] See also the discussion in Chapter 5, above, p. 145.

3. The Term 'Security'

When Shue talks about security as a precondition for rights, he seems to have in mind the absence of physical violence *directed specifically at the right-bearers, considered one by one*. The right to security is 'a right...not to be subjected to murder, torture, mayhem, rape, or assault' (p. 20). He is particularly interested in threats which are intended to have or actually do have the effect of preventing people from making the choices that their other rights are supposed to protect. So Shue has in mind individualized personal security; insecurity on his account just is an individual's being directly subject to evils like rape or murder or the threat of them. It is these evils in their most direct and personalized form that Shue sees as inimical to securing of other rights.

Maybe this distinguishes Shue's argument from the claims about security and rights that have been made since 9/11. Those who say, in the wake of terrorist attacks, that we must give up some of our rights for the sake of security do not necessarily mean security against physical attack of each and every one of us right-holders. They mean something more diffuse: the general security of the nation against attacks of this kind. If this is so, then maybe the two arguments are quite different since Shue is not interested in the premise of the 9/11 argument.

Certainly Shue is anxious to dissociate his thesis of security as a basic right from claims that are often made about the overriding importance of *national security*. He talks of the 'cancerous growth' of the concept of national security and he observes that it is 'used with an imprecision that would normally not be tolerated even on many less important concepts' (p. 168).[9] He acknowledges that national security was once supposed to have some connection to what he calls 'the physical security of the people in the nation' (p. 169), but he says that the concept has grown to become more or less entirely divorced from this, so that now it mainly connotes the integrity and power of the governmental apparatus and its ability to pursue its policies successfully.[10]

Another term that is sometimes used is 'homeland security' and that seems to be tied rather more closely to the incidence of physical attack on American civilians than national security is. But homeland security is still a bit more diffuse than the conception Shue seems to be using. We

[9] See also Nickel and Hasse, 'Review of *Basic Rights*,' 1586.
[10] See also Chapter 5, above, pp. 115–16.

say that we suffer a loss in homeland security when terrorist attacks take place or when the danger of terrorist attack is heightened, but yet the impact of those attacks—even when they are as devastating as the attacks of September 11—is confined to a tiny fraction of the American people. Almost 3,000 people were murdered in the attacks on the World Trade Center in 2001; but out of a population of 300,000,000, that is no more than 0.001 per cent. If we were to use Shue's conception focusing on individuals' being insecure, in the sense of being beaten, hurt, or murdered, then we might be forced to conclude that the actual extent of insecurity resulting from the attacks was very low.[11] Even if we take into account well-grounded fears of death or injury from future such attacks, an objective calculation at the individual level is not going to reveal very much insecurity, since the probability of any of us actually suffering the evil that is threatened is somewhat smaller than the insecurity we all accept when we drive on the freeway or engage in physical labor in a factory or a construction site. Now, it is clear nevertheless that the authorities responsible for homeland security do have to regard any further attacks on the scale of the events of September 11 as catastrophic events, to be avoided at almost any cost. They have to regard such threats to homeland security as matters of the greatest concern, even though their consummation would still leave the average resident of the United States with a vanishingly low probability of suffering death and injury as a result. Security in this 'homeland' conception is not detached entirely from the physical well-being of individual men and women in the way that the notion of national security seems to be. But it is not a simple function of individuals' being threatened.

The homeland conception is, I think, the notion of security that is appealed to when people say that it may be necessary to require us to give up some of our civil liberties in order to bring our security up to an acceptable level. As I have said, it is a more diffuse conception of security than Shue's. But I am not sure that Shue can avoid something like it at some stage in his analysis. And the something-like-it may generate conclusions that are very close to those of the 9/11 argument.

Even if one were to begin with Shue's more concrete conception of individualized security, one might still end up in a place not far from the homeland conception. Though the point of Shue's security is to avoid the situation in which particular individuals face death or violence or the threat of death and violence, as the cost of exercising their rights, the

---

[11] I think this individualistic approach is mistaken; I try to explain why in Waldron, 'Is this Torture Necessary?'

strategy for avoiding this prospect need not be as particularized as the prospect itself. True, we might provide security for each individual right-bearer by assigning him a personal bodyguard. But a more efficient and probably a more effective means is to use police forces to ensure a secure environment for everyone. This sort of provision treats security as something like a public good.[12] And under a regime of this kind, individuals benefit from security (in the enjoyment of their rights) not because their own particular security is attended to on a focused one-by-one basis but because threats to security in general are removed or reduced by less personalized means. The police do not wait till any particular death squad or paramilitary militia threatens a particular right-bearer. They outlaw these death squads and militias in general. The public authorities provide lighting in dark places and reliable police officers on patrol and on the beat. They reduce violence and the threat of violence by a variety of strategies to keep the crime rate down and to diminish the vulnerability of various classes of person. And everyone benefits from these efforts, just because they proceed on such a broad front. Using means like these to guarantee security to anyone means that security is guaranteed for many, for most, and—in the ideal case—for all.[13]

Does it make a difference that Shue wants to present security not just as a background condition for the enjoyment of rights but also as itself a basic right? On some accounts, a right to security is just a right correlative to a negative duty not to actually attack or harm others.[14] But Shue refuses to accept this view of the right to security. (Indeed his challenge to the simplistic distinction between rights correlative to negative duties and rights correlative to positive duties is one of the great virtues of *Basic Rights*.) He says:

Perhaps if one were dealing with some wilderness situation in which individuals' encounters with each other were infrequent and irregular, there might be some

---

[12] I mean a 'public good' in the sense of a good which is *non-competitive* (one person's enjoyment of it does not diminish the amount of it available for enjoyment by anyone else) and/or *non-excludable* (if it is made available to anyone in a given group, such as a whole society, it is necessarily made available to all members of that group).

[13] I acknowledge that this is a very rosy picture of law enforcement in most countries. Often the police are part of the problem, and often the public goods aspect is diminished or attenuated as certain neighborhoods are neglected and certain classes of individuals are made more vulnerable not less vulnerable as a result of law-enforcement activities. All I am trying to show is that Shue may not be able to avoid the sort of diffuse public-good conception as part of what the security ideal requires.

[14] For the traditional distinction between positive and negative rights (i.e. rights correlative to duties of positive action and duties of omission), see Cranston, 'Human Rights, Real and Supposed,' p. 43.

point in noting to someone: I am not asking you to cooperate with a system of guarantees to protect me from third parties, but only to refrain from attacking me yourself. But in an organized society, insofar as there were any such things as rights to physical security that were distinguishable from some other rights-to-be-protected-from-assaults-upon-physical-security, no one would have much interest in the bare rights to physical security. What people want and need...is protection of their rights. (p. 38)

Once this is accepted, then it is an open question whether the best way to protect security is to concentrate on thwarting possible violations one by one as they present themselves or to try and provide a secure environment as a sort of pubic good.

Joseph Raz has argued convincingly that the goods secured by rights often require the existence or provision of public goods, such as the good of a tolerant society or the good of a society in which certain socially-recognized options for the exercise of autonomy exist.[15] And Shue himself recognizes that this may be true in the case of subsistence. One of the examples he gives in *Basic Rights* of insufficient attention to subsistence is the introduction of a macroeconomic policy that encourages the production of cash crops for export. The implication seems to be that the basic contribution a government can make to subsistence is avoiding macroeconomic changes like this, and instead maintaining an economic environment in which people can live and hopefully flourish without being all the time on the edge of starvation. And I think he acknowledges this need for macro-strategies also in the case of security, when he says that

protection of rights to physical security necessitates police forces; criminal courts; penitentiaries; schools for training police, lawyers, and guards; and taxes to support an enormous system for the prevention, detection, and punishment of violations of personal security. All these activities and institutions are attempts at providing social guarantees for individuals' security so that they are not left to face alone forces that they cannot handle on their own. (pp. 37–8)

Once all this is accepted, then it is an easy step to something like the homeland security conception. If thousands of individuals are

---

[15] See Raz, *The Morality of Freedom*, pp. 198–207. Raz argues that public goods can't themselves be the subject of rights. But he confines this point to what he calls non-contingent public goods. See also the discussion in Réaume, 'Individuals, Groups, and Rights to Public Goods,' at 9–13 and Waldron, 'Can Communal Goods be Human Rights?' Security as I am imagining it, under the auspices of good policing, is a contingent public good in the relevant sense. On the other hand, there may be aspects of the idea of security which are non-contingent public goods: see the discussion in Chapter 5, above, pp. 159–60 and also in Loader and Walker, *Civilizing Security*.

threatened by sporadic terrorist attacks which it is difficult for them to guard against on their own, then the community has no choice but to adopt general strategies to combat and reduce the incidence of this evil.

4. Terrorist Attacks on Security as a Basic Right

Even granting all this, there may be a further distinction to be drawn, to distance Shue's thesis from the 9/11 argument. We might distinguish two ways in which lack of security can impact on one's rights. One—which he seems particularly concerned with—involves something like deliberate and direct intimidation relative to the exercise of one's rights. He writes:

No one can fully enjoy any right that is supposedly protected by society if someone can credibly threaten him or her with murder, rape, beating, etc., when he or she tries to enjoy the alleged right. (p. 21)

The other might be a more generalized fear that, so to speak, keeps people indoors, keeps them away from church or public meetings or polling places, not because they expect to be coerced *in the exercise of their rights*, but just because they are afraid of being mugged, for example, by people who have no interest apart from the particular circumstances of the mugging with the way their victims' rights are exercised. The man who robs me doesn't worry about whether I vote Democrat or worship as an Episcopalian or attend meetings of the ACLU; he just wants my money. And if fear of him or of people like him keeps me away from exercising those rights that is an unintended side-effect of his violence.

I think Shue's thesis about a basic right to security is more plausible when the threat of insecurity is understood in the first way than when it is understood in the second way. In the second way, the threat to the exercise of my civil and political rights posed by the mugger is rather like the threat posed to those rights by bad weather. The rain may keep me away from church or from the ACLU meeting as well. (Of course the mugging itself is deliberate and in that way unlike the weather; but we are talking about its collateral impact on the exercise of rights other than those affected immediately by the mugging itself.) On the other hand, Shue talks in a footnote of 'non-human threats to both security and subsistence' (p. 189 n. 17), which seems to imply that it may be the second sense that he is interested in. Certainly the second sense is appropriate for subsistence. For lack of subsistence can block or undermine the meaningful exercise of one's rights whether anyone intends that consequence or not. Shue does not really address the question of whether insecurity might be different from lack of subsistence in this regard.

Which category do terrorist attacks (such as the attacks of September 11) fit into? I am not sure. My inclination is to say that they fit into the second category: they are designed just to cause death and wreak havoc and enrage and humiliate the American government; any further impact on the way Americans exercise their civil and politcial rights was just a side-effect. But I have heard people say the opposite. The term 'terrorism' implies a desire for some effect on the society that is attacked which goes beyond the immediate death and havoc that is caused.[16] President Bush said that the terrorists who threaten us do so precisely because they hate our freedoms and want to frighten us away from the exercise of them.[17] But what if the terrorists' strategy is to provoke those who are supposed to protect us into curtailing or undermining our rights?[18] If the state's reaction to A's attack on B is to curtail B's rights, can we really say that it is A's attack that is the standard threat to rights? I don't think so. We certainly can't use that characterization to justify taking rights away from B for the sake of enhancing the security that B is supposed to need in order to enjoy his rights, for that would be to postulate the very same thing (the taking away of rights by the state in the face of terrorist attack) as both the problem and the solution!

5. The Indispensability of Security

I said there were two ways in which we might distinguish Shue's argument about security from the post-9/11 argument about security. We have considered whether there might be a distinction between the conceptions of security that are being used in the two arguments. Now we must consider as well the relation between security and rights, and see

---

[16] See also the discussion in Chapter 3, above, at pp. 76–7.

[17] See the quotation in Chapter 5 from President George W. Bush's Address to a Joint Session of Congress (September 20, 2001) on p. 163 (n. 93). ('Americans are asking, why do they hate us? They hate what we see right here in this chamber—a democratically elected government. Their leaders are self-appointed. They hate our freedoms—our freedom of religion, our freedom of speech, our freedom to vote and assemble and disagree with each other').

[18] See Chapter 3, above, p. 76.

whether the relation that Shue asserts is similar in relevant respects to the relation that has been envisaged in recent homeland security strategies.

The language that Shue uses is the language of indispensability. Security is an indispensable condition for the enjoyment of individual rights:

> No one can fully enjoy any right that is supposedly protected by society if someone can credibly threaten him with murder, rape, beating, etc., when he or she tries to enjoy the alleged right. Such threats to physical security are among the most serious and—in much of the world—the most widespread hindrances to the enjoyment of any right....In the absence of physical security people are unable to use any other rights that society may be said to be protecting without being liable to encounter many of the worst dangers they would encounter if society were not protecting the rights. (p. 21)

Indispensability here conveys one or both of two ideas. One is that an individual's security is a necessary condition for his enjoyment of any right. The other is that an individual's security is actually a part of what any other right is a right *to*. Shue uses the second formulation explicitly when he says that security 'is desirable as part of the enjoyment of any other right' (p. 21). And he uses the first formulation when he presents the abstract form of his argument in terms of a syllogism: 'If everyone has the right to y, and the enjoyment of x is necessary for the enjoyment of y, then everyone has a right to x' (p. 32). In fact the distinction between the two formulations doesn't really matter, since Shue sees no need to distinguish between, as it were, the essence of a right and what is necessary for its enjoyment. The distinction certainly makes no difference to four points that I would like to make about this indispensability relation.

Saying that one thing, x, is indispensable for or inherently necessary for another thing, y, raises a number of questions about the priority that should be accorded to x over y or vice versa. Some of those questions require us to look a little more closely at the indispensability relation and some require us to look skeptically at the issue of priorities. Let me begin with indispensability:

(i) How tight is the relation of indispensability supposed to be, as between security and rights, on Shue's account? People often seem to exercise (and sometimes even enjoy) their rights under the most adverse circumstances. Is Shue really saying that this *can never happen* in the absence of security? Shue is sensitive to the point and says this:

> A person could, of course, always try to enjoy some other right even if no social provision were made to protect his or her physical safety during attempts to

exercise the right. Suppose there is a right to peaceful assembly but it is not unusual for peaceful assemblies to be broken up and some of the participants beaten. . . . People could still try to assemble, and they might sometimes assemble safely. But it would obviously be misleading to say that that they are protected in their right to assemble . . . If they are as helpless against physical threats with the right protected as they would have been without the supposed protection, society is not actually protecting their exercise of the right to assembly. (p. 22)

And a little later he says that if people do not have 'guarantees' that they can assemble in security, then they have not been provided with assembly as a right' (p. 27). But I don't think this settles the issue.

The trouble is that security is not an all-or-nothing matter, but a matter of more or less. I may be provided with a guarantee of protection but not a cast-iron guarantee. The government may sincerely undertake to do its best for my security, but it may not be able to prevent every last gang of thugs from occasionally breaking up a public meeting. In this situation, I am not as helpless against attack as I would be if the government had done nothing at all. If I try (and often succeed) in exercising my rights in these circumstances, haven't I refuted at least a very strong version of Shue's claim that my security is absolutely indispensable for the enjoyment of my rights. This point seems particularly important when we consider security in the public good sense (i.e. in the sense discussed, above, in section 3). If the provision of security as a public good is less than perfect, or if it falls short of what might in certain circumstances be reasonably required, is it still plausible to say that the absence of security makes the enjoyment of rights impossible? Obviously not, for we have acknowledged that there might be a failure of something like homeland security and yet many individuals may face no actual threat at all.

I think that this shows a considerable gap in the 9/11 argument. When the avatars of homeland security justify curtailing a right for the sake of security, they do not usually mean that once this right is curtailed then everyone can be made perfectly secure. Instead they have in mind at best an incremental enhancement of security as a public good as a result of the curtailment: curtailing the right may allow us to move from (say) 51 to 52 per cent of the provision of security at an optimal level. Perhaps the curtailment is justified, but if it is, it is not because we need this curtailment in order to enjoy the rest of our rights. The rest of our rights, which we are going to have to exercise *anyway* in something less than perfect security, may not be much affected.

(ii) This leads to my second point. In a dangerous world, the provision of security is a voracious ideal. If we are looking for absolute security, there is no end to the resources that might have to be devoted to it. We could station a police officer every few yards and devote enormous resources to homeland security.[19] Maybe if we devoted the whole of the GNP, we might reduce to something approaching zero the threat of the sort of violence that undermines the enjoyment of rights. But then there would be nothing left for any other social program, let alone for any other program associated with rights. Since, on Shue's account, there are a number of necessary conditions for the enjoyment of rights (subsistence is another), it is not clear how we can or should proceed with this calculation.

(iii) One thing is sure: we must not regard the necessary conditions of the enjoyment of rights as having absolute priority over all other goals. Certainly we should not assign it lexical priority, in the Rawlsian sense.[20] Surely we do not want to devote all our resources and energy to fulfilling a necessary condition for rights, and nothing at all to the rights themselves. We need to find some balance here. Robert Goodin makes a similar point about national defense.[21] Defense, he notes, is sometimes presented as 'an indispensable prerequisite to everything else the nation might do' or as a 'precondition for pursuing other desirable goals.' But if that is how we understand it, we must occasionally allow those other goals to surface in public policy and to stake their claim to some of society's resources. We cannot infinitely postpone their enjoyment to the establishment of what is valued only as a necessary condition for their enjoyment.

When he introduced the notion of lexical priority, John Rawls observed that the idea should only be used in circumstances where the item accorded priority is limited in its demandingness and where there is some reasonable prospect of its being satisfied, so that other items further down the list can be attended to: '[U]nless the earlier principles have but a limited application and establish definite requirements which can be fulfilled, later principles will never come into play.'[22] Where this condition is not satisfied, we have to proceed on the basis of some sort of balancing, messy though that may seem. This may involve sometimes balancing the costs of rights against other social costs unconnected with

---

[19] See Walzer, *Spheres of Justice*, p. 67.
[20] See Rawls, *A Theory of Justice*, pp. 37–8.
[21] Goodin, *Political Theory and Public Policy*, pp. 232–3.
[22] Rawls, *Theory of Justice*, p. 38.

rights. It will certainly sometimes require balancing costs associated with the security that is necessary for rights, with costs associated with other aspects of the upholding of rights (including, no doubt, other necessary conditions).

(iv) In any case, lexical priority may not be appropriate as a way of operationalizing the importance of things which are valued only as necessary conditions for other values. A necessary condition for something desirable is *not worth supplying at all* unless there is a practicable possibility of also securing sufficient conditions for that desirable thing; if there is no such possibility, then we should just forget about the necessary conditions.[23] A necessary condition for me to visit the moon is that I should begin astronaut training right now, but even assuming that my visiting the moon is highly desirable, the necessary condition for it is simply of no interest since my visiting the moon is not going to happen. The effect of this point on the deontic logic of necessity and obligation is quite uninteresting. Suppose I have an obligation to ensure that person P enjoys a certain good, y. We cannot infer that I have an obligation to bring about something else (x) which is a necessary condition of P's enjoying y. If y cannot in fact be supplied to P under any circumstances (because sufficient conditions are not available), then I do not have an obligation to bring about x even if x itself *can* be brought about by me. The only ground for bringing about x in these circumstances would be if there were some reasonable prospect of sufficient conditions for y being available in the future, in which case bringing about x now would be a sort of advance preparation. Accordingly, if there are other insuperable obstacles to people's enjoyment of their rights, we may not be able to infer from the fact that security is a necessary condition for the enjoyment of their rights that therefore they have a right to security.

This point may be very important further down the line of the chain of necessary conditions. Shue's claim is that the enjoyment of individual rights among a given population depends on the individuals' in question enjoying security. Their individual security is a necessary condition for their effective enjoyment of their rights. But as we have seen, it may be a necessary condition for all these individuals' enjoying individual security in the relevant sense that the government provide a secure environment (by its homeland security strategy) in the sense discussed in section 3. And a case may be made that it is a necessary condition for *that* that (say)

---

[23] See Chapter 2, above, p. 44.

certain terrorist suspects be detained indefinitely. So we have a chain of necessary conditions:

detention of terrorist suspects
is necessary for
homeland security,
which is necessary for
individual security for individual right-bearers,
which is necessary for
individual right-bearers' enjoyment of their rights.

But if sufficient conditions are not available for any of these elements then we cannot infer that terrorists ought to be detained. Suppose the terrorist threat is so great that there is no reasonable prospect for the time being of establishing a secure environment for the enjoyment of rights. Then even though detaining the suspects is a necessary condition for a secure environment, it is like my going to astronaut school: it is a necessary condition for something that is not going to happen. It doesn't follow that we should not detain the suspects, but we cannot infer that they should be detained from the fact that their detention is necessary for something which is necessary for something which is necessary for the enjoyment of rights.

6. All Rights but One?

I have pursued these points about necessary conditions, priorities, and indispensability perhaps too fussily. But I did not do so for the sake of fiscal prudence or out of a concern about the cost-overruns that Shue's program might incur. My interest in this chapter is to see what, if anything, there is in common between Shue's argument about the relation between rights and security, and what I have called the 9/11 argument, namely, the argument that it may sometimes be necessary to sacrifice or limit certain rights in order to provide the security that rights in general presuppose. In the previous section, under heading (ii), I said that security was a voracious ideal. But the things that it might eat up are not just resources but rights, and if we give security too great a priority (or indeed lexical priority) over the rights that it is supposed to be a necessary condition for, we may find that much of what we are ultimately aiming to secure has been jettisoned for the sake of that security.

Abraham Lincoln famously asked, in regard to his unlawful Presidential suspension of *habeas corpus* in 1861, whether he was to let all the laws but one collapse and go unexecuted for the sake of upholding some particular law 'made in such extreme tenderness of the citizen's liberty, that practically it relieves more of the guilty than the innocent.'[24] Proponents of the 9/11 argument ask something similar about rights: are all the rights but a few to go unprotected, unsupported by the security that rights require, for the sake of protecting those few rights that might actually stand in the way of our providing the requisite security?

Where does Shue stand on this? I believe that Shue is not in a position to rule out the possibility that the post-9/11 argument envisages. There are two ways of reaching this conclusion. One is via the idea of the systematicity of rights. The other is via the exigencies of particular circumstances.

On the systematicity account, we might want to consider whether the right whose sacrifice seems to be required for the sake of security should really ever have been regarded as a right at all. (Or, if it is the limitation, rather than the wholesale sacrifice, of the right that seems to be called for in the name of security, we may want to consider whether the right should ever have been recognized in its unlimited form.) We might want to say that the importance of security represents a constraint on what counts as an acceptable set of individual rights. Just as we would not recognize a right that permitted a person to interfere with or undermine the rights of others, so (it might be argued), we should not recognize a right that is incompatible with conditions required for the security of others. This is analogous to the way in which Shue thinks about subsistence. Some people complain that securing subsistence for everyone might be incompatible with respecting property rights or rights to market freedom. But Shue's position seems to be that no such rights exist if they are incompatible with what is necessary for subsistence: 'property laws can be morally justified only if subsistence rights are fulfilled' (p. 124).[25]

Of course there is immense room for argument here—not only argument about the logic of necessity and indispensability considered in the previous paragraph, but also argument about the difference between qualifying property rights for the sake of immediate requirements of individual subsistence and qualifying property rights for the sake of a

[24] Abraham Lincoln, 'Message to Congress in Special Session,' July 4, 1861, quoted by Halbert, 'The Suspension of the Writ of Habeas Corpus by President Lincoln,' at 100.

[25] See also the discussion at the beginning of the 'Afterword' in *Basic Rights*, 2nd edition, p. 153.

particular macroeconomic strategy calculated to enhance subsistence in the medium or long term. Analogously, there is considerable room for argument in the space between qualifying a right whose exercise poses a direct threat to security and qualifying a right whose exercise or enjoyment may be incompatible with the particular homeland security strategy that we happen to be pursuing.

The systematicity approach assumes that, in some sense, we can settle in advance on a set of rights that are compossible *inter se* and compatible with the requirements of security.[26] Of course we have to do the figuring in real time, but the systematicity approach assumes that there is, objectively, a solution—something available to be figured out. The exigency approach is more skeptical about that. It does not assume that we have access to an objective set of rights whose natural law provenance ensures that they fit together rationally or coherently (p. 93). Instead we have to calculate and recalculate the effect on one another of the exercise of various rights in various circumstances. It assumes that no right is absolute, and that occasionally rights might have to be overridden or our sense of what rights we are entitled to rely on in particular circumstances may have to be revised. This is a troubling possibility, but Shue refuses to rule it out (p. 94).

A particularly troubling consequence of the exigency approach is that it might allow for the rights of *some people* to be overridden even when the similar rights of others are not. (This is unlikely on the systematicity approach since some sort of guarantee of equality of rights will operate alongside security and subsistence as an adequacy condition on any acceptable set of human rights.) So, for example, provision may be made for the detention without trial of people whose ethnicity and appearance are similar to those of a certain category of terrorists, even though it would be unthinkable to permit such detention in the case of citizens generally. Some of us have argued that this was characteristic of the Bush administration's homeland security strategy.[27] Though there was talk of a general trade-off of (say) liberty for security as though everyone were giving up a certain amount of liberty so that everyone could achieve greater security, in fact the trade-off was usually a matter of them-and-us—*their* liberty for *our* security. As Ronald Dworkin pointed out:

None of the administration's decisions and proposals will affect more than a tiny number of American citizens:... Most of us pay almost nothing in personal

---

[26] On compossibility, see Steiner, 'The Structure of a Set of Compossible Rights.'

[27] See, e.g. Cole, 'Their Liberties, Our Security' and Waldron, 'Is this Torture Necessary?'

freedom when such measures are used against those the President suspects of terrorism.[28]

Still, nothing in Shue's account affords any basis for ruling this sort of thing out as a matter of principle, at least on the exigency approach. Everything will depend on the particular dimensions of what is proposed and the case that can be made—subject to all the caveats of section 5—as to its necessity.

Elsewhere I have argued that if we are in the business of sacrificing or limiting rights for the sake of rights, we are required to pay particular attention to the logic of rights.[29] When Lincoln spoke of preserving 'all the laws but one,' he seemed to be using a simple maximizing approach: if not all the laws can be upheld, then we should uphold as many as possible. That may or may not be plausible in the case of laws. But when the currency of our calculation is rights, maximization is certainly not appropriate. Rights are inherently equal, and the only justification for the sort of unequal upholding of rights envisaged in the previous paragraph is that it is necessary to avoid even greater or more extensive inequality. So, for example, if we have to choose between two strategies for security, one that requires everyone in a community of (say) a quarter of a billion people to give up one right (for the sake of security) and 10,000 people in that same community to give up 10 rights each (for the sake of security) while all the others enjoy their rights intact, we should prefer the former strategy even though incomparably more rights in the aggregate are safeguarded by the latter strategy. There is not space here to pursue this matter further and, in any case, the philosophical study of such calculations remains fairly rudimentary. But it needs to be emphasized again and again that the mere fact that it is appropriate to contemplate trade-offs between rights and security does not license a more general move away from the egalitarian domain of rights to the more brutal logic of maximization. Trade-offs may seem to be the exclusive domain of the Benthamite economist; but the fact that trade-offs among rights are sometimes necessary shows that, in at least some cases, trade-offs need to be handled more carefully than one can expect economists to handle them.

For my money, these questions are much more likely to be handled with the appropriate care by someone like Henry Shue than by the latter-day proponents of the 9/11 argument. Shue does not discuss the

[28] Dworkin, 'The Threat to Patriotism.' See also Chapter 2, p. 34.
[29] See Chapter 2 above, p. 32.

issues about security exactly as I have posed them. But he does talk about trade-offs of similar kinds in other contexts, and this gives us an indication I think of how he would respond to the 9/11 argument. Shue does not deny the possibility that sometimes some rights, or some things that we thought were rights, might have to be sacrificed to secure other rights. But, in a discussion in *Basic Rights* of the limits on what we are required to do or to put up with for others, he draws the line at the sacrifice of anyone's *basic* rights. 'One is required,' says Shue, 'to sacrifice anything but one's basic rights in order to honor the basic rights of others' (p. 114). Why this line? As I understand it, Shue's position is that the sacrifice of anyone's basic rights means the sacrifice of the conditions that make it possible for that person meaningfully to enjoy and exercise any rights at all. And it is a consequence of what I believe is his acute sensitivity to the logic of the distribution of rights that he rules out this possibility. Even if innumerably more rights could be secured by this means, sacrificing some person as a rights-bearer—reducing him in effect to a non-person, a being who has no rights at all—is out of the question. Our responsibility with rights is to recognize everyone as a rights-bearer and to adjust our sense of what rights each person is to have under the discipline of this fundamental recognition.

What if basic rights of some have to sacrificed not just for the sake of rights but for the *basic* rights of others? In this case, Shue says, 'it is certainly not obvious which set of rights ought to be sacrificed' (pp. 166–7). One possibility he considers is that, in such a trade-off, a government (such as the U.S. government) is entitled to prefer the basic rights of its own citizens to the basic rights of foreigners. The most he is prepared to say in regard to this proposal is that government may elect to give priority to securing the basic rights of its own citizens over securing the basic rights of foreigners, but that this does not imply that it is entitled to violate the basic rights of foreigners—that is, act deliberately to undermine them—as a means to securing its own citizens' basic rights (p. 166).[30]

This sense of constraint is very important, both for what it represents about Shue's commitment to the logic of rights, and for its actual impact on the post-9/11 proposals. It is important to remember in evaluating various proposals for trade-offs that might enhance our security in a post-9/11 world, that at times of national panic the deprivations imposed on (or proposed for) members of vulnerable and identifiable

---

[30] Shue argues in an endnote (219n) that this does not involve reintroducing the distinction between positive and negative rights that, as we saw in section 4, he rejects.

minorities are often deprivations of security, not just deprivations of civil liberties or other ordinary rights. For example, those who have been beaten and tortured—some beaten and tortured to death[31]—by American intelligence operatives in the war against terrorism have suffered not just the loss of rights, but the radical loss of security. As I argued in section 2, the infliction of pain during interrogation renders a person not just less free—though he has to be made unfree (*held down*) in order to be tortured—but less safe, less secure in a very straightforward sense. The security that we all crave is security against violent attack, but that is exactly what many people lose when they are imprisoned in Guantánamo Bay or in 'black' U.S. prisons in Eastern Europe, or when they are 'rendered' by U.S. agents to foreign countries like Syria for torture by their authorities. Their security is sacrificed in order to make the rest of us more safe. That is an appalling prospect to contemplate on any account. But on Shue's account, it is particularly troubling, since he understands their security as not just a good to be enjoyed, but as a basic right, a condition for their having any other rights at all.

In Chapter 5, I argued that we should not treat security as a good to be maximized in society, but as something to be achieved, as far as possible, at an equal level for everyone. But that was not an easy argument to make.[32] Shue makes it much easier, however, by conceiving of security as a basic right. If security is the condition of the effective enjoyment of rights, then sacrificing anyone's security for the sake of others' is absolutely ruled out. What is commanded here by the logic of rights is peremptory and deafening: we are to do everything possible to avoid the situation in which anyone's security is comprehensively sacrificed for to do so is to act as though none of that person's rights matter, ultimately as though his personhood doesn't matter. Obviously there is still a little room for argument inasmuch as even the sacrifice of security can be conceived as a matter of more or less. But it is a sign of the importance of Shue's analysis that it locates the issue firmly on this ground of basic rights.

[31] 'In U.S. Report, Brutal Details of Two Afghan Inmates' Deaths,' *New York Times*, May 20, 2005.

[32] See also the argument about security in Williams, *In the Beginning was the Deed*, p. 4 ff.

7

Torture and Positive Law

The starting point of this chapter, written in the summer of 2004, was the dishonor that descended upon the United States earlier that year as a result of revelations about what was happening under American control in Abu Ghraib prison in Iraq. I mean more than the Abu Ghraib nightmare itself—the photographs of sexual humiliation, the dogs, the hoods, the wires, the beatings. I refer also to the emerging understanding that what took place there was not just a result of the depravity of a few poorly trained reservists, but the upshot of a policy determined by intelligence officials to have military police at the prison 'set favorable conditions' (that was the euphemism) for the interrogation of detainees.

The dishonor intensified when it was revealed that abuses were not isolated in this one prison, but that brutal interrogations were also being conducted by American officials elsewhere. We know now that a number of captured officers in Iraq and Afghanistan, including general officers, were severely beaten during interrogation by their American captors and in one case killed by suffocation.[1] We know too that terrorist suspects, enemy combatants, and others associated with the Taliban and Al Qaeda held by the U.S. in the camps at Guantánamo Bay were being interrogated using physical and psychological techniques that had been outlawed after their use by British forces against terrorist suspects in Northern Ireland in the early 1970s (outlawed by the European Court of Human Rights)[2] and outlawed after their use by security forces in Israel against terrorist suspects in the 1990s (outlawed by the Israeli Supreme Court).[3]

---

[1] See Miles Moffeit, 'Brutal Interrogation in Iraq: Five Detainees' Deaths probed,' *Denver Post*, May 19, 2004: ('Brutal interrogation techniques by U.S. military personnel are being investigated in connection with the deaths of at least five Iraqi prisoners.... The deaths include the killing in November of a high-level Iraqi general who was shoved into a sleeping bag and suffocated, according to the Pentagon report.')

[2] *Ireland v. United Kingdom* 25 Eur.Ct. H.R. 1 (1977).

[3] *Public Committee against Torture in Israel v. The State of Israel*, H.C. 5100/94, 53(4) P.D. 817 (1999).

Above all, my starting point was the realization that these abuses took place not just in the fog of war, but against a legal and political background set by discussions among lawyers and other officials in the White House, the Justice Department, and the Department of Defense about how to narrow the meaning and application of domestic and international legal prohibitions relating to torture.

It was dispiriting as well as shameful to have to turn our attention to this issue. In 1911 the author of the article on 'Torture' in the *Encyclopedia Britannica* wrote that 'the whole subject is now one of only historical interest as far as Europe is concerned.'[4] But it came to life again. With the growth of the ethnic-loyalty state and the security state in the twentieth century, with the emergence of anti-colonial insurgencies and other intractable forms of internal armed conflict, and with the rise of terrorism, torture has returned and 'flourished on a colossal scale.'[5] Nor is it just a rogue-state third-world banana-republic phenomenon: the use of torture has in recent decades disfigured the security polices of France (in Algeria), Britain (in Northern Ireland), Israel (in the Occupied Territories), and now the United States (in Iraq, Afghanistan, and Cuba).

I. Three Jurists

Perhaps what is remarkable is not that torture was used, but that it was being *defended* (or something very close to it was being defended) and defended not just by the hard men of state security agencies but by some well-known American jurists and law professors. Here are three examples:

A. John Yoo

Professor John Yoo now teaches law at the University of California at Berkeley. But while on leave from Boalt Hall as a Deputy Assistant

---

[4] *Encyclopedia Britannica* (11th edition, 1911), vol. 23, p. 75. See also Twining, 'Bentham on Torture,' 305.

[5] Cf. Shklar, 'The Liberalism of Fear,' p. 27: 'In Europe and North America torture had gradually been eliminated from the practices of government, and there was hope that it might eventually disappear everywhere. With the intelligence and loyalty requirements of the national warfare states that quickly developed [after 1914], torture returned and has flourished on a colossal scale.... [A]cute fear has again become the most common form of social control.'

Attorney-General in the Justice Department, Professor Yoo was the lead author of a January 2002 memo, persuading the Bush administration to withdraw the administration's recognition of the rules imposed by the Geneva Conventions so far as the treatment of prisoners belonging to Al Qaeda and the Taliban was concerned.[6] This pertained particularly to the issue of interrogation and torture. Despite the fact that the Geneva Conventions impose a prohibition on torture in relation to every single category of detainee they consider (civilians, POWs, captured insurgents, captured members of irregular forces), Professor Yoo argued that captured members of Al Qaeda and the Taliban were not protected by any such prohibition because the particular category of armed conflict in which they were involved was not explicitly mentioned in any of the Conventions under a description that the Bush administration would accept. Moreover Professor Yoo argued that the administration could not be constrained by any *inference* from the Conventions so far as torture was concerned, nor could it be constrained in this regard by *ius cogens* norms of customary international law.

B. Alan Dershowitz

Alan Dershowitz is a professor at Harvard Law School. In two well-publicized books, Professor Dershowitz argued that torture may be a not unacceptable method—morally and constitutionally—for use by United States officials if it is needed to extract information from terrorists that may lead to the immediate saving of lives.[7] He had in mind forms of non-lethal torture, such as (in his phrase) 'a sterilized needle inserted under the fingernails to produce unbearable pain without any threat to health or life.'[8] Professor Dershowitz wanted us to consider the possibility that it might be appropriate for torture of this kind to receive explicit authorization in the form of judicial torture warrants.

C. Jay Bybee

Jay Bybee was once a law professor at Louisiana State University and at the University of Nevada, and in March 2003 he was confirmed as a

---

[6] Yoo and Delahunty, 'Application of Treaties and Laws to Al Qaeda and Taliban Detainees.'

[7] Dershowitz, *Shouting Fire*, pp. 470–7 and Dershowitz, *Why Terrorism Works*, pp. 132–63. See also Dershowitz, 'Tortured Reasoning,' p. 257.

[8] Dershowitz, *Why Terrorism Works*, p. 144.

judge on the Ninth Circuit. Between 2001 and 2003 Judge Bybee was head of the Office of Legal Counsel in the Department of Justice, and in that capacity he put his name to a memorandum sent to the White House purporting to narrow the definition (or the administration's understanding of the definition) of 'torture' so that it did not cover all cases of the deliberate infliction of pain in the course of interrogation.[9] The word 'torture' and the prohibition on torture should be reserved, Bybee argued, only for the infliction of the sort of extreme pain that would be associated with death or organ failure. He also argued that legislation restricting the use of torture by U.S. forces under *any* definition might be unconstitutional as a restriction on the President's power as Commander-in-Chief.

These proposals did not arise in a vacuum. The United States suffered a catastrophic series of terrorist attacks on September 11, 2001 and in the wake of those attacks the Bush administration committed itself to a 'war on terror' and to an active doctrine of pre-emptive self-defense. In Al Qaeda it faces a resourceful enemy that obeys no legal restraints on armed conflict and may attack without warning at any time. The issue of torture arose because of the importance of intelligence in this conflict: success in protecting a country from terrorist attack depended on intelligence more than brute force; good intelligence was also necessary for protecting our armed forces from insurgent attack in countries like Afghanistan and Iraq which we occupied (allegedly in pursuit of the war on terror).

In 2003–4, I heard colleagues say that what the Bush administration was trying to do in regard to torture should be understood sympathetically in the light of these circumstances, and that we should be less reproachful of the administration's efforts to manipulate the definition of 'torture' than we might be in peacetime. I disagreed then and I disagree now; as I said in Chapter 1, I do not believe that 'everything is different' after September 11. The various municipal and international law prohibitions on torture were set up precisely to address the circumstances in which torture was likely to be most tempting. If the prohibitions did not hold fast in those circumstances, they would be of little use

---

[9] Bybee, 'Standards of Conduct for Interrogation under 18 U.S.C. 2340–2340A.' John Yoo has acknowledged that he had substantial involvement in the actual formulation of what I am calling the Bybee memorandum. See Maria L. La Ganga, 'Scholar Calmly Takes Heat for His Memos on Torture,' *L.A. Times*, May 16, 2005, at p. A1. However, because this memorandum went out under Judge Bybee's name, it is he who must take ultimate responsibility for the legal and ethical issues associated with its production.

in any circumstances. In what follows therefore I have considered the various attempts that were made to narrow or modify the prohibitions on torture as though they were attempts to narrow its *normal* meaning or its *normal* application. This is because those who set up the prohibitions envisaged that circumstances of stress and fear would be the normal habitat in which these provisions would have to operate.

I want to place particular emphasis on the fact that these efforts to modify the prohibition on torture were undertaken by *lawyers*.[10] Sure, our primary objection had to do with the immediate situation of those who suffered the treatment that Dershowitz, Bybee, and Yoo appeared to condone. But the defense of torture was also shocking as a jurisprudential matter. That views and proposals like these should be voiced by scholars who have devoted their lives to the law, to the study of the Rule of Law, and to the education of future generations of lawyers was a matter of dishonor for our profession. Reading the memoranda of Judge Bybee and Professor Yoo and the mooted proposal of Professor Dershowitz shook my faith in the integrity of the community of American jurists. At the very least, it indicated the necessity of our thinking more deeply about the nature of the rule against torture, its place in our legal system, and the responsibilities that lawyers (particularly lawyers working in government) have to uphold the integrity of our law in this regard.[11]

In what follows—and this is a long chapter—I want to do several things. In Part II of this chapter, I shall explore the idea that there is something wrong with trying to pin down the prohibition on torture with a precise legal definition. Insisting on exact definitions may sound very lawyerly, but there is something disturbing about it when the quest for precision is put to work in the service of a mentality that says, 'Give us a definition so we have something to work around, something to game, a determinate envelope to push.'

Part III of this chapter will consider whether the rule against torture can be regarded as an absolute. This is often treated as a moral question, but I also want to consider the idea of a legal absolute. The rule against

[10] See also Weisberg, 'Loose Professionalism, or Why Lawyers Take the Lead on Torture.'

[11] See Bilder and Vagts, 'Speaking Law to Power: Lawyers and Torture,' 691–5 (noting ethical requirements of the American Bar Association Model Rules of Professional Conduct and observing that 'it is only these professional qualities that protect against legal advice or advocacy that might undermine the national interest in respect for law, or subvert or erode the international legal order'). See also Chapter 10 below.

torture is often presented as a legal absolute, but in Part III, I want to consider the persuasiveness of claims made by Professor Dershowitz and others that we should be willing to recognize legal exceptions to this rule.

Part IV continues the exploration of the idea that the rule against torture may have extraordinary legal force. In Part IV, I want to defend the proposition that torture is utterly repugnant to the spirit of our law, and I want to explore the idea that narrowing or otherwise undermining the definition of torture might deal a body blow to the *corpus juris* that would go beyond the immediate effects on the mentality of torturers and the terror and suffering of their victims. I shall argue that the rule against torture operates in our law as an archetype—that is, as a rule which has significance not just in and of itself, but also as the embodiment of a pervasive principle. As the notion of a legal archetype is new and unfamiliar, I shall spend some time outlining and illustrating the jurisprudence that is necessary to make sense of this idea.

Finally, in Part V, I will extend the analysis to consider the relation between prohibitions on torture and the idea of the Rule of Law—specifically, the idea of subjecting the modern state to legal control. In this Part, I will consider also the application of the argument in Part IV to the role played by the prohibition on torture in international law and, in particular, the international law of human rights.

II. Definitions

A. The texts and the prohibitions

The law relating to torture comprises a variety of national, regional, and international norms. The basic provision of human rights law is found in the International Covenant on Civil and Political Rights (which I shall refer to as 'the Covenant'):

Article 7. No one shall be subjected to torture or to cruel, inhuman or degrading treatment or punishment. [. . .]

Article 4 of the Covenant provides that '[i]n time of public emergency which threatens the life of the nation and the existence of which is officially proclaimed, the States Parties to the present Covenant may take measures derogating from their obligations under the present Covenant to the extent strictly required by the exigencies of the situation,' but Article 4 also insists that no derogation from Article 7 may be made under that provision. The United States ratified the Covenant in 1994, though with the following reservation:

> [T]he United States considers itself bound by Article 7 to the extent that 'cruel, inhuman or degrading treatment or punishment' means the cruel and unusual treatment or punishment prohibited by the Fifth, Eighth, and/or Fourteenth Amendments to the Constitution of the United States.[12]

Besides the Covenant, we also have to consider a more specific document: the international Convention Against Torture (which I shall call 'the Convention') requires each state to 'take effective legislative, administrative, judicial or other measures to prevent acts of torture in any territory under its jurisdiction,' and to 'ensure that all acts of torture are offences under its criminal law.'[13] Again there is a non-derogation provision (implying in effect that states must establish an absolute rather than a conditional ban on torture),[14] and again the United States has made a similar reservation (relating not to torture, however, but to cruel, inhuman, and degrading treatment) in its ratification of the Convention.[15] Also the Convention does what the Covenant does not do (and also what other regional human rights instruments such as the European Convention on Human Rights do not do),[16] namely, it attempts a definition of torture:

> For the purposes of this Convention, torture means any act by which severe pain or suffering, whether physical or mental, is intentionally inflicted on a person for

---

[12] S. Exec. Rep. No. 102–23, at 22 (1992).

[13] Convention Against Torture, Articles 2(1) and 4(1). The Convention also imposes requirements of non-*refoulement* of refugees likely to face torture (Article 3), requirements to ensure that officials are prohibited from using torture and that the prohibition is included in their training (Article 10), requirements promptly to investigate allegations of torture (Article 12), to protect complainants against further ill-treatment or retaliation (Article 13), and to secure a right to redress and compensation for victims of torture (Article 14). There is also a prohibition on the use in legal proceedings or proceedings before any official tribunal of 'any statement which is established to have been made as a result of torture . . . except against a person accused of torture as evidence that the statement was made' (Article 15).

[14] Ibid., Article 2(2): 'No exceptional circumstances whatsoever, whether a state of war or a threat or war, internal political instability or any other public emergency, may be invoked as a justification of torture.'

[15] See S. Exec. Rep. No. 101–30, at 29–31 (1990).

[16] The relevant provisions of the European Convention on Human Rights are as follows. Article 3: 'No one shall be subjected to torture or to inhuman or degrading treatment or punishment.' Article 15: 'In time of war or other public emergency threatening the life of the nation any High Contracting Party may take measures derogating from its obligations under this Convention to the extent strictly required by the exigencies of the situation. . . . No derogation from . . . Article 3 . . . shall be made under this provision.'

such purposes as obtaining from him or a third person information or a confession, punishing him for an act he or a third person has committed or is suspected of having committed, or intimidating or coercing him or a third person, or for any reason based on discrimination of any kind, when such pain or suffering is inflicted by or at the instigation of or with the consent or acquiescence of a public official or other person acting in an official capacity. It does not include pain or suffering arising only from, inherent in or incidental to lawful sanctions.[17]

This definition, particularly in its reference to the *intentional* infliction of *severe* pain, was the starting point of the recent American discussion by Jay Bybee and others.

In pursuance of its obligations under the Convention, the United States has enacted legislation forbidding torture outside the United States by persons subject to U.S. jurisdiction.[18] The anti-torture statute[19] makes it an offense punishable by up to 20 years' imprisonment to commit, conspire, or attempt to commit torture (adding that this is punishable by death or life imprisonment if the victim of torture dies as a result). The statute defines torture as follows:

As used in this chapter,... 'torture' means an act committed by a person acting under the color of law specifically intended to inflict severe physical or mental pain or suffering (other than pain or suffering incidental to lawful sanctions) upon another person within his custody or physical control.[20]

And there is an additional definition of 'severe mental pain and suffering' in terms of 'prolonged mental harm' resulting from the threat of death or physical torture or the use of mind-altering substances on oneself or others.[21]

Finally, there are the Geneva Conventions, which deal with the treatment of various categories of vulnerable individuals in circumstances of armed conflict.[22] The best-known provision is Article 17 of the Third Geneva Convention, which provides that '[n]o physical or mental

---

[17] Convention Against Torture, Article 1(1).

[18] It is assumed that ordinary provisions of criminal and constitutional law sufficiently prohibit torture within the United States.

[19] 18 USC 2340A. (2000).   [20] 18 USC 2340(1).   [21] Ibid., (2).

[22] Geneva Convention for the Amelioration of the Condition of the Wounded and Sick in Armed Forces in the Field, opened for signature August 12, 1949 (Geneva Convention I); Geneva Convention for the Amelioration of the Condition of Wounded, Sick and Shipwrecked Members of Armed Forces at Sea, opened for signature August 12, 1949 (Geneva Convention II); Geneva Convention Relative to the Treatment of Prisoners of War, opened for signature August 12, 1949, (Geneva Convention III); Geneva Convention Relative to the Protection of Civilian Persons in Time of War, opened for signature August 12, 1949 (Geneva Convention IV).

torture, nor any other form of coercion, may be inflicted on prisoners of war to secure from them information of any kind whatever.'[23] In addition the four Geneva Conventions share a common Article—Article 3—which provides, among other things, that

Persons taking no active part in the hostilities, including members of armed forces who have laid down their arms...shall in all circumstances be treated humanely.... [T]he following acts are and shall remain prohibited at any time and in any place whatsoever with respect to the above-mentioned persons:...violence to life and person, in particular murder of all kinds, mutilation, cruel treatment and torture...[and] outrages upon personal dignity, in particular humiliating and degrading treatment.[24]

Common Article 3 applies to all the persons whom the Geneva Conventions protect, i.e. not just prisoners of war, but wounded soldiers, shipwrecked sailors, detained members of irregular forces, and so on.

These provisions, together with the protections that law routinely provides against serious assault and abuse, add up to an interlocking set of prohibitions on torture. They are what I have in mind when I refer, in what follows, to 'the prohibition on torture' (or 'the rule against torture'), though sometimes one element in this interlocking set, sometimes another, will be most prominent.

B. Rules and backgrounds

What is the effect of these provisions? How should we approach them as lawyers? Should we use the same strategies of interpretation as we use elsewhere in the law? Or is there something special about the prohibitions on torture that requires us to treat them more carefully or considerately? These are the questions that will occupy us throughout the remainder of this chapter.

I want to begin this discussion by considering the scope and application of the prohibitions on torture. John Yoo has suggested that the Geneva Conventions, read literally, apply to some captives or detainees but not others, and that they do not apply to Al Qaeda and Taliban detainees in the war on terror.[25] What sort of reading, what sort of

---

[23] Geneva Convention III, Article 17.
[24] Geneva Convention I, Article 3; Geneva Convention II, Article 3; Geneva Convention III, Article 3; Geneva Convention IV, Article 3.
[25] See Yoo and Delahunty, 'Application of Treaties and Laws to Al Qaeda and Taliban Detainees,' at pp. 1–2.

interpretive approach, is necessary to reach a conclusion like that? To answer this question, it is helpful to invoke the old distinction between *malum prohibitum* and *malum in se.*

On the *malum prohibitum* approach, we may think about the text of a given legal provision as introducing a prohibition into what was previously a realm of liberty. Consider the introduction of parking regulations as an analogy. Previously, we were at liberty to park our cars wherever we liked along the streets of our small town. But one day the town government adopts parking regulations, which restrict how long one can park. So now our freedom is limited. Those limits are defined by the regulations that have been enacted: the text of the regulations determines the extent of the prohibition, and we must consult the text to see exactly what is prohibited and what is left free. Over-parking is a *malum prohibitum* offense: it consists in violating the letter of the regulations. If the regulations had not been enacted, there would be no offense. And the corollary of this is that anything that is not explicitly prohibited by the regulations remains as free as before.

Compare this with a *mala in se* approach. Some things are just wrong, and would be wrong whether positive law prohibited them or not. What legal texts do is articulate this sense of wrongness and fill in the details to make that sense of wrongness administrable.[26] So, for example, a statute prohibiting murder characteristically does not make unlawful what was previously permissible; it simply expresses more clearly the unlawfulness of something which was impermissible all along. It follows that consulting the statutory provision in a rigidly textualist spirit might be inappropriate; it certainly would be inappropriate if one were assuming that anything not prohibited by the exact terms of the text must be regarded as something that one was entirely free to do.

The distinction between *malum prohibitum* and *malum in se* might seem to depend on natural law theory, in which some of law's functions are related to the administration of natural law prohibitions while other functions are related to positive law's capacity to generate new forms of requirement.[27] But that need not be so. All we need in order to make

---

[26] For an excellent discussion of what this involves, see Finnis, *Natural Law and Natural Rights*, pp. 281–90.

[27] See for example Blackstone, *Commentaries*, Vol. I, Ch. 2.: '[C]rimes and misdemesnors, that are forbidden by the superior laws, and therefore stiled mala in se, such as murder, theft, and perjury...contract no additional turpitude from being declared unlawful by the inferior legislature. For that legislature in all these cases acts only...in subordination to the great lawgiver, transcribing and publishing his precepts.'

sense of *malum in se* and distinguish it from *malum prohibitum*, is that there be some normative background to the prohibition which the law can recognize. That normative background may be a shared moral sense or it may be some sort of higher or background law, natural law perhaps or international law, to which the municipal legislature has some sort of obligation. Admittedly the distinction is not clear-cut. Even in our parking example, there will have been *some* background reasons governing the way it was appropriate to park even before the regulations were introduced: don't park unsafely or inconsiderately, don't block access, and so on; these reasons do not evaporate when the explicit regulations are introduced.

Now let us apply these distinctions to the rule against torture. I think it is obvious that the anti-torture statute cannot be construed according to model (i). It does not represent the first introduction of a prohibition into an area that was previously unregulated, and in which everyone was at liberty to do what he liked. On the contrary, the statute fulfilled a treaty obligation that the U.S. already had under the Convention, and it also applied and extended the spirit of existing criminal law and an existing and legally recognized sense of the inherent wrongness of torture. Something similar is true of the Convention itself and also of the Covenant. They themselves are not to be conceived as new pieces of positive international law encroaching into what was previously an area of freedom. Like all human rights instruments, they have what Gerald Neuman has called a suprapositive aspect: they are 'conceived as reflections of nonlegal principles that have normative force independent of their embodiment in law, or even superior to the positive legal system.'[28] Though formally they are treaties and, as such, based on the actual consent of the states that are party to them, they also represent a consensual acknowledgment of deeper background norms.

It might be thought that the Geneva Conventions are a special case because they are designed to limit armed conflict, and *there* the background or default position is indeed that anything goes. That is, it may be thought that armed forces are *normally* at liberty to do anything they like to enemy soldiers in time of war—bombard, shoot, kill, wound, maim, and terrify them—and that the function of the Geneva Conventions is precisely to introduce a degree of unprecedented regulation into what would otherwise be a horrifying realm of freedom.[29] So

---

[28] See Neuman, 'Human Rights and Constitutional Rights,' at 1892.
[29] I discuss and criticize this view in Chapter 4, above, at pp. 106–10.

it may be thought that approach (i) *is* appropriate for that case, and that therefore we have no choice but to consult the strict letter of the texts of the Conventions to see exactly what is prohibited and what has been left as a matter of military freedom. John Yoo's memorandum approached the Geneva Conventions in that spirit. He implied that absent the Conventions we would be entitled *to do anything we like* to enemy detainees; grudgingly, however, we must accept some limits (which we ourselves have negotiated and signed up for); but we have signed up for no more than the actual texts stipulate; when we run out of text, we revert to the default position, which is that we can do anything we like. Now—Yoo's reasoning continued—it so happens that as a result of military action in Afghanistan and Iraq, certain individuals have fallen into our hands as captives who do not have the precise attributes that the Geneva Conventions stipulate for persons protected by the prohibitions they have introduced. So—Yoo concluded—the textual prohibitions on maltreatment do not apply to these detainees, and we are back in the military default position: we can do with them whatever we like.[30]

Yoo's approach was wrong in three ways. First, its narrow textualism embodied a bewildering refusal to infer anything along the lines of *ejusdem generis* from the existing array of categories of detainees that *are* covered. The Geneva Conventions reiterate elementary protections (e.g. against torture) for one category of detainee, the same protections for a second category of detainee, the same protections for a third category of detainee, and so on. And now we have detainees in a fourth category that does not exactly fit the literal terms of the first three. It might be reasonable to think that the earlier categories give us a sense of *how to go on*—how to apply the underlying rule—in new kinds of cases. That is how lawyers generally proceed. (That is how we infer, for example, that the Third Amendment to the U.S. Constitution applies to the quartering of sailors, marines, and airmen as well as soldiers.)[31] But Professor Yoo proceeded as though the methods of analogy and inference and reasoned elaboration—the ordinary tools of our lawyerly trade—were utterly inappropriate in this case.

---

[30] This impression is based on Yoo and Delahunty, 'Application of Treaties and Laws to Al Qaeda and Taliban Detainees,' at p. 11 ('[M]embers of the al Qaeda organization do not receive the protection of the laws of war'); ibid. at p. 34: ('[C]ustomary international law of armed conflict in no way binds, as a legal matter, the President or the U.S. Armed Forces concerning the detention or trial of members of al Qaeda and the Taliban').

[31] See Schmidt, 'Could a CIA or FBI Agent Be Quartered in Your House During a War on Terrorism, Iraq or North Korea?' 645–6. But see Amar, 'Some New World Lessons for the Old World,' 493, arguing that omission of sailors is deliberate.

In any case, it is simply not true that the texts of the Geneva Conventions represent the first introduction of prohibitions into a previously unregulated area. The Geneva Conventions, like the Convention Against Torture and the International Covenant, respond to a strongly felt and well-established sense that certain abuses are beyond the pale, whether one is dealing with criminal suspects, political dissidents, or military detainees, and that they remain beyond the pale even in emergency situations or situations of armed conflict. There are certain things that are not to be done to human beings and these international instruments represent our acknowledgment by treaty of that fact. Professor Yoo asserted that the United States could not regard itself as bound by norms of customary international law or even *ius cogens* norms of international law: he thought that we must regard ourselves as having a free hand to deal with detainees except to the extent that the exact letter of our treaty obligations indicated otherwise.[32] But such argument as he provided for this assertion relied on the *mala prohibita* approach, which (as we have already seen) is inherently inappropriate in this area.

Thirdly, Yoo's analysis lacks a sense of the historic context in which the conventions governing captives and detainees were negotiated and reformulated in 1949. It has been suggested by Scott Horton that the modern Geneva Conventions are in part a response to experience during the Second World War.[33] The conventions then existing were vulnerable to being treated as a patchwork of rules with piecemeal coverage, encouraging Germany, for example, to argue that it could exclude from the benefit of their coverage various categories of detainee such as commandos, partisans, pilots engaged in acts of terror, and those who fought on behalf of a new kind of political entity (the Soviet Union). The conventions were renegotiated in 1949 precisely to prevent this sort of exploitation of loopholes, and it was quite discouraging to see American lawyers arguing for the inapplicability of the Conventions on grounds that are strikingly similar—new forms of warfare, new types of non-state entity, etc.—to those invoked by Germany in that period.

C. The interest in clear definitions

Let me turn now to the word 'torture' itself in these various provisions of municipal and international law. Some of the provisions—the Covenant for example—offer no elucidation of the meaning of the term. The

---

[32] Idem.   [33] See Horton, 'Through a Mirror, Darkly.'

ICCPR

Covenant just prohibits torture; it does not tell us what torture is. It seems to proceed on the theory that we know it when we see it,[34] or that we can recognize this evil using a sort of visceral 'puke' test.[35] In a 1990 Senate hearing, a Department of Justice official observed that 'there seems to be some degree of consensus that the concept involves conduct the mere mention of which sends chills down one's spine.'[36] Is this sufficient?

Well, the trouble is that we seem to puke or chill at different things. The response to the Abu Ghraib scandal indicated that there is far from a consensus in this matter. Muslim prisoners were humiliated by being made to simulate sexual activity with one another; they were beaten and their fingers and toes were stomped on; they were put in stress postures, hooded and wired, in fear of death if they so much as moved; they were set upon or put in fear of attack by dogs. Was this torture? Most commentators thought it was, but one or two American newspapers resisted the characterization, preferring the word 'abuse.'[37] Some conservative commentators suggested that what happened was no worse than hazing.[38] I guess they wanted to convey the point that if we use the word 'torture' to characterize what Americans did in Abu Ghraib prison, we might be depriving ourselves of the language we need to condemn much more vicious activities.[39]

[34] This was what Justice Potter Stewart said, notoriously, about obscenity in *Jacobellis v. Ohio* 378 US 184 (1964).

[35] Oliver Wendell Holmes once said that a law was not unconstitutional unless it made him want to 'puke.' (Letter to Harold Laski, October 23, 1906) in Howe (ed.), *Holmes-Laski Letters*, Vol. 2, p. 188.

[36] Hearing Before the Committee on Foreign Relations, United States Senate (101st Congress, Second Session) January 30, 1990 (Washington D.C.: U.S. Government Printing Office, 1990), p. 13.

[37] Geoffrey Nunberg, 'Don't Torture English to Soft-pedal Abuse,' *Newsday*, May 20, 2004, p. A50: '"Torture is torture is torture," Secretary of State Colin Powell said this week in an interview.... That depends on what papers you read. The media in France, Italy and Germany have been routinely using the word "torture" in the headings of their stories on the abuses in the Abu Ghraib prison.... But the American press has been more circumspect, sticking with vaguer terms such as "abuse" and "mistreatment." [T]hey may have been taking a cue from Defense Secretary Donald Rumsfeld. Asked about torture in the prison, he said, "What has been charged so far is abuse, which is different from torture. I'm not going to address the 'torture' word."'

[38] Frank Rich, "The War's Lost Weekend," *New York Times*, May 9, 2004, p. 2: '[A] former Army interrogation instructor, Tony Robinson, showed up on another Fox show...to assert that the prison photos did not show torture. "Frat hazing is worse than this," the self-styled expert said.'

[39] Similarly, Sir Gerald Fitzmaurice had asked this in his dissent in *Ireland v. United Kingdom* 25 Eur.Ct.H.R. 1 (1977), at 21: if the techniques that the British had used in Northern Ireland in the early 1970s—sleep deprivation, hooding, white noise, stress

Unlike the Covenant, the Convention Against Torture and the American anti-torture statute offer more than just a term and an appeal to our intuitions. Their definitional provisions offer us ways of analyzing torture in terms of what lawyers sometimes call 'the elements of the offense.' These provisions analyze torture as a certain sort of action, performed in a certain capacity, causing a certain sort of effect, done with a certain intent, for a certain purpose, and so on. Some of the elements in the statute and the Convention are the same: both, for example, distinguish torture from pain or suffering incidental to lawful sanctions. But debates about definition are likely to result from differences in the respective analyses: for example, the analyses of 'mental torture' are slightly different.[40] Now, I shall have some harsh things to say about the quest for definitional precision in the remainder of this section and the next. But nothing that is said in what follows is supposed to preclude or even frown upon the sort of analysis or analytic debate that I have just mentioned.

Instead, I want to consider a kind of complaint about definitional looseness (and an attempt to narrow the definition of 'torture') that goes well beyond this business of analyzing the elements of the offense. Both the Convention and the anti-torture statute refer to the intentional infliction of *severe* pain or suffering. Since pain can be more or less severe, evidently the word 'severe' is going to be a site for contestation as between those who think of torture in very broad terms and those who think of it in very narrow terms. The word looks as though it is supposed to restrict the application of the word 'torture.' But as with a requirement to take 'reasonable care' or a constitutional prohibition on 'excessive' bail, we are not told what exactly the restriction is, i.e. we are not told where exactly severity is on the spectrum of pain, and thus where the prohibition on torture is supposed to kick in.

We might ask: What is the point of this restriction? Why narrow the definition of torture so that it covers only *severe* pain? Some theorists have not sought a restrictive definition of this kind. Jeremy Bentham worried about 'the delusive power of words' in discussions of torture.[41]

---

postures, and severe limitations on food and water—were 'to be regarded as involving torture, how does one characterize e.g. having one's finger-nails torn out, being slowly impaled on a stake through the rectum, or roasted over an electric grid?'

[40] It is a weakness of this chapter that I say almost nothing about the definition of mental torture. That silence is not supposed to condone what the various Bush administration memoranda have said on that topic.

[41] Jeremy Bentham, *Of Torture*, manuscript reproduced in Twining, 'Bentham on Torture,' p. 308.

But his own definition was very wide. 'Torture,' he said, 'is where a person is made to suffer any violent pain of body in order to compel him to do something, which done...the penal application is immediately made to cease.'[42] Though he used the term 'violent' to qualify 'pain,' Bentham meant it to refer to the suddenness of the pain's onset, rather than its severity. So, for example, he applied the word 'torture' to the case of 'a Mother or Nurse seeing a child playing with a thing which he ought not to meddle with, and having forbidden him in vain pinches him till he lays it down.'[43] Evidently he thought the interests of clarity would be served by defining torture to include *all* cases of the sudden infliction of pain for the sake of immediate coercion. It is not surprising that Bentham would take this view. He was, after all, a consequentialist and the currency of his consequentialism is pain as well as pleasure. He thought the meanings of words should be adjusted to facilitate a substantive debate about which inflictions of pain are justified and which not, rather than assuming in advance that everything taken in by the term 'torture' is necessarily illegitimate and then debating the definitional ramifications of *that*.[44]

Most modern discussions, however, work from the opposite assumption. They begin with the sense that there is something seriously wrong with torture—even if it is not absolutely forbidden—and they approach the issue of definition on that basis. Marcy Strauss, for example, complains that

Amnesty International and others speak of torture when describing sexual abuse of women prisoners, police abuse of suspects by physical brutality, overcrowded cells, the use of implements such as stun guns, and the application of the death penalty.[45]

And she worries about the consequences of this casual expansion of the term: '[I]f virtually anything can constitute torture, the concept loses some of its ability to shock and disgust....[U]niversal condemnation may evaporate when the definition is so all encompassing.'[46] She implies

---

[42] Ibid., p. 309.   [43] Ibid., p. 310.

[44] Bentham said: 'There is no approving [torture] in the lump, without militating against reason and humanity: nor condemning it without falling into absurdities and contradictions' (ibid., p. 337).

[45] Strauss, 'Torture,' at 215.

[46] Ibid., 215. Some aspects of Professor Strauss's concern are unconvincing. She complains: 'Taking a particularly boring class is often referred to as 'torture' by many students' (ibid., 208 n. 16). But it's silly to object to figurative uses. The same students who complain that Professor Strauss's classes are 'torture' will also say that her term-tests are

that we have a certain normative investment in the term—we use it to mark a serious moral judgment—and we ought to adjust our definition so as to protect that investment.

What do those who are dissatisfied with the vagueness of the phrase 'severe pain or suffering' have in mind? What would be a more determinate definition? Presumably what they want is some sort of *measure* of severity, something to turn the existing vague standard into an operationalized rule. In section D we shall consider Jay Bybee's attempt to provide just such a measure. But here I want to discuss the very idea of such precision. What motivates the demand for a precise measure of severity? We know that in almost all cases when we replace a vague standard with an operationalized rule, the cost of diminishing vagueness is an increase in arbitrariness. We specify a number, but cases just a little bit below that number might seem to be excluded arbitrarily.[47] That sort of arbitrariness can itself reflect badly on the normative investment we have in the relevant provision. So why is this cost worth risking?

I think the argument in favor of precision goes like this. If the terms of a legal prohibition are indeterminate, the person to whom the prohibition is addressed may not know exactly what is required of him, and he may be left unsure as to how the enforcement powers of the state will be used against him. The effect is to chill that person's exercise of his liberty as he tries to avoid being taken by surprise by enforcement decisions.

Is this a compelling argument? We should begin by recalling that the prohibitions on torture contained in the Geneva Conventions and in the Convention Against Torture apply in the first instance to the state and state policy. Is the state in the same position as the ordinary individual in having a liberty-interest in bright lines and an interest in not having

---

murder, but that is not a ground for worrying about the legal definition of 'murder.' We should remember too that there is a common figurative use of the word 'torture' in law— the idea of 'torturing' the meaning of a word or a phrase to yield a particular result. For example, in *Terry v. Ohio*, 392 U.S. 1 (1968), at 16: '[I]t is nothing less than sheer torture of the English language to suggest that a careful exploration of the outer surfaces of a person's clothing all over his or her body in an attempt to find weapons is not a "search." '

[47] Cf. Kennedy, 'Form and Substance,' at 1689: 'Suppose that the reason for creating a class of persons who lack capacity is the belief that immature people lack the faculty of free will. Setting the age of majority at 21 years will incapacitate many but not all of those who lack this faculty. And it will incapacitate some who actually possess it. From the point of view of the purpose of the rules, this combined over and underinclusiveness amounts not just to licensing but to requiring official arbitrariness. If we adopt the rule, it is because of a judgment that this kind of arbitrariness is less serious than the arbitrariness and uncertainty that would result from empowering the official to apply the standard of "free will" directly to the facts of each case.'

its freedom of action chilled?[48] I don't think so: we set up the state to preserve and enlarge *our* liberty; the state itself is not conceived as a beneficiary of our libertarian concern.[49] Even the basic logic of liberty seems inapplicable. In the case of individuals, we invoke the old principle that everything which is not expressly forbidden is permitted. But it is far from clear that this should be a principle applying to the state.[50] Indeed, constitutional doctrine often works the other way round: in the United States, everything which is not explicitly entrusted to the federal government is forbidden to it; it does not have plenary power.[51]

However, although the prohibition on torture is intended in the first place as a constraint on state policy, soldiers and other officials do also have an interest as individuals in anticipating war crimes or other prosecutions. The anti-torture statute purports to fulfill the United States' obligations under the Convention Against Torture by defining torture as an individual criminal offense. Many would say that inasmuch as that statute threatens serious punishment, there is an obligation to provide a tight definition. If that obligation is not fulfilled, they will say, then lenity requires that the defendant be given the benefit of whatever ambiguity we find in the statute.[52]

Against all this, we need to remember that the charge of torture is unlikely to come 'out of the blue' or to be entirely unanticipated by someone already engaged in the deliberate infliction of pain on prisoners: 'I am shocked—*shocked!*—to find that "water-boarding" or squeezing prisoners' genitals or setting dogs on them is regarded as torture.' For remember we are talking about a particular element in the definition of torture: the severity element. The potential defendant we have

---

[48] There is an English doctrine that the state or its officials should be treated just like any other individual. See Dicey, *Introduction to the Study of the Law of the Constitution*, pp. 114–15. But see Harlow and Rawlings, *Law and Administration*, pp. 38–47 and Waldron, *The Law*, pp. 39–42, suggesting that this doctrine is now generally and rightly in disrepute.

[49] See also the argument of Chapter 10, below.

[50] Cf. Harris, 'The Third Source of Authority,' 633–6.

[51] Is the state entitled, as we sometimes think individuals are entitled (cf. Hayek, *The Constitution of Liberty*, pp. 139–40, to a legally predictable environment in which it can exercise whatever liberty it has? I was intrigued by a suggestion to this effect by Justice Scalia in his dissent in *Rasul v. Bush* 124 S.Ct. 2686 (U.S. Jun 28, 2004) at 2706: 'Normally, we consider the interests of those who have relied on our decisions. Today, the Court springs a trap on the Executive, subjecting Guantanamo Bay to the oversight of the federal courts even though it has never before been thought to be within their jurisdiction—and thus making it a foolish place to have housed alien wartime detainees.'

[52] Cf. *Staples v. United States*, 511 U.S. 600, 619 (1994) (lenity requires that 'ambiguous criminal statute[s] . . . be construed in favor of the accused').

to consider is one who already knows that he is inflicting considerable pain; that is his intention. It seems to me that the working definition of torture in this statute already gives him all the warning he needs that there is a huge risk in relying upon some casuistry about 'severity' as a defense against allegations of torture.

One other point in this connection. Even if there is a legitimate interest on the part of potential individual defendants in having a precise definition of torture, it is evident from the tone and direction of the Bybee and Yoo memoranda that they were attempting to exploit this in the interests of *state* policy. They appealed to the principle of lenity, ostensibly in the interests of the individual soldier, but actually in order to foster a particular sort of definition which is more easily exploited in the interests of the state. Defining the sort of bright line that lenity calls for has the effect of carving out space for an official policy of coercive interrogation that would be much more problematic if the administration did not present itself as pandering to the individual interest in definitions. As we think about the case that can be made for precision, we need to remember that this is how any argument based on lenity is likely to be exploited.

Let us return now to the general question of precision in law. One way of thinking about the need for precise definition involves asking whether the person constrained by the norm in question—state or individual—has a legitimate interest in pressing up as close as possible to the norm, and thus a legitimate interest in having a bright line rule stipulating exactly what is permitted and exactly what is forbidden by the norm. The idea is that the offense may be understood as a threshold on a continuum of some sort; the subject knows that he is on the continuum and that there is a point at which his conduct might be stigmatized as criminal; and the question is whether he has a legitimate interest in being able to move as close to that point as possible. If he *does* have such an interest, then he has an interest in having the precise location of the crucial point on the continuum settled clearly in advance.[53] If he does not, then the demand for precision may be treated less sympathetically.

An example of someone who has such a legitimate interest might be a taxpayer who says, 'I have an interest in arranging my affairs to lower my tax liability much as possible, so I need to know exactly how much I can deduct for entertainment expenses.' Another example is the driver who

---

[53] Some material here is adapted from Waldron, 'Vagueness in Law and Language,' 534–6.

says, 'I have an interest in knowing how fast I can go without breaking the speed limit.' For those cases, there does seem to be a legitimate interest in having clear definitions. Compare them however to some other cases: the husband who says, 'I have an interest in pushing my wife round a bit and I need to know exactly how far I can go before it counts as domestic violence'; or the professor who says 'I have an interest in flirting with my students and I need to know exactly how far I can go without falling foul of the sexual harassment rules.' *There are some scales one really shouldn't be on,* and with respect to which one really does not have a legitimate interest in knowing precisely how far along the scale one is permitted to go.

Let us apply this to the prohibition on torture. In regard to torture, is there an interest in being able to press up against clear and bright line rules, analogous to the taxpayer's interest in pushing his entertainment deductions to the limit or the driver's interest in going at exactly 65 mph? The most common argument goes like this. Interrogators have an interest in being as coercive as possible and in being able to inflict as much pain as possible short of violating the prohibition on torture. After all, the point of interrogation is to get people to do what they don't want to do and for that reason pressure of some sort is necessary, to elicit information that the subject would rather not reveal. Since interrogation *as such* is not out of bounds, it may be thought interrogators obviously do have a legitimate interest in being on a continuum of pressure and it is just a question of how far along that continuum we ought to allow them to go. If we fail to specify that point, we might chill *any* use of pressure in interrogation, even what might turn out to be legitimate pressure.[54]

What is wrong with that argument? Well, it is true that all interrogation *puts pressure* on people to reveal what they would rather not reveal. But there are ways in which the law can pressure people while still respecting them as persons and without using any form of brutality. And it is quite wrong to suggest that these forms of respectful pressure are on the same scale as torture, just further down the line. So for example: a hostile witness under *sub poena* on the witness stand (in a case where there is no issue of self-incrimination) is *pressured* to answer questions truthfully and give information that he would rather not give. The examination or cross-examination may be grueling, and there are

---

[54] See Bradley Graham, 'Abuse Probes' Impact Concerns the Military; Chilling Effect on Operations Is Cited,' *Washington Post*, August 29, 2004, p. A20.

penalties of contempt for refusing to answer and perjury for answering falsely. These are forms of pressure, but they are not on a continuum of brutality with torture. Certainly the penalties for contempt and perjury are coercive: they impose unwelcome costs on certain options otherwise available to the witness.[55] Even so, there is a difference of quality, not just a difference of degree, between the coercion posed by legally established penalties for non-compliance and the sort of force that involves using pain to twist the agency and break the will of the person being interrogated. I doubt that Professor Dershowitz would agree with what I have just said. Dershowitz argues that

> imprisoning a witness who refuses to testify after being given immunity is designed to be punitive—that is painful. Such imprisonment can, on occasion, produce more pain...than non-lethal torture. Yet we continue to threaten and use the pain of imprisonment to loosen the tongues of reluctant witnesses.[56]

The mistake lies in Dershowitz's equation of 'punitive' and 'painful.' Though pain can be used as punishment, only the crudest utilitarian would suggest that all punishment is necessarily painful. Imprisonment works coercively because it is undesired, not because it is, in any literal sense, painful. And it is the literal sense that is needed if we are to say that torture and imprisonment are on a continuum.

Some have argued that there might be a continuum of discomfort associated with interrogation, and we are entitled to ask how far along *that* continuum we are permitted to be. After all, we are not required to provide comfortable furniture for the subject of interrogation to sit in. So, one might ask, 'Are we required to ensure that the back of the chair that the subject sits in does not hurt his back or that the seat is not too hard?' If the answer is 'No,' then surely that means we *are* on a continuum with some of the techniques of interrogation that are arguably torture, like the Israeli technique of shackling a subject in a stress position in a very small tilted chair (the *Shabeh*).[57]

To answer this, it is important to understand that torture is a crime of specific intent: it involves the use of pain deliberately and specifically to *break the will* of the subject. Failing to provide a comfortable armchair for the interrogation room may or may not be permissible; but it is in a different category from specifically choosing or designing furniture in a way calculated to break the will of the subject by the excruciating

---

[55] For a more complete account of coercion see Nozick, 'Coercion,' p. 101.
[56] Dershowitz, *Why Terrorism Works*, p. 147.
[57] See Public Committee, *Torture in Israel/Palestine: The Black Book*, pp. 113 and 125.

pain of having to sit in it. That latter choice *is* on a continuum with torture—and I want to question whether that's a continuum an official has a legitimate reason for being on. The former choice—failing to provide an armchair or a cushion—is not.

If I am right about all this, then there is every reason to be suspicious about the attempts made in the Bush administration memoranda to pin down a definition of torture and to try to stipulate precisely the point of severity at which the prohibition on torture is supposed to kick in. Far from being the epitome of good lawyering, this enterprise represented an attempt to weaken or undermine the prohibition by portraying it as something like a speed limit, which we are entitled to push up against as closely as we can, and in regard to which there might even be a margin of toleration which a good-hearted enforcement officer, familiar with our situation and its exigencies, might be willing to recognize. These suspicions are confirmed I think by the character of the actual attempts that have been made to give the prohibition on torture this sort of spurious precision.

D. The Bybee memorandum

I have talked a little about the August 2002 memorandum written for the CIA and the White House by Jay Bybee, chief of the Office of Legal Counsel in the Department of Justice.[58] Now I want to focus on it more specifically. Its 50 pages give what some have described as the most lenient interpretation conceivable to the anti-torture Convention and other anti-torture provisions.[59] (Though subsequently it was officially repudiated, in fact large sections of the Bybee memorandum were incorporated more or less verbatim into what is now known as the Haynes memorandum, produced by a working group set up in the Pentagon in January 2003 to reconsider interrogation methods.)[60]

---

[58] Bybee, 'Standards of Conduct for Interrogation.'

[59] See, e.g. Angell, 'Ethics, Torture, and Marginal Memoranda,' at 559 and Traynor, 'Citizenship in a Time of Repression,' 5. See also Confirmation Hearing on the Nomination of Alberto R. Gonzales to be Attorney-General of the United States: Hearing Before the S. Comm. on the Judiciary, 109th Cong. 534–7 (2005) (statement of Harold Hongju Koh, Dean of Yale Law School) (describing the Bybee memorandum as 'perhaps the most clearly erroneous legal opinion I have ever read,' as offering 'a definition of torture so narrow that it would have exculpated Saddam Hussein,' and as 'a stunning failure of lawyerly craft').

[60] Haynes, 'Counter-Resistance Techniques.' For discussion of the relation between the Bybee and the Haynes memoranda, see Herman Schwartz, 'Judgeship Nominees; Twisting the Law on Interrogating Detainees,' *Newsday*, August 18, 2004, p. A39.

According to Bybee, it is plain that the relevant legal provisions prohibit as torture 'only extreme acts' and penalize as torture 'only the most egregious conduct.' He notes that the American ratification of the Convention Against Torture was accompanied by the following understanding:

The United States understands that, in order to constitute torture, an act must be a deliberate and calculated act of an extremely cruel and inhuman nature, specifically intended to inflict excruciating and agonizing physical or mental pain or suffering.[61]

In discussions at the time, it was suggested that the word 'torture' should be 'reserved for extreme deliberate and unusually cruel practices, for example, sustained systematic beatings, application of electric currents to sensitive parts of the body and tying up or hanging in positions that cause extreme pain.'[62] Administration officials added that such 'rough treatment as generally falls into the category of "police brutality," while deplorable, does not amount to "torture."'[63] Although it is conceded that this sort of brutality might amount to 'inhuman treatment,' Bybee noted that the U.S. made a reservation to that part of the Convention Against Torture too, saying that the prohibition on inhuman treatment does not apply to the extent that it purports to prohibit anything permitted by the U.S. Constitution as currently interpreted.[64] From all this, Bybee concluded that 'certain acts may be cruel, inhuman, or degrading, but still not produce pain and suffering of the requisite intensity to fall within [the] proscription against torture.'[65]

It is clear, then, what sort of continuum Bybee thought interrogators should be on, in relation to which they would have an interest in knowing the precise location of a torture threshold. It is not a continuum of pressure, nor is it a continuum of unwelcome penalties, nor is it a continuum of discomfort. Interrogators, in Bybee's opinion, are permitted to work somewhere along the continuum of *the deliberate infliction of pain* and the question is: 'Where is the bright-line along that continuum where the specific prohibition on torture kicks in?' If we could not answer this, Bybee feared, our interrogators might be chilled from *any*

---

[61] Bybee, 'Standards of Conduct for Interrogation,' p. 16.   [62] Ibid., pp. 16–17.
[63] These comments came in the comments that accompanied the Administration's recommendation of the treaty to the Senate—U.S. Reservations, Declarations, and Understandings, Convention Against Torture and Other Cruel, Inhuman or Degrading Treatment or Punishment, 138 Cong. Rec. S17486–01 (daily ed. October 27, 1990).
[64] Bybee, 'Standards of Conduct for Interrogation,' p. 17.   [65] Ibid., at p. 1.

sort of deliberate infliction of pain on detainees. And that, he implied, would be a bad thing. Or, he noted, American interrogators are not very strongly or categorically prohibited from working somewhere along a continuum of *inhuman and degrading treatment*, and the question is where precisely on that continuum of inhumanity and degradation do they cross the line into torture. People needed to have a sense of where that line is, Bybee suggested, for if they did not, they might be chilled from *any* sort of infliction of degradation or from *any* sort of inhuman treatment. And we would not want that to be chilled, or at any rate we would not want that to be chilled as much as torture is.

I leave readers to decide whether this was a legally reputable exercise. Bybee purported to draw some support from the jurisprudence of the European Convention of Human Rights (ECHR), even though the ECHR does not apply to the United States. The leading case is one I have already mentioned—*Ireland v. United Kingdom* (1977),[66] in which the European Court of Human Rights assessed methods of interrogation used by the British in Northern Ireland. Five techniques of what was called 'interrogation-in-depth' were at issue: sleep deprivation, hooding, white noise, stress postures, and severe limitations on food and water. In holding that the use of these methods did not constitute torture, the Court observed:

> it appears...that it was the intention that the Convention, with its distinction between 'torture' and 'inhuman or degrading treatment', should by the first of these terms attach a special stigma to deliberate inhuman treatment causing very serious and cruel suffering.[67]

Bybee read that as reinforcing his view that 'torture' and 'inhuman or degrading treatment' should be regarded as different zones on the same scale, with the first being an extreme version of the second.[68] (This is important because, as I said at the outset, the methods condemned in *Ireland v. UK* were very similar to the methods that were being used in Guantánamo Bay at the time Bybee wrote his memorandum.)

However, Bybee failed to mention two things about this decision. He failed to mention that in *Ireland v. UK*, the European Commission of Human Rights[69] concluded that the five techniques, in combination

---

[66] *Ireland v. United Kingdom* 25 Eur.Ct.H.R. 1 (1977).   [67] Ibid., para 168.

[68] Bybee, 'Standards of Conduct for Interrogation,' p. 29. See also pp. 283–4, below.

[69] The European Commission of Human Rights is like an investigating magistracy for the European Court of Human Rights. Its report is presented first to the Court, and then the Court makes a final determination.

were torture and not just inhuman or degrading treatment. Both parties to the suit and a minority of judges on the Court accepted this determination.[70] More important, Bybee failed to mention that *both* categories of conduct were and are *absolutely* prohibited under the ECHR. The five techniques may not have been termed torture by the Court; but since the Court determined that their application treated the suspects in an inhuman and degrading manner, they were prohibited nonetheless. The fact that there is a verbal distinction in Article 3 of the ECHR between torture and inhuman and degrading treatment does not mark an effective normative distinction in the ECHR scheme, so far as the strength and immovability of these prohibitions is concerned. The Article 15 non-derogation provision applies to both, and the Court's comments about 'special stigma' do not affect that.[71] One does not have to be a legal realist to reckon that since the normative consequences of the discrimination between torture and inhuman and degrading treatment are different as between the ECHR and the American torture statute (together with its background in the Convention Against Torture), any extrapolation of support from an approach taken under the former is likely to be suspect.

All that goes to the general character of Bybee's analysis. Let us turn now to its detail. How, exactly, did Bybee propose to pin down a meaning for 'severe pain or suffering'? It is all very well to talk about 'requisite intensity,' but how are we to determine the appropriate measure of severity? With a dictionary in hand, Bybee essayed a proliferation of adjectives—'excruciating,' 'agonizing,' and the like. But they all seemed to defy operationalization in the same way: the intensity, the severity, the agonizing or excruciating character of pain are all subjective and to a certain extent inscrutable phenomena.[72] One thing Bybee said, in an attempt to give the definition of torture a somewhat less phenomenological basis, was that 'the adjective "severe" conveys that the pain or

---

[70] Dissenting Judge Zekia said this was an issue on which the Court should have deferred to the fact-finder (i.e. the Commission), especially when its finding was uncontested by the parties.

[71] Indeed, had the Court been confronted with the situation Bybee thought *he* was confronted with—a situation in which there is a weaker prohibition on abuse that is merely inhuman, degrading, and cruel than there is on torture—I think it is unlikely that the Court would have rejected the Commission's characterization of the five techniques as torture.

[72] Cf. Strauss, 'Torture,' 211: 'Defining torture based on the degree of pain is also fruitless. The amount of physical abuse that causes "significant" pain cannot be measured objectively, and would provide little guidance to interrogators.'

suffering must be of such a high level of intensity that the pain is difficult for the subject to endure.'[73] But that is not going to give him the distinction he wants. Presumably that is the whole point of *any* pain imposed deliberately in cruel and inhuman interrogation, not just the extreme cases Bybee wants to isolate.

A more promising approach involves drawing on statutes governing medical administration, where Bybee said that attempts to define the phrase 'severe pain' had already been made. He wrote this:

Congress's use of the phrase 'severe pain' elsewhere in the United States Code can shed more light on its meaning.... Significantly, the phrase 'severe pain' appears in statutes defining an emergency medical condition for the purpose of providing health benefits. (see, e.g., 8 U.S.C. §1369 (2000); 42 U.S.C. §1395w-22 (2000); id. §1395x (2000); id. § 1395dd (2000); id. §1396b (2000); id. §1396u-2 (2000). These statutes define an emergency condition as one 'manifesting itself by acute symptoms of sufficient severity (including *severe pain*) such that a prudent lay person, who possesses an average knowledge of health and medicine) could reasonably expect the absence of immediate medical attention to result in—placing the health of the individual ... (i) in serious jeopardy, (ii) serious impairment to bodily functions, or (iii) serious dysfunction of any bodily organ or part.' Id. §1395w-22(d)(3)(B) (emphasis added). Although these statutes address a substantially different subject from §2340, they are nonetheless helpful for understanding what constitutes severe pain.[74]

From this, Bybee concluded that 'physical pain amounting to torture must be equivalent in intensity to the pain accompanying serious physical injury, such as organ failure, impairment of body function, or even death.'[75]

It is hard to know where to start in criticizing this 'analysis.' One could comment on the strange assumption that a term like 'severe pain' takes no color from its context or from the particular purpose of the provision in which it is found, but that it unproblematically means the same in a medical administration statute (with the purposes characteristically associated with statutes of this kind) as it does in an anti-torture statute (with the purposes characteristically associated with statutes of that kind). Never mind that the latter provision is intended to fulfill our international obligations under the Convention, while the former addresses the resource problems of

---

[73] Bybee, 'Standards of Conduct for Interrogation,' p. 5.   [74] Ibid., pp. 5–6.
[75] Ibid., p. 6.

our quite peculiar health care regime. Bybee thought the medical administration statute could still cast some light on the definition of torture.

Even that glimmer of light flickers out when we consider a couple of glaring defects of basic logic in the detail of the analysis itself. First, the statutory provision that Bybee quoted uses conditions (i) through (iii) to define the phrase 'emergency condition,' not to define 'severe pain.' The medical administration statute says that severe symptoms (including severe pain) add up to an emergency condition if conditions (i), (ii), or (iii) are satisfied. But since the anti-torture statute does not use the term 'emergency condition,' conditions (i) to (iii) are irrelevant to its interpretation.[76] Secondly, Bybee's analysis reversed the causality implicit in the medical administration statute: that statute refers to the likelihood that a severe condition will *lead to* organic impairment or dysfunction if left untreated, whereas what Bybee inferrred from it was that pain counted as severe only if it was associated with (which is naturally read as 'caused by') organic impairment or dysfunction.

The quality of Bybee's legal work here was a disgrace when one considers the service to which this analysis is being put. Bybee is an intelligent man, these were obvious mistakes, and the Office of Legal Counsel—as the agency charged with special responsibility for the legal integrity of executive action—had a duty to take care with this most important of issues.[77] Bybee's mistakes distorted the character of the legal prohibition on torture and strove to create an impression in his audience that there was more room for the lawful infliction of pain in interrogation than a casual acquaintance with the anti-torture statute might suggest. Fortunately someone in administration felt that he had gone too far: this part of Bybee's memorandum was not incorporated into the Haynes memorandum which took on board most of the rest of it, and much of the Bybee approach to the definition of torture appears to have been rejected by the administration in its most recent deliverances on the subject.[78]

[76] Using these conditions to define 'severe pain' would be like taking the following statement—'A dog (particularly a large dog) is a Dalmatian if it has a white coat with black spots'—to imply that the definition of 'large dog' required a white coat and black spots. I am grateful to Bill Dailey for this analogy.

[77] For a clear and accessible account of the responsibility of the Justice Department's Office of Legal Counsel, see Goldsmith, *The Terror Presidency*, pp. 32–9.

[78] Ibid., p. 153. See Neil A. Lewis, 'U.S. Spells Out New Definition Curbing Torture,' *New York Times*, January 1, 2005, p. A1.

III. Absolutes

A. Legal contingency: is nothing sacred?

I now want to step back from all this and ask: What is it about these definitional shenanigans that seems so disturbing? After all, we know there is an element of contingency and manipulation in the definition of any legal rule. As circumstances change, amendments in the law or changes of interpretation seem appropriate.[79] Legal prohibitions are not set in stone. Changing the definition of offenses or reinterpreting open-ended phrases is part of the normal life of any body of positive law. Why should the law relating to torture be any different?

Well for one thing, we seem to be dealing in this case with not just fine-tuning but a wholesale attempt to gut our commitment to a certain basic norm. As I mentioned earlier, the Bybee memorandum maintained that *none* of the legislation enacted pursuant to the Convention Against Torture could be construed as applying to interrogations authorized under the President's Commander-in-Chief powers.[80] It does not matter what the legislative definition of torture is; those who act under Presidential authority in time of war cannot be construed as covered by it; any attempt to extend prohibitions on torture to modes of interrogation authorized by the President would be unconstitutional.[81] This was not just tinkering with the detail of positive law; it amounted to a comprehensive assault on our traditional understanding of the whole legal regime relating to torture. Even so we still have to acknowledge that the life of the law is sometimes to change or reinterpret whole paradigms (particularly in constitutional law, where we suddenly decide that a whole area of lawmaking thought out-of-bounds is in-bounds or vice versa).[82] Why is it so shocking in this instance?

---

[79] See also the discussion in the Introduction and in Chapter 2 of this book.

[80] Bybee, 'Standards of Conduct for Interrogation,' pp. 35–6: 'Section 2340A may be unconstitutional if applied to interrogations undertaken of enemy combatants pursuant to the President's Commander-in-Chief powers. We find that in the circumstances of the current war against al-Qaeda and its allies, prosecution under Section 2340A may be barred because enforcement of the statute would represent an unconstitutional infringement of the President's authority to conduct war.'

[81] Bybee, 'Standards of Conduct for Interrogation,' p. 35: 'Congress may no more regulate the President's ability to detain and interrogate enemy combatants than it may regulate his ability to direct troop movements on the battlefield.'

[82] See for example the discussion in *Planned Parenthood of Southeastern Pennsylvania v. Casey*, 505 U.S. 833 (1992) at 861–6 of cases like *West Coast Hotel Co. v. Parrish*, 300 U.S. 379 (1937) which overruled whole swathes of existing constitutional doctrine.

The question can be generalized. Law in all its features and all the detail of its terms and application is contingent on politics and circumstances—that's the lesson of legal positivism. Nothing is beyond revision or repudiation. Why then do we have this sense that something *sacred* is being violated in the Bybee memo or in John Yoo's arguments or in the proposal Alan Dershowitz invites us to consider? Can a provision of positive law *be* sacred, in anything approaching a literal sense, so that it is wrong to even touch or approach its formulation? Is there a literal meaning of 'sacred' in this secular age?

Some among the drafters of the European Convention seemed to think so. I am not usually one for citing legislative history, but in this case it is instructive. The following motion was proposed in the *travaux préparatoires* for the ECHR in 1949 by a United Kingdom delegate, a Mr F.S. Cocks:

[T]he Consultative Assembly takes this opportunity of declaring that all forms of physical torture . . are inconsistent with civilized society, are offences against heaven and humanity, and must be prohibited. It declares that this prohibition must be absolute, and that torture cannot be permitted for any purpose whatsoever, neither for extracting evidence, for saving life nor even for the safety of the State. It believes that it would be better even for society to perish than for it to permit this relic of barbarism to remain.[83]

Lamenting the rise of torture in the twentieth century, Mr Cocks added this in his speech moving this proposal:

I feel that this is the occasion when this Assembly should condemn in the most forthright and absolute fashion this retrogression into barbarism. I say that to take the straight beautiful bodies of men and women and to maim and mutilate them by torture is a crime against high heaven and the holy spirit of man. I say it is a sin against the Holy Ghost for which there is no forgiveness.[84]

Mr Cock's fellow delegates applauded his sentiments—nobody disagreed with his fierce absolutism on this issue—but they thought this was inappropriate to include in their report. And you can see their point. It's all very well to talk about 'the sin against the Holy Ghost'[85] and 'crimes against high heaven and humanity,' but these are not exactly legal ideas,

---

[83] Council of Europe, *Collected Edition of the 'Travaux Préparatoires' of the European Convention on Human Rights*, Vol. II (August–November 1949), pp. 36–40.

[84] Ibid., p. 40. (I would like to acknowledge Peters, *Torture*, pp. 145–6 (1985) for this reference.) See also the discussion of the use of religious ideas in Chapter 8, below.

[85] The reference is to Mark 3:29 and Luke 12:10; but those passages seem to indicate that the sin against the Holy Ghost is a form of blasphemy or denial.

and it's unlikely that they resonate even with my good-hearted readers let alone steely-eyed lawyers in the Justice Department.

So: can we make sense—without resorting to religious ideas—of the idea of a non-contingent prohibition, a prohibition so deeply embedded that it cannot be modified or truncated in this way?

There are some fairly well-known ways of conceiving the indispensability of certain legal norms. We have already considered the distinction between *mala in se* and *mala prohibita*. There is H.L.A. Hart's idea of 'the minimum content of natural law'—certain kinds of rule that a legal system couldn't possibly do without, given humans as they are and the world as it is.[86] Less philosophically, we understand that there are things that in theory lawmakers *might* do but are in fact very unlikely to do: 'If a legislature decided that all blue-eyed babies should be murdered, the preservation of blue-eyed babies would be illegal; but legislators must go mad before they could pass such a law, and subjects be idiotic before they could submit to it.'[87]

There are also various legal ways to diminish the vulnerability of a norm to revision, redefinition, or repeal: (i) A rule might be entrenched in a constitution as proof against casual or bare majoritarian alteration. (ii) A provision of international law might acquire the status of *ius cogens*, as proof against the vagaries of consent that dominate treaty-based international law. (iii) A human rights norm might be associated with an explicit non-derogation clause as proof against the thought that it is all right to abandon rights-based scruples in times of emergency. In fact there have been attempts in all three of these ways to insulate the prohibition against torture against the contingency of positive law: the Eighth Amendment to the U.S. Constitution might be taken as an example of (i), the identification of international norms against torture as *ius cogens* is an example of (ii),[88] and of course the non-derogation

---

[86] See Hart, *The Concept of Law*, pp. 193–200. Hart, 'Positivism and the Separation of Law and Morals,' 623, put it this way: '[S]uppose that men were to become invulnerable to attack by each other, were clad perhaps like giant land crabs with an impenetrable carapace...In such circumstances (the details of which can be left to science fiction) rules forbidding the free use of violence would not have the necessary nonarbitrary status which they have for us, constituted as we are in a world like ours. At present, and until such radical changes supervene, such rules are so fundamental that if a legal system did not have them there would be no point in having any other rules at all.'

[87] Cf. Dicey, *Introduction to the Study of the Law of the Constitution*, p. 33 (quoting Stephen, *Science of Ethics*, p. 143).

[88] See *In re Estate of Ferdinand E. Marcos* 25 F.3d 1467, 1475 (9th Cir. 1994): 'The right to be free from official torture is fundamental and universal, a right deserving of the highest stature under international law, a norm of *jus cogens*. The crack of the whip,

provisions of the European Convention on Human Rights in relation to Article 3 of that Convention offer a fine example of (iii).[89] But all of these are themselves positive law devices and they too are subject to manipulation. Constitutions can be reinterpreted: for example, the Eighth Amendment prohibition on cruelty is construed nowadays not to cover any maltreatment that is not imposed as punishment in the context of the criminal process.[90] And even usually rights-respecting regimes can limit or weaken their support for apparently compelling international obligations by definitional or other maneuvers: Professor Yoo argued that the U.S. President could not be bound by customary international law; Judge Bybee said that there could be no legislative constraints on the President's ability to authorize torture; and the English Court of Appeal recently determined that the prohibition in the Convention Against Torture on using information obtained by torture (e.g. for the purpose of determining whether an individual's detention as a terrorist suspect was justified) applied only to information that had been extracted by torture conducted by agents of the detaining state.[91] In the end, a legal prohibition is only as strong as the moral and political consensus that supports it.

And there's the difficulty. In these troubled times, it is not hard to make the idea of an absolute prohibition on torture or any absolute prohibition look silly, as a matter of moral philosophy. I don't mean that everyone is a consequentialist. There are good deontological accounts of the rule against

---

the clamp of the thumb screw, the crush of the iron maiden, and, in these more efficient modern times, the shock of the electric cattle prod are forms of torture that the international order will not tolerate.'

[89] ECHR, Article 15. Also Article 7 of the Covenant which explicitly states that 'no one shall be subjected to torture or to cruel, inhuman or degrading treatment or punishment,' but Article 4.2 of the Covenant also, and just as explicitly, states that '[n]o derogation' from Article 7 is permitted.

[90] *Ingraham v. Wright* 430 U.S. 651 (1977), which holds that this prohibition applies only to 'punishment imposed as part of the criminal process.'

[91] *A and others v. Secretary of State for the Home Department* [2004] All ER (D) 62 (Aug), Court of Appeal, 11 August 2004: 'The Secretary of State could not rely on a statement which his agents had procured by torture, or with his agent's connivance at torture. He was not, however, precluded from relying…on evidence coming into his hands which had or might have been obtained through torture by agencies of other states over which he had no power of direction.' (This despite the simple and unconditional nature of Convention Against Torture, Article 15: 'Each State Party shall ensure that any statement which is established to have been made as a result of torture shall not be invoked as evidence in any proceedings, except against a person accused of torture as evidence that the statement was made.') This decision of the Court of Appeal was overturned by the House of Lords in *A. (F.C.) and others v. Home Secretary*, House of Lords decision, December 8, 2005.

torture, but they stop short of absolutism:[92] the principle defended by deontologists almost always turns out to be wobbly when sufficient pressure is applied. Even among those who are not already Bentham-style consequentialists, most are moderates in their deontology: they are willing to abandon even cherished absolutes in the face of what Robert Nozick once called 'catastrophic moral horror.'[93] For a culture supposedly committed to human rights, we have amazing difficulty in even conceiving—without some sort of squirm—the idea of genuine moral absolutes. Academics in particular are so frightened of being branded 'unrealistic' that we will fall over ourselves at the slightest provocation to opine that *of course* moral restraints must be abandoned when the stakes are high enough. Extreme circumstances can make moral absolutes look ridiculous; and men in our position cannot afford to be made to look ridiculous.

B. The Dershowitz strategy

This tendency is exacerbated by the way we pose the question of torture to ourselves. Law school classes and moral philosophy classes thrive on hypotheticals that involve grotesque disproportion between the pain that a torturer might inflict on an informant and the pain that might be averted by timely use of the information extracted from him:[94] a little bit of pain from the needles for him versus a hundred thousand people saved from nuclear incineration.[95] Of course after September 11, 2001, the

[92] See, e.g. Nagel, 'Autonomy and Deontology,' pp. 156–7, and Sussman, 'What's Wrong with Torture?' *Philosophy and Public Affairs*. But as Sussman points out (ibid., pp. 2–3) giving an account of inherent wrongness of torture is one thing, giving an account which shows that what is inherently wrong may never in any circumstances be done is another. 'Inherently' does not mean the same as 'absolutely.'

[93] Nozick, *Anarchy, State, and Utopia*, p. 30n: 'The question of whether these side constraints are absolute, or whether they may be violated in order to avoid catastrophic moral horror, and if the latter, what the resulting structure might look like, is one I hope largely to avoid.' See also Kadish, 'Torture, the State and the Individual,' at 346: 'The use of torture is so profound a violation of a human right that *almost* nothing can redeem it—*almost*, because one cannot rule out a case in which the lives of many innocent persons will surely be saved by its use against a single person...' (my emphasis). See also the discussion of 'threshold deontology' in Meisels, *The Trouble with Terror*, p. 174 ff.

[94] Samuel Scheffler has suggested to me in conversation that there is a distinction between hypothetical cases that are designed to test philosophically what our views (about torture, for example) are based on, and hypothetical cases like the ones posed by Alan Dershowitz, which are designed to tempt us away from moral absolutes. (See also the discussion in Chapter 1, above, at pp. 6–7.)

[95] See Dershowitz, *Why Terrorism Works*, p. 132. It is a tradition reaching back to Jeremy Bentham, who writes in a passage quoted in Dershowitz, *Why Terrorism Works*, p. 143:

> Suppose...a suspicion was entertained...that at this very time a considerable number of individuals are actually suffering, by illegal violence inflictions equal in

hypotheticals were beginning to look a little less fantastic. Alan Dershowitz asked: '[W]hat if on September 11 law enforcement officials had "arrested terrorists boarding one of the planes and learned that other planes, then airborne, were heading towards unknown occupied buildings?" Would they not have been justified in torturing the terrorists in their custody— just enough to get the information that would allow the target buildings to be evacuated?'[96] How could anyone object to the use of torture if it were dedicated specifically to saving thousands of lives in a case like this?[97]

Should it worry us that once one goes down this road, the justification of torture—indeed the justification of *anything*—is a matter of simple arithmetic coupled with the professor's ingenuity in concocting the appropriate fact situation? As Seth Kreimer has observed, a sufficiently large fear of catastrophe could conceivably authorize almost any plausibly efficacious government action.[98] The tactics used to discredit absolute prohibitions on torture are tactics that can show in the end, 'to borrow the formula of Dostoevsky's Ivan Karamazov,... [that] everything is permitted.'[99] Dershowitz conceded the point, acknowledging that there was something disingenuous about his own suggestion that judicial torture warrants would be issued to authorize nothing but *non-lethal* torture.[100] If the number of lives that could be saved were twice that of the number necessary to justify non-lethal torture, why not justify lethal torture or torture with *un*sterilized needles? Indeed, why just torture? Why not judicial rape warrants? Why not terrorism itself? The same kind of hypotheticals will take care of these inhibitions as well.

intensity to those which if inflicted by the hand of justice, would universally be spoken of under the name of torture. For the purpose of rescuing from torture these hundred innocents, should any scruple be made of applying equal or superior torture, to extract the requisite information from the mouth of one criminal, who having it in his power to make known the place where at this time the enormity was being practiced, should refuse to do so?

Bentham referred to the anti-torture sentiment here (in the face of this sort of example) as 'blind and vulgar humanity' of those who 'to save one criminal, should determine to abandon 100 innocent persons to the same fate.' (See Twining, 'Bentham on Torture,' 347 ff.)

[96] Dershowitz, *Why Terrorism Works*, p. 477.

[97] Luban, 'Liberalism and the Unpleasant Question of Torture,' 12, has developed an exemplary diagnosis of arguments of this kind: 'The idea is to force the liberal prohibitionist to admit that yes, even he or even she would agree to torture in at least this one situation. Once the prohibitionist admits that,... all that is left is haggling about the price. No longer can the prohibitionist claim the moral high ground;... [s]he's down in the mud with them, and the only question left is how much further down she will go.'

[98] Kreimer, 'Too Close to the Rack and the Screw,' 306.   [99] Idem.

[100] Dershowitz, *Why Terrorism Works*, p. 146.

Still, a mere expression of this concern does not answer Dershowitz's question. Should we not be willing to allow the authorization of torture at least in a 'ticking bomb' case—make it a ticking nuclear bomb in your home town, if you like—where we are sure that the detainee we are proposing to torture has the information that will save thousands of lives and that he will give it up only if subjected to excruciating pain?

For what it is worth, my own answer to this question is a simple 'No.' I draw the line at torture. I suspect that almost all of my readers will draw the line somewhere, to prohibit some actions even under the most extreme circumstances—if it is not torture of the terrorist, they will draw the line at torturing the terrorist's relatives, or raping the terrorist, or raping the terrorist's relatives, all of which can be posited (with a logic similar to Dershowitz's) to be the necessary means of eliciting the information. Then the boot is simply on the other foot: Why is it so easy to abandon one absolute (against torturing terrorists) while remaining committed to other absolutes (against, for instance, raping terrorists' children)? We can all be persuaded to draw the line somewhere, and I say we should draw it where the law requires it, and where the human rights tradition has insisted it should be drawn.

But in any case, one's answer is less important than one's estimation of the question. An affirmative answer is meant to make us feel patriotic and tough-minded. But the question that is supposed to elicit this response is at best silly and at worst deeply corrupt. It is silly because torture is seldom used in the real world to elicit startling facts about particular ticking bombs; it is used by American interrogators and others to accumulate lots of small pieces of relatively insignificant information which may become important only when accumulated with other pieces of similar information elicited by this or other means. And it is corrupt because it attempts to use a far-fetched scenario, more at home in a television thriller than in the real world,[101] deliberately to undermine the integrity of certain moral positions.[102]

---

[101] I am told that the Fox television series *24* sometimes made use of Dershowitz-type scenarios to present acts of torture in a heroic light. See also Teresa Wiltz, 'Torture's Tortured Cultural Roots,' *Washington Post*, May 3, 2005, at p. C1 ('If you're addicted to Fox's *24*, you probably cheered on Jack Bauer when, in a recent episode, he snapped the fingers of a suspect who was, shall we say, reluctant to talk.... Torture's a no-brainer here. Jack's got to save us all from imminent thermonuclear annihilation.'). For an example of the use of Fox's *24* to elicit support for the torture of terrorist suspects by United States interrogators, see Cal Thomas, 'Restrictions Won't Win War on Terror for Us,' *South Florida Sun-Sentinel*, May 4, 2005, at p. 25A.

[102] For a critique by David Luban of the use of these hypotheticals, see n. 97 above.

One set of replies to this question—and to my mind, they are quite convincing replies—say that even if the basic fact-situation is no longer so fantastic (in light of the bizarre horrors of September 11), nevertheless the framing of the hypothetical *is* still far-fetched, inasmuch as it asks us to assume that torture warrants will work exactly as Professor Dershowitz says they should work.[103] The hypothetical asks us to assume that the power to authorize torture will not be abused, that intelligence officials will not lie about what is at stake or about the availability of the information, that the readiness to issue torture warrants in one case (where they may be justified by the sort of circumstances Dershowitz cites) will not lead to their extension to other cases (where the circumstances are somewhat less compelling), that a professional corps of torturers will not emerge who stand around looking for work,[104] that the existence of a law allowing torture in some cases will not change the office-politics of police and security agencies to undermine and disempower those who argue against torture in other cases, and so on.

Professor Dershowitz has ventured the opinion that if his torture-warrant idea had been taken seriously, it is less likely that the abuses at Abu Ghraib prison in Iraq would have occurred.[105] This takes optimism to the point of irresponsibility. What we know about Abu Ghraib and other recent cases is that against the background of any given regulatory regime in these matters, there will be some who are prepared to 'push

---

[103] The best version of this answer comes from Shue, 'Torture,' 124, who points out that precious few real-world cases have the clean precision of the philosopher's hypothetical; the philosophers' cases remain fanciful in their closure conditions and in the assurances we are given that the authority to torture will not expand and will not be abused. See also the discussion in Chapter 2 above, at pp. 41–2.

[104] Kreimer, 'Too Close to the Rack and the Screw,' 322: 'Modern regimes seem to find that torture is most effectively deployed by a corps of trained officers who can dispense it with cold and measured precision, and such bureaucrats will predictably seek outlets for their skills.' See also Luban, 'Liberalism and the Unpleasant Question of Torture,' 15–16: 'Should we create a professional cadre of trained torturers? That means a group of interrogators who know the techniques, who have learned to overcome their instinctive revulsion against causing physical pain, and who acquire the legendary surgeon's arrogance about their own infallibility.'

[105] Dershowitz, 'When Torture Is The Least Evil Of Terrible Options,' p. 20: 'Abu Ghraib occurred precisely because U.S. policy consisted of rampant hypocrisy: our President and Secretary of Defense publicly announced an absolute prohibition on all torture, and then with a wink and a nod sent a clear message to soldiers to do what you have to do to get information and to soften up suspects for interrogation. Because there was no warrant—indeed no official authorization for any extraordinary interrogation methods—there were no standards, no limitations and no accountability. I doubt whether any President, Secretary of Defense or Chief Justice would ever have given written authorization to beat or sexually humiliate low-value detainees.'

the envelope' trespassing into territory that goes beyond what is legally permitted.[106] Moreover there will always be individuals who act in a way that is simply abusive *relative to whatever authorization is given them.* There is, as Henry Shue notes, 'considerable evidence of all torture's metastatic tendency.'[107] In the last hundred years or so it has shown itself not to be the sort of thing that can be kept under rational control. Indeed, *it is already expanding.* The torture at Abu Ghraib had nothing to do with 'ticking bomb' terrorism. It was intended to 'soften up' detainees so that U.S. military intelligence could get information from them about likely attacks by Iraqi insurgents against American occupiers.

The important point is that the use of torture is not an area in which human motives are trustworthy. Sadism, sexual sadism, the pleasure of indulging brutality, the love of power, and the enjoyment of the humiliation of others—these all-too-human characteristics need to be kept very tightly under control, especially in the context of war and terror, where many of the usual restraints on human action are already loosened.[108] If ever there was a case for Augustinian suspicion of the idea that basic human depravity can be channeled to social advantage, this is it. Remember too that we are not asking whether these motives can be judicially regulated in the abstract. We are asking whether they can be regulated in the kind of circumstances of fear, anger, stress, danger, panic, and terror in which, realistically, the hypothetical case must be posed.

Considerations like these might furnish a pragmatic case for upholding the rule against torture as a legal absolute, even if we cannot make a case in purely philosophical terms for a moral absolute.[109] However, I do not want to stop there. Though I think the pragmatic case for a legal absolute is exactly right, in the rest of this chapter I want to explore an additional idea. This is the idea that certain things might be just repugnant to the spirit of our law, and that torture may be one of them.

---

[106] Cf. Kreimer, 'Too Close to the Rack and the Screw,' 322–3: 'Some officials will tend to view their legally permitted scope of action as the starting point from which to push the envelope in pursuit of their appointed task.... The wider the scope of legally permitted action, the wider the resulting expansion of extralegal physical pressure.'

[107] Shue, 'Torture,' 143.

[108] Incidentally, it is worth noting the role that the pornographic character of modern American culture played in determining the sort of images and tableaux that seemed appealing to the torturers at Abu Ghraib. (Is it asking too much to expect that those who 'defend to the death' our right to suffuse society with pornographic imagery might acknowledge this as one of its not-entirely-harmless effects?)

[109] Cf. Gross, 'Are Torture Warrants Warranted?' 1481.

Specifically I want to make and explore the claim that the rule against torture plays an important emblematic role so far as the spirit of our law is concerned.

IV. Archetypes

A. Repugnance to law

Why does the prospect of judicially authorizing torture (whether it is called 'torture' or not) shock the conscience of a scrupulous lawyer? Is it simply that the unthinkable has become thinkable? Or is it something about the specific effect *on law*—perhaps a more systemic corrupting effect—of this abomination's becoming one of the normal items on the menu of practical consideration?

Maybe there are certain things we can imagine justifying in theory but whose permissibility would have such an impact on the rest of the law that it would be a strong or conclusive reason for not permitting them. An analogy I have found helpful in thinking about this is the argument about slavery in *Somerset's case*,[110] made famous in recent jurisprudence by its discussion in Robert Cover's book *Justice Accused*.[111] James Somerset was an African slave belonging to a resident of Virginia, who was brought to England by his master in 1769. Somerset made a bid for freedom, running away from his master, but was apprehended and detained aboard ship for a voyage to Jamaica (where his master proposed to resell him). A writ of habeas corpus was brought on Somerset's behalf, and of course counsel for the detainers argued that the English courts were required to recognize Somerset's slave status and his master's property rights as a matter of private international law. Counsel for the petitioner, though, opposed that argument in terms that I want to draw on. He asked:

[S]hall an attempt to introduce perpetual servitude here to this island [Great Britain] hope for countenance?...[T]he laws, the genius and spirit of the constitution, forbid the approach of slavery; will not suffer it's existence here....I mean, the proof of our mild and just constitution is ill adapted to the reception of arbitrary maxims and practices.[112]

---

[110] *Somerset v. Stewart* 1 Lofft's Rep. 1; 98 Eng. Rep. 499 (1772).
[111] See Cover, *Justice Accused*, pp. 16–17 and 87–8.
[112] *Somerset v. Stewart*, 1 Lofft's Rep. 1; 98 Eng. Rep. 499, at 500 (1772).

After some hesitation, Lord Mansfield agreed with this argument and ordered that Somerset be discharged: '[T]he state of slavery is of such a nature that it is incapable of being introduced on any reasons...but only by positive law....It is so odious, that nothing can be suffered to support it, but positive law.'[113] Lord Mansfield was evidently not denying that there could be a valid law in England establishing slavery. Though he drew on the fact that natural law prohibits slavery, his position was not the classic natural law doctrine '*lex iniusta non est lex*'— that such an edict would be too unjust to deserve the status 'law.' If Parliament established slavery, then slavery would be the law, and English lawyers would just have to put up with the traumatic shock this would deal to the rest of their principles about liberty. The prospect of that shock, though, is one of the things that convinced Lord Mansfield that nothing short of explicit parliamentary legislation could be permitted to require this. The affront to liberty implicit in a person's legal confinement on the basis that he is another man's chattel is 'so high an act of dominion' that nothing but an explicit enactment would do to legitimate it. That is why any attempt to bring it in by the back door—or to bring in its effects so far as liberty is concerned—would have to be resisted.

Something analogous is true of torture. There is no question but that it *could* be introduced into our law, directly by legislation, or indirectly by so narrowing a definition that torture was being authorized *de jure* in all but name. But its introduction—openly (as Alan Dershowitz was contemplating) or surreptitiously (as Jay Bybee seemed to be urging)— would be contrary to 'the genius and spirit' of our law. For there is in the heritage of Anglo-American law a long tradition of rejecting torture and of regarding it as alien to our jurisprudence. True, torture warrants were issued under Elizabeth I and James I. But they were issued in the exercise of prerogative power, not by the courts. Blackstone's comment on this is telling. He observes that the refusal to authorize torture was an early point of pride for the English judiciary:

[W]hen, upon the assassination of Villiers duke of Buckingham..., it was proposed in the privy council to put the assassin to the rack, in order to discover his accomplices; the judges, being consulted, declared unanimously, to their own honour and the honour of the English law, that no such proceeding was allowable by the laws of England.[114]

---

[113] Ibid., at 510.   [114] Blackstone, *Commentaries*, Vol. 4, pp. 257–8.

Actually a case can be made that torture is now to be regarded as alien to *any* system of law. It may *once* have been intimately bound up with the civilian law of proofs,[115] but as Edward Peters observes, '[a]fter the end of the eighteenth century, torture...came to be considered...the supreme enemy of humanitarian jurisprudence...and the greatest threat to law and reason that the nineteenth century could imagine.'[116] Be that as it may, torture is certainly seen by most jurists—or has been seen by most jurists until very recently—as inherently alien to *our* legal heritage.

Thus American judges have always been anxious to distance themselves from what they refer to as 'the kind of custodial interrogation that was once employed by the Star Chamber, by the Germans of the 1930's and early 1940's.'[117]

There have been, and are now, certain foreign nations with governments...which convict individuals with testimony obtained by police organizations possessed of an unrestrained power to seize persons suspected of crimes against the state, hold them in secret custody, and wring from them confessions by physical or mental torture. So long as the Constitution remains the basic law of our Republic, America will not have that kind of government.[118]

Torture is seen as characteristic not of free, but of tyrannical governments:

Tyrannical governments had immemorially utilized dictatorial criminal procedure and punishment to make scapegoats of the weak, or of helpless political, religious, or racial minorities and those who differed, who would not conform and who resisted tyranny.... The rack, the thumbscrew, the wheel, solitary confinement, protracted questioning and cross questioning, and other ingenious forms of entrapment of the helpless or unpopular had left their wake of mutilated bodies and shattered minds along the way to the cross, the guillotine, the stake and the hangman's noose.[119]

Torture may be something that happens elsewhere in the world, but not in a free country, or not in (what used to be referred to as) a Christian country,[120] or at any rate, not under the law of a country like ours. Our

---

[115] See Langbein, *Torture and the Law of Proof.*

[116] Peters, *Torture*, p. 75. See also *Filártiga v. Peña-Irala*, 630 F.2d 876, 890 (2d Cir. 1980) ('[T]he torturer has become—like the pirate and slave trader before him—*hostis humani generis*, an enemy of all mankind.').

[117] *Chavez v. Martinez*, 123 S. Ct. 1994, 2012 (2003) (Stevens, J., dissenting in part).

[118] *Ashcraft et al. v. State of Tennessee.* 322 U.S. 143 (1944).

[119] *Chambers v. Florida* 309 US 227 (1940) at 236–8.

[120] The availability of torture under Muslim governments used to be cited as a ground for the practice of allowing consular officers to deal with American sailors or merchants

constitutional arrangements are spurred precisely by the desire to set the face of our law against such 'ancient evils.'[121]

In section D, I shall pursue the threads of these pervasive concerns more extensively, but first I want to say something more abstract about the model of law that I am assuming when I say that torture is incompatible with the spirit of our legal system.

B. Positivism and legal archetypes

One of the things that people have found consistently wrong with the jurisprudence of legal positivism is that it views law simply as a heap or accumulation of rules, each of which might be amended, repealed, or reinterpreted with little effect on any of the others.[122] This way of viewing law attracts two sorts of criticisms. First, it does not give enough attention to the importance of structure and system in the law, i.e. to the way various provisions, precedents, and doctrines hang together, adding up to a whole that is greater than the sum of its parts.[123] Secondly, the positivist picture fails to give adequate consideration to things other than rules—background principles, policies, purposes, and the like, which pervade the law even if they are not explicitly posited.

charged or embroiled in disputes while in foreign ports. See *In re Ross v. McIntyre*, 140 U.S. 453 (1891) at 462–3:

> The practice of European governments to send officers to reside in foreign countries, authorized to exercise a limited jurisdiction over vessels and seamen of their country, to...assist in adjusting their disputes...goes back to a very early period...In other than Christian countries they were, by treaty stipulations, usually clothed with authority to hear complaints against their countrymen, and to sit in judgment upon them when charged with public offenses. After the rise of Islamism, and the spread of its followers over western Asia and other countries bordering on the Mediterranean, the exercise of this judicial authority became a matter of great concern. The intense hostility of the people of Moslem faith to all other sects, and particularly to Christians, affected all...proceedings had in their tribunals. Even the rules of evidence adopted by them placed those of different faith on unequal grounds in any controversy with them. For this cause, and by reason of...the frequent use of torture to enforce confession from parties accused, it was a matter of deep interest to Christian governments [to] withdraw the trial of their subjects...from the arbitrary and despotic action of the local officials.

[121] *Chambers v. Florida* 309 U.S. 227 (1940) at 236.

[122] There is a similar (though more general) complaint about positivism in Fallon, 'Reflections on the Hart and Wechsler Paradigm,' at 953. Admittedly this is something of a caricature of legal positivism as a philosophical theory. For a positivist's discussion of the inter-connectedness of norms in a legal system, see Raz, *Practical Reason and Norms*, p. 107 ff.

[123] See also Waldron, 'Transcendental Nonsense and System in the Law,' at 24–6.

The latter was of course Ronald Dworkin's criticism,[124] outlined by him as the basis of a new jurisprudence in which law is understood to include not just rules, but also principles, policies, and other sorts of norms and reasons which operate quite unlike rules. These Dworkinian elements operate more like moral considerations; only they are distinctively legal, being emergent features of actually existing legal systems and varying from country to country in a way that moral considerations do not. Policies, principles, and so on operate as background features; they do their work behind the legal rules, pervading doctrine, filling in gaps, helping us with hard cases, providing touchstones for legal argument, and in a sense capturing the underlying spirit of whole areas of doctrine. One of the theoretical claims I want to advance in this chapter is that the prohibition on torture operates not only as a rule, but also just like one of those background features that Dworkin has identified.

On the first criticism—that positivism does not give enough attention to structure and system—what I have in mind is not global holism at the level of the entire *corpus juris*, but more local holisms in particular areas of law.[125] A very easy example would be the way in which the separate provisions of a single statute work together, united by their contribution to a common statutory purpose. A statute is not just a heap of little laws. It operates as an integrated whole and the purpose of the whole statute explains what is being aimed at and also how the enterprise of aiming at that goal or purpose is organized. That, as I said, is an easy example. But it is not hard to understand also how different statutes might work together, or how an array of different precedents and doctrines work together to embody a common purpose or legal policy. Think of the way rules governing contract formation come together with rules about consideration, duty, breach, damages, and liability to add up to a more or less coherent package of market freedom and contractual responsibility. What we might regard as distinct legal provisions interact to constitute a unified realm of legal meaning and purpose, a structured array of norms with a distinctive spirit of its own.

My emphasis here on local structure has something in common with Langdellian formalism.[126] But I do not want to be read as suggesting that there is anything natural or given about the cohering of laws in these various areas. Langdell believed contract law was in and of itself

---

[124] See Dworkin, *Taking Rights Seriously*, pp. 22–31.
[125] See Dworkin, *Law's Empire*, pp. 250–4 on 'local priority.'
[126] For a discussion of Langdellian formalism, see Grey, 'Langdell's Orthodoxy.'

a structure of reason, while some of his followers thought the law of contract embodied the nostrums of *laissez-faire* economics.[127] Modern formalists like Ernest Weinrib believe tort law necessarily embodies the spirit of Aristotlean corrective justice.[128] I do not take such a view. The spirit of a cluster of laws is not something given; it is something we create, albeit sometimes implicitly. It emerges from the way in which, over time, *we* treat the laws *we* have concocted. We begin to see that together the provisions and precedents in question embody a certain principle; our seeing them in that way becomes a shared and settled background feature of the legal landscape; and we begin to construct legal arguments that turn on their embodying that principle.

Let us return for a moment to the easy example—the single statute comprising hundreds of provisions. Sometimes in a complex statute there is a section explicitly stating the statute's purpose. In other cases, the purpose is implicit and we have to infer it from our reading of the statute as a whole. The same two possibilities arise with regard to larger clusters of law. Sometimes we have to infer the underlying principle or policy, e.g. in the way Dworkin suggests in his theory of interpretation.[129] Sometimes, however—and this is where I go beyond Dworkin— there is one provision in the cluster which by virtue of its force, clarity, and vividness expresses the spirit that animates the whole area of law. It becomes a sort of emblem, token, or icon of the whole: I shall say it becomes an *archetype* of the spirit of the area of law in question.[130]

The term 'archetype' is known in philosophy by its Lockean and Jungian senses. For John Locke, the archetype of a general idea was either the particular experience on which that idea was based, or (in the case of a complex idea) the original mental concoction which gave rise to persistence of the general idea.[131] For Carl Jung, an archetype is an image, theme, or idea that haunts and pervades a mind or haunts and pervades our collective consciousness: a sort of 'myth motif.'[132] My use

[127] See the discussion in Duxbury, *Patterns of American Jurisprudence*, pp. 25–32.

[128] See Weinrib, 'Understanding Tort Law,' and Weinrib, *The Idea of Private Law.*

[129] Dworkin, *Law's Empire*, chs 2 and 7.

[130] The phrase 'legal archetype' is not original with me, though its meaning is not usually elaborated as I have elaborated it. See Kirkland, 'Efficacy of Post-divorce Mediation and Evaluation Services,' at 188: 'The best interests standard exists independently of our work as a...legal archetype that can always be utilized as a "true North" type objective standard to guide through individual issues.'

[131] Locke, *Essay Concerning Human Understanding*, pp. 376–7 (Bk II, ch. 31, sect. 3).

[132] Jung conceived of the archetypes as autonomous structures within the collective unconscious. They were pre-existent, self-generating 'forces of nature.' In Jung, *Memories, Dreams, Reflections*, pp. 392–3, Jung wrote: 'The archetype is...an irrepresentable,

of 'archetype' is rather straightforward in contrast to these esoteric bodies of thought. It is closer to Jung's than to Locke's in the following (crude) sense: I am talking about the archetype as something shared by the participants in a given legal system, not just as a feature of an individual mind. On the other hand, my usage is closer to Locke's than to Jung's in repudiating any idea that a given archetype is inevitable or predetermined.

When I use the term 'archetype,' I mean a particular provision in a system of norms which has a significance going beyond its immediate normative content, a significance stemming from the fact that it sums up or makes vivid to us the point, purpose, principle, or policy of a whole area of law. Like a Dworkinian principle, the archetype performs a background function in a given legal system. But archetypes differ from Dworkinian principles and policies in that they *also* operate as foreground provisions. They do foreground work as rules or precedents; but *in doing that work* they sum up the spirit of a whole body of law that goes beyond what they might be thought to require on their own terms. The idea of an archetype, then, is the idea of a rule or positive law provision that operates not just on its own account, and does not just stand simply in a cumulative relation to other provisions, but that also operates in a way that expresses or epitomizes the spirit of a whole structured area of doctrine, and does so vividly, effectively, publicly, establishing the significance of that area for the entire legal enterprise.

I will say more about the way the rule against torture operates as an archetype in our law in section D. But it may help us get our bearings at this stage if I mention some *other* examples of legal archetypes, i.e. provisions or precedents which do this double duty of operating themselves as rules or requirements but also as emblems or icons of whole areas of legal principle or policy.

The best example, I think, is given by the habeas corpus statutes. The importance of 'the Great Writ' is not exhausted by what it does in itself, overwhelmingly important though that is. Habeas corpus is also archetypal of the whole orientation of our legal tradition towards liberty, in the physical sense of freedom from confinement. It is archetypal too of law's set against arbitrariness in regard to actions that impact upon the rights of the subject. This is an aspect of habeas corpus that has often been commented on; it is referred to as 'the bulwark of liberty'[133] and 'the

---

unconscious, pre-existent form that seems to be part of the inherited structure of the psyche and can therefore manifest itself spontaneously anywhere, at any time...'

[133] Anonymous, 'The Suspension of Habeas Corpus During the War of the Rebellion,' at 454.

crystallization of the freedom of the individual'[134] and its constant use is seen as a way of 'slowly educating the bench, the bar, police, prosecutors, and the mass of citizens to the highest traditions of Anglo-American law.'[135] To say that habeas corpus is archetypal is not to say that it is absolute or comprehensive in its coverage. The great writ, as we all know, is subject to suspension and may be limited in its application. Calling it an archetype is without prejudice to all of that: archetypes stand for general principles or policies in the law, and principles or policies may differ in their weight.[136] What is necessary for an archetype is that a foreground provision of the law does this sort of double duty, in regard to its own immediate normative effect and with regard to a broader principle—of whatever strength and extent—that it seems to epitomize.

Another example might be the way in which the Second Amendment's protection of the right of the people to bear arms is archetypal of a general attitude towards gun control. True, the direct impact of the constitutional provision is limited so far as the validity of gun control statutes is concerned: Second Amendment challenges to weapons possession convictions are almost always denied.[137] However, to the extent that the law relating to weapons possession is more permissive here than the gun control law of most other countries, the Second Amendment operates as an archetype of the general spirit of such permissiveness. Though any repeal or truncation of the Amendment would not immediately change the constitutional validity of most gun control legislation, it would undermine the shared sense of a general policy in the law that is tolerant of the possession of firearms. In a recent book, David Williams has invoked something very like this idea of an archetype to explain the importance of the Amendment.[138] Besides their direct legal impact, Williams argues, constitutional provisions also furnish 'large mythic stories addressed primarily to the citizenry as a whole and designed to explain to them their fundamental civic morality.'[139] Williams separates the legal character from the iconic character of

[134] Grant, 'Suspension of the Habeas Corpus in Strikes,' 249.

[135] Pollak, 'Proposals to Curtail Federal Habeas Corpus,' at 66.

[136] Cf. Dworkin, *Taking Rights Seriously*, p. 26.

[137] See, e.g. *U.S. v. Emerson*, 270 F.3d 203 (5th Cir. (Tex.) Oct 16, 2001) and *Silveira v. Lockyer*, 312 F.3d 1052, (9th Cir. (Cal.) Dec 05, 2002). But see more recently *District of Columbia v. Heller*, 128 S.Ct. 2783 (2008).

[138] Williams, *The Mythic Meanings of the Second Amendment*.

[139] Ibid., pp. 4–5; Williams is particularly interested in the fact that there are two myths, not one, associated with the Second Amendment—a revolutionary states' militias myth and an individual frontiersman myth—and these compete for the iconic force of the Amendment itself. I am indebted here to a review of Williams's book by Banner, 'The Second Amendment, So Far,' at 909.

constitutional provisions more sharply than I want to: I am interested in the way legal icons or archetypes function (in a Dworkinian fashion) in the law as well as in the 'folk-loric' reception or popular understanding of the law. But I think both are important in considering legal archetypes. Certainly both are important in considering the archetypal status of the prohibition on torture.

Precedents are sometimes archetypes. The best example is the most obvious. In itself *Brown v. Board of Education*[140] is authority for a fairly narrow proposition about segregation in schools, and its immediate effect in desegregation was notoriously slow and limited. But its archetypal power is staggering and in the years since 1954 it has become an icon of the law's commitment to demolish the structures of *de jure* (and perhaps also *de facto*) segregation, and to pursue and discredit forms of discrimination and badges of racial inferiority wherever they crop up in American law or public administration.[141] Ronald Dworkin famously distinguished between the 'enactment force' and the 'gravitational force' of precedents.[142] The enactment force is the rule laid down in a particular case that *stare decisis* might command other courts to follow. But the gravitational force is more diffuse and extensive: 'Judges and lawyers do not think that the force of precedents is exhausted, as a statute would be, by the linguistic limits of some particular phrase.... [T]he earlier decision exerts a gravitational force on later decisions even when these later decisions lie outside its particular orbit.'[143] While it is true that this gravitational force accumulates as the significance of a precedent develops through a line of cases, nevertheless it is possible that an early member of the relevant series of cases may acquire iconic significance in relation to the gravitational force. It may become an archetype because it was seen at the time as a test case or it was widely regarded as a striking victory or because it seemed to epitomize more clearly than subsequent or earlier cases what was at stake in this area of the law: *Brown* has all these features and it is, so to speak, the archetype of archetypes, so far as case law is concerned.

My examples so far are all from public or constitutional law. But there are archetypes in private law too: the doctrine of adverse possession in property law might be regarded as archetypal of the law's interest in settlement and predictability; the rule about not inquiring into the adequacy of consideration is archetypal of contract law's commitment to

---

[140] 349 U.S. 294 (1954).   [141] See Balkin, 'Brown as Icon,' pp. 3–4.
[142] Dworkin, *Taking Rights Seriously*, p. 110 ff.   [143] Ibid., p. 111.

market-based notions of fairness; *Donoghue v. Stevenson*[144] is archetypal in the English law of negligence; and so on.

Finally a couple of foreign examples (though my first example— habeas corpus—also applies throughout the Anglo-American legal world, not just in the United States). The Canadian Charter of Rights and Freedoms contains a clause that allows the national and provincial legislatures to legislate 'notwithstanding' the operative sections of the Charter.[145] Canadian constitutional lawyers tell us two things about this provision. First, it is very rarely invoked;[146] and secondly that it never-theless captures a very important part of the spirit of Canadian constitu-tionalism, namely a commitment to democratic dialogue between the legislatures and the courts.[147] In this case, the 'notwithstanding' clause is archetypal of the commitment to dialogue, and repealing it might have a substantial and extensive effect on the spirit of dialogue even though the clause is not widely used. I don't mean to suggest that all archetypes have this characteristic of not being widely used in relation to their direct legal impact. I mean simply that an archetype is a provi-sion which both has its own direct legal effect and which also epitomizes something in, on, or around the law that goes beyond the ambit of its own provisions.

A final example, even less familiar to American audiences, comes from my native New Zealand. Considered in itself the Treaty of Waitangi[148] signed in 1840 by representatives of the British Crown and Maori chiefs has limited and disputable significance. But it is now the keystone to a whole area of 'Treaty law' that goes beyond the text of the Treaty itself, and includes numerous more recent statutes, precedents, findings, and settlements. Modern Treaty law embodies an attitude towards race

---

[144] *Donoghue v. Stevenson* [1932] A.C. 562 (H.L.).

[145] Canadian Charter of Rights and Freedoms, section 33: '(1) Parliament or the leg-islature of a province may expressly declare in an Act of Parliament or of the legislature, as the case may be, that the Act or a provision thereof shall operate notwithstanding a provision included in section 2 or sections 7 to 15 of this Charter. (2) An Act or a provi-sion of an Act in respect of which a declaration made under this section is in effect shall have such operation as it would have but for the provision of this Charter referred to in the declaration.'

[146] See Kahana, 'The Notwithstanding Mechanism and Public Discussion.' It has mostly been invoked in the very controversial context of *Québecois* resistance to more general constitutional demands.

[147] See, e.g. Hogg and Bushell, 'The Charter Dialogue between Courts and Legislatures.'

[148] For the text of the Treaty, see <http://www.nzhistory.net.nz/politics/treaty/read-the-treaty/english-text> (last visited on January 13, 2010).

relations and historic injustice in New Zealand that is no older than 1975.[149] But we would be making a mistake if we thought that the 1840 Treaty itself could be discarded without loss or 'read down' in a radical or destructive way. The Treaty of Waitangi is important not just for the understanding of its own provisions but as an epitomizing emblem of a whole range of legal commitments. Take it away, or read it out of existence, and those commitments would take on a different and more fragile and fragmented character.

C. What is the rule against torture archetypal *of*?

My aim in this part of the chapter has been to argue that, individually or collectively, the various prohibitions on torture that we have discussed amount to a legal archetype and that this ought to affect our view of what is at stake when we consider amending them, limiting their application, or defining them out of existence. But what are these provisions archetypal of? What is the policy, principle, or spirit of an area of law that this archetype embodies and conveys? I don't want to say that it is archetypal of a general hostility to torture. That is a matter of its direct content. Its archetypal character goes beyond this to some more abstract principle or policy implicit in our law.

The rule against torture is archetypal of a certain policy having to do with the relation between law and force, and with law's forcefulness with regard to the persons it rules. The prohibition on torture is expressive of an important underlying policy of the law, which we might try to capture in the following way:

Law is not brutal in its operation; law is not savage; law does not rule through abject fear and terror, or by breaking the will of those whom it confronts. If law is forceful or coercive, it gets its way by methods which respect rather than mutilate the dignity and agency of those who are its subjects.

The idea is that even where law has to operate forcefully, there will not be the connection that has existed in other times or places between law and *brutality*. People may fear and be deterred by legal sanctions, they may dread lawsuits, they may even on occasion be literally forced against their will by legal means or by legally empowered officials to do things or go places they would not otherwise do or go to. But even when this

---

[149] See Treaty of Waitangi Act 1975 and *New Zealand Maori Council v. Attorney-General* [1987] 1 NZLR 641 (Court of Appeal).

happens, they will not be herded like cattle or broken like horses; they will not be beaten like dumb animals or treated just as bodies to be manipulated. Instead, there will be an enduring connection between the spirit of law and respect for human dignity—respect for human dignity even *in extremis*, even in situations where law is at its most forceful and its subjects at their most vulnerable. I think the rule against torture functions as an archetype of this very general policy. It is vividly emblematic of our determination to sever the link between law and brutality, between law and terror, and between law and the enterprise of trying to break a person's will.

No one denies that law has to be forceful and final. The finality of law means that it is important for law to prevail in the last analysis, and, as Max Weber puts it, 'the threat of force, and in the case of need its actual use…is always the last resort when others have failed.'[150] But forcefulness can take many forms, and—as I mentioned already in my discussion of compelled testimony—not all of it involves the sort of savage breaking of the will that is the aim of torture and the aim too of many of the cruel, inhuman, and degrading methods that the Bush administration would like to distinguish from torture for the purpose of maintaining lip service to the prohibition. Nor does all legal forcefulness involve the torturer's enterprise (and the enterprise of those who use the cruel, inhuman, and degrading methods that the administration would like to distinguish from torture) of inducing a regression of the subject into an infantile state, where the elementary demands of the body supplant almost all adult thought. The force of ordinary legal sanctions and incentives does not work like that, nor does the literal force of physical control and confinement. For example, when a defendant charged with a serious offense is brought into a courtroom, he is brought in whether he likes it or not, and when he is punished, he is subject to penalties that are definitely unwelcome and that he would avoid if he could; in these instances there is no doubt that he is subject to force, that he is coerced. But in these cases force and coercion do not work by reducing him to a quivering mass of 'bestial desperate terror,'[151] which is the aim of every torturer (and the aim of those interrogators who would inflict cruel, degrading, and inhuman treatment which they say does not quite amount to torture). So: when I say that the prohibition on torture is an archetype of our determination to draw a line between law and savagery

---

[150] Weber, *Economy and Society*, p. 54.
[151] Arendt, *The Origins of Totalitarianism*, p. 441.

or between law and brutality, I am not looking piously to some sort of paradise of force-free law. I am looking rather to the well-understood idea that law can be forceful without compromising the dignity of those whom it constrains and punishes.[152]

That our law keeps perfect faith with this commitment may be doubted. Defendants are sometimes kept silent and passive in American courtrooms by the use of technology which enables the judge to subject them to electric shocks if they misbehave.[153] Reports of prisoners being 'herded' with cattle prods emerge from time to time.[154] Conditions in our prisons are *de facto* terrorizing and well-known to be so, even if they are not officially approved or authorized; and we know that prosecutors feel free to make use of defendants' dread of this brutalization as a tactic in plea-bargaining.[155] Some would say too that the use of the death penalty represents a residuum of savagery in our system that shows the limits of our adherence to the principle that I am talking about.[156]

All this can be conceded. Now, those who oppose these various kinds of brutality and abuse sometimes do so simply on moral grounds: they mobilize the standard moral outrage that one would expect such practices to evoke. But often they oppose and criticize these practices using moral resources drawn from *within* the legal tradition—constitutional resources in many cases, but also a broader and more diffuse sense that there is an affront to the deeper traditions of Anglo-American law in abuse of this kind. I believe that the familiar prohibition on torture serves as an archetype of those traditions, and it is that archetype that I am trying to bring into focus in this chapter.

---

[152] Those—like Sarat and Kearns, 'A Journey Through Forgetting: Toward a Jurisprudence of Violence'—who maintain dogmatically that law is always violent and that the most important feature about it is that it works its will, in Robert Cover's phrase, 'in a field of pain and death' (Cover, 'Violence and the Word'), will be unimpressed by the distinctions I am making. For them, law's complicity with torture in the cases I have discussed is just business as usual.

[153] See, e.g. Harriet Chiang, 'Justices Limit Stun Belts in Court,' *San Francisco Chronicle*, August 23, 2002, p. A7 and William Glaberson, 'Electric Restraint's Use Stirs Charges of Cruelty to Inmates,' *New York Times*, June 8, 1999, p. A1.

[154] See, e.g. '37 Prisoners Sent to Texas Sue Missouri,' *St. Louis Post-Dispatch* (Missouri), September 18, 1997, p. 3B: 'Missouri prisoners alleging abuse in a jail in Texas have sued their home state and officials responsible for running the jail where a videotape showed inmates apparently being beaten and shocked with stun guns,' and Mike Bucsko and Robert Dvorchak, 'Lawsuits Describe Racist Prison Rife with Brutality,' *Pittsburgh Post-Gazette*, April 26, 1998, p. B1.

[155] Dershowitz, *Why Terrorism Works*, at pp. 147–9.

[156] Sarat and Kearns, 'A Journey through Forgetting,' at pp. 221–3.

D. The rule against torture as an archetype in American law

In this section, I offer a preliminary account of the way in which the prohibition on torture—or rather the interlocking set of prohibitions that I outlined in Part I—operates as an archetype of a more general policy pervading American law. I shall give examples mainly from constitutional law, showing in particular the status of this archetype in relation to Eighth Amendment and Due Process concerns. I shall also say something which is a little less formal about the relation between this archetype and other features of our legal and law enforcement culture, particularly the campaign that has been waged—relatively successfully in recent years—to eliminate police brutality as a normal incident of law enforcement behavior in the United States.

To begin, a word about what we are looking for when we search for evidence of a provision's archetypal status. When I say that the prohibition against torture is archetypal in regard to a given body of law, I don't mean that that body of law is primarily or even mainly concerned with torture. It may have relatively little to do with torture, or it may be concerned with the regulation of a wide range of conduct, in which torture does not figure with any particular prominence. The claim that I am looking to support is more complex. It has two aspects: first, that the body of law in question is pervaded by a certain principle or policy, and second that the prohibition against torture is archetypal of that policy or principle. A claim of the first sort is not easy to verify. It was part of Ronald Dworkin's original argument against modern positivism, that there can be no litmus test for recognizing principles in the law of the type that an H.L.A. Hart-type 'rule of recognition' might provide. A rule of recognition tests for the pedigree of a putative legal norm: how was it enacted and by whom? But such a test of pedigree will not work for the more diffuse principles and policies that Dworkin and we are interested in:

The origin of these as legal principles lies not in a particular decision of some legislature or court, but in a sense of appropriateness developed in the profession and the public over time. Their continued power depends upon this sense of appropriateness being sustained. . . . True, if we were challenged to back up our claim that some principle is a principle of law, we would mention any prior cases in which the principle was cited, or figured in the argument. We would also mention any statute that seemed to exemplify that principle. . . . Unless we could find some such institutional support, we would probably fail to make out our case. . . . Yet we could not devise any formula for testing how much and what kind of institutional support is necessary to make a principle a legal principle.... We argue for a particular principle by grappling with a whole lot of shifting, developing and interacting standards (themselves principles rather than rules) about institutional responsibility, statutory interpretation, the persuasive force of various sorts of precedent, the relation of all these to contemporary moral practices, and hosts of other such standards.[157]

As for the second, it too can be difficult to substantiate. The claim that a given provision is archetypal of a certain policy or principle is in part a subjective one: this is how it strikes the jurist. In some instances, it may be clear that this is not just how it strikes one author, but that this is how it strikes everyone: we all think of this as an archetype. Some of the examples I mentioned earlier—habeas corpus and *Brown v. Board of Education*—are clear instances of uncontested archetypes. But it is not only a matter of the impression one gets. We can give the claim that a certain provision is archetypal a slightly more substantial cast, to the extent that citings or elaborations by courts of the principle or policy in question are sometimes or characteristically accompanied by references to the alleged archetype—perhaps as rhetoric or as image—even when the archetype's immediate function is not in play. So I turn now to a number of areas of American law where, it seems to me, the prohibition on torture features in this way in epitomizing a more pervasive policy of non-brutality.

(i) It has been said of the constitutional prohibition on cruel and unusual punishment that the original impetus for the Eighth Amendment came from the framers' repugnance towards the use of torture, which was regarded as incompatible with the liberties of Englishmen.[158] The primary concern of the drafters was to proscribe ' "torture[s]" and other "barbar[ous]" methods of punishment.'[159] Even for those sentenced to death, the Court has held for more than a century that 'punishments

---

[157] Dworkin, *Taking Rights Seriously*, p. 40. Whether or not these considerations provide the basis for an interesting criticism of Hart's theory of legal recognition is not something we shall consider here. For a sample of the gallons of ink that have been spilled in that controversy, see Raz, 'Legal Principles and the Limits of Law,' p. 73.

[158] *Ingraham v. Wright*, 430 U.S. 651 (1977), at 665 (Powell J., for the Court): 'The Americans who adopted the language of this part of the English Bill of Rights in framing their own State and Federal Constitutions 100 years later feared the imposition of torture and other cruel punishments not only by judges acting beyond their lawful authority, but also by legislatures engaged in making the laws by which judicial authority would be measured.' See also *Estelle v. Gamble*, 429 U.S. 97 (1976), at 102.

[159] *In re Kemmler*, 136 U.S. 436, 447 (1890) ('Punishments are cruel when they involve torture or a lingering death.'). See also Granucci, 'Nor Cruel and Unusual Punishment Inflicted,' at 842.

of torture…and all others in the same line of unnecessary cruelty, are forbidden.'[160] 'Wanton infliction of physical pain' is a formula that is commonly used,[161] and it is used in a way that indicates reference to a continuum on which torture is conceived as the most vivid and alarming point.[162] We see this, for example, in what has been said in our courts about prison rape,[163] about the withholding of medical treatment from prisoners,[164] and about the use of flogging, hitching posts, and other forms of corporal punishment in our prisons.[165] In a similar way, judicial resistance in recent years to the use of corporal punishment in prisons has used the idea of torture as a reference point, even though corporal punishment is not identified necessarily as torture.[166]

(ii) Consider also the role of the prohibition on torture in epitomizing the constitutional requirements of procedural due process. Reference to torture is common in the jurisprudence of due process and

---

[160] *Wilkerson v. Utah*, 99 U.S. 130, 136 (1879).

[161] See e.g. *Furman v. Georgia*, 408 U.S. 238, at 392 and *Kent v. Johnson*, 821 F.2d 1220 ((Mich.) 1987), at 1229.

[162] Also *Holt v. Sarver* 309 F.Supp. 362, at 380, discussing meaning of 'cruel and unusual punishment': 'The term cannot be defined with specificity. It is flexible and tends to broaden as society tends to pay more regard to human decency and dignity and becomes, or likes to think that it becomes, more humane. Generally speaking, a punishment that amounts to torture, or that is grossly excessive in proportion to the offense for which it is imposed, or that is inherently unfair, or that is unnecessarily degrading, or that is shocking or disgusting to people of reasonable sensitivity is a "cruel and unusual" punishment.'

[163] *U.S. v. Bailey*, 444 U.S. 394 (1980), at 423–4 (Blackmun J., dissenting): '[F]ailure to use reasonable measures to protect an inmate from violence inflicted by other inmates also constitutes cruel and unusual punishment. Homosexual rape or other violence serves no penological purpose. Such brutality is the equivalent of torture, and is offensive to any modern standard of human dignity. Prisoners must depend, and rightly so, upon the prison administrators for protection from abuse of this kind.'

[164] *Estelle v. Gamble*, 429 U.S. 97 (1976), at 103: 'An inmate must rely on prison authorities to treat his medical needs; if the authorities fail to do so, those needs will not be met. In the worst cases, such a failure may actually produce physical "torture or a lingering death," [citation omitted] the evils of most immediate concern to the drafters of the Amendment. In less serious cases, denial of medical care may result in pain and suffering which no one suggests would serve any penological purpose.'

[165] The Supreme Court has condemned the practice of handcuffing prisoners to hitching posts as a form of punishment, formal or informal, for disciplinary infractions, citing a Fifth Circuit observation that '[w]e have no difficulty in reaching the conclusion that these forms of corporal punishment run afoul of the Eighth Amendment, offend contemporary concepts of decency, human dignity, and precepts of civilization which we profess to possess.' *Gates v. Collier*, 501 F.2d 1291 (5th Cir.1974), 1306, cited in *Hope v. Pelzer*, 536 U.S. 730 (2002), at 737.

[166] See *Jackson v. Bishop*. 404 F.2d 571 (8th Cir. 1968) (prison use of strap for whipping unconstitutional). See also the excellent discussion in Rubin and Feeley, 'Judicial Policy Making and Litigation against the Government.'

self-incrimination. Principles of procedural due process are expressed by saying things like '[t]he rack and torture chamber may not be substituted for the witness stand,'[167] and the privilege against self-incrimination we are told was designed primarily to prevent 'a recurrence of the Inquisition and the Star Chamber, even if not in their stark brutality.'[168] Here—as with the Eighth Amendment jurisprudence—the point is not to remind us that torture is prohibited, but to use our clear grip on that well-known prohibition to illuminate and motivate other prohibitions that are perhaps less extreme but more pervasive and important in the ordinary life of the law.[169]

The connection between this use of the torture archetype and the non-brutality principle is particularly clear in the opinion of Justice Frankfurter in *Rochin v. California* (1952).[170] In that case, narcotics detectives directed a doctor to force an emetic solution through a tube into the stomach of a suspect against his will. The suspect's vomiting brought up two morphine capsules he had swallowed when he first saw the detectives. The morphine was introduced into evidence, and the suspect was convicted of unlawful possession. The Supreme Court reversed the conviction, holding that '[f]orce so brutal and so offensive to human dignity'[171] was constitutionally prohibited and that there was little difference between forcing a confession from a suspect's lips and forcing a substance from his body. Justice Frankfurter said famously of Mr Rochin's treatment, 'These...are methods too close to the rack and the screw.'[172] Referring to some earlier decisions about the use of

---

[167] *Brown v. Mississippi*, 297 U.S. 278, 285–6 (1936).

[168] *Pennsylvania v. Muniz*, 496 U.S. 582, 596, citing *Ullmann v. United States*, 350 U.S. 422, (1956). Consider also this from *U.S. v. Balsys*, 524 U.S. 666, 701–2 (1998), Justice Ginsburg, dissenting: 'The privilege against self-incrimination, "closely linked historically with the abolition of torture," is properly regarded as a "landmar[k] in man's struggle to make himself civilized"' (citing Griswold, *The Fifth Amendment Today*, 7).

[169] See also *United States v. White* 322 U.S. 694 (1944) 697–8: '[T]he constitutional privilege against self-incrimination...grows out of the high...regard of our jurisprudence for conducting criminal trials and investigatory proceedings upon a plane of dignity, humanity and impartiality. It is designed to prevent the use of legal process to force from the lips of the accused individual the evidence necessary to convict him.... Physical torture and other less violent but equally reprehensible modes of compelling the production of incriminating evidence are thereby avoided.'

[170] 342 U.S. 165 (1952).   [171] Ibid., 174.

[172] The whole passage reads: '[T]he proceedings by which this conviction was obtained do more than offend some fastidious squeamishness or private sentimentalism about combating crime too energetically. This is conduct that shocks the conscience. Illegally breaking into the privacy of the petitioner, the struggle to open his mouth and remove what was there, the forcible extraction of his stomach's contents—this course of

coerced confessions, he went on to talk in general terms about the principle at stake in the condemnation of the coercion in this case:

> These decisions are not arbitrary exceptions to the comprehensive right of States to fashion their own rules of evidence for criminal trials. They are not sports in our constitutional law but applications of a general principle. They are only instances of the general requirement that States in their prosecutions respect certain decencies of civilized conduct.... To attempt in this case to distinguish what lawyers call 'real evidence' from verbal evidence is to ignore the reasons for excluding coerced confessions.... Coerced confessions offend the community's sense of fair play and decency. So here, to sanction the brutal conduct which naturally enough was condemned by the court whose judgment is before us, would be to afford brutality the cloak of law. Nothing would be more calculated to discredit law and thereby to brutalize the temper of a society.[173]

Once again, we don't need to define Mr Rochin's treatment as torture in order to see how the prohibition on torture is key to the Supreme Court's invocation of this more general non-brutality principle to condemn this apparently novel form of coercion. In recent years, the Court has repeated this approach: 'Determining what constitutes unconstitutional compulsion involves a question of judgment: courts must decide whether the consequences of an inmate's choice to remain silent are closer to the physical torture against which the Constitution clearly protects or the de minimis harms against which it does not.'[174] My guess is that if the prohibition on torture itself becomes shaky or uncertain as a legal standard, we will have to find new points of orientation to help us in our application of whatever is left of the non-brutality principle articulated in *Rochin*.

(iii) The importance of the prohibition on torture for the jurisprudence of *substantive* due process is a little less clear. In a rather confusing set of opinions in *Chavez v. Martinez* (2003),[175] a plurality on the Supreme Court rejected the position that torture to obtain relevant information is a constitutionally acceptable law enforcement technique if the information is not introduced at trial. There was considerable disagreement about the facts in *Chavez*, but there seemed to be a consensus that the Court's reliance in other abuse cases on the Fifth Amendment's

---

proceeding by agents of government to obtain evidence is bound to offend even hardened sensibilities. They are methods too close to the rack and the screw to permit of constitutional differentiation.' Ibid., 172.

[173] Ibid., at 173–4.   [174] *McKune v. Lile*, 536 U.S. 24, 26 (2002).
[175] 538 U.S. 760, 773 (2003).

Self-Incrimination Clause 'do[es] not mean that police torture or other abuse that results in a confession is constitutionally permissible so long as the statements are not used at trial.'[176] As Justice Kennedy put it, '[a] constitutional right is traduced the moment torture or its close equivalents are brought to bear. Constitutional protection for a tortured suspect is not held in abeyance until some later criminal proceeding takes place.'[177] So I think one can say at least this: if there is anything to the substantive due process idea, the claim that torture for any purpose is unconstitutional comes close to capturing the minimum.

Seth Kreimer has taken all this a little further with the suggestion that the prohibition on torture should be understood as connected with the constitutional protection of bodily integrity and autonomy interests.[178] One of the reasons physical torture is constitutionally out of the question, Kreimer says, is that the constitution protects bodily integrity against invasion[179] and physical torture always involves such an invasion. Indeed he cites anti-slavery provisions as relevant in this regard:

In American law before the Civil War, one of the defining differences between slavery and other domestic relations was precisely that the body of the slave was subject to the master's 'uncontrolled authority'; physical assault could yield no legal redress. Indeed, the standard form of a legal suit for freedom was an action for battery against the purported master. A constitutional prohibition of slavery brings with it a presumption that the bodies of citizens are subject to neither the 'uncontrolled authority' of the state nor that of any private party.[180]

Likewise with autonomy. Kreimer argues that torture is constitutionally suspect for the same reason all assaults on autonomy are suspect:

The pain of torture by design negates the vision of humanity that lies at the core of a liberal democracy. Justice Kennedy recently set forth the constitutional importance of the 'autonomy of self' in *Lawrence v. Texas*....Torture seeks to shatter that autonomy. Torture's evil extends beyond the physical; extreme pain totally occupies the psychic world; the agony of torture is designed to make

---

[176] Ibid. Also Justice Stevens said the type of brutal police conduct involved 'constitutes an immediate deprivation of the prisoner's constitutionally protected interest in liberty.' (Ibid. at 784 (Stevens, J., concurring in part and dissenting in part).

[177] 236. Ibid. at 789–90 (Kennedy, J., concurring in part and dissenting in part).

[178] Kreimer, 'Too Close to the Rack and the Screw.'

[179] See, e.g. *Cruzan v. Director of Minnesota Department of Health*, 497 U.S. 261, 287 (1990) (O'Connor, J., concurring): 'Because our notions of liberty are inextricably entwined with our idea of physical freedom and self-determination, the Court has often deemed state incursions into the body repugnant to the interests protected by the Due Process Clause'—cited by Kreimer, 'Too Close to the Rack and the Screw,' at 296.

[180] Ibid., 295–6.

choice impossible. Effective torture is intended to induce the subject to abandon her own volition and become the instrument of the torturer by revealing information. Such government occupation of the self is at odds with constitutional mandate.[181]

Now, the immediate point of Kreimer's discussion is to refute Alan Dershowitz's suggestion that any constitutional prohibition on torture is actually quite limited in its operation and that Dershowitz's own proposal for judicial torture warrants may not pose any great constitutional difficulty. Kreimer's purpose is to highlight the resources available in our constitutional tradition for attacking the use of torture that Dershowitz is contemplating. But it is worth also considering how the argument might be pushed in the opposite direction: and that is what I am doing here. The constitutional resources that might be used by Kreimer to oppose torture might also be understood as constitutional resources whose security depends upon the integrity of the prohibition on torture. Undermine that integrity, and our conception of the constitutional scheme as something which *as a whole* protects dignity, autonomy, and bodily liberty begins to unravel.

(iv) It is not only in the decisions of the courts that we find an array of doctrines and principles epitomized by the prohibition on torture. We find it also in regard to the general culture of law enforcement. 'The third degree' used to be a pervasive feature of the culture of policing. The fact that it has now largely disappeared from the culture of policing represents an enormous change in that culture.[182] It is not just a matter of a few changes in positive law or in the regulations with which police behavior is disciplined. To eliminate this sort of violence (once it is established), you need to change the entire basis on which police officers are trained to respond (and hold themselves and each other ready to respond) in dangerous or threatening situations. It is a matter of changing a whole ethos—patterns of training, supervision, camaraderie, peer support, conceptions of good and bad policing as shared among low-ranking officers, and the expectations of the public. Moreover it cannot be done piecemeal: it requires a broad-fronted transformation of attitude, impulse, and expectation. You can't just have a bit of restraint here and a bit of abuse there; the prohibition needs to be incorporated into

---

[181] Ibid., 298–9.
[182] President's Commission, *The Challenge of Crime in a Free Society*, at p. 93: '[T]oday the third degree is almost nonexistent...' On the huge cultural changes that were necessary to eliminate coercion in police station houses, see Fyfe and Skolnick, *Above the Law*.

the whole training and peer relations and supervision and disciplinary regimen.

Now we know that the shift away from police brutality is imperfect and cases of abuse still surface from time to time. Still, what is remarkable is the scale of the change and the way it has been incorporated into the ethos of policing generally. As an established and respectable practice in police culture, the third degree has been eliminated, and we have moved onto a whole new footing so far as interrogations are concerned. This has not been easy, and we have to consider whether this hard-won achievement might begin to unravel, if officers are expected once again to become familiar—at first-hand or by having to turn a blind eye—with the techniques of abusive interrogation. We know that already unease is recorded among FBI officers about interrogations conducted by Department of Defense officials, and there are disturbing reports too of Department officials masquerading as FBI officers in torture sessions, to lessen the chance that the FBI will pursue investigation of reported abuses.[183] This is how the contagion and the unraveling begin.

I mentioned earlier that American officials argued at the time of the ratification of the Convention Against Torture that such 'rough treatment as generally falls into the category of "police brutality," while deplorable, does not amount to "torture".' Even if they are right about that, the very considerable reduction in police brutality may not be so easily separable from the widespread abhorrence of torture. The mentality that assumes that torture is way out of bounds may be crucial for the permanent suppression of police brutality. And so there are serious questions about how much of that we will be able to hang on to if torture secures any sort of authorized foothold in the practice of law enforcement.

E. Undermining an archetype

I have said that the prohibition on torture is a legal archetype, which means that, in some sense, *other law* depends on its integrity. But *in what sense* does other law depend on the integrity of this prohibition? What sort of hypothesis am I propounding when I talk about the impact on the rest of our law of undermining current restrictions on the deliberate infliction of pain as an aid to interrogation? Is it a prediction? Or

---

[183] Neil A. Lewis and David Johnston, 'New F.B.I. Files Describe Abuse of Iraq Inmates,' *New York Times*, December 21, 2004.

does it involve some other sort of concern about law's character? In the last few sections, I have spoken loosely about something that looks like a domino effect, an unraveling of surrounding law once the torture prohibition is tampered with. But what exactly is this domino effect, this unraveling supposed to involve?

It sounds like some sort of 'slippery slope' argument and you may think it needs to be treated with all the caution that 'slippery slope' arguments deserve.[184] I did use something like a slippery slope argument in section III(B), when I argued for a pragmatic absolute. But the archetype idea is the reverse of a slippery slope argument. It is sometimes argued that if we relax some lesser constitutional inhibition, we will be on the downward slide towards an abomination like torture. But I am arguing in the other direction: starting at the bottom of the so-called slippery slope, I am arguing that if we mess with the prohibition on torture, we may find it harder to defend some arguably less important requirements that—in the conventional mode of argument—are perched above torture on the slippery slope. The idea is that our confidence that what lies at the bottom of the slope (torture) is wrong informs and supports our confidence that the lesser evils that lie above torture are wrong too. Our beliefs that flogging in prisons is wrong, that coerced confessions are wrong, that pumping a person's stomach for narcotics evidence is wrong, that police brutality is wrong—these beliefs may each of them be uncertain and a little shaky, but the confidence we have in them depends partly on analogies we have constructed between them and torture or on a sense that what is wrong with torture gives us some insight into what is wrong with these other evils. If we undermine the sense that torture is absolutely out of the question, then we lose a crucial point of reference for sustaining these other less confident beliefs.

The case I am making is in part an empirical one, and it is open in principle to empirical refutation. Presented with solid evidence that a legal system that permitted torture was nevertheless able to maintain the rest of the adjacent law about non-brutality intact over the long or medium term, I would have to abandon my concern about the systemic effects of messing with these provisions. Of course, the empirical argument in either direction is complicated. It is complicated first by the sense that we cannot assume stability or any particular trajectory for

---

[184] See e.g., Schauer, 'Slippery Slopes.' For full discussion of the form of argument, see Volokh, 'The Mechanisms of the Slippery Slope,' Rizzo and Whitman, 'The Camel's Nose is in the Tent,' and Lode, 'Slippery Slope Arguments and Legal Reasoning.'

the rest of our law absent any assault on the prohibition on torture; we may be at a loss to say what would have happened had the torture not been undermined and thus at a loss to determine how far the assault on the prohibition has caused us to deviate from that baseline. And it is complicated, secondly, by the possibility that the very factors that led us to undermine the prohibition on torture may have also led us to undermine the adjacent law, in which case it will be hard to show that it was the undermining of the prohibition as such that had the deleterious effect. Actual causation, baselines, and null hypotheses in this area are notoriously difficult to establish.

The difficulties are compounded by the fact that the specific mechanism suggested here has to do with the role of argument. My claim assumes that the life of the law depends, in large part, on argumentation. It assumes that argument is not (as some Legal Realists suggested) just decoration in the law, but a medium through which legal positions are sustained, modified, and elaborated.[185] Above all, it assumes that whether a given argument works or has a chance of success in sustaining a legal position depends on what decisions have already been made in the law. That last point is very important. In law, we don't just argue pragmatically for what we think is the best result; we argue by analogy with results already established, or we argue for general propositions on the basis of existing decisions that already appear to embody them. Philosophical defenses of this mode of argumentation can be given (as they have been in Dworkin's work on integrity, for example).[186] But whether one finds that jurisprudence convincing or not, there is no doubt as a matter of fact that this is how legal argumentation does take place and this is how arguments have whatever effect they have in preventing or promoting legal change.

One other point needs to be mentioned also. Critics of 'slippery-slope' and other similar models of argumentation sometimes say that the slide from one position to another can always be prevented provided the person evaluating the arguments can tell a good argument from a bad one and distinguish between positions that are superficially similar. That may be true of some philosophically sophisticated individuals. But in legal systems, we evaluate arguments together and we have to concern ourselves with the prospects for *socially accepted* arguments

---

[185] See, e.g. Frank, *Law and the Modern Mind*, p. 111.
[186] Dworkin, *Law's Empire*, chs 5–6.

and *socially convincing* distinctions.[187] In general, law makes available an institutional matrix for the presentation and evaluation of arguments, a social way of presenting and evaluating arguments that is supposed to affect what actually happens at the level of the whole society. Any estimation of empirical likelihoods, then, must take all this complexity into account.

We are not dealing then with any simple empirical prediction. But the presence of complexity and methodological difficulty is not a reason for discounting or ignoring the hypothesis we are considering, nor should we be in the business of presuming that the archetype-effect will not accrue unless there is clear and simplistically-discernable evidence that it will. We could as easily and as appropriately work with the opposite presumption. If it is said that we do not or cannot know what the effect on the rest of the legal system will be of our messing with the prohibition on torture, then given what we know *might* be at stake, we have reason to approach the matter with much more caution than the Bush administration lawyers displayed.

In any case the claim of this chapter goes beyond a purely empirical projection of the likelihood that one type of legal change will lead to another. There is also a more qualitative concern about the corruption of our legal system as a result of undermining the prohibition on torture. Consider analogous concerns about the corruption of an individual. Suppose an individual, previously honest, is offered a bribe. Friends may warn him against the first act of dishonesty, not just for itself, but because of what it is likely to do to his character. Part of that is concern about the effect on future decisions of this man via the change in his character that this decision has led to. But corruption is more than just an enhanced probability of future dishonest acts. It involves a present inherent loss: now the man no longer has the sort of character that is set against dishonesty; he no longer has the standing to condemn and oppose dishonesty that an honest man would have.

Or suppose—a worse case, but one more analogous to the torture possibility—that someone has decided that in office he will accept bribes

---

[187] Cf. Rizzo and Whitman, 'The Camel's Nose is in the Tent,' 570–1: 'The process by which arguments are accepted and decisions made is a social one that derives from the decisions of many individuals. No single decision maker can control the evolution of the discussion. The person who makes [a slippery slope argument] does not necessarily claim that the listener himself will be the perpetrator of the future bad decision. Rather, he draws attention to the structure of the discussion that will shape the decisions of many decision makers involved in a social process.'

but that in other areas of his personal and professional life he will maintain honesty, and not steal or cheat on his taxes etc. He may think that he can maintain this firewall between one sort of dishonesty and other sorts, but the cost to him is that he has to maintain it artificially. He no longer refrains from stealing for the reasons that are common to the condemnation of stealing and bribery; he refrains from stealing because even though it is like the acts he is willing to commit, he has simply determined that his dishonesty will go thus far and no further. That is a moral loss attendant on his corruption: an inability now to follow the force of a certain sort of reason, an attenuation of moral insight so far as bribery, stealing, and other forms of dishonesty are concerned.

The damage done to our system of law by undermining the prohibition on torture is, I think, just like this. If we were to permit the torture of Al Qaeda and Taliban detainees, or if we were to define what most of us regard as torture as not really 'torture' at all to enable our officials to inflict pain on them while questioning them, or if we were to set up a Dershowitz regime of judicial torture warrants, maybe only a few score detainees would be affected in the first instance. But the character of our legal system would be corrupted. We would be moving from a situation in which our law had a certain character—a general virtue of non-brutality—to a situation in which that character would be compromised or corrupted by the permitting of this most brutal of practices. We would have given up the lynch-pin of the modern doctrine that law will not operate savagely or countenance brutality. We would no longer be able to state that doctrine in any categorical form. Instead we would have to say, more cautiously and with greater reservation: 'In *most* cases the law will not permit or countenance brutality, but since torture is now permitted in a (hopefully) small and carefully cabined class of cases, we cannot rule out the possibility that in other cases the use of brutal tactics will also be permitted to agents of the law.' In other words, the repudiation of brutality would become a *technical* matter ('Sometimes it is repudiated, sometimes it is not') rather than a shining issue of principle.

Of course the pre-9/11 character of our legal system was imperfect, just as the honesty of any given individual is imperfect. There were already pockets of brutality in our law—capital punishment, on some accounts, residual police brutality of the Rodney King variety, and the regular 'leverage' of prison rape and other unlawful phenomena by prosecutors in the course of plea-bargaining—and we see from Alan Dershowitz's example that their existence is already exploitable for an argument by analogy in favor of torture.[188] Our general commitment to the non-brutality principle is not so secure that we can assume it will remain intact if we add one more set of deviations. In any case, it is not just one more set of deviations. The *archetypal* character of the prohibition on torture means that it plays a crucial and high-visibility role in regard to the principle. As we have seen, the prohibition on torture is a point of reference to which we return over and over again in articulating legally what is wrong with cruel punishment or how to tell a punishment which is cruel from one which is not: we do not equate cruelty with torture, but we use torture to illuminate our rejection of cruelty. And the same is true of procedural due process constraints, certain liberty-based constraints of substantive due process, and our general repudiation of brutality in law enforcement. So—in order to see what might go wrong as a result of undermining the prohibition on torture, we have to imagine Eighth Amendment jurisprudence without this point of reference—arguing about cruelty with the assumption that torture, at any rate, is wholly out of the question. Or we have to imagine Fifth Amendment jurisprudence without this point of reference; we have to imagine arguing about coerced confessions and self-incrimination against the background of an assumption that torture is sometimes legally permissible. The halting and hesitant character of such argumentation would itself be a blight on our law in addition to the actual abuses that resulted. Or rather the two would not be separated: because law is an argumentative practice, the empirical consequences for our law would be bound up with the corruption of our ability to make arguments of a certain kind or to assert principles which put torture unequivocally beyond the pale and used that to provide a vivid and convincing basis for the elaboration of a general principle of non-brutality.

V. The State

A. 'Engine of State' and the Rule of Law

I have been arguing that the prohibition on torture is a legal archetype emblematic of our determination to break the connection between law and brutality and to reinforce its commitment to human dignity even when law is at its most forceful and its subjects are at their most

---

[188] Dershowitz, *Why Terrorism Works*, pp. 147–9.

vulnerable. But in its modern revival, torture does not present itself as an aspect of *legal* practice. It presents instead as an aspect of *state* practice, by which I mean it involves agents of the state seeking to acquire information needed for security or military or counter-insurgency purposes, rather than (say) police, prosecutors, or agents of a court seeking to obtain information which can then be put to some forensic use.

For the most part, this has been true throughout our tradition. Our legal heritage has not been entirely uncontaminated by torture. But to the extent that torture was authorized in England in earlier centuries it was not used as part of the judicial process; this contrasts with the Continent where torture was intimately bound up with the law of proofs.[189] So, for example, William Blackstone observed that the rack in Tudor times, particularly under the first Queen Elizabeth, was 'occasionally used as an engine of state, [but] not of law.'[190] And that is true too of most of what has been under discussion in this chapter. The Yoo and Bybee memoranda address the issue of the legality of certain courses of action that might be undertaken by soldiers, military police, intelligence operatives, or other state officials and authorized at the highest level by the executive. But they are not proposing that torture be incorporated into criminal procedure in the way that it was, for example in the law of proofs in Continental Europe until the eighteenth century. I guess the suggestion that Professor Dershowitz raises *can* be read as a way of introducing torture into the fabric of the law, with its specific provision for judicial torture warrants. But even Dershowitz is primarily concerned with judicial authorization of state torture for state purposes, not judicial authorization of state torture as a mode of input into the criminal process.

So what is the relevance of my argument about *legal* archetypes to a practice which no one proposes to connect specifically with law? Why be so preoccupied with the trauma to *law* of what is essentially a matter of *power*?

---

[189] Alan Dershowitz's account of the relation between torture and the law of proofs is garbled and comprehensively misreads the account in Langbein, *Torture and the Law of Proofs*. The law of proofs was not, as Dershowitz suggests it was (Dershowitz, *Why Terrorism Works*, p. 155), an aspect of Anglo-Saxon law. Contrary to what Dershowitz suggests (ibid., p. 157), the torture warrants which Langbein says were issued in England in the sixteenth and seventeenth centuries had nothing to do with the law of proofs. And the introduction of trial by jury, with an entitlement to evaluate circumstantial evidence unconstrained by anything like the law of proofs, occurred in England centuries before the 1600s, which is when Dershowitz suggests it was introduced (ibid., p. 157).

[190] Blackstone, *Commentaries*, Vol. IV, p. 267.

Well, one point is that 'engines of state' and 'engines of law' are not so widely separated as the Blackstone observation might lead us to believe. Even if one were to take the view that what is done by American officials in holding cells in Iraq, Afghanistan, or Guantánamo Bay is done in relation to the waging of war in a state of emergency rather than as part of a legally constituted practice, still the thought that torture (or something very like torture) is permitted would be a legally disturbing thought. For we know that, in general, there is a danger that abuses undertaken in extraordinary circumstances (extraordinary relative to the administration of law and order at home) can come back to haunt or infect the practices of the domestic legal system. This a concern voiced by Edmund Burke in his apprehensions about the effect on England of the unchecked abuses of Warren Hastings in India,[191] and it is voiced too—though as sad diagnosis—by Hannah Arendt, as she offers the tradition of racist and oppressive administration in the African colonies as part of her explanation of the easy acceptance of the most atrocious modes of oppression in mid-twentieth century Europe.[192] The warning has been sounded often enough: 'Don't imagine that you can maintain a firewall between what is done by your soldiers and spies abroad to those they demonize as terrorists or insurgents, and what will be done at home to those who can be designated as enemies of society.'[193] You may say that there is a distinction between what we do when we are at war, and what we do in peacetime, and we shouldn't be too paranoid that the first will infect the second. Saying that may offer some reassurance about the prospect of insulating the engines of law from the exigencies of *some* wars. But is it really a basis for confidence in regard to the sort of war in which we are said to be currently involved—a war against terror as such, a war without end and with no boundaries, a war fought in the American homeland as well as in the cities, plains, and mountains of Afghanistan and Iraq?

A second point is that although we are dealing with torture as 'an engine of state,' still the issue of legality has been made central. Maybe

---

[191] See Edmund Burke, 'Speech in General Reply (on the impeachment of Warren Hastings, Esq.),' 194–225 (rev. ed. 1867) ('[T]he House of Commons has already well considered what may be our future moral and political condition, when the persons who come from that school of pride, insolence, corruption, and tyranny are more intimately mixed up with us of purer morals. Nothing but contamination can be the result...').

[192] Arendt, *The Origins of Totalitarianism*, pp. 185–86, 215–16, 221.

[193] Bear in mind also that some of the reservists involved in the abuse at Abu Ghraib were prison guards in civilian life. It is of course disturbing to think that that explains their abusive behavior in Iraq; it is also disturbing to think about causation back in the opposite direction.

there are hard men in our intelligence agencies who are prepared to say (whenever they can get away with it): 'Just torture them, get the information, and we'll sort out the legal niceties later.' But even if this is happening, a remarkable feature of the modern debate is that an effort is also being made to see whether something like torture can be accommodated *within the very legal framework that purports to prohibit it*. The American executive seems to be interested in the prospects for a regime of cruelty and pain in interrogation that is legally authorized or at least not categorically and unconditionally prohibited.[194] An effort is being made to see whether the law can be stretched or deformed to actually permit and authorize this sort of thing. They don't just take the prisoners to the waterboards; they want to drag the law along with them. The effect on law, in other words, is unavoidable.

A third point addresses the issue of *the Rule of Law*—the enterprise of subjecting what Blackstone called 'the engines of state' to legal regulation and restraint. We hold ourselves committed to a general and quite aggressive principle of legality, which means that law doesn't just have a little sphere of its own in which to operate, but expands to govern and regulate every aspect of official practice. I think the central claim of this chapter applies to that aspiration as well: that is, I think we should be concerned about the effect *on the Rule of Law* of a weakening or an undermining of the legal prohibition on torture. We have seen how the prohibition on torture operates as an archetype of various parts of American constitutional law and of law enforcement culture generally. I believe it also operates as an archetype of the ideal we call the Rule of Law. That agents of the state will not be permitted to torture those who fall into its hands seems an elementary incident of the Rule of Law as it is understood in the modern world. If this protection is not assured, then the prospects for the Rule of Law generally look bleak indeed.

True, we must acknowledge that the Rule of Law ideal has many meanings,[195] and I can imagine Alan Dershowitz saying that the formal regulation of torture might be as much a triumph for the Rule of Law as its prohibition.[196] I am not being sarcastic: I think Dershowitz really

---

[194] Should we be pleased that the Bush administration cares enough about legality to embark on this debate? Or should we be appalled? Is it a tribute to law? Or is it an affront (like trying to get an honorable father's favor for a thoroughly disreputable friend)?

[195] See Waldron, 'Is the Rule of Law an Essentially Contested Concept?'

[196] I can imagine Professor Dershowitz even seeing it as an achievement. What greater tribute could there be to the Rule of Law than that it is capable of *regularizing* the abomination of torture rather than leaving it beyond the pale of legal regulation? For the opposite view, see Kadish, 'Torture, the State and the Individual,' 355.

is concerned that the alternative to his proposal is not 'no torture' but torture conducted *sub rosa*, torture conducted beneath legal notice and with law's complicity or silence. I believe he thinks that that is much worse for the Rule of Law than the judicial-torture-warrant regime he has in mind.[197]

Nevertheless, a case can be made that it is the prohibition which is really archetypal in this regard. Think back to Judith Shklar's concern, mentioned at the very beginning of this chapter, about the danger that 'acute fear' will again become 'the most common form of social control.'[198] States in the twentieth century (and now apparently also in the twenty-first century) suffer from a standing temptation to try and get their way by terrorizing the populations under their authority with the immense security apparatus they control and the dreadful prospects of torture, disappearance, and other violence that they can deploy against their internal enemies. Much more than mere arbitrariness and lack of regulation, this is the apprehension that most of us have about the modern state. The Rule of Law offers a way of responding to that apprehension for, as we have seen, law (at least in the heritage of our jurisprudence) has set its face against brutality, and has found ways of remaining forceful and final in human affairs without savaging or terrorizing its subjects. The promise of the Rule of Law, then, is the promise that this sort of ethos can increasingly inform the practices of the state and not just the practices of courts, police, jailers, prosecutors etc. In this way, *a state subject to law* becomes not just a state whose excesses are predictable or a state whose actions are subject to forms, procedures, and warrants; it becomes a state whose exercise of power is imbued with this broader spirit of the repudiation of brutality. That is the hope, and I think the prohibition on torture is an archetype of that hope: it is archetypal of what law can offer, and in its application to the state, it is archetypal of the project of bringing power under this sort of control.

This point can be stated also the other way round: to be willing to abandon the prohibition on torture or to define it out of existence is to be willing—among other things—to sit back and watch how much

---

[197] See Dershowitz, *Why Terrorism Works*, p. 150. See also the insistence on 'the truthful road of the rule of law' by the Israeli Landau Commission, rejecting 'the way...of the hypocrites: they declare that they abide by the rule of law, but turn a blind eye to what goes on beneath the surface'—Landau Commission, 'Report of Commission of Inquiry,' at pp. 183–4. (The Landau Commission recommended legal approval for 'a moderate measure of physical pressure' in interrogation: ibid., p. 184).

[198] Shklar, 'Liberalism of Fear,' p. 27.

of that enterprise unravels. It is to contemplate with equanimity the prospect that the ideal of the Rule of Law will no longer hold out this clear promise: that the state that it aims to control will be permitted in some areas and to at least a certain extent to operate towards individuals who are wholly within its power with methods of brutality that law itself recoils from.

B. An archetype of international law

I have said that the prohibition on torture is archetypal of our particular legal heritage, and that it is also archetypal of a certain sort of commitment to the Rule of Law. Beyond that, we may ask about its archetypal status in international law, particularly international humanitarian law and the law of human rights.

I think a case can be made, similar to the case I made in Part IV, that the prohibition on torture also operates as an archetype in these areas. Consider, for example, its prominence in the law relating to the treatment of prisoners in wartime. The rule against the torture of prisoners may not be the best known of the Geneva Convention provisions. (That honor probably belongs to the image of a prisoner's having an obligation to disclose only his 'name, rank, and number.') But if it is less prominent in the public imagination, it is only because it is more taken for granted. We implicitly understand that while prisoner-of-war camps are uncomfortable and the circumstances of the prisoners often straitened, there is something inherently unlawful about the torture of prisoners.[199] And this is not just because of the stringency of the provision itself. Torture of prisoners threatens to undermine the integrity of

---

[199] When captured British airmen appeared on Iraqi television during the first Gulf War in 1991 showing clear evidence of having been beaten, allied outrage was immediate. See Maureen Dowd, 'War in the Gulf: the Oval Office; Bush Calls Iraqis "Brutal" to Pilots,' *New York Times*, January 22, 1991, p. A10: 'President Bush vowed today to hold President Saddam Hussein accountable for what he called 'the brutal parading of allied pilots,' an act that he denounced as a 'direct violation of every convention that protects prisoners.' Iraq released videotapes on Sunday in which seven men identified as allied pilots gave robotic answers to Iraqi questions....Several of the pilots' faces appeared bruised in the tapes, which were broadcast today in the United States. The appearance of the men, along with the wooden delivery of their responses, led military analysts to believe that the pilots were coerced.' See also John Bulloch et al., 'Crisis in the Gulf,' *The Independent* (London), January 27, 1991, p. 13: '[B]y parading US and British pilots on Baghdad television, the argument for war crimes trials moves on to the agenda again, bringing with it the possibility of pursuing the war into Iraq after a withdrawal from Kuwait.'

the surrender/incarceration regime: if we can torture prisoners, then we can do anything to them, and if we can do anything to them, then the willingness of defeated soldiers to surrender will be quite limited.[200] The whole enterprise of attempting to mitigate the horrors of war by making provision for an *hors de combat* status for individual soldiers in the face of certain defeat depends on their confidence, underwritten by law, that surrender and incarceration is better than death in combat. But torture (or interrogation practices that come close to torture) threatens that confidence and thus the whole basis of the regime.

What about human rights law? Certainly torture is widely understood as the paradigmatic human rights abuse. It is the sort of evil that arouses human rights passions and drives human rights campaigns. The idea of a human rights code which lacked a prohibition on torture is barely intelligible to us. Now it is true that even human rights advocates accept the idea that rights are subject to interpretation and subject also to limitation to meet 'the just requirements of morality, public order and the general welfare in a democratic society.'[201] And few are so immoderate in their human rights advocacy that they do not accept that '[i]n time of public emergency which threatens the life of the nation' the human rights obligations of the state may be limited.[202] People are willing to accept that the human rights regime does not unravel altogether when detention without trial is permitted or when habeas corpus is suspended or when free speech or freedom of assembly is limited in times of grave emergency. But were we to put up for acceptance as an integral part of the main body of human rights law the proposition that people may be *tortured* in times of emergency, I think people would sense that the whole game was being given away, that human rights law itself was entering a crisis.

But what if we are only proposing to violate not the rule against torture but only the international norm relating to cruel, inhuman, or degrading treatment? Maybe that can be abandoned without wider

---

[200] Parks, 'Teaching the Law of War,' at pp. 5–6: '[T]actical rationale is being used to support legal principles; our service men and women are taught that these principles are absolute and may not be waived when convenient. . . . [A] lack of humane treatment may induce an enemy to fight to the death rather than surrender, thereby leading to increased friendly casualties. The instruction is candid, however, in admitting that humane treatment of enemy prisoners of war will not guarantee equal treatment for our captured servicemen, as we learned in World War II, Korea, and Vietnam; but it is emphasized that inhumane treatment will most assuredly lead to equivalent actions by the enemy.'

[201] Universal Declaration of Human Rights, Article 29(2).

[202] International Covenant on Civil and Political Rights, Article 4(1).

damage to the human rights regime? I have serious doubts about this. For one thing, the administration has also been toying with the redescription of a considerable amount of what was previously regarded as torture to re-categorize as merely—merely!—'cruel, inhuman, and degrading treatment.'[203] The human rights community is not easily fooled, and it would be an archetypal blow to its endeavor if the rule which in fact prohibits torture were to unravel under this sort of definitional pressure. For another thing, we must not become so jaded that the phrase 'cruel, inhuman, and degrading treatment' simply trips off the tongue as something much less taboo than torture. It may be vague, but it is not a technical term. And it is not just a pious aspiration: the word 'inhuman' means much more than merely 'inhumane.'[204] 'Inhuman treatment' means what it says, and its antonymic connection with the phrase 'human rights' is not just happenstance. To treat a person inhumanly is to treat him in the way that no human should ever be treated. On this basis it would not be hard to argue that the prohibition on inhuman treatment (for example, in the UDHR, the Covenant, and ECHR) is as much a paradigm of the international human rights movement as the absolute prohibition on torture.

I said in section IV(E) that dire predictions about the effect of undermining an archetype are partly empirical, but they also have partly to do with the sense of corruption and demoralization that the collapse of an archetype would induce. Archetypes make law visible, they dramatize its more abstract principles, and they serve as icons or symbols of its deepest commitments. By the same token, the demise of an archetype sends a powerful message about a change in the character of the relevant law. As Sanford Kadish has observed:

> The deliberate infliction of pain and suffering upon a person by agents of the state is an abominable practice. Since World War II, progress has been made internationally to mark the perpetrators of such practices as outlaws. This progress has been made by proclamations and conventions which have condemned these practices without qualification.... Any claim by a state that it is free to inflict pain and suffering upon a person when it finds the circumstances sufficiently exigent threatens to undermine that painfully won and still fragile consensus.... If any state is free of the restraint whenever it is satisfied that the stakes are high enough to justify it, then the ground gained since WWII threatens to be lost.... Lost would be the opportunity immediately to condemn as outlaw any state engaging in these practices. Judgment would be a far more

---

[203] See Chapter 9, below.   [204] See Chapter 9, below, pp. 303–4.

complicated process of assessing the proffered justification and delving into all the circumstances.[205]

If in this way the rule against torture changes from a matter of shining principle in the 'Global Bill of Rights' to become a technical matter—a matter of counterintuitive lawyers' definitions and a maze of exceptions and provisions for derogation—then we would lose our sense of international law's ability to confront the horrors of our time clearly and decisively. Law's mission in these areas is much more vulnerable to demoralization than it is in domestic law, where people have learned to live with a gap between legal technicality on the one hand and the clear demands of morality on the other.

We also need to consider the effect on the international human rights regime of the collapse of the archetype in relation to the *United States* in particular. That is, we need to consider the demoralizing impact of defection from the anti-torture consensus, by not just another rogue state but the world's one remaining super-power. An archetype can be the commitment embodied in a particular precedent as well as in a general rule. The expressed willingness of one very powerful state to subject itself to legal restraint where its interests are most gravely at stake sends a message that international law is to be taken seriously. But the abandonment of the archetype by such a state sends a message too: that international law may be of no account if even the most powerful regime—the one that can most afford to sustain damage—is willing to dispense with legal restraint for the sake of a tactical advantage.[206] Some may say gloomily

---

[205] Kadish, 'Torture, the State and the Individual,' 354.

[206] Cf. Strauss, 'Torture,' 257: '[O]nce the United States employs torture, it is likely that such practices would spread worldwide. At a minimum, the nation would lose its ability to condemn torture or other unacceptable acts of cruelty perpetrated in other parts of the world. Even if we could assure the world that torture would be utilized only in extreme circumstances, any moral leadership would be destroyed.' See also Levinson, op. cit., at p. 2053, who quotes Oona Hathaway as offering 'in conversation' a special reason for the United States, above all other countries, to adhere absolutely to the rule against torture: 'This involves what might be termed the "contagion effect" if the United States is widely believed to accept torture (either directly or by its allies) as a proper means of fighting the war against terrorism. The United States is, for better and, most definitely, for worse, the "new Rome," the giant colossus striding the world and claiming to speak on behalf of good against evil. Part of being such a colossus may be the need to accept certain costs that lesser countries need not be expected to pay. Our very size and power (and moral pretensions) may require that we limit our responses in a way that might not be necessary for smaller countries far more "existentially" threatened by their enemies than the United States has yet been demonstrated to be. If we give up the no-torture taboo, then why shouldn't any other country in the world be equally free to proclaim its freedom from the solemn covenant entered into through the United Nations Convention?'

that American moral leadership in humanitarian law and international law generally has already been squandered to such an extent that little further damage can be done. I suspect that is too pessimistic. The events of the last few years may be an aberration, and it is not unreasonable to think that the United States might still redeem the promise of its historic leadership position in favor of the international Rule of Law.[207] But if it were to put itself so far beyond the pale of international humanitarian and human rights law as to permit torture or something like torture as a regular feature of state practice, then there might be no way back to that position of leadership.

So far in this section I have considered the rule against torture as an archetype of the substantive law of human rights and the treatment of prisoners. We may want to consider it also as an archetype of international law *as such*, as an archetype of the way in which international law operates. We know that the rule against torture functions as one of the most vivid modern exemplars of *ius cogens* in international law, that is, of the idea that some norms have a status which transcends the ordinary requirement of subscription to treaty as the basis of the bindingness of international law.[208] However, it is not the only exemplar. Traditionally, the paradigms of an offense prohibited by *ius cogens* were piracy and the slave trade; even if the rule against torture ceased to be regarded as *ius cogens*, these other rules would continue to afford clear examples of peremptory norms subject to universal jurisdiction.

Much more disturbing, however, was the way in which Bush administration jurisprudence threatened to undermine the delicate systematics of treaty-based international law. International law operates and can be enforced to a certain extent on its account and through its own institutions and agencies. But particularly in human rights law and humanitarian law, international covenants and conventions operate best when they are matched by parallel provisions of national constitutions and legislation. Indeed, as we saw in Part II of this chapter, the Convention Against Torture requires those who are party to it to ensure that they have made legislative or other legal provision to outlaw torture by their own governmental officials both at home and abroad. Without this convergence—without what Gerald Neuman has termed 'dual positivization'[209]—the international law provisions would be much more like the

---

[207] See John F. Murphy, *The United States and the Rule of Law in International Affairs*, pp. 355–9. (See also p. 16 above.)

[208] Wedgwood, 'International Criminal Law and Augusto Pinochet,' at 836. See also Bassiouni, *Crimes against Humanity in International Criminal Law*, at p. 489.

[209] See Neuman, 'Human Rights and Constitutional Rights.'

meaningless verbal flatulence that their denigrators often accuse them of being. But even with such convergence, there is still a danger to the legal regime. Suppose governments generally were to adopt the stance that Jay Bybee has urged for the United States—that in his military decision-making the U.S. President cannot possibly be subject to legislation mandated by international conventions, that any such legislation would be unconstitutional just because it constrained his freedom of action as Commander-in-Chief. (After all, there is nothing unique to the American constitution about this stance: the Commander-in-Chief authority in the United States is a power which, in American constitutional theory, every civilian government should have.)[210] Such a stance might make it impossible for international law to regulate armed conflict at all: certainly it would make its *ex ante* regulation very difficult and wholly dependent on the willingness of national executives to choose to limit the means used in interrogations conducted under their military or national security authority. Enforcement of international obligations would depend wholly on war crimes prosecutions after the fact, and the United States has already repudiated the jurisdiction that an International Criminal Court would have over such matters. Someone might respond to all this by saying: 'Well, surely *every* provision of international law is hostage in the end to the consent of states to be bound by the relevant treaties.' Maybe so. But the mode of operation of international law in matters like this has been for states to enter into treaty obligations *in advance and in general*, not for national executives to be able to pick and choose in detail and in the midst of particular hostilities the constraints that they will and will not accept. Yet that is what the Bybee doctrine amounts to. If we accept that international law needs dual positivization, of the sort that I have described, then we can see that the administration's attitude towards torture might well deal a body blow to the normal mode of operation of human rights law.

VI. Conclusion

Let me end with a few cautionary remarks about the concept of legal archetype that I have been using. First, I don't want to exaggerate the significance of undermining a legal archetype, either in general or in this special case of torture. Undermining an archetype will usually have an effect on the general morale of the law in a given area. It may become

---

[210] See Hamilton, Madison, and Jay, *Federalist Papers*, no. 74, at p. 422.

much harder for us to hang on to a proper sense of why the surrounding law is important and to convey that sense to the public. For example, if we start issuing torture warrants, it may be harder to hang on to a proper sense of the importance of the exclusionary rule for involuntary confessions. Or if 'inhuman treatment' is not banned from our interrogation centers, it may be harder to hang on to the conviction that flogging is not an acceptable punishment. But I am not saying that all this surrounding law necessarily unravels, the instant we diminish the force of the archetype. It's more that each of the surrounding provisions will be kind of thrown back on its own resources and each will be only as resilient (in the face of attempts at repeal, amendment, or redefinition) as the particular arguments that can be summoned in its favor. It will lose the benefit of the archetype's gravitational force. It will derive less or it will derive nothing from the more general sense of the overall point of this whole area of law, previously epitomized in the archetype.

I guess it's possible that our sense of the purpose, policy, or principle behind the area of law in question will find another archetype if the existing archetype is damaged. But remember that archetypes do dual duty: they do not just epitomize the spirit of the law; they also contribute to it with their primary normative force. So any attempt to find a second archetype when the first archetype is damaged is not just like finding a new logo for a corporation. Instead it involves a damaged policy or an injured principle going in search of a compromised archetype to enable us to retrieve and protect whatever is left of the broken spirit of the law.

Secondly, I should not exaggerate the significance of something's being an archetype. From a normative point of view, archetypes might be good or bad; they may be archetypal of good law or bad law. *Lochner v. New York* (1905)[211] is or was archetypal of a certain approach to economic regulation which married the freedom-of-contract provisions of the U.S. Constitution to the dogmas of *laissez-faire* economics, and that archetype was discredited when the general legal doctrine was discredited.[212] (Indeed, the shock to the system of disrupting or undermining an archetype may well be part of an effective strategy for necessary legal reform.) Archetype is not a natural law idea. An archetype is only as important as the spirit of the area of surrounding law that it epitomizes. And it is up to us to make that estimation.

---

[211] *Lochner v. New York* 198 U.S. 45 (1905).
[212] See, e.g. *West Coast Hotel Co. v. Parrish*, 300 U.S. 379, 392–3 (1937).

Of course natural law ideas may determine our judgment of the importance of a given archetype and the area of law it stands for. That is certainly the case with torture. I believe—and I hope that most of my readers share this belief—that the prohibition on torture does epitomize something very important in the 'spirit and genius' of our law, and that we mess with it at our peril. It's not something to be taken lightly, if we take seriously what I have referred to as the more general policy of breaking the link between law and brutality. I also think that what I have referred to as the general dissociation of law from brutality has a natural law basis, too. But again that's not why I call the prohibition on torture an archetype. Archetype is a structural idea; natural law (or less grandly, our basic moral sense) comes into play to determine the importance of the structures involved and to determine too the value of what we might lose if an archetype is damaged.

One final caveat. There are all sorts of reasons to be concerned about torture, and I am under no illusion that I have focused on the most important. The most important issue about torture remains the moral issue of the deliberate infliction of pain, the suffering that results, the insult to dignity, and the demoralization and depravity that is almost always associated with this enterprise whether it is legalized or not. The issue of the relation between the prohibition on torture and the rest of the law, the issue of archetypes, is *a second-tier issue*. By that I mean it does not confront the primary wrongness of torture; it is a second-tier issue like the issue of our proven inability to keep torture under control, or the fatuousness of the suggestion made by Professor Dershowitz and others that we can confine its application to exactly the cases in which it might be thought justified. Given that we are sometimes tongue-tied about what is really wrong with an evil like torture, work at this second tier is surely worth doing. Or it is surely worth doing anyway, as part of the general division of labor, even if others are managing to produce a first-tier account of the evil.[213]

I have found this second-tier thinking about archetypes helpful in my general thinking about law. I have found it helpful as a way of thinking about what it is for law to structure itself and present itself in a certain light. I have found it helpful to think about archetypes as a general topic in legal philosophy, as a corrective to some of the simplicities of legal positivism, and as an interesting elaboration of Dworkin's jurisprudence. Most of all, I have found this exploration helpful in understanding what

[213] See, e.g. Sussman, 'What's Wrong with Torture?'

the prohibition on torture symbolizes. By thinking about the prohibition as an archetype I have been able to reach a clearer and more substantive sense of what we aspire to in our jurisprudence: a body of law and a Rule of Law that renounce savagery and a state that pursues its purposes (even its most urgent purposes) and secures its citizens (even its most endangered citizens) honorably and without recourse to brutality and terror.

8

What Can Christian Teaching Add to the Debate about Torture?

It is a matter of shame, but in the years 2002–8 in the United States we had no choice but to open and conduct a national debate about torture—and not just a debate about how to prevent torture by corrupt and tyrannical regimes elsewhere in the world, but a debate about whether torture is a legitimate means for *our* government to use as it seeks information to act on in the war against terrorism and in the effort to suppress insurgencies in Afghanistan and Iraq. The debate engaged the voices and passions of all sorts of people—executive officials (including the President and Vice President of the United States), government and military lawyers, legal scholars and moral philosophers, newspaper and magazine columnists, senators and congressmen, human rights agencies and activists, and—most important—ordinary citizens, organized and unorganized. It is a debate that the rest of the world has watched with fascination and horror, as Americans pondered publicly whether they would remain part of the international human rights consensus that torture is utterly beyond the pale.

For most of this period, the voices of Christian leaders—clergy and lay people—were silent. Maybe I am slighting one or two brave men and women who spoke out against torture from the beginning. But by and large they were not heard, or their voices were not noticed as distinctively *Christian* voices. Those of us who were actively engaged in this debate listened for—yearned for and strained to hear—a contribution by the churches, and our impression (at least as late as 2006) was that interventions by church leaders in this debate were late and hesitant, at best. In November 2005, both the U.S. Conference of Catholic Bishops and the National Council of Churches applauded the lead given by the U.S. Senate (in the McCain Amendment), condemning any use of torture as unacceptable; but this was the USCCB and the NCC following the lead of elected legislators, three years after the torture debate had begun, rather than giving any lead of their own. A National Religious Campaign against Torture got underway in a conference at the Princeton Theological Seminary in January 2006.[1] But again this was four years after the earliest torture memos emerged, 18 months after the Abu Ghraib abuse was brought to public attention.

There is no point speculating about why the Christian response has been so late.[2] What I should like to do in this chapter is to convey a sense of what—until very recently—has been missing from the debate on account of the silence of the churches. It is sometimes said that secular morality—secular ethics, secular conceptions of human rights—can get by quite well on their own, without any religious input. Almost all professional moral philosophers that I know believe this. No doubt they would think it good to have the support of church people for urgent moral campaigns against this or that evil or in favor of this or that moral initiative. But that is what it would be: support for positions that are already well-thought-through. Secular moralists say they have nothing to learn intellectually from any distinctively Christian ethics; they can do it all on their own, by reading and rereading Aristotle, Kant, Bentham, or John Rawls or by elaborating the logic of their own considered judgments and those of their friends in what they call 'reflective equilibrium.'[3] This is a very common view. Personally I believe it is catastrophically inadequate in the case of the debate about torture and inadequate on many other issues as well.[4] But again, the point is not to criticize the secular moralists: they have done all they can on this issue with the resources available to them and at least they did it when it needed to be done, against a backdrop of silence from those who usually go around saying that secular ethics is truncated or impoverished. The point is not to criticize what they have done but to show, even at this late stage, what *else* we can do on the basis of Christian commitments.[5]

---

[1] This chapter was originally presented at the conference at Princeton Theological Seminary in 2006, which inaugurated that group. Since then other similar groups have emerged, notably 'Evangelicals against Torture,' under the leadership of David Gushee.

[2] I have heard it said that some church leaders were reluctant to speak out on torture until they were sure that criticism on this issue would not diminish the political capital that the Bush administration might need in order to secure the confirmation of conservative nominees to the U.S. Supreme Court.

[3] For the idea of 'reflective equilibrium,' see Rawls, *A Theory of Justice*, pp. 48–51.

[4] For some general discussion on the prospects of a purely secular theory of ethics and rights, see Waldron, *God, Locke and Equality*, pp. 235–43.

[5] For some critical discussion of the Rawlsian view that we should eschew religious and other deep philosophical conceptions in public discourse, see Waldron, 'Public Reason and "Justification" in the Courtroom.'

1. The Torture Debate

Let me begin with a review of what the debate was about. Mark Danner's book, *Torture and Truth* charts the sorry story of origins of the American debate about torture in the last four years and it is an indispensable starting point for mature consideration of this topic.[6]

The debate arose, first of all, amidst the anger and fear that welled up in the United States in response to the terrorist attacks of September 11, 2001. It was predicated on a belief that these murderous attacks were likely to be repeated, and by an understanding that prevention of future attacks would require *information—timely* information—about terrorist networks and their plans and capacities. And so we had to consider how this information could be secured and how we might quickly figure out and unravel the structures and operations of these clandestine organizations. Early on, torture was prominent among the methods that were contemplated, and the debate quickly became one about whether *any means necessary* should be used to avoid these murderous attacks or whether there were some means that were absolutely ruled out despite the fact that they could help us save hundreds, perhaps thousands of lives. So here we have a first question that might be put to Christian church leaders: *Do the churches have anything to teach us on this issue of means and ends, and on the question of whether there are certain means that are to be utterly ruled out of consideration?*

Secondly, in some circles, considerable intellectual energy was devoted to the elaboration of *hypothetical* scenarios in which, it was said, torture would seem to be *obviously* justified—indeed scenarios in which, according to one commentator, torture would be *required*, a matter of moral duty.[7] These are the 'ticking bomb' scenarios, familiar to many who watch shows such as the Fox Network's *24*.[8] We are to imagine, with the omniscience that television gives us, that terrorists have planted a nuclear device in Manhattan and that we have captured

---

[6] Danner, *Torture and Truth: America, Abu Ghraib, and the War on Terror.* For background on the torture debates, see also Greenberg, *The Torture Debate in America.*

[7] See Dershowitz, *Why Terrorism Works,* pp. 131–63, and Krauthammer, 'The Truth about Torture: It's Time to be Honest about Doing Terrible Things,' *The Weekly Standard,* December 5, 2005.

[8] For an example of the use of Fox's *24* to elicit support for the torture of terrorist suspects by United States interrogators, see Cal Thomas, 'Restrictions Won't Win War on Terror for Us,' *South Florida Sun-Sentinel,* May 4, 2005, at p. 25A.

one of them who undoubtedly knows where the bomb is, but will not tell. Apparently, our fellow Americans divide into a majority who believe that torturing the captive is obviously the right thing to do (and boast that they themselves would be ready to do it, if only they knew how), and a minority who maintain that even in this scenario (or any realistic equivalent of it) torture must remain forbidden. Within that minority there is a further group that regards these thought-experiments as inherently corrupting.[9] It would be interesting to know what the churches have to say about that last point: *What can the churches add to our understanding of the health and wisdom of this sort of casuistry and about the use (or abuse) of moral thinking involved in these hypothetical speculations about 'ticking bombs' etc.?*

The debate about torture was inspired, thirdly, by a deliberate attempt on the part of certain lawyers working in the White House and in the Departments of Justice and Defense in 2002 and 2003, to see if anything could be done to blur the framework of international, military, constitutional, and domestic law that many of us had assumed put torture completely beyond the pale so far as the interrogation of prisoners and detainees was concerned. There was an attempt to narrow the definition of torture and make it a technical term, so the prohibition would cover much less than most people supposed. There was an attempt to restrict the application of the Geneva Conventions, so that Taliban and Al Qaeda captives would not be covered by safeguards prohibiting 'mutilation, cruel treatment and torture; ... [and] outrages upon personal dignity' against those who had laid down their arms in any sort of conflict. There was an attempt to deny that the United States was bound by international human rights covenants prohibiting cruel, inhuman, or degrading treatment. And there was an overarching insistence that the President and those under his command could not be bound by *any* law—domestic or international—that might constrain his ability to wage a war against terror. This aspect of the debate concerned the integrity of the rules and standards of positive law,[10] and it may be thought that this is an essentially legal matter, quite distinct from the concerns of bishops and theologians. But actually the integrity of positive law is itself usually regarded as a matter of value and concern from a Christian point of view. So it is worth asking: *Can the churches contribute anything to our understanding of the value of legal stability and legal clarity in an area like this?*

---

[9] See, e.g. Luban, 'Liberalism, Torture, and the Ticking Bomb,' at 1440–5.
[10] See the discussion in Chapter 7, above, at pp. 222–47.

Fourthly, the debate focused on the ethical and legal dilemmas—real, not imaginary—facing soldiers, law enforcement officials, and intelligence operatives in relation to the actual occurrence of abusive interrogation procedures. What are these persons to do when they see such abuses taking place, when they see beatings, waterboardings, dogs set upon prisoners, prisoners shackled in stress positions for days on end? What should they do when they are ordered, in vague if not explicit terms, to participate in such abuse or facilitate it or turn a blind eye to it? What are they to do when they are warned officially or unofficially against bringing such abuses to public attention or the attention of higher authority? How should they reconcile the ethics and honor of their profession—as soldiers, lawyers, perhaps even doctors and chaplains—with what are said to be the needs of their country at a time of crisis? We have learned of the growth of a torture culture in the United States through the activities of leakers and whistleblowers, and we have heard too of the anguish that good-hearted men and women in government and in the military have faced as they wrestle with these issues. Each of us can imagine being in their situation, or imagine that our sons and daughters are in their situation, and we wonder what we should do in their place and what moral courage we could summon up. Once again there are questions to put to the church leaders in this connection. *How is a Christian to think about reconciling law, professional ethics, and the exigencies of national security? What counsel can be offered to young and frightened soldiers who want to do what is right even in the midst of what they see as considerable pressure from peers and superiors to connive or participate in what is wrong?*[11]

Fifthly, and most vividly, the torture debate was galvanized by a lurid picture of what a regime of torture in the real world would actually involve. I refer of course to the descent into depravity by American soldiers at Abu Ghraib prison in Iraq, luridly illustrated in photographs published around the world in April 2004, with catastrophic consequences for the reputation of the United States and the honor of its military.[12] What we want here is not just condemnation to pile upon condemnation, and not just a pursuit of the guilty further up the chain of command. What we need is a sense of how to think about Abu Ghraib. *Do the churches offer us anything to choose between the 'few bad apples' characterization of these abuses and an alternative characterization*

---

[11] See Lazreg, *Torture and the Twilight of Empire*, pp. 173–212 and the review of that book in Waldron, 'Review Article: Clean Torture by Modern Democracies.'

[12] See Danner, *Torture and Truth*, pp. 216–24.

*which might regard this sort of depravity as inevitable when frail human
beings are freed from the constraints that are supposed to hold them back
from an abyss of horror?*

2. Assaults on Clarity

A friend of mine, a priest, expressed doubt about whether it is appropriate for the churches to speak out against torture when the facts remain unclear. We know some of the truth about Abu Ghraib, and there are well confirmed eye-witness accounts of 'waterboarding' and other abusive techniques at Guantánamo Bay and elsewhere. But there was a lot of secrecy, rumor, and contradictory speculation about extraordinary rendition, secret bases in places like Romania and Poland, and so on. We just don't know the facts, said my friend, and we shouldn't leap to judgment, especially in these troubled times.

My friend is quite right that some of the facts were unclear and that it would be wrong to judge on the basis of unconfirmed evidence. But what we needed from the churches was not the adjudication of any particular factual claim, but some help in furnishing a clear and unequivocal *framework* in which the issue of torture could be discussed. We know, for a fact, that administration lawyers strove mightily in 2002 and 2003 to undermine the clarity of the legal framework relating to torture. They argued that the laws applied to some detainees and not others; they mounted repeated assaults on the definition of torture, trying to shrink it down so that the prohibition would cover only the most extreme and egregious acts; they lampooned the conventions and institutions of international law and human rights law; and they put forward all sorts of general exceptions, most prominently for any act authorized by the President in his capacity as Commander-in-Chief.[13] The aim was to create an atmosphere of confusion in which honorable people, inside and outside the armed forces, would come to think of the rule against torture as a muddled and difficult technical issue rather than a clear and uncompromising prohibition. All this has been done against a background in which the moral consensus against torture was already being corroded by fear and anger among the general population and by

---

[13] See the White House, Defense Department and Justice Department memoranda reprinted in Danner, *Torture and Truth*, pp. 78–216 and in Greenberg and Dratel (eds) *The Torture Papers*. See also Chapter 7, above, pp. 194–8 and 207–12.

the irresponsible intellectual contortions of opinion-leaders. In reaction to this, good-hearted people have been struggling mightily to restore the integrity of the battered moral framework in which our understanding of torture had previously been located. Without a secure framework, our judgments are chaotic, even arbitrary.[14] It is in respect of that enterprise of the repair of a moral framework that the voices of church leaders have been most sorely missed.

3. Contributions from Christian Teaching

My personal conviction is that torture is an abomination, to be excluded from consideration in all circumstances, even in the ticking-bomb scenarios that commentators like Alan Dershowitz and Charles Krauthammer are fond of imagining. I am told that this is an idealistic position, a sort of naïve Kantianism utterly inappropriate for use as a standard for public action in the real world. Yet the absolutist position is not just conjured up out of my own personal fastidiousness. It is what the law requires and it is found in all human rights conventions. These, we should remember, are *public* documents; they are not treatises of personal ethics but conventions establishing minimum legal standards for the exercise of state power. As such, they prohibit torture categorically and absolutely, explicitly withholding from the prohibition on torture the provision for derogation in times of emergency that they allow for other human rights norms. They do this on the basis of the most elementary regard for human dignity and respect for the sacredness of the human individual, even *in extremis* when the individual is at his most isolated, dangerous, and despised. When I regret that the churches have not been more vociferous on this issue, when I look forward to their increasing interventions in the torture debate, I naturally expect that the Christian position will coincide with and lend support to the absolute legal prohibition I have outlined.[15]

But there is of course something impudent about that expectation. Church teaching is not guaranteed to fall in with *Waldron's* moral views

---

[14] See O'Donovan, *The Ways of Judgment*, pp. 8–11 for a fine discussion, in political theology, of the restoration of a moral framework as indispensable aim and aspect of judgment.

[15] For a striking example, see the quotations from the discussion of torture in the *travaux préparatoires* for the European Convention on Human Rights in 1949, quoted in Chapter 7 at p. 214.

or those of anyone else. Nor is it guaranteed to coincide with the conventional wisdom of the law. Christian teaching can be surprising, and on many issues it ought to be disconcerting and reproachful of our legal conventions and personal ethical assumptions. Also, we need to remember that torture historically has not always been beyond the pale from a Christian point of view (though it is centuries since the Puritans tortured to death those they suspected of witchcraft or since Vatican authorities felt it appropriate to put instruments of torment on display to coerce Galileo to recant or modify his scientific views). Moreover, it should be acknowledged that some of those in modern America who are willing to countenance the use of torture against terrorist suspects claim to do so for the best of motives, for moral reasons, to save innocent lives in circumstances where there seems to be no humane alternative. It is not inconceivable that this position might be endorsed from a Christian perspective, since there are values on both sides that a Christian must respect.

So I do not purport to say what a Christian *must* think on this matter, though certainly many of us would be surprised to find the churches falling in with the sweaty television fantasies, the brutal patriotic swaggering, the dishonorable lawyering, the irresponsible academic speculation, the contemptuous name-calling, and the simplistic means/end calculations that pass for moral reasoning in the secular debate.

When I say that the churches' voices have been missing from this debate, what I mostly mean is that there are concepts, frameworks, and resources in Christian moral thinking that ought to be available for responsible use in that debate—perhaps for use by thoughtful people on both sides—to supplement the rather ashen and impoverished moral vocabulary of secular commentators. Let me offer six examples of moral resources that might be useful in this debate, resources that Christian contributors can make better sense of and more articulate use of, in thinking about torture than their secular counterparts.

1. Absolute prohibitions. Christians understand the idea of a moral absolute, of a prohibition that is not to suffer infringement, whatever the circumstances or whatever the advantages of violating it. Secular moral philosophers mostly squirm at this idea: even deontologists furnish their ethics with some sort of 'out' to accommodate the possibility of what Robert Nozick referred to as 'catastrophic moral horror.'[16] The reason is

---

[16] Nozick, *Anarchy, State, and Utopia*, p. 30n: 'The question of whether these side constraints are absolute, or whether they may be violated in order to avoid catastrophic moral horror, and if the latter, what the resulting structure might look like, is one I hope largely to avoid.' See also pp. 216–17 above.

plain. For the secular theorist, moral prohibitions are rooted in the same terrain of value that nourishes our sense of the advantages that might accrue from a violation in particular circumstances. We say that torture is banned on account of an affront to human dignity, but we only need to imagine the consequences for human dignity of a thousand people being blown up to see that this value pulls us in both directions.[17] By contrast, a prohibition based on divine command has credentials that transcend all such calculations. As an expression of what God requires of us, individually and collectively, it is to be understood as categorical and uncompromising. Once again, I have no right to insist that this should actually *be* the Christian position on torture. But a Christian will not immediately take it off the table as an option, as a consequentialist or even a secular deontologist might.

2. The sacredness of the human person. The case against torture is rooted in respect for human dignity. But there are different ways of understanding that. Christians will not see human dignity as something we happen to be in favor of, or as a goal to be promoted. They will respond to it, as to the sacred, as to the holy presence of the image of God (*imago Dei*) in every human person. The idea of the sacred is not one that secular philosophers have wholly ignored.[18] But it is not an easy notion for us to make sense of, as it defies the sort of counting and manipulation that we usually associate with 'our' values. I am told that secular moral thought *can* make sense of the objectivity of value—values that do not depend on what we think, are not relative to our desires or customs or cultures. That is reassuring. But the notion that the value accorded to a person (or a thing or a place) might come from somewhere altogether beyond human life and imagining is a form of *radical* objectivity that goes beyond common-or-garden moral realism. And this, I think, is something that has proved very hard for secular theory to capture.

3. The sacredness of norms. Putting these first two points together, we might generate a sense—which even moral realists cannot attain—that certain norms (certain rules or principles) are not to be meddled with, or that it is not for us to manipulate them, reformulate them, or try to read them up or down on account of their under- or over-inclusiveness. Even when we think of moral norms as objective, we think of our activity in formulating and reformulating them as perfectly compatible with

---

[17] See Dershowitz, *Why Terrorism Works*, pp. 142–3.
[18] Ronald Dworkin essayed a secular translation of *the sacred* in his book *Life's Dominion*, pp. 68–101.

their objective existence. There is no sense that their objective given-ness compels us simply to take notice of them and comply rather than quibble and reformulate. The status of objectivity is something we paste on to a norm after we have done with it all that we can. It is not understood itself as a mode of moral apprehension.

Something similar is true of our approach to law, though there at least some jurisprudes get closer to the idea of a norm that is simply *given* to us. When most jurists think of positive law, they think of ourselves as constantly tinkering with it, to adjust its formulation in the light of what they take to be its purpose. But not all jurists approach positive law in this way. Modern textualists have come close to a sense that enacted norms might be beyond such meddling, on account of their provenance: *this* and not anything else is what the framers enacted or what the democratic legislature voted for; therefore *this* and not anything else is what commands our respect. That is a hint of what I have in mind. But an ethics which attends to divine command can take this much further, and imagine that sacred source and sacred substance come together in some particular prohibition, and that it is the given task of human law to approximate the inviolability of divine law on both these fronts. In other words, religious thinking can furnish not only with the notion that certain things are taboo and untouchable, but also with the idea that the very norms that protect those things might be taboo and untouchable and that meddling with those norms might already be a sin.

4. Tainted goods. Defenses of torture depend upon an apprehension that certain goods can be attained by a problematic means and that whatever else we might say about a particular means' being prohibited, we cannot deny the value of what its violation might secure. If we might secure safety by torture, then our use of this means might be objectionable, but at least no one can deny the value of the safety. Well, Christians need not accept this. They are in a position to say that certain goods might be objectively *tainted* on account of the methods that were used to achieve them. Thus even if we acknowledge that security and safety are of great importance, Christians understand that they are not the highest goods and that they can sometimes be purchased at too a high a price. Again, without begging any questions as to the ultimate position that church leaders should adopt, we need to leave open the possibility we are buying contaminated goods—goods ultimately not worth having—if the price of our security is torture.

One understanding of this will draw on the experience of ancient Israel and the warnings of the prophets: that even a people who have reason to regard themselves as God's elect—and many Americans have thought their republic should be viewed in this light—should fear that God will turn his back on them, even in this world, on account of their willingness to toy with abominations like torture. If we justify torture, we may have to justify it in its God-forsaken character.

Another understanding points to what we may ultimately lose if we enjoy goods secured in a certain way: 'For what shall it profit a man, if he shall gain the whole world, and lose his own soul?' (Mark 8:36). We need to take care how we seek the goods and avoid the dangers of this world, because we face goods and dangers beyond this world that are a lot more important than those.

A third and even deeper understanding points not just to what we may endanger (our country and its honor), or what else we may lose (our souls and our salvation), but to the burden of 'enjoying' the very goods we have sought to secure in this way. Living safe in the knowledge that our security was purchased on the back of a waterboard, the muzzle of a snarling dog, or the live end of an electrode is a hideous thing. Let me put this more affirmatively. It is not often realized how much our affection for due process and the Rule of Law is bound up with the character of our enjoyment of the goods and the safety that law provides. Having committed ourselves to the Rule of Law, we know something about the character of the goods we enjoy: they have not been secured for us arbitrarily or oppressively. But take away the Rule of Law, and introduce brutality and the infliction of torment, then our personal safety or the safety of our streets is a reproach to us, a tainted and clammy form of satisfaction that we can enjoy only with our consciences turned off.

5. Guilt and innocence. People sometimes say that we owe moral obligations only to the innocent, not to those who are complicit in terrorist activity. The heroes of human rights requirements are decent, valiant men and women. But terrorist suspects are like animals, they say. The English philosopher John Locke summed up this position when he said that 'one may destroy a Man who makes war upon him, . . . for the same Reason, that he may kill a *Wolf* or a *Lyon*; because such Men are not under the ties of the Common Law of Reason, have no other Rule, but that of Force and Violence, and so may be treated as Beasts of Prey.'[19]

---

[19] Locke, *Two Treatises of Government*, p. 279. For a critique, see Waldron, *God, Locke, and Equality*, pp. 145–7.

There is no doubt that we may treat the guilty in ways that it would be wrong to treat the innocent.[20] But it doesn't follow that we may treat the guilty any way we like,[21] or that it is permissible to exploit and instrumentalize their pain and terror for our purposes. And here there is a distinctive Christian doctrine available. Church leaders know and can remind us that there is a perspective from which we are none of us innocent, and they can remind us that a religiously-grounded requirement to respect human dignity is utterly invariant as between the treatment of saints and the treatment of those accused of the most heinous crimes. When our Savior Christ imagined Himself reproaching us on the Day of Judgment, in the great story of the sheep and the goats—'I was...in prison, and ye visited me not' (Matthew 25:31–46)—He did not distinguish between those in prison who were guilty and those in prison who were innocent. He did not say we owed duties only to prisoners accused of some offenses and not others. He warned us that inasmuch as we failed to minister in this regard to any of 'the *least* of these my brethren,' we failed to minister to Him, and I suspect He meant 'least' not just in the sense of lowliest, but the least considerable, even the most hated and despicable of 'these my brethren' (that is, of *any* human being we might have anything to do with). The most fundamental concerns invoked by the image of God in each human being and the commandments to respect and pay tribute to that image are utterly indiscriminate. The churches can remind us that the proposition that we owe moral

---

[20] I leave aside the point that there is no evidence of trials being held to distinguish guilt from innocence *in advance* of subjecting terrorist suspects to torture. We just torture those who happen to fall into our hands.

[21] In a 2005 decision, the Supreme Court of Israel considered the Israeli government's policy of preventative strikes aimed at killing members of terrorist organizations in the West Bank and the Gaza Strip even when they were not immediately engaged in terrorist activities. President (Emeritus) Aharon Barak prefaced his opinion with this observation (*The Public Committee against Torture in Israel and Palestinian Society for the Protection of Human Rights and the Environment v. The Government of Israel and others* (HCJ 769/02) December 11, 2005, §25):

> Needless to say, unlawful combatants are not beyond the law. They are not 'outlaws.' God created them as well in his image; their human dignity as well is to be honored; they as well enjoy and are entitled to protection...by customary international law.

The reference here to the image of God is intended to pull us up short and remind us that, although we are dealing with someone who will kill and maim scores of innocent people given the opportunity and one who is justly liable through his actions and intentions to deadly force, still we are not just talking about a wild beast or something that may be killed as though its life did not matter. The unlawful combatant is also *man-created-in-the-image-of-God* and the status associated with that characterization imposes radical limits on how lightly we treat the question of what is to be done with him. I discuss this further in Waldron, 'The Image of God: Rights, Reason, and Order.'

duties only to the good, or to those who are not suspected of terrorism, is a blasphemy that a Christian should have nothing to do with.

6. *The depraved and the demonic.* I have mentioned already the sense of personal taint that might attach to the use of forbidden means to secure some desired good. We need to remember, too, the old wisdom that torture harms the soul of the torturer, even as it breaks the spirit of his victim. This is not just rhetoric; it is an alert to very great spiritual danger. Abu Ghraib showed how an atmosphere where abuse of prisoners was permitted or encouraged, or where the legal and military restraints on it were made unclear, became one in which depravity flourished: sexual assault, pornographic tableaux, the use of animals, foul and blasphemous imprecations, and screeching hideous fear and brutality. This was not just high jinks, 'animal house on the night shift,' a few bad apples unaccountably rotting in an otherwise impeccable barrel. Everything we know about the exercise of the sort of power and brutality that torture involves indicates that this is a gateway for the demonic to enter human affairs. Use of torture involves immediate spiritual danger to the persons and organizations involved, and to the people (us) in whose name this is done. Church leaders understand this, and they should say it. If torture is thought to be defensible, or if the relaxation of the tight constraints upon abuse of prisoners is thought to be defensible, a case should have to be made that it is defensible in spite of this demonic element, not in denial of it.

4. Religious Abuse

Besides this moral vocabulary, and the richer stock of principles, ideals, and resources that church folks can use to characterize what is at stake, there are two other more vivid and troubling points that should be present to the minds of Christians in the torture debate.

The first is something about religion itself. It has to do with the relation between torture and the religion of those who are being tortured, and it is distinctive of what American interrogators have been doing to some of those who have fallen into their hands. Many or most of our captives are Muslims. Their terrorism is associated in the public mind with Islamic fundamentalism. And their captors and interrogators have felt free to treat their Islamic beliefs, their reverence for scripture, and the requirements of Islamic prayer and worship as points of vulnerability for cruelty, humiliation, and degradation. Let me say it plainly: religion itself has been made a target of torture. Devout religious belief has been perceived by those acting in our name as an opportunity for inhuman treatment to break the spirit of those from whom we want to elicit information. Korans have been abused, the Prophet mocked, the name of God blasphemed, and schedules of prayer frustrated and interrupted. In one appalling incident, an American woman interrogator smeared a Muslim detainee with red liquid she took from her pants, giving him the impression that this was menstrual blood, preventing him from washing, and knowing that he would not regard himself while thus defiled as able to pray. The hope was that a tactic like this would break his heart so that he would tell his American captors what they wanted to know.[22]

Muslims pray to God, as we do (though they believe different things and say different things). If there is a thought among military interrogators that it is all right to interfere with Muslim prayer, because it is not real religion, because it is meaningless, 'their' God not being 'our' God, then church leaders need to disabuse them of that impression. If there is a thought that it is all right to treat people's religion as something about them that we can manipulate—forcing them to curse Islam, threatening to beat them unless they thank Jesus they are alive—then church leaders need to warn them and their superiors about the gravity of this type of conduct.[23] The torturers may respond that the trivialities of a foreign religion pale into insignificance compared with the seriousness of the security interest in interrogation. The war on terror, they will say, is not a game. Church leaders can respond by reminding them that messing with a man's religion in this way is not a game either, not a trivial offense, but one of the worst things one can do. They can tell them it is playing with fire.

5. Torture and Crucifixion

The last point I will raise is one we need to approach with the greatest caution, but which can never be far from the mind of a Christian contemplating the issue of torture. Our Savior Christ, we know, was not just

---

[22] See Saar and Novak, *Inside the Wire: A Military Intelligence Soldier's Eyewitness Account of Life at Guantanamo*, pp. 225–8 and Jeff Jacoby, 'Saying Nothing Is Torture In Itself,' *The Boston Globe*, January 30, 2005, p. K11.

[23] Mark Danner, *Torture and Truth*, p. 227, reports that Ameen Sa'eed al Sheikh included the following in a sworn statement of January 16, 2004, concerning his experience at the hands of American guards at Abu Ghraib: 'Then they handcuffed me and hung me to the bed. They ordered me to curse Islam and because they started to hit my broken leg, I cursed my religion. They ordered me to thank Jesus that I'm alive. And I did what they ordered me.'

put to death; as we say in the creed, He *suffered* under Pontius Pilate. He was tortured with flogging and a crown of thorns. He was mocked and spat upon. As He was being crucified—itself the extremity of torture, even unto death—His tormentors took the opportunity to disparage His faith: 'He trusted in God; let him deliver him now, if he will have him' (Matthew 25:43).

We are charged, on our souls' peril, to remember all this. It is not to be exploited for cinematic entertainment, and it would be wrong to treat Christ's passion and crucifixion simply as the archetype of a human rights violation. We cannot infer a ban on torture from the fact of Christ's passion any more than we can infer a ban on capital punishment from His crucifixion.[24] This is a holy thing, not to be used for political purposes.

Still, it is there, and we need to think about our relation to it. Our primary relation is as sinners, saved by the cross, despite its having been our dereliction that made the cross necessary: in the words of the old hymn, *Herzliebster Jesu*: ''Twas I, Lord Jesus, I it was denied thee; I crucified thee.'[25] This is not a comfortable thought, though the passion of Jesus remains our chief hope. Even less comforting in this context, however, are the words of the warning that I have already mentioned, in the story of the sheep and the goats (Matthew 25:31–46). The thought here is difficult, but it goes something like this. Almost all of us can be confident that *we* will not suffer the torture our officials are complicit in; *we* will not bear the degradation that has been practiced in our name. Our complicity, our silence, or our denial are things to be borne not by us, but by others at our hands. But our pastors can do us a service with the reminder, given vivid form in the cross and passion held before our eyes, of *who one of those others may be*: 'Verily I say unto you, Inasmuch as ye have done it unto one of the least of these my brethren, ye have done it unto me.' We could do worse than think about torture in that light.

[24] If there are direct ethical lessons to be learned, they are those of 1 Peter 2: 20–24.

[25] The hymn's title (in English) is 'Ah, Holy Jesus, How Hast Thou Offended?' translated by Robert Bridges from the German of Johann Heermann (1585–1647). The full stanza, the second of the hymn, is as follows: 'Who was the guilty? Who brought this upon thee? | Alas, my treason, Jesus, hath undone thee. | 'Twas I, Lord Jesus, I it was denied thee: | I crucified thee.'

9

Cruel, Inhuman, and Degrading Treatment: The Words Themselves

When I wrote the articles that have become Chapters 7 and 8 of this book, I said very little about a set of accompanying prohibitions that we find in many of the conventions and statutes that outlaw torture: I mean the prohibitions on cruel, inhuman, and degrading treatment and punishment. In this chapter, I want to consider the meaning of these predicates 'cruel,' 'inhuman,' and 'degrading' and to reflect on the way in which we might approach provisions like these in the law.

I. The Law on Cruel, Inhuman, and Degrading Treatment

The Universal Declaration of Human Rights of 1948 (UDHR) and the International Covenant on Civil and Political Rights (ICCPR) both provide that '[n]o one shall be subjected to torture or to cruel, inhuman, or degrading treatment or punishment.'[1] A great many national and regional Bills of Rights say something similar. The formulation of the European Convention on Human Rights (ECHR) is very well known: 'No one shall be subjected to torture or to inhuman or degrading treatment or punishment.'[2] There are similar provisions in the South African Constitution,[3]

---

[1] UDHR, Article 5; ICCPR, Article 7.

[2] ECHR, Article 3: 'No one shall be subjected to torture or to inhuman or degrading treatment or punishment.' The non-derogation provision—Article 15(2)—that makes the ECHR prohibition on torture absolute also applies to the prohibition on inhuman and degrading treatment.

[3] South African Constitution, Article 12(1): 'Everyone has the right to freedom and security of the person, which includes the right...not to be tortured in any way; and not to be treated or punished in a cruel, inhuman or degrading way.'

the Constitution of Brazil,[4] and the New Zealand Bill of Rights Act.[5] The Canadian Charter uses the older language of 'cruel and unusual' treatment or punishment,[6] used also in the U.S. Bill of Rights[7] and (with slight variations) in most U.S. State Constitutions,[8] and adapted there more or less word-for-word from the English Bill of Rights of 1689.[9]

In addition to these general provisions, similar language is used in some more specific international instruments. The UN Convention Against Torture (UNCAT) uses the language of cruel, inhuman, and degrading treatment in one of its supplementary provisions (supplementary to its main prohibition on torture).[10] Slightly different language is used in the Rome Statute of the International Criminal Court; that statute prohibits not only 'torture' as a crime against humanity but also '[o]ther inhumane acts of a similar character intentionally causing great suffering, or serious injury to body or to mental or physical health.' It also prohibits as war crimes 'inhuman treatment,' and 'outrages upon personal dignity, in particular humiliating and degrading treatment.' Common Article 3 of the Geneva Conventions requires 'humane' treatment for persons taking no active part in hostilities (including prisoners and detainees), and it contains a prohibition on 'cruel treatment and torture' and on 'outrages upon personal dignity, in particular, humiliating and degrading treatment.'[11]

I used to think the most important thing about these provisions was that they erected a sort of *cordon sanitaire* around the much more important prohibition on torture—a 'fence around the wall,' designed not just to keep police, spies, and interrogators from crossing the torture

---

[4] Constitution of the Federal Republic of Brazil, Article 5 (III): *'[N]inguém será submetido a tortura nem a tratamento desumano ou degradante.'*

[5] New Zealand Bill of Rights Act 1990, section 9: 'Everyone has the right not to be subjected to torture or to cruel, degrading, or disproportionately severe treatment or punishment.' This statute also includes the following requirement, in section 23(5): 'Everyone deprived of liberty shall be treated with humanity and with respect for the inherent dignity of the person.' This is based on a similar provision in ICCPR, Article 10(1).

[6] Canadian Charter of Rights and Freedoms, Article 12.

[7] U.S. Constitution, Eighth Amendment.

[8] See, e.g. New York State Constitution, Article 1, sect. 5 (cruel *and* unusual); Constitution of the State of Texas, Article 1.13 ('cruel *or* unusual').

[9] Bill of Rights, December 16, 1689: '[T]he...lords spiritual and temporal, and commons...do...(as their ancestors in like case have usually done) for the vindicating and asserting their ancient rights and liberties, declare...10. That excessive bail ought not to be required, nor excessive fines imposed; nor cruel and unusual punishments inflicted.'

[10] UNCAT, Article 16(1): 'Each State Party shall undertake to prevent in any territory under its jurisdiction other acts of cruel, inhuman or degrading treatment or punishment which do not amount to torture as defined...'

[11] Geneva Conventions, Common Article 3.

threshold but to keep them from even approaching it.[12] In this chapter, however, I proceed on a different assumption; I am going to assume that 'cruel,' 'inhuman,' and 'degrading' have work of their own to do. They are not just ancillary to the torture prohibition; indeed they apply even when there is no question of any interrogational purpose. For Americans the issues of inhuman treatment and outrages on personal dignity have come up in the last 10 years mainly in relation to the treatment of detainees in the war on terror, but elsewhere in the world these prohibitions are oriented towards regular law enforcement as well. Article 3 of the ECHR, for example, has been mostly used to correct routine police and prison brutality in Turkey, Eastern Europe, and the former Soviet Union.

II. Indeterminacy and Elaboration

If we accept that these provisions have work of their own to do, how should we go about interpreting them? What are we to say about the meaning of predicates like 'cruel,' 'inhuman,' and 'degrading' in human rights law and phrases like 'outrages on personal dignity'? Almost everyone agrees that these standards are contestable.[13] They deploy highly charged value-terms—terms that the authors of one treatise say, 'tend to be over-used in ordinary speech.'[14] And many officials (including the President of the United States)[15] have professed themselves alarmed and bewildered by their indeterminacy.[16]

---

[12] On the other hand, in Chapter 7, pp. 203–7, I also suggested that this *cordon sanitaire* function might be performed by the relative indeterminacy of the term 'torture' itself rather than by these accompanying standards. See also the discussion of the sacredness of norms in Chapter 8, pp. 269–70.

[13] For some reflection on different kinds of indeterminacy—e.g. ambiguity, vagueness (in the technical sense), and contestability—see Waldron, 'Vagueness in Law and Language.'

[14] Harris, O'Boyle, and Warbrick, *Law Of The European Convention On Human Rights*, p. 88: 'The terms "inhuman" and "degrading" ... have no clear legal meaning and tend to be over-used in ordinary speech.'

[15] President Bush said in 2006: 'It's very vague. What does that mean, "outrages upon human dignity"? That's a statement that is wide open to interpretation.... [T]he standards are so vague that our professionals won't be able to carry forward the program, because they don't want to be tried as war criminals.... These are decent, honorable citizens who are on the front line of protecting the American people, and they expect our government to give them clarity about what is right and what is wrong in the law.' *Press Conference of the President*, September 15, 2006: <http://www.nytimes.com/2006/09/15/washington/15bush_transcript.html?pagewanted=6> (last visited January 13, 2010).

[16] Occasionally such professions of bewilderment elicit a skeptical response. The White House Press Corps has been known to make fun of the late Tony Snow's protestations

Even with the best will in the world, it is not easy to figure out what these provisions forbid. Inasmuch as they use evaluative predicates rather than descriptive ones, they present themselves as *standards* rather than rules. I believe it is important to keep faith with this presentation. At the same time, we face the difficulty of finding a reasonable way to elaborate these standards, for the evaluative predicates they use are certainly capable of meaning different things to different people. Let us consider some possibilities.

A. Refuse to deal with it

One possible response is to throw up one's hands and refuse to deal with the provisions on the ground that they are simply too indeterminate to be justiciable. This is what some federal courts have done when these standards have been invoked in the United States in Alien Tort Statute (ATS) litigation. The ATS, dating from 1791, entitles an alien to sue a foreign tortfeasor for (among other things) violations of the law of nations.[17] It is something of an historic anomaly, but it is about as close as we get in the American system to the sort of *ius cogens* jurisdiction that some foreign courts have assumed over human rights abuses (e.g. in the *Pinochet* case).[18]

Now the federal courts have been very cautious in their approach to ATS litigation, especially where actions are brought against high foreign

about vagueness. See e.g. *White House Press Briefing* (September 14, 2006) at <http://www.presidency.ucsb.edu/ws/index.php?pid=60247> (last visited on January 13, 2010).

> MR. SNOW: Some of the language in...Common Article III...is vague. In the case of Common Article III, of course, you have had some of—the 'prohibitions against cruel, inhumane or degrading treatment or punishment'—that's important to figure out what that means. As you know, in—Q: It's vague to you? MR. SNOW: Yes, it is. Q: [You m]ean, cruel, inhuman, degrading? MR. SNOW: Yes, because you have to specify exactly what you mean. Q: Keep smiling. (Laughter.) MR. SNOW: Please permit me to continue.

Readers will also remember the healthy and robust derision that was directed from Capitol Hill at Attorney-General nominee Mukasey's claim that he didn't know whether waterboarding was torture. See Editorial, 'In Arrogant Defense of Torture,' *New York Times*, December 9, 2007, p. 9: 'The new attorney general, Michael Mukasey, twisted himself into knots during his confirmation hearing, refusing to say whether waterboarding was torture and therefore illegal.'

[17] The Alien Tort Statute 1791: 'The district courts shall have original jurisdiction of any civil action by an alien for a tort only, committed in violation of the law of nations or a treaty of the United States.'

[18] Compare the assertion of universal jurisdiction in *Regina v. Bow Street Metropolitan Stipendiary Magistrate and Others, ex parte Pinochet* [2000] 1 A.C. 147.

government officials.[19] They are also quite cautious about the 'law of nations' idea in light of the insistence of the Supreme Court in *Sosa v. Alvarez-Machain* (2004), that any new claim for a violation of an individual's human rights under the ATS must 'rest on a norm of international character accepted by the civilized world and defined with a specificity comparable to the features of the 18th-century paradigm' of the law of nations.[20] It is generally accepted that the international norm against torture crosses this threshold.[21] But courts have divided on the question of how this plays out with regard to prohibitions on cruel, inhuman, and degrading treatment. The Eleventh Circuit in *Aldana v. Del Monte* (2005) maintained that the ATS covers only violations of customary international law; it denied that one could simply extrapolate 'law of nations' standards from human rights conventions.[22] But others have done just that.[23]

In a case against Argentinian officials involved in torture and disappearances, a District Court in California complained about the relativity of the 'degrading' standard:

> From our necessarily global perspective, conduct...which is humiliating or even grossly humiliating in one cultural context is of no moment in another. An international tort which appears and disappears as one travels around the world is clearly lacking in that level of common understanding necessary to create universal consensus....To be actionable under the Alien Tort Statute the proposed tort must be characterized by universal consensus in the international community. Plaintiffs' submissions fail to establish that there is anything even remotely approaching universal consensus as to what constitutes 'cruel, inhuman or degrading treatment.' Absent this consensus in the internal community as to the tort's content it is not actionable under the Alien Tort Statute.[24]

The court concluded that in the absence of clear and categorical definitions, it had no way of knowing what conduct was actionable under a 'cruel, inhuman, and degrading treatment' standard. And so it refused to recognize violation of this standard as a tort.

More recently, however, federal judges have shown themselves willing to work with these standards even if they remain ragged around

[19] See *Tachiona v. U.S.* 386 F.3d 205 C.A.2 (N.Y.), 2004.
[20] *Sosa v. Alvarez-Machain* 542 U.S. 692 (2004), at 725.
[21] See *Filártiga v. Peña-Irala* 630 F.2d 876 C.A.N.Y. (1980).
[22] *Aldana v. Del Monte Fresh Produce* 416 F.3d 1242 C.A.11 (Fla.), 2005, at 1247.
[23] See *Mehinovic v. Vuckovic,* 198 F.Supp.2d 1322, 1347 (N.D.Ga.2002).
[24] *Forti v. Suarez-Mason* 694 F.Supp. 707, at 712 (N.D. Cal., 1988).

the edges.[25] One district court said that

[i]t is not necessary that every aspect of... 'cruel, inhuman or degrading treatment' be fully defined and universally agreed upon before a given action meriting the label is clearly proscribed under international law, any more than it is necessary to define all acts that may constitute 'torture'... in order to recognize certain conduct as actionable misconduct under that rubric.[26]

In 2002, in a case dealing with human rights abuses in Zimbabwe, Judge Victor Marrero in the Southern District of New York made the point that federal courts have a responsibility to help remedy the definitional indeterminacy of 'cruel, inhuman or degrading treatment'; they should not just cite that indeterminacy as grounds for dismissing a suit. Judge Marrero said that in an area of law 'where uncertainty persists by dearth of precedent, declining to render decision that otherwise may help clarify or enlarge international practice... creates a self-fulfilling prophecy and retards the growth of customary international law.'[27] In that case, Judge Marrero engaged in a quite sophisticated discussion of the definitional question, including a holding that 'degrading' might apply to post-mortem mistreatment of a human body.[28] Eventually, the holding of liability against Mugabe and his party ZANU-PF was reversed on grounds of diplomatic immunity.[29] But it was not reversed on the ground of indeterminacy.

B. Use more familiar language

A second approach is to link the problematic provision to language that we find more familiar or more congenial. So, for example, the United

---

[25] See, e.g. *Jama v. United States Immigration and Nat. Serv.*, 22 F.Supp.2d 353, 363 D.N.J. 1998); *Mehinovic*, 198 F.Supp.2d at 1347–8.

[26] *Xuncax v. Gramajo*, 886 F.Supp. 162, 186 (D. Mass. 1995). Also a court in California—in *Doe v. Qi*, 349 F.Supp.2d 1258 (N.D.Cal.2004)—observed that 'the fact that there [is] doubt at the margins—a fact that inheres in any definition—does not negate the essence and application of that definition in clear cases.'

[27] *Tachiona v. Mugabe* 234 F.Supp.2d 401 S.D.N.Y., 2002. at 437 (Victor Marrero judge).

[28] Ibid., at 438: 'By any measure of decency, the public dragging of a lifeless body, especially in front of the victim's own home, for close kin and neighbors to behold the gruesome spectacle, would rank as a degradation and mean affront to human dignity.'

[29] Judge Marrero had already held that Robert Mugabe himself had something like head-of-state immunity: *Tachiona v. Mugabe* 169 F.Supp.2d 259 S.D.N.Y., 2001. And the Second Circuit held in 2004 that diplomatic immunity provided for U.N. delegations precluded service upon Mugabe as an agent for ZANU-PF. (See *Tachiona v. U.S.* 386 F.3d 205 C.A.2 (N.Y.), 2004.)

States entered a well-known reservation when it ratified the ICCPR and the CAT.

[T]he United States considers itself bound…only insofar as the term 'cruel, inhuman or degrading treatment or punishment' means the cruel, unusual and inhumane treatment or punishment prohibited by the Fifth, Eighth, and/or Fourteenth Amendments to the Constitution of the United States.[30]

The idea seemed to be that if we moved from the text of the conventions to terminology that was more familiar from our own constitutional law, we would have a better idea of where we stood. The shift is not to language that is any less evaluative or any more determinate; but at least we know the history of its elaboration.

In his confirmation hearings in 2005, former Attorney-General Alberto Gonzalez told the Senate that the effect of these reservations was to incorporate American geographic limitations on the application of constitutional rights into our obligations under the Treaty.[31] Aliens 'interrogated by the U.S. outside the United States enjoy no substantive rights under the Fifth, Eighth and 14th Amendment,' he said. And he added that there was therefore 'no legal prohibition applying to us under the "Convention Against Torture" on cruel, inhuman or degrading treatment with respect to aliens overseas.'[32] This was a mistake.[33] On its terms, the reservation concerns only definitions, not jurisdiction. I doubt very much whether a jurisdictional or geographic reservation would be valid.[34] And certainly it *would* have been invalid had it

---

[30] <http://www1.umn.edu/humanrts/usdocs/tortres.html> (last visited January 13, 2010). Something exactly similar accompanied our ratification of the ICCPR.

[31] This account of Gonzalez's testimony is adapted from Forcese, 'A New Geography of Abuse,' at 908–9.

[32] Ibid., 909, citing *Confirmation Hearing on the Nomination of Alberto R. Gonzales to be Attorney General of the United States: Hearings Before the S. Judiciary Comm.,* 109th Cong. 121 (2005). For a view similar to Gonzalez's, see McCarthy, 'The International-Law Trap': '[I]t is well established that the Constitution of the United States does not apply outside U.S. territory. The Constitution's Bill of Rights protections are unavailing for aliens who are outside our geographic jurisdiction.'

[33] Forcese, 'A New Geography of Abuse,' makes a more elaborate argument, but I think he comes up with the same conclusion.

[34] Some countries denounced our reservation even as it stood. For example, Sweden said of the U.S. position, 'A reservation by which a State modifies or excludes the application of the most fundamental provisions of the Covenant, or limits its responsibilities under that treaty by invoking general principles of national law, may cast doubts upon the commitment of the reserving State to the object and purpose of the Covenant.' (<http://www.iilj.org/courses/documents/USReservationsandOtherStatesObjections. pdf> last visited on January 13, 2010). I believe the U.S. reservation *would* have been invalid had it amounted to a determination not to apply the relevant provision at all in our treatment of certain categories of aliens in certain places.

amounted to a determination not to apply the relevant provision at all in our treatment of certain categories of aliens in certain places.

In any case, no such reservation qualifies American commitments under Common Article 3 of the Geneva Conventions. When the U.S. Supreme Court established in *Hamdan*[35] that Common Article 3 applies to our treatment of alien detainees at Guantánamo Bay, it made the task of parsing phrases like 'cruel treatment' and 'outrages upon personal dignity' quite urgent.

The Detainee Treatment Act of 2005[36] purported to establish a statutory equivalent to the reservations associated with our ratification of the ICCPR and UNCAT. Section 1003(a) provides that '[n]o individual in the custody or under the physical control of the United States Government, regardless of nationality or physical location, shall be subject to cruel, inhuman, or degrading treatment or punishment,' and section 1003(d) tells us that

In this section, the term 'cruel, inhuman, or degrading treatment or punishment' means the cruel, unusual, and inhumane treatment or punishment prohibited by the Fifth, Eighth, and Fourteenth Amendments to the Constitution of the United States, as defined in the United States Reservations, Declarations and Understandings to the United Nations Convention Against Torture and Other Forms of Cruel, Inhuman or Degrading Treatment or Punishment done at New York, December 10, 1984.

However, a statutory stipulation like this cannot have the authority of a reservation. While it is important that countries enact legislation to give domestic effect to their treaty obligations, such legislation cannot lessen the force of those obligations or alter their content as a matter of international law.

C. A quantitative approach

These first two maneuvers are ways of trying to avoid the actual words used in these provisions. If we do try to focus on the words themselves, what sort of approach should we take to their meaning?

One approach is to see these terms as simply picking up levels of the infliction of suffering that in its intensity falls short of the intensity of torture but are also banned—in the case of the ECHR by exactly the Article (Article 3) that prohibits torture. Bernhard Schlink, for example, has ventured the suggestion that '[w]hatever the wording, the distinction

---

[35] *Hamdan v. Rumsfeld*, 548 U.S. 557 (2006).
[36] This statute forms part of the Department of Defense Appropriations Act of 2006 (Title X, H.R. 2863).

between torture and cruel, inhuman and degrading treatment is one of intensity.'[37]

Thus there was a stage at which the European Court of Human Rights and the attendant scholarship distinguished between the terms but only in a crude quantitative way, marked by differences in the intensity of the suffering that was inflicted.[38] The idea was that degrading treatment is painful, painful enough to get over the minimum threshold of Article 3, but not as painful as inhuman treatment; inhuman treatment is very painful, but not as painful as torture; torture is the most painful of all and so needs a special stigma attached to it, etc.[39] The only qualitative distinction toyed with at this stage was that the basis of the distinction between torture and inhuman treatment might be the purposive element in torture. Elements of this quantitative approach still persist in ECHR law.[40]

D. Reasoned elaboration

I have emphasized that the provisions we are looking at are standards, rather than rules.[41] Can the problem of construing them be solved by converting them into rules or by supplanting them with rules defined by the decisions of courts? It might seem so. If the courts decide that solitary confinement is inhuman, then we can take the provision prohibiting inhuman treatment to be a provision prohibiting (*inter alia*) solitary confinement. If they decide that shackling prisoners is degrading, then we take the provision prohibiting degrading treatment to prohibit shackling. As the precedents build up,

---

[37] See Schlink, 'The Problem with "Torture Lite",' 86.

[38] Of course these measures of inherent suffering might be complicated in a sort of Benthamite way by 'duration' etc. See Meyerfield, 'Playing by our own Rules,' 93: 'One might even argue that there are circumstances in which cruel, inhuman, or degrading treatment not rising to the level of torture is worse than torture. Some forms of torture, such as waterboarding, last only for seconds. When ill treatment less severe than torture is extended for months and years, one could argue that such treatment is worse than very brief torture.' For the quantitative dimensions of Jeremy Bentham's felicific calculus, see Bentham, *Introduction to the Principles of Morals and Legislation*, pp. 38–40.

[39] The ECtHR famously said in the 1970s in *Ireland v. United Kingdom*, Series A, No. 25, ECtHR, 18 January 1978, '[I]t appears...that it was the intention that the Convention, with its distinction between "torture" and "inhuman or degrading treatment," should by the first of these terms attach a special stigma to deliberate inhuman treatment causing very serious and cruel suffering.'

[40] Scholars still routinely refer to the prohibition on 'degrading' treatment as 'the lowest form of an absolute right on the graded scale of ill-treatment under Article 3'—see, e.g. Mowbray, *Cases and Materials on the European Convention on Human Rights*, p. 227, citing Arai-Takahashi, 'Grading Scale of Degradation,' at 420.

[41] For the rules/standards distinction, see Sullivan, 'The Supreme Court, 1991 Term—Foreword: The Justices of Rules and Standards.'

we replace vague evaluative terms with lists of practices that are prohibited, practices that can be identified descriptively rather than by evaluative reasoning. In time, the list usurps the standard; the list becomes the effective norm in our application of the provision; the list is what is referred to when an agency is trying to ensure that it is in compliance.

What I have just described is a version of what is sometimes called 'reasoned elaboration,' as set out in the writings of the Legal Process School: courts and agencies take a relatively indeterminate standard and elaborate it by developing a set of much more determinate rules (sometimes called 'subsidiary guides'), which can then be used in people's self-application of the standard.[42]

This approach is illustrated in the best developed body of case law on 'inhuman and degrading treatment,' coming from the European Court of Human Rights (ECtHR) administering Article 3 of the ECHR: 'No one shall be subjected to torture or to inhuman or degrading treatment or punishment.' Through its precedents the ECtHR has established a set of principles,[43] presumptions,[44] and benchmarks[45] on various issues

---

[42] Cf. the discussion of 'The Reasoned Elaboration of Avowedly Determinate Directions' in Hart and Sacks, *The Legal Process*, pp. 150–1.

[43] The principles tend to be reiterated in virtually every case, more or less in exactly the words used in previous cases, at the beginning of substantive assessment of Article 3 complaints. The recitation goes something like this (from *Wainwright v. United Kingdom* (2007) 44 E.H.R.R. 40 at §41):

Ill-treatment must attain a minimum level of severity if it is to fall within the scope of Art.3 of the Convention. The assessment of this minimum level of severity is relative; it depends on all the circumstances of the case, such as the duration of the treatment, its physical and mental effects and, in some cases, the sex, age and health of the victim. In considering whether a treatment is 'degrading' within the meaning of Art.3, the Court will have regard to whether its object is to humiliate and debase the person concerned and whether, as far as the consequences are concerned, it adversely affected his or her personality in a manner incompatible with Art.3. Though it may be noted that the absence of such a purpose does not conclusively rule out a finding of a violation. Furthermore, the suffering and humiliation must in any event go beyond the inevitable element of suffering or humiliation connected with a given form of legitimate treatment or punishment, as in, for example, measures depriving a person of their liberty.

[44] An example of a presumption is the following: '[W]here an individual is taken into custody in good health but is found to be injured by the time of release, it is incumbent on the State to provide a plausible explanation of how those injuries were caused and to produce evidence casting doubt on the victim's allegations, particularly if those allegations were corroborated by medical reports, failing which a clear issue arises under Art.3 of the Convention.' *Yavuz v. Turkey* (2007) 45 E.H.R.R. 16 at §38. (This is pursuant to a general principle that '[i]n respect of persons deprived of their liberty, recourse to physical force which has not been made strictly necessary by their own conduct diminishes human dignity and is in principle an infringement of the right set forth in Art.3.' *Menesheva v. Russia* (2007) 44 E.H.R.R. 56.

[45] For the idea of 'benchmarks', see Schmuck, 'The European Committee for the Prevention of Torture and Inhuman or Degrading Treatment or Punishment,' at 79. The

relating to the circumstances in which official action might count as inhuman and degrading.

It is a good and usable jurisprudence.[46] Maybe there are one or two instances where Americans would feel the Europeans have been over-fastidious. Some worry that Article 3 as currently interpreted would forbid even standard U.S. police interrogation techniques.[47] The Reagan administration's concern about the language of 'inhuman and degrading'—which motivated the reservation discussed at the beginning

ECtHR avails itself of benchmarks set by various regional agencies. See e.g. *Kalashnikov v. Russia* (2003) 36 E.H.R.R. 34 at §97: '[T]he Court recalls that the European Committee for the Prevention of Torture and Inhuman or Degrading Treatment of Punishment has set 7m² per prisoner as an approximate, desirable guideline for a detention cell, that is 56m² for eight inmates.'

[46] And it has been used in the United States as well in some ATS cases. U.S. courts used the work of the ECtHR in *Xuncax v. Gramajo*, 886 F.Supp. 162, 186 and 189 (D. Mass. 1995), citing *The Greek Case*, Y.B.Eur.Conv. on H.R. 186, 461–5 (1969) and *East African Asians v. United Kingdom*, 3 Eur. H.R.Rep. 76 at §§ 207–9 (1973). And the ECtHR used the work that American courts did in *Rochin v. California*, 342 U.S. 165 (1952): see *Jalloh v. Germany* (2007) 44 E.H.R.R. 32, at §§49–52.

Let me add something about the use by courts in one jurisdiction of the work done by courts in other jurisdictions. The fact that these phrases are used in international, regional, and national rights documents means that there is case law all over the world devoted to the question of their meaning. To illustrate this, see the recent decision by the Supreme Court of New Zealand in *Taunoa v. Attorney-General* [2008] 1 NZLR 429. The Court had to determine some difficult questions about the application of the New Zealand Bill of Rights Act to the behavior modification regime applied in Auckland prison to prisoners whose conduct was violent or disruptive. The regime involved solitary confinement, loss of exercise and other privileges, and constant invasive searches. The question was whether the regime violated the requirement of section 23(5) that '[e]veryone deprived of liberty shall be treated with humanity and with respect for the inherent dignity of the person,' and if so, whether it also violated the more serious prohibition in section 9 on 'torture or … cruel, degrading, or disproportionately severe treatment or punishment.' The Court held unanimously that the former provision was violated but—by a 4–1 majority (Chief Justice Sian Elias dissenting)—that the latter, more serious prohibition was not. (The Court also divided on the question of monetary remedies.) It is a long and interesting set of opinions. Not the least of its interest is the approach taken by the Court to the citation of foreign law: the New Zealand Court cited 22 American cases, 9 Canadian cases, 18 cases decided by the ECtHR, 3 South African cases, 8 UK cases (plus 6 Privy Council decisions), and 10 decisions by the UN Human Rights Commission, as well as 17 New Zealand cases.

[47] A footnote to the notorious Bybee torture memorandum—Bybee, 'Standards of Conduct for Interrogation under 18 U.S.C. 2340–2340A,' pp. 17–18, n. 9—reads as follows: 'The vagueness of 'cruel, inhuman and degrading treatment' enables the term to have a far-ranging reach. Article 3 of the [ECHR] similarly prohibits such treatment. The [ECtHR] has construed this phrase broadly, even assessing whether such treatment has occurred from the subjective stand point of the victim.' The Bybee memorandum refers also to Ho, 'Possible Interpretations of Common Article 3,' finding that [the ECtHR]'s construction of inhuman or degrading treatment 'is broad enough to arguably forbid even standard U.S. law enforcement interrogation techniques, which endeavor to break down a detainee's "moral resistance" to answering questions.'

of this chapter—is said to have arisen out of its knowledge of a European case in which prison authorities' failure to recognize a sex change was determined to be inhuman and degrading.[48] And one might also mention a suggestion in one case—not, however, adopted by the Court— that flight paths into Heathrow airport imposed inhuman treatment on those who had to live under them.[49] But mostly the Court has held firm to its principle that Article 3 should not be cheapened by overuse.[50]

For all the sophistication and moderation of these precedents, there is one thing that is missed in the ECtHR case law and in the text-books that summarize it. No one spends much time reflecting on the meaning of the predicates that are incorporated in the Article 3 standard— 'inhuman' and 'degrading'—and explaining how the Court is guided by their meanings in generating its principles, presumptions, and benchmarks. The Court simply announces its finding that certain practices are inhuman or degrading while others are not, or announces a principle that it is going to use in determining what is degrading or what is inhuman. Sometimes principles for the elaboration of Article 3 are necessary inferences from the place that the Article is supposed to occupy in a legal system and their explanation is more or less self-evident. For example, nobody thinks that the prohibition on degrading treatment is supposed to preclude *any* stigmatizing aspect of punishment; and so we have the principle that in order to count as degrading treatment 'the suffering and humiliation must...go beyond the inevitable element of suffering or humiliation connected with a given form of legitimate treatment or punishment, as in, for example, measures depriving a person of their liberty.'[51] But other principles cry out for an explanation that would tie them more closely to an understanding of the language of the text.

Consider, for example, the cases—still distressingly common in Eastern Europe, Turkey, and Russia—in which someone is made to 'disappear' by

---

[48] This is asserted ibid., at 17, citing a decision by the European Commission on Human Rights, December 15, 1977, in *X v. Federal Republic of Germany* (No. 6694/74), 11 Dec. & Rep. 16).

[49] *Hatton v. UK* (2003) 37 E.H.R.R. 28.

[50] For example, it has refused to apply it to force-feeding to avoid death by hunger strike or solitary confinement or even the death penalty *per se*. On force-feeding, see *Nevmerzhitsky v. Ukraine* (2006) 43 E.H.R.R. 32, ECHR at §94. On solitary confinement, see *Iorgov v. Bulgaria* (2005) 40 E.H.R.R. 7, ECHR. And on the death penalty, see *Öcalan v. Turkey* (2005) 41 E.H.R.R. 45, ECHR (Grand Chamber) 163. (Though the Parliamentary Assembly of the Council of Europe has recently 'reaffirmed its beliefs that the application of the death penalty constitutes inhuman and degrading punishment,' the ECtHR has not said that the death penalty is inhuman and degrading.)

[51] See, e.g. *Kudla v. Poland* (Judgment of October 26, 2000), para. 92.

the authorities and frenzied inquiries by their parents or loved ones are dismissed with callous indifference. That the Court has been receptive to these claims is to its great credit; it has dealt with them carefully and sensitively. But the manner in which it articulates a relation between the text of Article 3 and the principles it lays down for dealing with such cases leaves a lot to be desired. In the earliest cases, the reasoning went like this:

The court notes that ill-treatment must attain a minimum level of severity if it is to fall within the scope of art 3 . . . It recalls in this respect that the applicant approached the public prosecutor in the days following his disappearance in the definite belief that he had been taken into custody. . . . However, the public prosecutor gave no serious consideration to her complaint. . . . As a result, she has been left with the anguish of knowing that her son had been detained and that there is a complete absence of official information as to his subsequent fate. This anguish has endured over a prolonged period of time. Having regard to the circumstances described above as well as to the fact that the complainant was the mother of the victim of a human rights violation and herself the victim of the authorities' complacency in the face of her anguish and distress, the court finds that the respondent state is in breach of art 3 in respect of the applicant.[52]

What is happening here is that there is a finding of anguish and distress caused by the authorities' indifference, and an announcement that this rises to the level of severity required for a violation of Article 3. Nothing more. In later cases, additional principles are introduced:

Whether a family member of a 'disappeared person' is a victim of treatment contrary to Art.3 will depend on the existence of special factors which give the suffering of the relative a dimension and character distinct from the emotional distress which may be regarded as inevitably caused to relatives of a victim of serious violations of human rights. Relevant elements will include the proximity of the family tie, the particular circumstances of the relationship, the extent to which the family member witnessed the events in question, the involvement of the family members in the attempts to obtain information about the disappeared person and the way in which the authorities responded to those enquiries.[53]

But again these subsidiary principles are simply announced, not explained. There is no sense that it might be worth discussing *why* the word 'inhuman' or the word 'degrading' apply to these recurrent dismissals of parental inquiries. Is it *degrading* inasmuch as the parent is

---

[52] *Kurt v. Turkey* (15/1997/799/1002), ECtHR, 5 BHRC 1, 25 May 1998 at §§133–4.

[53] *Gongadze v. Ukraine* (2006) 43 E.H.R.R. 44 at §184, citing *Orhan v. Turkey* [2002] ECHR 25656/94 (18 June 2002).

treated as though her anxiety amounted to nothing, as though she had no right to make such an inquiry, or as though officials could treat an inquiry from someone like her as beneath contempt? The subsidiary principle that requires us to look at 'the way in which the authorities responded to [the] enquiries' suggests something along these lines, but it is not spelled out. Is the conduct *inhuman*, inasmuch as any decent human being would understand a mother's need to find out what had happened to her son, and would have to be particularly hard-hearted to ignore her distress? Is it inhuman because it predictably leads to a level of suffering that no human can reasonably be expected to endure? The subsidiary principle that requires us to look at 'the proximity of the family tie' suggests something along these lines, but again there is no attempt to spell it out.

The scholars don't attempt any analysis either. The principles and precedents are simply listed in the treatises and commentaries; the chapters on Article 3 in these textbooks consist of nothing but a succession of such citations—sentence plus footnote, sentence plus footnote.[54] The impression they convey is that a lawyer working in this area does not need to understand the elaborative relation between the principles and precedents and the text of the Article.

There is a danger that an exclusive focus on the subsidiary rules might detract from the sort of thoughtfulness that the standard initially seemed to invite. The standard invites us to reflect upon and argue about whether a given practice is degrading or inhuman. But now we simply consult a list of rules. The result is a decline in the level of the moral argument—I mean the level of abstraction, but perhaps also the quality of moral argument—that the standard seemed to require.

Also, it is not clear how this approach helps when a court is confronted with an unprecedented practice alleged to be inhuman or degrading. How should a court approach the task of establishing a new precedent in this area? How should counsel in such a case frame their arguments? Should they proceed by a process of analogy with the list of practices already condemned as violations of the standard? Or should they go back to the original standard and reflect on the fundamentals of *its* application to this new set of circumstances? I believe the latter

---

[54] See e.g. Harris, O'Boyle, and Warbrick, *Law of the European Convention on Human Rights*, at pp. 34–58; Gomien, Harris, and Zwaak, *Law and Practice of the European Convention*, pp. 108–18; Mowbray, *Cases and Materials on the European Convention on Human Rights* pp. 172–227; Ovey and White, *European Convention on Human Rights*, pp. 58–66.

is by far the better approach to take. And it is probably inevitable anyway, given that anything other than a mechanical analogy with practices already prohibited will require us to reflect upon whether the new practice is *relevantly* similar—where 'relevantly' necessarily takes us back to some understanding of the original standard itself. In effect, what I am saying is that the 'list of precedents' (or list of subsidiary rules) approach can function as a useful guide only for those whose orientation to the law is primarily to predict the behavior of the courts and figure out what is necessary to keep on the right side of their decisions. But it cannot be the basis on which the courts themselves approach the matter. This is more or less the point that used to be made against Legal Realists and others who tried to define 'law' in terms of predictions about what the courts would do; such a definition is of little help to a court when it is actually in the throes of deciding what to do. That task requires active argument, not the paradox of self-prediction.[55]

E. The purposive approach

Another familiar lawyerly approach to these matters is to try to interpret problematic/indeterminate provisions in terms of their purpose or policy behind their enactment. The assumption is that the text cannot provide much in the way of assistance. Since the words—their indeterminacy or their contested character—are the problem, they cannot be part of the solution. And so one tries to look for other evidence of what the framers of these provisions were getting at. Of course it is an open question whether the underlying principles or policies are any more determinate than the text itself. As H.L.A. Hart once observed, indeterminacy of purpose is at least as much of a contributing factor to indeterminacy as the open texture of the language.[56] But the idea that this is the only place we can look has a very strong grip on the legal mind.

In general, attempts to talk purposively about these provisions usually just invites bland generalities, which take us away from their specifics. For example: it is sometimes said that underlying the Eighth Amendment is a broader principle of human dignity:

A punishment is 'cruel and unusual' . . . if it does not comport with human dignity. The primary principle is that a punishment must not be so severe as to

---

[55] For the predictive approach, see Holmes, 'The Path of the Law,' 699–700, and for this criticism of it, see Hart, *The Concept of Law*, pp. 10–11.

[56] Hart, *The Concept of Law*, p. 128.

be degrading to the dignity of human beings.... The true significance of these punishments *[sc. those prohibited by the Eighth Amendment]* is that they treat members of the human race as nonhumans, as objects to be toyed with and discarded. They are thus inconsistent with the fundamental premise of the Clause that even the vilest criminal remains a human being possessed of common human dignity.[57]

No doubt something about human dignity is conveyed whenever these terms—'cruel,' 'inhuman,' and 'degrading'—are used.[58] But the dignitarian reading encourages jurists to treat the 'cruel and unusual' formulation of the Eighth Amendment as though it also conveyed a prohibition on inhuman and degrading treatment—indeed as though it was intended as a broad catch-all dignitarian restraint.[59] This is a distraction when we have modern human rights and humanitarian law provisions that explicitly use all three terms and we are considering their distinct meanings one by one.

Constitutional interpretation in the U.S. sometimes orients itself to what is thought to be the original intention behind difficult phrases like 'cruel and unusual punishment' in the Eighth Amendment. Originalists believe that the provisions of a statute, treaty, or constitution should be understood now in the way that it was understood by those who framed, signed, voted for, or ratified it. This methodology is often thought to involve attending to what the original framers would have wanted done with the text so far as its application to various practices is concerned.[60] We are supposed to ask: 'would James Madison have approved

---

[57] *Furman v. Georgia*, 408 U.S. 238 (1972), at 271–3 (Brennan J.).

[58] See for example the discussion in Chapter 7, pp. 235–42, of the prohibition on torture as the archetype of a non-brutality principle.

[59] *Furman v. Georgia* 408 U.S. 238 (1972), Brennan J. concurring, at 270–3: 'At bottom, then, the Cruel and Unusual Punishments Clause prohibits the infliction of uncivilized and inhuman punishments. The State, even as it punishes, must treat its members with respect for their intrinsic worth as human beings. A punishment is "cruel and unusual," therefore, if it does not comport with human dignity.... The primary principle is that a punishment must not be so severe as to be degrading to the dignity of human beings.... Pain, certainly, may be a factor in the judgment.... More than the presence of pain, however, is comprehended in the judgment that the extreme severity of a punishment makes it degrading to the dignity of human beings.... The true significance of these punishments is that they treat members of the human race as nonhumans, as objects to be toyed with and discarded. They are thus inconsistent with the fundamental premise of the Clause that even the vilest criminal remains a human being possessed of common human dignity.' (For a similar approach in Canada, see *R. v. Smith*, [1987] 1 S.C.R. 1045.)

[60] This is an approach no self-respecting textualist would ever take to a statute; and the puzzling thing is why certain American textualists give up that inhibition when it comes to constitutional provisions.

of the death penalty?' for example, and the answer is supposed to help us dispose of the question of whether the death penalty is 'cruel' for the purposes of the Eighth Amendment.[61] This is sometimes called 'intended-application originalism.'

I shall say a little but more about this approach in section F, below. The most important thing to say, however, is that intended-application originalism is unlikely to work for 'inhuman' and 'degrading.' We have no real information about the original intention behind the relevant provisions of the ICCPR or the ECHR.[62] For example, no one seems to know why 'cruel' was present in Article 7 of the ICCPR but absent in Article 3 of the ECHR.[63] All we know is that the framers of the ECHR wanted to ban inhuman and degrading treatment. No one knows why these terms were chosen or what the people who chose them had in mind. It just seemed obvious that standards like these needed to be set up.

F. Ordinary language

I think that in the end there is no alternative to a steadfast focus on the ordinary meaning of the words themselves: 'cruel,' 'inhuman,' and 'degrading.' What is the natural language meaning of these words? What do they convey in themselves? What would someone think they meant if they had just been introduced into a conversation? My approach is going to involve what for many scholars will seem a distressing and perhaps annoying deference to the dictionary. It focuses on the complications and components of word-meaning that it is exactly the function of a good dictionary to record. I am well aware that words do many things in law besides conveying their dictionary definitions. Attention to word-meaning is not the be-all or end-all. But still it can be illuminating. The situation is redolent of what J.L. Austin said in his defense of ordinary language analysis: '[O]rdinary language is not the last word: in principle it can everywhere be supplemented and improved upon and superseded.

---

[61] For a critique of intended-application originalism, see Dworkin, *Freedom's Law*, pp. 13–14 and Dworkin, 'Comment' (in Scalia, *A Matter of Interpretation*).

[62] In any case, I have never heard an American defend the use of intended-application originalism with regard to twentieth century constitutional provisions. It usually relies for its plausibility on historical distance and perhaps also on the presence of a sort of mythic aura of original virtue that surrounds figures like the framers of 1787.

[63] The omission of 'cruel' in ECHR and the addition of 'degrading' to earlier drafts was not seen as particularly significant. Evans and Morgan, *Preventing Torture*, at p. 72 suggest that there was no debate in the *travaux préparatoires* on the significance of the particular terms.

Only remember, it is the *first* word.'[64] I worry sometimes that in our rush to the bottom line we miss some of the nuance and illumination that ordinary language can provide in helping us appreciate the standards that are being invoked here.

Some readers may think this is a mistake. They may follow Arthur Chaskalson, former President of the Constitutional Court of South Africa, who said this in an early decision of that Court on the death penalty—

In the ordinary meaning of the words, the death sentence is undoubtedly a cruel punishment.... It is also an inhuman punishment for it '... involves, by its very nature, a denial of the executed person's humanity,' and it is degrading because it strips the convicted person of all dignity and treats him or her as an object to be eliminated by the State.[65]

—but then went on to say:

The question is not, however, whether the death sentence is a cruel, inhuman or degrading punishment in the ordinary meaning of these words but whether it is a cruel, inhuman or degrading punishment *within the meaning of section 11(2) of our Constitution.*[66]

I am afraid that, as it stands, this is unhelpful. The case in which Chaskalson said this was one of the earliest cases facing the new South African Constitutional Court. The Court had to *decide* what meaning to attribute to these words for constitutional purposes. There was no well-established technical meaning there already to appeal to. If technical meanings are relevant at all, our inquiry in the first instance must be into how a technical meaning for 'cruel,' 'inhuman,' and 'degrading' is to be arrived at, and it seems to me obvious that, in this regard, we cannot avoid taking the ordinary meaning of these terms as our starting point at least.

---

[64] Austin, 'A Plea for Excuses,' at 8: '[O]ur common stock of words embodies all the distinctions men have found worth drawing, and the connections they have found worth marking, in the lifetimes of many generations: these surely are likely to be more numerous, more sound, since they have stood up to the long test of the survival of the fittest, and more subtle, at least in all ordinary and reasonably practical matters, than any that you or I are likely to think up in our arm-chairs of an afternoon—the most favoured alternative method.... Certainly, then, ordinary language is not the last word: in principle it can everywhere be supplemented and improved upon and superseded. Only remember, it is the *first* word.'

[65] Chaskalson P., in *S v. Makwanyane and another* [1995] South African Constitutional Court.

[66] Idem. (my emphasis).

The approach that I want to take might be called *textualist*, though I want to eschew the connection commonly made between textualism and originalism, particularly intended-application originalism. As I said in section E, originalists believe that the provisions of a statute, treaty, or constitution should be understood now in the way that they were understood by those who framed, signed, voted for, or ratified them. If this involves attention to the original word-meaning, well and good. The best guide to the intentions of the framers who used these terms are the intentions linguistically associated with them as a matter of word-meaning—i.e. the intentions whose conveyance it is the social role of the words in question to indicate.[67] But if it goes beyond what I referred to earlier as 'intended-application originalism,' then it loses its connection to the text. The trouble with intended-application originalism is that it does not take seriously the meaning of the words used in the relevant provisions, because it treats the same language—the same text—differently depending on who counts as the relevant class of framers and what they were historically inclined to do or approve. And it does this even if there is no independent evidence that the word-meaning has changed from one context to another.

So, for example, a jurist taking this approach is going to interpret the same phrase 'cruel...punishment' one way as it occurs in the English Bill of Rights of 1689, another way as it occurs in the Texas Constitution of 1876, and a third way in the Canadian Charter of 1982. In each case, he will be looking at the judgments about cruelty that the framers were inclined to make. The Canadian framers probably took it for granted that capital punishment was out of the question; the British framers probably had the opposite assumption. Now there is no independent reason to suppose that the word-meaning of 'cruel' has changed significantly over this 400-year period—certainly the dictionary records no such change. What have changed are people's views about cruelty, not the meaning of the word. But intended-application originalists are not interested in word-meaning.

I am interested in word-meaning, and in following this approach, I shall proceed on the basis of six assumptions.

(i) Evaluative language. The terms we are considering are patently evaluative. As I said at the outset, we should not lose sight of this, and we should not approach the interpretation of the relevant provisions

---

[67] See the discussion in Raz, 'Intention in Interpretation,' pp. 265–6 and see also Grice, *Studies in the Way of Words*, p. 111.

thinking that this is some sort of mistake or failure of nerve on the part of the drafters. We should not use the opportunity that interpretation presents to correct or supplant the evaluative character of these terms and try to convert what is presented to us as a standard into a rule or set of rules. Constitutional, humanitarian, or human rights provisions governing punishment and adverse treatment might have been framed using descriptive rather than evaluative predicates;[68] but the ones we have were not. It seems to me that the elaboration of a standard is not the same as the elaboration of a rule; nor should we assume that the elaboration of a standard involves replacing it with a rule.

(ii) Particular, not all-purpose, evaluations. I shall assume that provisions prohibiting cruel, inhuman, and degrading treatment invite us to make particular, rather than all-purpose, evaluations. 'Cruel,' 'inhuman,' and 'degrading' don't just mean 'bad.'[69] As one scholar puts it, 'inhuman or degrading treatment' is not a 'catch-all concept that encapsulates almost every conceivable manifestation of unbecoming conduct.'[70] We are invited to look for a particular sort of badness or inappropriateness and it is the purpose of the word-meanings of 'cruel' and 'inhuman' and 'degrading' to indicate to us what that particular sort of badness is supposed to be.

(iii) Unpacking evaluations. The elaboration of a standard—at least in the first instance—should involve some movement from general evaluative ideas to more specific but still evaluative ideas. We take a term like 'inhuman' and try to open up the specific evaluations—often the quite complex evaluations—that it involves, rather than scuttling away from the realm of evaluation altogether.

---

[68] An example of a provision (in this ball-park) that is much more descriptive, much more rule-like, is Article 18 of the Constitution of Argentina which says (in translation): '...Death penalty for political causes, any kind of tortures and whipping, are forever abolished. The prisons of the Nation shall be healthy and clean, for the security and not for the punishment of the prisoners confined therein; and any measure taken with the pretext of precaution which may lead to mortify them beyond the demands of security, shall render liable the judge who authorizes it.' There is still some indeterminacy here; but there has been a conscious effort to refer descriptively to particular practices, such as whipping and the death penalty, rather than to rely on evaluative terms like 'cruel' or 'inhuman.'

[69] I follow ECtHR judge Gerald Fitzmaurice in *Tyrer v. United Kingdom*, judgment of 25 April 1978 Series A No 26., sep. opinion, para. 14. (quoted by Evans and Morgan, *Preventing Torture*, at p. 89), in saying that '[t]he fact that a certain practice is felt to be distasteful, undesirable or morally wrong...is not sufficient ground in itself for holding it to [be inhuman or degrading].'

[70] Van der Vyver, 'Torture as a Crime under International Law,' 448.

This process requires a good ear. One has to be alert to the way the terms function in ordinary language and the role they perform in ordinary moral discourse. Beyond that one will look for clues in etymology and literary usage—not because these dictate our analysis, but because they may be suggestive of levels of complexity we might otherwise miss.

Often it is assumed that there is nothing to be said about the meaning of value terms: they just express attitudes. This is a mistake. Just because a word or phrase is evaluative and hence contestable does not mean that we might not gain from reflecting upon its meaning. A single evaluative word often packs into its conventional linguistic meaning resources that can be useful for the elaboration of the provisions in which it appears.[71] Not all evaluations are simple. Some are complex combinations of description and evaluation tangled together and not readily separable; we sometimes call these 'thick' moral predicates (as opposed to thin ones like 'good' and 'right' and 'reasonable'). Some evaluations nest inside one another, directing our evaluative attention at each level to some particular aspect of a situation.

(iv) The path not chosen. We should be attentive to the fact that a particular set of words has been chosen and that others have not been chosen. On their terms, the norms we are considering do not prohibit 'unjust' treatment, for example, or 'inefficient' or 'overly expensive' punishment. Our evaluative language is very rich: and these provisions draw on some of these riches and not others.

(v) Different terms mean different things. I shall assume that the use of more than one term is supposed to indicate more than one meaning. The United Nations Human Rights Committee is on record as saying that it is not necessary 'to establish sharp distinctions between the different kinds of punishment or treatment.'[72] But I shall not follow them in that. I will not say, with Lord Bingham, that '[d]espite the semantic difference between the expressions "cruel and unusual treatment or punishment" . . . and "inhuman or degrading treatment or punishment" (as in the European Convention), it seems clear that the essential thrust of these provisions, however expressed, is the same, and their meaning has been assimilated.'[73] We may find a certain measure of overlap;

---

[71] See e.g. Foot, 'Moral Arguments' and 'Moral Beliefs,' analyzing evaluative terms like 'pride,' 'harm,' 'rudeness,' 'justice,' etc.
[72] HRC, General Comment No. 20/44 (2 April 1992), cited by Evans and Morgan, *Preventing Torture*, at p. 76.
[73] *Reyes v. The Queen* [2002] 2 A.C. 235 (Privy Council), at §30.

but that is something for us to uncover in our analysis, not to assume *ex ante*.

(vi) No distractions. The provisions we are considering prohibit treatment or punishment which is cruel, inhuman, or degrading, *whatever else it is.* So, for example, if someone thinks that waterboarding is *necessary* in certain circumstances to prevent terrorist attacks, that does not affect the question of whether it is inhuman, nor does it affect the consequences of its being judged inhuman. If it is inhuman, then it is prohibited by the provisions we are considering whether it is thought necessary for defense against terrorism or not. The logic of these provisions is clear:

$$[X \text{ is cruel } or \text{ inhuman } or \text{ degrading}] \rightarrow [X \text{ is prohibited}]$$

There is no room in the antecedent of this conditional to consider anything like necessity or any other aspects of X's desirability. (This point is sustained partly by the categorical language of the Articles and partly by the explicit statement in the ICCPR and the ECHR that no derogation is to be made from these provisions in time of emergency.)[74] We are certainly not permitted to follow the reverse logic, a realist logic proceeding on the basis of *modus tollens*:

(1) If X is inhuman then X is prohibited;
(2) But because X is necessary, it is unthinkable that X should be prohibited;
therefore, (3) X cannot be regarded as inhuman.

My working assumption is that the meaning of 'inhuman' generates independent input into the syllogism, so that we cannot manipulate the term to reach whatever result we think is necessary.

I do not mean that attendant circumstances can never be relevant to a determination of whether treatment is inhuman or degrading. For example, ECtHR doctrine holds that shackling a prisoner is degrading unless the shackling is necessary to stop the prisoner from harming others. Someone might ask: what is the difference between *this* invocation of an attendant possibility of harm to others to justify what would otherwise be degrading, and (say) the invocation of the danger of terrorist attack to justify what would otherwise be degrading treatment during interrogation?[75]

---

[74] See ICCPR, Article 4(2) and ECHR, Article 15(2).
[75] I am grateful to Rachel Barkow and Cristina Rodriguez for pressing this point.

The question is a fair one, but I think it can be answered. In the shackling case, what is degrading is the use of chains without any valid justification. Once the justification is clear, the element of degradation evaporates. But in the interrogation case, we choose treatment that is inherently degrading because we think that it is precisely the *degradation* that will get the detainee to talk. In other words, the purpose of avoiding future attacks is not a way of undermining the claim that the interrogation technique is degrading; it is a way of justifying the selection of a degrading technique. And as such it is prohibited by the provisions we are considering.[76]

Some scholars have argued that a prohibition on (say) cruel punishment is going to work differently in a society which believes that God mandates amputation for theft and stoning for adultery.[77] But that need not be true. It is quite consistent to say of a punishment that it is cruel *and* that God ordains it: God may be cruel.[78] The question of whether

---

[76] I recently came across a novel way of trying to undermine this point. In a letter dated December 2007 (facsimile on file with author), Brian Benczkowski, a Principal Deputy Assistant Attorney-General in the Office of Legal Counsel in the Justice Department considered whether the identity of a detainee or the information he was thought to possess might affect our interpretation of Common Article 3 safeguards. Mr Benczkowski thought the answer was probably 'no,' but he noted this possible exception:

> [S]ome prohibitions under Common Article 3, such as the prohibition on 'outrages upon personal dignity,' do invite consideration of the circumstances surrounding the action.... [A] general policy to shave detainees for hygienic and security purposes would not be an 'outrage upon personal dignity,' but the targeted decision to shave the beard of a devout Sikh for the purpose of humiliation and abuse would present a much more serious issue. In such an example, the identity of the detainee and the purpose underlying the act would clearly be relevant. Similarly, the fact that an act is undertaken to prevent a threatened terrorist attack, rather than for the purpose of humiliation and abuse, would be relevant to a reasonable observer in measuring the outrageousness of the act.

Mr Benczkowski's analysis depends on moving from the quite specific phrase 'outrage upon personal dignity' to the more general standard of 'outrageousness.' Obviously whether an action is outrageous or not depends, among other things, on whether we are trying to achieve something important—such as averting a terrorist attack—by its means. But that does not affect the question of whether it is an outrage upon personal dignity. The fact that the word 'outrage' is used in the latter phrase does not entitle us to assume that what is deployed here is a general standard of outrageousness. Also, Benczkowski's analysis suggests assuming that if the purpose of an action like shaving a Sikh's beard is to elicit valuable information from him, then the purpose cannot be humiliation. But this is a mistake. The purpose is to elicit the information *by humiliating him*: the humiliation is intended as a means and the eliciting of information is intended as an end.

[77] See e.g. the discussion in An-Na'im, 'Toward a Cross-Cultural Approach to Defining International Standards of Human Rights,' at p. 33. See also Asad, 'On Torture, or Cruel, Inhuman, and Degrading Treatment', at p. 119.

[78] Cf. Isaiah 13:9: 'Behold, the day of the Lord comes, cruel, with both wrath and fierce anger, to lay the land desolate; and He will destroy its sinners from it' and also

something is cruel or inhuman is one aspect of its overall evaluation; the question of whether God ordains it is another. The position of the ICCPR is that cruel punishment is prohibited absolutely *whether God is thought to have ordained it or not.* Of course someone who thinks that God *has* ordained cruel punishment may be reluctant to sign up for the ICCPR prohibition. That just shows that human rights are demanding; indeed, it is a measure of how demanding they are.

III. The Words Themselves

After all this throat clearing, let us turn now to the particular predicates that are used in these provisions: 'cruel,' 'inhuman,' and 'degrading.'

A. 'Cruel'

'Cruel,' obviously, is a term of condemnation. The *Oxford English Dictionary*'s definition of 'cruel' indicates a range of attitudes towards others' distress or suffering that are properly regarded as wrong or seriously inappropriate.

Of persons (also *transf.* and *fig.* of things): Disposed to inflict suffering; indifferent to or taking pleasure in another's pain or distress; destitute of kindness or compassion; merciless, pitiless, hard-hearted.... Of actions, etc.: Proceeding from or showing indifference to or pleasure in another's distress.[79]

Distress and suffering normally excite concern and aversion; except in pathological cases, they are not the subject of pleasure or satisfaction in an observer. The disposition to inflict suffering, for its own sake, and taking pleasure in another's pain or distress are usually regarded as paradigms of wrongness. But, as the dictionary indicates, it is not only the conscious and active attitudes towards suffering that the term 'cruelty' captures; it also encompasses hard-heartedness or indifference towards suffering. In between deliberate sadism and cold-hearted indifference, 'cruel' also connotes the absence of attitudes that are appropriate when suffering is inflicted or otherwise going on: it connotes the absence of compassion or pity or mercy.

Jeremiah 30: 14: 'I have wounded you with the wound of an enemy, with the chastisement of a cruel one, for the multitude of your iniquities' (KJV).

[79] *Oxford English Dictionary*, online edition.

What makes a certain attitude towards suffering or distress appropriate or inappropriate? Sometimes the answer is to be found in the background norms of a certain institution. In old-fashioned family law, 'cruelty' as a matrimonial offense is understood relative to the love and mutual support generally reckoned among the conditions of a decent marriage. But it is not always so relative. The very idea of 'cruelty' supposes, I think, that there are certain attitudes which are *inherently* appropriate when there is a question of suffering or distress: compassion, pity, concern, etc. And there are certain attitudes inherently *in*appropriate: pleasure in another's suffering, unconcern, or indifference.

Though many of the rights provisions we are considering talk very generally about 'cruel treatment,' the term takes on a particular flavor in the context of punishment. It does so because punishment seems to involve a reversal of ordinary attitudes towards suffering: it seems that we deliberately choose sanctions that will cause suffering to those upon whom they are imposed. Some say this is part of the definition of punishment: H.L.A. Hart, for example, defines punishment in terms of 'pain or other consequences normally considered unpleasant.'[80] I think it is part of the meaning of punishment that the sanction is imposed because it is (thought to be) undesired by the victim; it is something he would prefer to avoid. But it need not involve pain or suffering: fines are punishments, and so is imprisonment, even when it consists (as it should) of nothing more than the unwanted deprivation of liberty. Even in cases where we do set out to impose as punishment a sanction that will cause distress, we think it appropriate that the imposition of distress be measured and that there should be a strong aversion to imposing more distress than is merited or than is necessary. The condemnatory implications of 'cruel' are rightly applied to anyone who takes advantage of the opportunities afforded by lawful punishment to inflict greater suffering than is appropriate, or to inflict suffering without the appropriate attention to necessity and proportion.

The dictionary suggests that 'cruel' is a word to be applied primarily to the agents whose attitudes to suffering or distress are revealed in their action or inaction. That is the primary meaning. Its application to the condition of the victim—the person experiencing the distress or suffering—is secondary, an extension of that. (So the dictionary also says that 'cruel' can be used '[o]f conditions, circumstances, etc.: Causing or

---

[80] Hart, *Punishment and Responsibility*, p. 4.

characterized by great suffering; extremely painful or distressing; *col-loq.* = severe, hard.') Mediating the two uses—'cruel person' and 'cruel condition'—is of course 'cruel action,' though I reckon that partakes more of the agent-oriented sense than the victim-oriented sense. And I would put 'cruel treatment' and 'cruel punishment' in that category too. They characterize actions or events in terms of the presence of inappropriate attitudes towards suffering or the absence of appropriate attitudes towards suffering.

I noted earlier that in the American jurisprudence on 'cruel and unusual punishment,' it is sometimes said that there is a broader principle of human dignity underlying the Eighth Amendment.[81] But, in fact, out of the three predicates we are considering, 'cruel' seems to be the one that is the least dignitarian in its connotations. Degradation is obviously a dignitarian idea, and so is inhumanity, at least if it is used in a victim-oriented as opposed to an agent-oriented way. (We shall consider this in more detail in our discussion of 'inhuman' in section B below.) But 'cruel' seems to focus on pain and distress, which is something suffered by animals as well as humans. We talk easily and I think non-figuratively about cruelty to animals. In that case, the term has more or less exactly the same use as it does in the case of cruelty to humans: it refers to an inappropriate attitude towards suffering or distress. I think, therefore, that if we are trying to capture the distinct meaning that 'cruel' is supposed to convey in a provision like Article 7 of the ICCPR—'No one shall be subjected...to cruel, inhuman, or degrading treatment or punishment'—we should not say that what it conveys is a distinctive standard of human dignity.

Having said that, U.S. case law on the Eighth Amendment is an obvious place to look for a consideration of what 'cruel' means in the context of a prohibition on 'cruel, inhuman, and degrading' treatment. But one has to be very careful with this body of case law, for a number of reasons. First, there is the distracting presence of 'unusual' in the Eighth Amendment formulation: for a punishment to violate the Eighth Amendment, it must be both 'cruel and unusual.'[82] Secondly, in its early years, the administration of the Eighth Amendment and its state equivalents had to be reconciled with the requirements of slavery.

---

[81] See, e.g. *Furman v. Georgia*, 408 U.S. 238 (1972), at 271–3.

[82] *Harmelin v. Michigan*, 501 U.S. 957, 967 (1991). Some U.S. State Constitutions by contrast prohibit 'cruel *or* unusual punishments.' (The 1876 Constitution of Texas is an example: Article 1(13) says that '[e]xcessive bail shall not be required, nor excessive fines imposed, nor cruel *or* unusual punishment inflicted' (my emphasis).

There might have been prohibitions on cruelty, but in slave codes those had to be read as prohibitions on '*excessive* whipping, beating, cutting or wounding' and '*unnecessary* tearing and biting with dogs.'[83] What Colin Dayan has called 'the twisted logic of slavery' infested the jurisprudence of the Eighth Amendment.[84] (The persistence of corporal punishment (whipping) in prisons until well into the middle of the twentieth century, and the difficulty of using Eighth Amendment arguments against it, is just one illustration of this.)[85] Thirdly, in its modern manifestations, American Eighth Amendment jurisprudence has been particularly preoccupied with the death penalty, whereas this is a marginal consideration in most other advanced democracies.

Fourthly, Eighth Amendment jurisprudence, like American constitutionalism generally, has been disfigured in recent years by the work of 'originalists,' who maintain that the proper approach to understanding rights provisions is to try to determine how members of the founding generation would have applied these terms 200 or more years ago. I have already ventured some observations about this. Let me just add that in no other jurisdiction in the world is this methodology deployed; nowhere else in the world is it taken seriously.

A final point is that the 'cruel and unusual' formulation of the Eighth Amendment is sometimes read (particularly by its liberal interpreters) as though it also conveyed a prohibition on inhuman and degrading treatment—indeed as though it was intended as a broad catch-all dignitarian restraint.[86] This, as I have already observed, is a distraction when we have modern human rights and humanitarian law provisions that explicitly use all three terms and we are considering their distinct meanings one by one.

---

[83] See, e.g. Dayan, *The Story of Cruel and Unusual*, p. 13.   [84] Ibid., at p. 16.
[85] See *Jackson v. Bishop*, 404 F.2d 571, 577–9 (8th Cir. 1968).
[86] *Furman v. Georgia* 408 U.S. 238 (1972), Brennan J. concurring, at 270–3: 'At bottom, then, the Cruel and Unusual Punishments Clause prohibits the infliction of uncivilized and inhuman punishments. The State, even as it punishes, must treat its members with respect for their intrinsic worth as human beings. A punishment is "cruel and unusual," therefore, if it does not comport with human dignity. . . . The primary principle is that a punishment must not be so severe as to be degrading to the dignity of human beings. . . . Pain, certainly, may be a factor in the judgment. . . . More than the presence of pain, however, is comprehended in the judgment that the extreme severity of a punishment makes it degrading to the dignity of human beings. . . . The true significance of these punishments is that they treat members of the human race as nonhumans, as objects to be toyed with and discarded. They are thus inconsistent with the fundamental premise of the Clause that even the vilest criminal remains a human being possessed of common human dignity.'

B. 'Inhuman'

The first thing to note about 'inhuman' is that it does not mean the same as 'inhumane.' The confusion is very common. On February 17, 2008, a fine op-ed piece by an Air Force Colonel and former Guantánamo prosecutor on the use of waterboarding was subbed by the *New York Times* with the internal headline 'Waterboarding is Inhumane'—which is *not* what the author said in his article. He said it was inhuman.[87] In fact, both terms are used in the human rights and humanitarian law provisions we are considering. Article 7 of the ICCPR prohibits inhuman treatment, while Article 10(1) of that Covenant also requires that '[a]ll persons deprived of their liberty shall be treated with humanity.' Common Article 3 of the Geneva Conventions does not use 'inhuman.' Instead it says that '[p]ersons taking no active part in hostilities...shall in all circumstances be treated humanely...' According to the *Oxford English Dictionary*, 'inhumane' in its modern use is 'a word of milder meaning than *inhuman*.'[88] Accordingly a prohibition on 'inhumane conduct' is much more demanding than a prohibition on 'inhuman conduct.'[89] (So, if one wants to discredit an accusation of 'inhuman'

---

[87] Morris Davis, 'Unforgiveable Behavior, Inadmissible Evidence,' *New York Times*, February 17, 2008, Opinion p. 12. In the same issue of the *New York Times*, a news story on John McCain said that legislation that he helped sponsor in 2005 'already prohibits the C.I.A. from "cruel, inhumane or degrading treatment."' It is not clear whether the quotation marks here are supposed to indicate what McCain said or whether it is just the reporter's ignorance that the relevant legislation prohibits inhuman treatment not inhumane treatment. (Michael Cooper, 'McCain Draws Criticism on Torture Bill,' *New York Times*, Sunday, February 17, p. A27.) Both the *New York Times* and the *Wall Street Journal* said that McCain's legislation prohibited inhumane treatment when it was passed into law. David Rogers, 'Bush Accepts McCain's Torture-Ban Amendment,' *The Wall Street Journal*, December 16, 2005, p. A6. Elisabeth Bumiller, 'For President, Final Say on a Bill Sometimes Comes After the Signing,' *New York Times*, January 16, 2006, p. A1. Also the 'inhumane' version is used over and over again in Richard W. Stevenson and Joel Brinkley, 'More Questions as Rice Asserts Detainee Policy,' *New York Times* December 8, 2005, p. A1.

[88] The *Oxford English Dictionary* says there was a time when the two expressions meant the same thing and were used interchangeably, but it notes that by the nineteenth century, 'inhumane' had become an obsolete variant of inhuman. And the dictionary says that '*inhumane* in current use has been formed afresh on *humane*, in order to provide an exact negative to the latter, and [is] thus a word of milder meaning than *inhuman*.' The dictionary defines 'inhumane' as 'destitute of compassion for misery or suffering in men or animals.'

[89] There is an excellent discussion of 'inhuman' and 'inhumane' in the opinion of Elias CJ in *Taunoa v. Attorney-General* [2008] 1 NZLR 429, at §79. Considering that section 23(5) of the New Zealand Bill of Rights Act requires that '[e]veryone deprived of liberty shall be treated with humanity and with respect for the inherent dignity of the person' in

treatment' as invoking a standard which is excessively demanding, one rewrites it as an accusation of 'inhumane treatment.' I believe this happens often in the American debate). In the rest of the discussion in this section, I shall focus on the meaning of 'inhuman,' the term used in Article 7 of the ICCPR.

The term 'inhuman' seems to refer to the absence of something to do with our common humanity or the presence of something at odds with it. There is something about being human that makes particularly problematic either (a) the act of inflicting of the treatment referred to as inhuman or (b) the suffering of the treatment referred to as inhuman. Of these alternatives, the dictionary seems to favor (a). According to the *Oxford English Dictionary*, 'inhuman,' as applied to persons, means '[n]ot having the qualities proper or natural to a human being; esp. destitute of natural kindness or pity; brutal, unfeeling, cruel.' And as applied to actions or conduct, it means '[b]rutal, savage, barbarous, cruel.' As in the case of 'cruel,' these definitions apply the predicate to the person meting out the treatment. It is the person meting out the treatment who is inhuman, who does not have 'the qualities proper or natural to a human being.' The term picks out what David Hume called 'the *vice* of inhumanity.'[90]

In the case of 'cruel,' the application of the word to the suffering itself, as opposed to the inflictor's attitude to the suffering, seems obviously figurative. But in the case of 'inhuman' I am not so sure. Milton used the phrase 'inhuman suffering' in the last book of *Paradise Lost*,[91] and

addition to the broader section 9 prohibition on 'cruel, degrading, or disproportionately severe treatment or punishment,' the Chief Justice said this:

> A requirement to treat people with humanity and respect for the inherent dignity of the person imposes a requirement of humane treatment. That seems to me to be the natural and contextual effect of the words 'with humanity'. A principal meaning of 'humanity' relates to 'humane'. In the context of the New Zealand Bill of Rights Act, the words 'with humanity' are I think properly to be contrasted with the concept of 'inhuman treatment', which underlies s 9 and its equivalent statements in other comparable instruments. On this view, s 23(5) is concerned to ensure that prisoners are treated 'humanely' while s 9 is concerned with the prevention of treatment properly characterised as 'inhuman'. The concepts are not the same, although they overlap because inhuman treatment will always be inhumane. Inhuman treatment is however different in quality. It amounts to denial of humanity. That is I think consistent with modern usage which contrasts 'inhuman' with 'inhumane'.

This is exactly the kind of discussion whose absence I was lamenting in my account of the ECtHR jurisprudence in section IV(D) above.

[90] Hume, *A Treatise of Human Nature*, Bk III, Pt 3, ch. iii, p. 606 (my emphasis).

[91] 'Can thus | Th' Image of God in man created once | So goodly and erect, though faultie since, | To such unsightly sufferings be debas't | Under inhuman pains?' (Milton, *Paradise Lost*, x, 507–11).

we might give that a quite distinct meaning, along the following lines. Suffering might be described as inhuman if it were thought that no human could or should have to put up with it, rather than inhuman because, in some normative sense, no human could or should be able to inflict it.[92] Relying now on my own linguistic intuitions rather than the dictionary, I believe that this independent victim-centered meaning of 'inhuman' may well be involved in our best understanding of the term in the human rights provisions we are considering. I shall explore it shortly. But first I want to give the agent-centered approach its due.

The agent-centered approach might include inhuman treatment of an animal: recall Cordelia's expostulation in *King Lear* when she hears of the storm her father was exposed to by her sisters: 'Mine enemy's dog,/ Though he had bit me, should have stood that night/Against my fire.'[93] The idea would be that, in the circumstances, no human could treat a dog in this way—maybe on account of what Jean-Jacques Rousseau called our 'innate repugnance at seeing a fellow-creature suffer.'[94] But it would be odd to describe the dog's suffering as, in itself, inhuman.

Judge Fitzmaurice in his separate opinion in the European Court on British maltreatment of detainees in Northern Ireland in the 1970s said that

the concept of 'inhuman treatment' should be confined to kinds of treatment that...no member of the human species ought to inflict on another, or could so inflict without doing grave violence to the human, as opposed to animal, element in his or her make-up.[95]

That is an agent-centered emphasis—treatment that would do 'grave violence to the human, as opposed to animal, element in [the agent's] make-up.' But it is also relational in the sense of referring to treatment that no member of the human species ought to inflict *on another member of the human species,* as opposed to treatment that Cordelia would not apply to her enemy's dog. There are certain things that humans cannot

---

[92] Twining, 'Torture and Philosophy,' thinks it is obvious that the terms are victim-centered: 'words like inhuman and degrading, and, more important, the kinds of concern that lie behind them, refer directly to the situation, and the rights, of the victim rather than to the blameworthiness of the behaviour of the agent.'

[93] Shakespeare, *King Lear*, Act 4, sc 7.

[94] Rousseau described this 'force of natural compassion' as a 'pure emotion of nature,' prior to all kinds of reflection.' Rousseau, *Discourse on Inequality*, Part One.

[95] Separate opinion in *Ireland v. United Kingdom* (Application no. 5310/71), 18 January 1978, quoted by Evans and Morgan, *Preventing Torture*, who observe, however, that this view has not prevailed.

or should not be able to do to other humans (whatever they can do to dogs). This relationality might be explained by sympathy. David Hume observed that '[a]ll human creatures are related to us by resemblance. Their persons, therefore, their interests, their passions, their pains and pleasures must strike upon us in a lively manner, and produce an emotion similar to the original one.'[96] The idea is that the suffering of another human resonates with us—we know what it is like to be a human in pain—and it might be thought that there is an extent of human suffering whose resonance in the person inflicting it would normally excite such sympathetic anguish as would lead him to pity his victim and desist.

Now this certainly will not work as a psychological hypothesis. There are sadists who enjoy the infliction of suffering that those who talk of 'inhumanity' say no human could tolerate inflicting, and these sadists are and remain members of the human species. There are torturers who, even if they do not derive pleasure from inflicting such suffering, are nevertheless willing to do so for what they regard as good purposes— and they too remain members of our species. Humans can be brutal, savage, cruel, and pitiless in the suffering they are prepared to inflict. We may want to label them inhuman, yet they remain human beings. The inhuman, as Levinas put it, comes to us through the human.[97]

The term 'inhuman' is evidently a normative not a descriptive one; but it is not simply a term of condemnation. The substance of the claim is that persons who behave in this way are being in some sense *untrue* to their undoubted humanity. Maybe we can resolve this with talk of pathology: a sense of normal human moral development that places limits on what one can bear in the way of this fellow feeling, and then a pathology defined by contrast with that pattern of normal development. So someone's ability to inflict this suffering leads us to classify him as a monster, a pervert, or as sick or damaged. But we have to conjoin this with an acknowledgement that many people of whom we say this remain unconcerned and cheerfully steadfast in their brutality.

Earlier I suggested that 'inhuman' might have a distinct victim-centered meaning: something that no human can endure or perhaps that no human can be expected to endure. This is a different sort of invocation of our human qualities than we saw in the agent-centered approach.

---

[96] Hume, *A Treatise of Human Nature*, Bk II, Pt 2, ch. vii, p. 368 ff. (on compassion).
[97] Levinas, *Sur L'esprit de Genève*, p. 164, quoted in Alford, 'Levinas and Political Theory,' at 157.

It looks to the limitations of our nature: the weight we can bear, the pain we can endure, the loneliness we can put up with, and so on.

It is not easy to parse this meaning of 'inhuman.' What does it mean for a person not to be able, as a human, to put up with something or to endure it? Does that predict what will happen—death, physical collapse, nervous collapse, madness—if he tries? We may say, for example, that the human capacity for bearing pain is limited: but what are we saying will happen if the threshold is exceeded? We saw in the case of the agent-centered meaning of inhuman that the implicit claim may be normative rather than descriptive. The same may be true of the victim-oriented sense. Perhaps we should talk not about suffering that no human can endure, but about suffering that no human should reasonably be expected to endure. But if we adopt such a formulation, we should treat it carefully: it doesn't mean the same as 'suffering that it is not reasonable to impose on a human being.' We are looking to a value-laden notion of human endurance as a way of interpreting a provision that limits the treatment we are entitled to impose. We are not jumping directly to a judgment about what treatment is permissible and what is not. Inhuman treatment is supposed to be a ground of impermissibility, not equivalent to impermissibility. I think that 'inhuman treatment' in the victim-oriented sense refers to treatment which cannot be endured in a way that enables the person suffering it to continue the basic elements of human functioning. These are elements like self-control, rational thought, care of self, ability to speak and converse, and so on. Any such list will reflect what we value about elementary human functioning, and so of course it will be contestable. But we have now focused the evaluative contestability on this particular issue, rather than leaving it at the more general level of contestation about what it is permissible to do to people.

I believe these ideas are particularly important in the context of punishment. Inasmuch as they regulate the types and conditions of punishment, provisions like ICCPR Article 7 and ECHR Article 3 impose a requirement that any punishment inflicted should be bearable—should be something that a person can endure, without abandoning his elementary human functioning. One ought to be able to do one's time, take one's licks. Even going to one's execution is something that a human can do; and to the extent that these provisions affect the death penalty, there is an implicit requirement that it be administered in a way that enables the persons to whom it is applied to function as human beings up until the point at which their lives are extinguished.

Is inhuman treatment just about the infliction of suffering? I think a lot of what we have said might be applied to other aspects of human experience as well. Treatment may be described as inhuman if it fails in sensitivity to the most basic needs and rhythms of a human life:[98] the need to sleep, to defecate or urinate, the need for daylight and exercise, and perhaps even the need for human company. We can imagine what it is like not to be allowed to use a toilet; we can imagine what it is like to be deprived of sleep. This commonality of human experience seems to be what is being appealed to in some shape or form with this standard.

Above all, we should remember the context. These standards are supposed to operate in regard to situations like detention, incarceration, captivity: situations of more or less comprehensive vulnerability of a person; and total control by others of a person's living situation. I think the provisions we are considering require those in total control of another's living situation to think about the conditions that are being imposed, and whether they are conditions minimally fit for a human, with characteristic human needs, life-rhythms etc.

C. 'Degrading'

'Degrading' might be thought to have the same duality as we noticed with 'inhuman': in the context of torture, we sometimes talk of treatment that degrades the torturer as well as the victim of torture. But I think it is clear that in the human rights context, 'degrading' is mostly a victim-impact term.

The *Oxford English Dictionary* defines 'degrade' rather formalistically as meaning '[t]o reduce from a higher to a lower rank, to depose from . . . a position of honour or estimation.'[99] The connection with rank is an important one. But it needs to be understood against the background of the way in which ideas about human dignity have evolved in our moral vocabulary. Rank is in the first instance a hierarchical idea, and the formal sense of degradation seems to involve taking someone down a notch or two in the hierarchy.

Someone is degraded if he is treated in a way that corresponds to a lower rank than he actually has: treating a queen like an ordinary lady

---

[98] One of the meanings that the Merriam-Webster Dictionary gives to 'inhuman' is 'not worthy of or conforming to the needs of human beings.'

[99] The OED also notes that it has a specialized meaning referring to the formal deposition of a person 'from his degree, rank, or position of honour as an act of punishment, [e.g.] as [in] degrad[ing] . . . a military officer, [or] a graduate of a university.'

is degrading or treating a professor like a graduate student. This use of degrading can certainly be relevant to the treatment of detainees in time of war. Fans of the David Lean movie, *The Bridge on the River Kwai*[100] will recall the long sequence in which Colonel Nicholson, played by Alec Guinness, insists to the Japanese commander of a prisoner-of-war camp that he and his officers are exempt by the laws of war from manual labor, even though the private soldiers under his command may legitimately be forced to work. Nicholson clearly believes that forcing the officers to work would be degrading, and he suffers a great deal as a result of the Japanese reaction to his refusal to accept this degrading treatment. However, it is pretty clear that the reference to degrading treatment in the modern Geneva Conventions is not about insensitivity to military rank. It depends on an idea of dignity that is more egalitarian than that.

The word 'dignity' *has* traditionally had a hierarchical reference: one talked, for example, about the dignity of a king or the dignity of a general.[101] I have argued elsewhere that the modern notion of *human* dignity does not cut loose from the idea of rank; instead it involves an upwards equalization of rank, so that we now try to accord to every human being something of the dignity, rank, and expectation of respect that was formerly accorded to nobility.[102] (I got this idea from Gregory Vlastos,[103] and James Whitman has also pursued in his work the idea of 'an extension of formerly high-status treatment to all sectors of the population.')[104]

Vlastos's idea is a constructive one: this is what we have decided to do. But there are also more ontological theories about the *inherent* dignity and high rank of every human person. One idea is that the human species has a rank that is much higher than any other natural species—higher than the animals, a little lower than the angels—by virtue of our reason and our moral powers. A connected idea is that each human has

---

[100] *The Bridge on the River Kwai* (Columbia Pictures, 1957), directed by David Lean. The movie was based on a 1954 novel by Pierre Boulle, *The Bridge over the River Kwai*.

[101] Consider this OED citation from the statute taking the crown away from Richard II—'1399 Rolls Parl. III. 424/1 Ye renounsed and cessed of the State of Kyng, and of Lordeshipp and of all the Dignite and Wirsshipp that longed therto.'

[102] Waldron, 'Dignity and Rank.'

[103] Vlastos, 'Justice and Equality,' pp. 54–5.

[104] Whitman, '"Human Dignity" in Europe and the United States,' 110–11, argues that '[t]he core idea of "human dignity" in Continental Europe is that old forms of low-status treatment are no longer acceptable.... "Human dignity," as we find it on the Continent today, has been formed by a pattern of leveling up, by an extension of formerly high-status treatment to all sectors of the population.'

a high rank by virtue of being created in the image of God. Associated with both of these is an insistence that this ontological dignity is the birthright of every human, and that, for example, racial discrimination is to be condemned as degrading treatment precisely because it involves the denial of this notion of the dignity of human beings as such.

The idea of an 'outrage' on human dignity—as used in Common Article 3 of the Geneva Conventions—is a particularly interesting one. 'Outrage' is a complaint one makes in high dudgeon about one's disrespectful treatment, but it also conveys the point that the slight to dignity is serious not trivial, and would strike almost any observer as a degradation.

It may be useful to outline four kinds of outrage to dignity, four species of serious degradation. Following Margalit's classification in *The Decent Society*, I call these (α) bestialization; (β) instrumentalization; (γ) infantilization; (δ) demonization.[105]

(α) Bestialization. The 'higher than the animals' sense of human dignity gives us a natural sense of 'degrading treatment': it is treatment that is more fit for an animal than for a human, treatment of a person as though he were an animal, as though he were reduced from the high equal status of *human* to mere animality. It can be treatment that is insufficiently sensitive to the differences between humans and animals, the differences in virtue of which humans are supposed to have special status. So for example a human is degraded by being bred like an animal, used as a beast of burden, beaten like an animal, herded like an animal, treated as though he did not have language, reason or understanding, or any power of self-control. Or it could include treating a person as though he did not have any religious life or sense of religious obligation, or as though the human (or *this* human) were one of those animals who are indifferent to separation from offspring or mate. It might also include cases of post-mortem ill-treatment: eating human flesh, for example, or failing to properly bury a human, or dragging a corpse.[106]

(β) Instrumentalization. We exploit animals as though they were mere means, objects to be manipulated for our purposes. This can generate a broader sense of degrading treatment associated with the Kantian meaning of indignity—being used as a mere means, being used in a way that is

---

[105] The account that I give is similar to that found in Margalit, *The Decent Society*, though his account is about humiliation, not degradation.
[106] See *Tachiona v. Mugabe* 234 F.Supp.2d 401 S.D.N.Y., 2002. at 438 and the discussion of that case in section II(A), above, p. 281, n. 28.

not sufficiently respectful of humanity as an end in itself.[107] This sense of degradation may be particularly important with regard to *sexual* abuse.

(γ) *Infantilization.* A third type of 'degradation' might have to do with the special dignity associated with human adulthood: an adult has achieved full human status and is capably of standing upright on his or her own account, in a way that (say) an infant is not. So it is degrading to treat an adult human as though he or she were an infant or in ways appropriate to treating an infant. This is particularly important with elementary issues about care of self, including taking care of urination and defecation. A number of the European cases have dealt with treatment that involves a person 'being forced to relieve bodily functions in [one's] clothing.'[108] And we know to our shame that this has been an issue in some recent forms of American mistreatment as well.[109] And again, we must remember the context: we are talking about vulnerable people in total institutions, with very limited powers to control their own self-presentation.

(δ) *Demonization.* The prohibition on inhuman and degrading treatment has particular importance in the way we treat our enemies or terrorists or criminals, those we have most reason to fear and despise. And obviously one of the functions of the 'degrading treatment' standard is to limit the extent to which we can treat someone who is bad or hostile as though he were simply a vile embodiment of evil. There are specific prohibitions in the Geneva Conventions against putting prisoners on display. And we might also mention in this connection the ancient biblical injunction in Deuteronomy 25:2–3, on the number of stripes that may be used if someone is sentenced to be beaten: 'Forty stripes may be given him, but not more, lest...your brother be degraded in your sight.'[110]

I have said that 'degrading' is an impact word. How important is it that the degradation be experienced subjectively as humiliating?[111] Some

---

[107] Kant, *Groundwork of the Metaphysics of Morals*, pp. 37–8.

[108] *Hurtado v. Switzerland*, Application no. 1754/90, Judgment of 28 January 1994.

[109] See, e.g. Meyer, *The Dark Side*, p. 207.

[110] Deuteronomy 25:2–3 (ESV). See also Martin Luther's observation in 'Lectures on Deuteronomy,' 248, that the purpose of this limit is 'so that your brother and his humanity should not be made contemptible...in your presence.'

[111] The fact that it is a victim-term does not necessarily mean that it is a term referring to subjective experience (in the way that the term 'humiliating' clearly does). Nor does it settle the matter of specific intention. In ECHR jurisprudence, a relevant factor in considering whether treatment was 'degrading' is whether its object was to humiliate the person concerned. But the absence of such a purpose does not conclusively rule out a finding of violation of Article 3.

ECHR commentators suggest that the connection is definitional,[112] but this is not so, at least not in my dictionary. However it is very common in the case law to emphasize the subjective element almost to the exclusion of everything else. Treatment is degrading, we are told, if it arouses in its victim 'feelings of fear, anguish and inferiority capable of humiliating and debasing them.'[113] (And it is worth bearing in mind that the Common Article 3 of the Geneva Conventions does also use the word 'humiliating'.)

It is an interesting question whether treatment can be 'degrading' if the person subject to it is unaware of it. In a recent English decision, the English High Court grappled with this, drawing upon considerable European (ECtHR) authority, and concluded:

Treatment is capable of being 'degrading' within the meaning of article 3, whether or not there is awareness on the part of the victim. However unconscious or unaware of ill-treatment a particular patient may be, treatment which has the effect on those who witness it of degrading the individual may come within article 3. It is enough if judged by the standard of right-thinking bystanders it would be viewed as humiliating or debasing the victim, showing a lack of respect for, or diminishing, his or her human dignity.[114]

I think this is right. Often when the European treatise writers consider a distinction between objective and subjective here, they have in mind a distinction between what the particular victim actually felt and what would be felt by a reasonable victim.[115] But what I have been talking about with categories of bestial, instrumental, infantile, and demonic degradation focuses in the first instance on what objectively happens to the person

---

[112] Harris, O'Boyle, and Warbrick, *Law of the European Convention on Human Rights*, at p. 80.

[113] *Tysiaogonc v. Poland* (2007) 45 E.H.R.R. 42, ECHR Paragraph 67, citing *Ireland v. United Kingdom* (A/25) (1979–80) 2 E.H.R.R. 25 at [167]. Also the International Criminal Tribunal for Rwanda defined degrading and humiliating treatment as '[s]ubjecting victims to treatment designed to subvert their self-regard.' [*Prosecutor v. Musema*, Case No. ICTR-96-13-A, Judgment and Sentence, §285 (Jan. 27, 2000)]. However, in some contexts this is left open; the ITFY defined this offense as requiring: 'an act or an omission which would be generally considered to cause serious humiliation, degradation or otherwise be a serious attack on human dignity.' *Prosecutor v. Kunarac, Kovac, & Vokovic*, Case No. IT-96-23 and IT-96-23/1 (Appeals Chamber), Judgment, 161 (June 12, 2002).

[114] *Regina (Burke) v. General Medical* Council (Official Solicitor intervening) [2005] Q.B. 424, at §178.

[115] Berndt, 'Ghost Detainees,' 1717: 'In analyzing behavior under this standard, the ICTY looked to both a subjective factor—whether or not the victim had experienced an outrage on personal dignity—as well as an objective factor—whether humiliation was so intense that a reasonable person would be outraged. The humiliation must be real and serious.'

in relation to some objective standard of dignity. If anyone's conscious reaction is emphasized it is the reasonable on-looker, not the victim.

But of course we do need to add that human degradation, even in an objective sense, is usually accompanied by a serious decline in self-regard. A term that is sometimes used is 'debasement.' Now we say that coinage can be debased, but a silver dollar does not know that it is being debased when it is alloyed or clipped. Human dignity does have a conscious component, if only because our dignity is thought to be based on conscious aspects of our being such as reason, understanding, autonomy, free will, and so on. And often too human dignity is associated with an element of normative self-regard. So, in the case of humans, debasement may not be possible without some conscious impact, though whether that is subjectively experienced as humiliation or anguish is a further question.

IV. The Moral Reading

In Part II of this chapter, I emphasized that the provisions we have been reflecting upon are *standards*, not rules; they use evaluative rather than descriptive predicates. As I said then, one approach to standards is to view them as inchoate rules, formulated in half-baked fashion by the lawmaker, and awaiting determinate elaboration and reconstruction by the courts. I said that I prefer an approach which takes more seriously the normative significance of the evaluative terminology that is used. The evaluative terms are not just blanks to be filled in. They require us to make evaluations of a certain sort and it is our task to figure specifically what kinds of evaluations these are. As we have just seen, this is a daunting but—I hope you will agree—an enriching task.

But excavating the meaning and resonance of these evaluative terms can detain us only so long. We do have to figure out whether we are supposed to be evaluating something the agent did or something the victim suffered; we have to figure out whether the evaluation required is predicated upon or conditioned by any other idea (such as a notion of elementary human functioning); we have to figure out whether there is any factual component in the judgment we are invited to make (e.g. a judgment about the victim's subjective consciousness of the treatment alleged to be degrading). All this has to be addressed. But when it is, then the value judgments that we have homed in on actually have to be made. Is there anything more we can say about that stage of the process?

Ronald Dworkin has used the term 'the moral reading' to refer to an approach to provisions like these which accepts the challenge to actually make the value judgment that their word-meaning indicates and make it in one's own voice (rather than as a ventriloquist for the framers).[116] Taking the evaluative character of these predicates seriously, Dworkin reads them as instructions to the norm-applier—an official in the first instance, a court in the final analysis—to go ahead and actually make a value judgment, i.e. to think about and try to the best of one's ability to make the judgment that is indicated by the evaluative terminology. Depending on one's moral self-confidence, this can be a lonely, a vertiginous, or an exhilarating responsibility.

True, the norm-applier is not entirely on his own. The provision does already indicate a certain value judgment by the norm-*framer* which binds us all: namely, if something *is* cruel, inhuman, or degrading then it is utterly forbidden. That we have no control over; that is given to us in the text as written. But the provision instructs the norm-applier to determine what *is* cruel, inhuman, and degrading and to make that value judgment in reference to the particular case under discussion. I have argued that we can unpack each of these evaluative predicates a little bit, without losing sight of the evaluative element. So Dworkin's approach would suggest that each norm-applier should ask himself as honestly as he can and in as objective a spirit as he can muster, certain quite specific evaluative questions. 'What attitudes towards suffering really are seriously inappropriate?' (What really is cruel?) 'What forms of treatment really are such that no human should reasonably be expected to endure them?' (What really is inhuman?) 'What is the special dignity that all humans have, and what counts as a derogation from it?' (What really is degrading or an outrage on human dignity?)'

On Dworkin's approach, the norm-applier is to ask these questions as complicated moral questions, and to try to get to the objective right answer—that is, to the moral truth about cruelty, inhumanity, and degradation and about the other moral issues that they embed. Any sensible person will recognize of course that as with all objective inquiries, what you get is the speaker's best opinion, and opinions will differ. But the formation of the opinion is supposed to be governed by the discipline of presenting the question and the answer in an objective spirit.

I should say that I am not entirely comfortable with this. On Dworkin's account, the norm-applier engages his or her own critical

---

[116] Dworkin, *Freedom's Law: The Moral Reading of the Constitution*, pp. 2–3 and 7–12.

views on what counts as inhuman and degrading. But I think a better way to understand these provisions is that they purport to elicit some shared sense of positive morality, some 'common conscience' we already share,[117] some code that already exists or resonates among us. I believe that these provisions, these standards, make an appeal to social facts and not just to individual moral judgment; they evoke positive morality not critical morality or the philosopher's 'moral reality.'[118] They appeal to what is supposed to be a more or less shared sense among us of how one person responds as a human to another human, a more or less shared sense of what humans can and should be expected to endure, a more or less shared sense of basic human dignity, a more or less shared sense of what it is to respond appropriately to the elementary exigencies of human life. The provisions we have been studying remind us that we share such a sense (if we do), they bring it to the forefront of our attention, and they require us to apply it in these circumstances. We sometimes think of these standards as prohibiting conduct that 'shocks the conscience.'[119] Again, I prefer to think of that not as an appeal to the moral sensibility of the solitary individual, but to some sort of shared conscience, ('con-science' in the etymological sense of 'knowing together'). Of course this is a massive act of faith in social morality, but it seems to me more satisfactory to view these provisions in this social and positive light than to see them simply as invitations to make our own individual moral judgments.

Some may say that this talk of shared standards and common conscience works perhaps for a single society, but that it is much more problematic in the case of human rights standards that supposedly govern all or almost all the nations of the earth. Given the massive moral differences that exist between peoples and cultures, how can the provisions we have been studying possibly be read as credible invocations of a common positive morality?

We have to be careful how we understand the impact of cultural relativity on the operation of these provisions. Sometimes the relativity of cultural and religious standards is referenced specifically in our understanding of the provisions. It is commonly observed that something

---

[117] Sanford Levinson in an essay entitled 'In Quest of a Common Conscience,' at p. 243, asks: '[I]s there some meaningful test of conscience which rests, ultimately, on the belief (or hope) that there is what might be called a "common conscience"?'

[118] For this distinction, see Hart, *The Concept of Law*, pp. 180–4.

[119] See also use of this phrase in Eighth Amendment jurisprudence, e.g. in *Chavez v. Martinez*, 538 U.S. 760 (2003).

that is experienced as 'degrading' in one culture may not be experienced as degrading in another. For a Muslim man it might seem degrading to be shaved or forced into close proximity with a scantily clad woman, whereas this would not necessarily be degrading to an American. At another level of abstraction, however, the meaning of degradation remains constant here: it connotes (or includes) something like being forced to violate one's fundamental norms of chastity, modesty, or piety. The meaning is the same, but different norms are referenced in the two cases. I think the court in *Forti v. Suarez-Mason* made a silly mistake when it complained about the relativity of the 'degrading' standard.[120] In every culture, it is degrading to be forced to violate one's own deeply held principles of modesty. The principles may vary from context to context but the standard which prohibits degradation remains the same.

This leads to a larger point. Whatever the relativists think, the fact is that 164 nations have signed (and most of those have ratified) the ICCPR, which includes the provision condemning cruel, inhuman, and degrading treatment and punishment. No doubt some governments have done this for the most opportunistic and hypocritical of reasons. Still, we are entitled to ask of the various nations that signed it in good faith: what—given the well-known facts about variations in peoples' views about cruelty, inhumanity, and degradation—should we suppose they were committing themselves to?

One possibility is that each nation thought itself entitled to read Article 7 in accordance with its own moral traditions.[121] Another possibility is that the representatives of the nations of the earth took themselves to be aspiring to standards that they thought did or could transcend the particularity of cultures and moral traditions. Terms like 'humanity' and 'inhumanity' for example seem to express such an aspiration: they seem to suggest that, for all the moral differences that there

---

[120] See *Forti v. Suarez-Mason* 694 F. Supp. 707, at 712 (N.D. Cal.,1988.): Noting that 'conduct...which is...grossly humiliating in one cultural context is of no moment in another,' it concluded that 'an international tort which appears and disappears as one travels around the world is clearly lacking in that level of common understanding necessary to create universal consensus.' (Analogously, religious persecution in one country may prevent someone from following Jewish ritual on a Saturday, and religious persecution in another country may prevent someone from practicing Catholic ritual on a Sunday. But it would be silly to say that a right which changes from Saturday to Sunday cannot be a universal right!)

[121] This seems to have been the American attitude, as expressed in the reservations discussed in section II(B) of this chapter, pp. 281–3 above.

are among peoples, still there are standards that define the way in which any human being should respond to the predicament of others or define extremities that no human being should be expected to endure. I believe it is a common feature of all moral cultures in the modern world that they have such an idea (which of course does not mean that the idea amounts to the same thing in every society). I am not resting anything here on the existence of moral universals; but I am suggesting that every moral culture in the modern world contains materials which are oriented in a universalistic direction. So it may be that there are enough universalistically-oriented materials in the morality of every society to make intelligible a public and international commitment by the government of that society to play its role in nurturing and upholding common standards and aspirations in the world.

As the United States has found to its cost and shame over the past seven years, a commitment to standards like Article 7 of the ICCPR or Common Article 3 of the Geneva Convention commits us to privileging some elements over other elements in our moral and cultural repertoire. We like to swagger around and blow things up; we like movies and TV shows in which the hero breaks people's arms in order to elicit vital information.[122] But our culture is also riddled with powerful universalistic humanitarian and dignitarian ideas about the proper and respectful treatment due to every human being. Our commitments to these conventions require us to privilege the latter over the former. It is not a matter of submitting to funny foreign standards; it is about privileging some of our own (that we share with others). I think something similar—though no doubt with somewhat different content—is true of every society.

One final point, in further qualification of Dworkin's moral reading. Whether we imagine ourselves asking an objective moral question at the level of critical morality or a social question about common conscience at the level of positive morality, different people (even in the same culture) are inevitably going to have their own takes on the matter; they will disagree, even when they think of themselves as asking and answering

---

[122] See Teresa Wiltz, 'Torture's Tortured Cultural Roots,' *Washington Post*, May 3, 2005, at C1: 'If you're addicted to Fox's "24," you probably cheered on Jack Bauer when, in a recent episode, he snapped the fingers of a suspect who was, shall we say, reluctant to talk.... Torture's a no-brainer here. Jack's got to save us all from imminent thermonuclear annihilation.'). For an example of the use of Fox's *24* to elicit support for the torture of terrorist suspects by United States interrogators, see Cal Thomas, 'Restrictions Won't Win War on Terror for Us,' *South Florida Sun-Sentinel*, May 4, 2005, at p. 25A.

the same question, even when they take themselves to be invoking standards that they think are shared. We should not panic at the prospect of these disagreements. The provisions we have been dealing with seem to invite them: they invite us to state and argue about our different views about what is cruel, what is inhuman, and what is degrading. There is a mentality afflicting some lawyers which sees things as spinning out of control when norms are deployed whose meanings people disagree about. It is a mentality that cannot see any difference between contestation, on the one hand, and, on the other hand, a situation that leaves each norm-applier at liberty to apply his or her own subjective preferences.

I think this mentality is misguided and deplorable. At worst it lays the ground for a sort of studied disingenuous moral obtuseness, as though one had never heard of the terms 'inhuman' and 'degrading' before— 'Who knows what these words mean?'—and a cynical opportunism which sees their contestedness as a chance to muddy the waters and undermine the operation of any standards at all in this area.

I said that we should keep faith with the fact that standards, not rules, have been laid down in this area.[123] That means adopting a positive rather than a pusillanimous view of the possibilities of argumentation. Those who framed and promoted these standards were intelligent men; even an originalist must acknowledge that. They didn't doubt for a moment that these provisions would be contestable. But they figured that in a world where people were locked up and interrogated and in general made vulnerable to the sharp end of official action, it was better to have such practices shadowed by a debate about cruelty, inhumanity, and degradation—a debate sponsored and focused by the law— than to leave these practices unregulated. And it seems clear to me that the application of standards of this kind, contested and indeterminate though their outcomes might be, differs quite considerably from a system where there is no provision at all for substantive assessment of such practices; and it differs too from a system which operates with nothing but determinate rules in this regard (such as 'No sleep deprivation,' 'No capital punishment') without sponsoring any opportunity to debate these at a more abstract level. That is the spirit in which I have approached these provisions, and I hope that, in Part III, I was able to indicate how complex and textured that debate can be and how it can be structured by a sensitive unpacking of the evaluative predicates used

---

[123] The following paragraph is adapted from Waldron, 'Law,' pp. 190–1.

in the law. It is not a complete account of the use of 'cruel,' 'inhuman,' and 'degrading' in the law but it is a beginning, and I hope it will inspire others. I believe it represents an important and indispensable dimension of the analysis that is necessary if these terms are to do the work we want them to in constitutional international human rights, and international humanitarian law.

10

The Rule of International Law

How should we think about the Rule of Law in the international arena? Asking about the Rule of Law in the international arena is not just asking whether there *is* such a thing as international law, or what we think of particular treaties (such as human rights covenants) or of the value of customary international law or of the enforceability of international law in our own courts. The phrase 'the Rule of Law' brings to mind a particular set of values and principles associated with the idea of legality.[1] These values and principles are the ancient focus of our allegiance as lawyers. The Rule of Law is one of the most important sources of the dignity and honor of our profession and an awareness of the principles and values that it comprises ought to be part of our professional ethos, something that disciplines the spirit and attitude that we bring to our work. True, it is not the only value we serve. As lawyers, we serve justice too, for justice is part of law's promise.[2] And of course we serve the interests of our clients and of society generally. But the Rule of Law constrains us in everything we do for these other goals: we pursue justice and the social good through the Rule of Law, not around it or in spite of it. In this chapter I want to talk particularly about the obligations the Rule of Law imposes upon lawyers, acting in various capacities. Like everything else in this book, it is written with issues of terrorism and the treatment of terrorist suspects in mind; but I hope the ideas developed in this chapter will also have some broader application.

Is it clear what the Rule of Law demands of us in the international arena? Many people think it demands less in the international arena—that it demands less of a national government, for example, than it demands of a national government in the domestic arena—not just

---

[1] For good accounts of these values and principles, see Fuller, *The Morality of Law*, pp. 33–94; Raz, *The Rule of Law and its Virtue* at pp. 212–19; Rawls, *A Theory Of Justice*, at pp. 236–9; and Finnis, *Natural Law And Natural Rights*, at pp. 270–6.

[2] See Waldron, 'Does Law Promise Justice?'

because there is less international law, but also because a different attitude towards law and the Rule of Law is appropriate in international
affairs. I do not agree with that suggestion and in what follows, I shall
give a number of reasons for rejecting it.

1. The Rule of Law for Individuals in the National Arena

Let us begin by thinking what the Rule of Law requires of us in the
national arena. Usually we think of the Rule of Law as being a requirement placed on governments: the government must exercise its power
through the application of general rules, it must limit the discretion of
its officials, it must not impose penalties on people without due process,
and so on. But the Rule of Law applies to the individual too. Let us begin
with the individual. Suppose I am an ordinary citizen; what does the
Rule of Law require of me? It requires certainly that I should obey the
laws that apply to me. I should be alert to changes in the law; I should
arrange things with my legal advisors to keep me informed as to what
my legal obligations are, in my particular business or area of activity;
I should refrain from taking the law into my own hands; and I should not
act in any way that impedes, harms, or undermines the operation of the
legal system. All of this applies to me as an ordinary citizen; all of this is
something that I can properly expect my legal advisers to help me with.

As I go about my business, I may find that there are areas in which
the law imposes minimal demands on me or no demands at all—many
areas where it leaves me free, leaves me to my own devices. This is not a
matter of regret. Allegiance to the Rule of Law does not mean I have to
wish for more law (or less freedom) than there is, nor does it require that
I play any part in bringing fresh law into existence if I do not want it.
I must obey the law where it does exist; but I have no particular obligation where it does not. It is not up to individual citizens or businessmen
to do the lawmakers' job for them—for example, to extend the scope
of the law's constraint (in accordance with common sense, morality, the
spirit of the law, social purposes, or anything else) if the sources of law
do not disclose an unambiguous enactment to that effect. We can even
go further. On most conceptions of the Rule of Law, individual citizens
are entitled to insist that the law be public and clear, not murky and
uncertain, stated clearly in a text not buried in doctrine. If the state is
going to have an impact on individuals by way of penalty, restriction,

loss, or incapacity then they are entitled to advance notice of this in the form of clear promulgated laws.[3] To the extent that the law that impacts upon them is unclear, then individuals are entitled to the benefit of that uncertainty.[4] In the absence of clearly stated constraint laid down in a promulgated legal text (like an enacted rule or a well-known precedent), there is a presumption in favor of individual freedom: everything is permitted if it is not clearly forbidden. It is not inappropriate for lawyers to help their clients navigate the legal system with this in mind—looking for ambiguities and loopholes, taking advantage of them where they exist, not going out of one's way to defer to laws whose application to a client's case is ambiguous or unclear.

The reason why all this is legitimate and entirely consistent with legality is that (on most accounts), the whole point of the Rule of Law is to secure individual freedom by providing a predictable environment in which individuals can act freely, plan their affairs, and make their decisions.[5] The elimination of uncertainty in the interests of freedom, the furnishing of an environment conducive to the exercise of individual autonomy: that is the *raison d'être* of the Rule of Law. And so it is perfectly appropriate to approach legal matters in this arena with the freedom of the individual—freedom from any restrictions that are not promulgated clearly in advance—in mind.

2. The Rule of Law Applied to the Government

What happens when we turn our attention from the individual to the government? (For the moment, we are still in the national arena; we are still leaving international law to one side.) Unlike the individual, the administration does not have an inherent interest in freedom of action in the national arena. It does not have an interest in being unconstrained by law in the way that the individual does. Quite the contrary: it is an important part of our tradition that the government should in all things

---

[3] See Dicey, *Introduction to the Study of the Law of the Constitution*, p. 110: when we talk about the Rule of Law, '[w]e mean, in the first place, that no man is punishable or can be lawfully made to suffer in body or goods except for a distinct breach of law established in the ordinary legal manner before the ordinary Courts of the land. In this sense the Rule of Law is contrasted with every system of government based on the exercise by persons in authority of wide, arbitrary, or discretionary powers of constraint.'

[4] See, e.g. *Staples v. United States*, 511 U.S. 600, 619 n. 17 (1994).

[5] See especially Hayek, *The Constitution of Liberty*, chs 9–10.

act in accordance with law, under the auspices of the ideal that we live in a nation of laws, not men, so far as governance is concerned. So the presumption for the government goes in a direction exactly opposite to the presumption for the individual. Governmental freedom is not the *raison d'être* of the Rule of Law. The Rule of Law does not favor freedom or unregulated discretion for the government. On the contrary, the government is required to go out of its way, to bend over backwards to ensure that legality and the Rule of Law are honored in the administration of our society. For the citizen, absence of regulation represents an opportunity for individual freedom. But this is not the case with absence of regulation so far as the state is concerned. If official discretion is left unregulated, if power exists without a process to channel and discipline its exercise, if officials find themselves in a position to impose penalties or losses upon individuals without clear legal guidelines—that is not an opportunity, but rather a defect, a danger, and a matter of regret so far as the Rule of Law is concerned. A government committed to legality should feel impelled to remedy this situation—facilitate and take responsibility for the emergence of new law to fill the gap—in a way that does not correspond to any equivalent obligation on the part of an individual citizen faced with the silence of the laws so far as some aspect of his or her own conduct is concerned. So while it is definitely not true from the citizens' perspective that 'the more law the better' or that it is better for more rather than less of their conduct to be governed by the law, something like that *is* true of the government. It *is* true that the more law, the better, so far as the regulation of government discretion is concerned—or at least that is true from the perspective of the Rule of Law, even if it has to be qualified from the perspective of other ideals that apply to the government.[6]

Accordingly, the responsibilities of a lawyer advising the government are different from the responsibilities of a lawyer advising the private citizen or the individual businessman. The lawyer's job in private practice is certainly not to counsel law-breaking, but the lawyer may legitimately look for loopholes or ways of avoiding the impact of regulation and restraint on the freedom of his or her client. In government service, however, things are different. There, the lawyer's job is to hold the government to its responsibility under the Rule of Law. Government

---

6 The Rule of Law is just one of the normative ideals that apply to government action. Others, such as efficiency or even security may sometimes pull in a different direction. For some reflection on the limits of the Rule of Law as a political ideal, see Fuller, *The Morality of Law*, at pp. 168–77 and Raz, 'The Rule of Law and its Virtue,' at pp. 226–9.

lawyers should not be in the business of looking for pockets of unregulated discretion or loopholes in such regulations as do exist. They should not be advising their political bosses that they are entitled to avoid the impact of legal constraint where it is ambiguous or unclear. Nor should they complain when their expectations of governmental freedom from constraint are frustrated—that is, when legal constraint turns up in an area where they had been under the impression that the government had a free hand.[7] Instead, they should proceed on the basis that the government is to act in accordance with law in *all* its operations, bearing in mind all the time that this general sense of constraint is not applied gratuitously, but applied precisely to foster the sort of environment in which *individuals* can enjoy their liberty. The administration subjects itself to constraint by law so that citizens can enjoy freedom under law. The government's own freedom of action is not a value, or at least not an intrinsic value as it is for individual citizens. This is an important contrast of ethos and attitude.

3. The Rule of Law for Governments in the International Arena

Now we move to the international sphere. Imagine you are a lawyer in the State Department, the Defense Department, or the White House, or working in the Justice Department in the Office of Legal Counsel, advising the administration on its responsibilities under international law. Which of our models from national law is appropriate for thinking about what the Rule of Law requires of you in the international domain?

It is tempting to say that the individual model is appropriate. It is true that you are acting for a government, but in the international realm, governments are just like individuals: in Hobbes' language, 'commonwealths once instituted take on the personal qualities of men.'[8] As individual

---

[7] Compare, however, the misplaced concern of Justice Scalia, in his dissent in *Rasul v. Bush* 124 S. Ct. 2686, 2706 (2004) about whether the administration's expectations of freedom are entitled to respect:

> Normally, we consider the interests of those who have relied on our decisions. Today, the Court springs a trap on the Executive, subjecting Guantanamo Bay to the oversight of the federal courts even though it has never before been thought to be within their jurisdiction—and thus making it a foolish place to have housed alien wartime detainees.

[8] Hobbes, *On the Citizen*, p. 156 (ch. 14, sect. 4).

humans are the subjects of domestic law, so nation-states are the individual subjects of international law. And so—the argument goes—the administration and its lawyers should have the benefit of the same sort of attitude towards the Rule of Law in the international realm as individuals and their lawyers have in relation to the law of the land. The same logic applies. The administration should respect any law that is clearly applicable—the clear text of any treaty it has entered into, for example—but only to the extent that it is manifestly and unambiguously on point. On this theory, any unclarity should be resolved in favor of liberty—in favor, that is, of the freedom of action of the individual sovereign state. The state is entitled to treat international legal restraints in a rigorously textual spirit; they apply where they clearly apply; but there is no requirement to stretch or extend their meaning to constrain governmental freedom of action in areas where they are unclear.[9] Also, on this approach, a national government is not required to go out of its way to establish international law. It need not wish for more laws (though it may); nor is it required to strive to bring what jurists sometimes call 'soft law' into clearer focus so that it can play a larger part in regulating or constraining sovereign states.[10] In the national sphere, the individual citizen is entitled to regard the absence of law or the unclarity of law as an opportunity for the exercise of freedom, and so—on the analogy we are considering—an individual government is entitled to regard the absence of international law or gaps in international law or the ambiguity of international law as an opportunity so far as the exercise of its sovereign freedom is concerned.

In my view this whole way of looking at things is a mistake, and the analogy on which it is based is misconceived. The state is quite unlike an individual or natural person; certainly it is quite unlike an individual so far as the value of its freedom of action is concerned. Whether you consider it in its national aspect or in its international aspect, its sovereignty is an artificial construct, not something whose value is to be assumed as a first principle of normative analysis. In its national aspect, the state is a particular tissue of legal organization: it is the upshot of organizing certain rules of public life in a particular way.[11] Its sovereignty is something made, not assumed, and made for the benefit of those whose interests it protects. In its international aspect, the sovereignty and sovereign

---

[9] For an argument that this is the approach of Bush administration lawyers to the Geneva Conventions, see Chapter 7 above, pp. 194–8.

[10] For the idea of 'soft law,' see the discussion in Handl et al., 'A Hard Look at Soft Law.'

[11] For this way of regarding the state, see Kelsen, *Introduction to the Problems of Legal Theory*, at p. 99.

freedom of the individual state is equally an artifact of international law. What its sovereignty is and what it amounts to is determined by the rules of the international order.[12]

I am not saying the sovereign state is not entitled to respect as the basic unit of international law. But respect comes in many shapes and sizes. The respect that the state is entitled to is already bound up with its status as a law-constituted and law-governed entity. It is not to be regarded in the light of an anarchic individual, being dragged kicking and screaming under the umbrella of law for the first time by some sort of international social contract. The point was made long ago by Immanuel Kant, and made in a way that was actually intended to blunt the censoriousness of certain enthusiasts for international law:

> [T]he obligation which men in a lawless condition have under the natural law, and which requires them to abandon the state of nature, does not quite apply to states under the law of nations, for as states they already have an internal juridical constitution and have thus outgrown compulsion from others to submit to a more extended lawful constitution according to their ideas of right.[13]

If a government has reason to resist the application of international law to itself—international law, as such, or any particular treaty or custom—it does so not as an individual defending his or her freedom, but as a law-imbued entity which already constrains its conduct with rules of its own. Accordingly, any case that is to be made for resisting the application of international law should be based on legality rather than the repudiation of legality. For example, one can imagine a state indicating that it prefers to be bound by the human rights constraints contained in its own constitution rather than by those contained in an international instrument (and qualifying its ratification of the latter accordingly); in my view, there is nothing incompatible with the Rule of Law in that.[14] But this is quite different from a state associating its

---

[12] See Hart, *The Concept of Law*, at p. 223: '[I]f in fact we find that there exists among states a given form of international authority, the sovereignty of states is to that extent limited, and it has just that extent which the rules allow. Hence we can only know which states are sovereign, and what the extent of their sovereignty is, when we know what the rules are...'

[13] Kant, *Perpetual Peace*, at p. 18.

[14] This might apply, for example, to some of the qualifications on the U.S. government's ratification of the Convention Against Torture (See S. Exec. Rep. No. 101-30, at 29–31 (1990)):

> The Senate's advice and consent is subject to the following reservations: (1) That the United States considers itself bound by the obligation under article 16 to prevent 'cruel, inhuman or degrading treatment or punishment,' only insofar as the term

sovereignty with the desire to be free from legal restraint altogether. In that regard, as Kant also noticed in his essay on perpetual peace, there is something odd about the state treating its majesty as a sovereign republic—something which at home is bound up with the very idea of legality and constitutionalism—as a license to demand freedom from international constraint, or as a platform from which it gives only the most grudging bow to the Rule of Law, when it looks outwards rather than inwards.[15] In the international realm, the state remains a creature of law, a tissue of legality, imbued with the idea of law, governed in the way that states are supposed to be governed, so far as the Rule of Law is concerned.

I want to go a little deeper into this because I am aware that it challenges some of the ways we are accustomed to thinking about international law. We often say that states are the subjects of international law,[16] which seems to imply (by the analogy I have rejected) that states are just like individuals in the national arena. But we need to understand that the state is not *just* a subject of international law; it is additionally both a *source* and an *official* of international law. International law regulates a small community of a few hundred members, compared to the millions that are regulated by domestic law. And it is horizontal law, rather than vertical law, law depending largely on treaty between states or the emergence of customs among states for the generation of new norms. So, regulating a sovereign state in international law is more like regulating a lawmaker in national law than like regulating a private individual.[17] It is true that in the national arena individuals can also be sources of law—through contract, for example. The difference is that in the national arena, there are substantial sources of law that are not dependent on individuals in this way, whereas this is much less the case

'cruel, inhuman or degrading treatment or punishment' means the cruel, unusual and inhumane treatment or punishment prohibited by the Fifth, Eighth, and/or Fourteenth Amendments to the Constitution of the United States.

It might even apply to the U.S. government's refusal to be bound by the International Criminal Court, if such refusal is based on a good faith affirmation that legality is better served by the extensive legal procedures it has for regulating and disciplining the conduct of its own military etc. in theaters outside the United States.

[15] Kant, *Perpetual Peace*, at p. 16.

[16] See Brownlie, *Principles of Public International Law*, p. 58 and Henkin et al., *International Law: Cases and Materials*, p. 241.

[17] Cf. Chayes, 'A Common Lawyer Looks at International Law,' at 1410: 'If states are the "subjects" of international law, they are so, not as private persons are the "subjects" of national legal systems, but as government bodies are the "subjects" of constitutional arrangements.'

in the international arena. States may be subjects of international law, but they are also much more like legislators than most legal subjects, and they both have and should embody special duties of respect for legality commensurate with that status.

States are not just makers of the international order; they are also its officials. International law has few executive resources of its own. It depends on its individual subjects—sovereign nation-states—for the enforcement of its provisions and the integrity of its rule. Governments are the officials or officers of the international legal system.[18] So advising a government in the realm of international law is much more like advising an executive official in the national arena than like advising a private individual or business. And as I said before, advising such a client cannot be conceived on the model of finding loopholes or trying to minimize the extent that law constrains one's client's freedom of action.

Another way to understand my position is to remind ourselves of the obvious point that states are not themselves people, they are not themselves human individuals. In the last resort they are not the bearers of ultimate value. They exist for the sake of human individuals. To use Kant's terminology, they are not ends in themselves, but means for the nurture, protection, and freedom of those who *are* ends in themselves.[19] We acknowledge this in the philosophy of national law, when we say that the state exists for the sake of its citizens, not the other way round. And the same is true in the international arena, where states are recognized by international law as in some sense trustees for the people committed to their care.[20] As trustees they are supposed to operate lawfully and in a way that is mindful that the peaceful and ordered world that we seek in international law—a world in which violence is restrained or mitigated, a world in which travel, trade, and cooperation are possible—is something we seek not for the sake of national sovereigns themselves, but for the sake of the millions of men and women, and the communities and the businesses, who are committed to their care. They are the ones who are likely to suffer if the international order is disrupted; they are the ones whose prosperity is secure when the international order is

---

[18] Here is an analogy: sometimes we say that a lawyer works not just as a counselor for his client, but also as an officer of the law, or an officer of the court. For a useful discussion of this idea, see Gaetke, 'Lawyers as Officers of the Court,' and Cohen, 'Lawyer Role, Agency Law, and the Characterization "Officer of the Court." '

[19] See Kant, *Groundwork of the Metaphysics of Morals*, pp. 36–7 for the idea of persons as ends-in-themselves.

[20] See Roth, *Governmental Illegitimacy in International Law* for an interesting discussion.

secure. Their well-being, not the well-being of sovereigns, is the ultimate *telos* of international law.[21] Nowhere is this clearer than in the role of international law in articulating a set of common standards for the protection of human rights. A pedant might see this as a departure from the intergovernmental character of international law.[22] I see it as the consummation of the point I made a moment ago about trusteeship—that ultimately international law is oriented to the well-being of human individuals, rather than the freedom of states.

The analogy that I have been arguing against is sometimes bolstered by the fact that so much of international law seems to arise out of treaties, and by the idea that treaties can be thought of as analogous to contracts between businesses or individuals. And again, the claim would be that we are bound only and at most by our explicit undertakings; we are not—people say—bound to extend the spirit of those undertakings into any grey areas to which they do not clearly apply and we are entitled to look for loopholes in our contracts and take advantage of their ambiguity. My view is that we need to be very careful with this analogy also. It makes most sense in regard to bilateral treaties that regulate particular aspects of trade or border-relations, for example. But in other areas, treaty-making is much more like voluntarily participating in legislation than it is like striking a commercial bargain. This is certainly true of multilateral treaties. This sort of treaty-making has a jurisgenerative aspect. And the responsibility of those who enter into a multilateral human rights convention (such as the Torture Convention, for example) is like that of a legislature that passes law constraining its own freedom of action—like Congress passing the Religious Freedom Restoration Act.[23]

So: the Rule of Law in the international realm constrains the administration not in the way that domestic law constrains an individual, but in the way that domestic law constrains a lawmaker. Governments are bound in this arena, as in any arena, to show themselves devoted to the principle of legality in all their dealings. They are not to think in terms of a sphere of executive discretion where they can act unconstrained and lawlessly.

---

[21] So, when it is said in traditional international law doctrine that the individual is only an object of international law (not a subject)—Oppenheim, *International Law: A Treatise*, p. 99—we might read 'object' in the sense of *telos*.

[22] See the discussion of the various ways of thinking about this in D'Zurilla, 'Individual Responsibility for Torture under International Law.'

[23] Cf. Chayes, 'A Common Lawyer Looks at International Law,' at 1410.

All this affects how lawyers should think of themselves when they advise the government on matters of international law—working, as I said, in the Justice Department or the White House. These lawyers should remember that they are acting for and advising an entity which is not just limited by law but law-governed in its very essence—a nation of laws, not men in *all* its operations. Their advice should be given with the integrity of the international legal order in mind. Legal advice given in this spirit should not be grudging as to legality, as though the Rule of Law in the international arena were an inconvenience to get around or an envelope to be pushed. Legal advice should certainly not be given in a spirit of studied recklessness or deliberately cultivated obtuseness as to the nature and extent of the obligations of international law. Instead legal advice should be given in a spirit that takes for granted the importance of the international legal order and the obligatory character of its provisions.

4. A Warning

My comments have been abstract and jurisprudential, but you will understand from the rest of this volume that these are not abstract issues. The ethics of lawyering in relation to international law and human rights constraints is a live concern at present in the United States. You know the situations that I am gesturing at. I am thinking of the advice given by lawyers in the Office of Legal Counsel concerning the applicability of Common Article 3 of the Geneva Conventions to Al Qaeda and Taliban detainees in the war against terrorism.[24] I am thinking too of the advice given by lawyers in the same office concerning the legality of torture and of cruel, inhuman, and degrading treatment in the course of interrogation.[25] There is law to govern these matters, but the Bush administration was advised by lawyers in the Office of Legal Counsel and elsewhere—some of whom are present at this session today—in a way that treated that law as though it were an inconvenience to be ignored, an order to be muddied, a framework to be overridden, rather than in a way that defended its integrity as an order in which we can take our rightful place

---

[24] See Yoo and Delahunty, 'Application of Treaties and Laws to Al Qaeda and Taliban Detainees.' (See pp. 194–8 above.)

[25] See Bybee, Jay, 'Standards of Conduct for Interrogation under 18 U.S.C. 2340–2340A.' (See pp. 207–12 above.)

as a nation, among other nations, under law and subject to the principles of legality.

Personally I believe that the sort of lawyering that has gone on in these settings in recent years has entailed grave breaches of professional ethics, amounting in some cases to complicity in war crimes.[26] Those who have done this—and I include some members of this organization, some of the people in this room—are going to have to live now with the personal and reputational consequences as well as the damage they have done to the honor and reputation of their country, in relation to the Rule of Law.

In December 2005, Robert Keohane wrote a letter to the *Financial Times*, protesting something that had been written in an opinion piece concerning Jack Goldsmith, formerly in the office of Legal Counsel, now a Professor at Harvard Law School. The piece that Keohane objected to had suggested that Goldsmith might be subject to criminal prosecution for the legal advice he gave the U.S. government (advice concerning extraordinary renditions). Professor Keohane disagreed. He maintained that Goldsmith had acted more honorably than that. He said that 'when he became assistant attorney-general, [Goldsmith] withdrew one of the Yoo memos well before it became public, and [that] he resigned as a result of disputes with vice-president Dick Cheney's top legal adviser, David Addington.'[27] What struck me about this exchange was not so much the merits of the particular issue concerning the actions of Professor Goldsmith.[28] What struck me was rather that things have come to a sad pass, when it is necessary to undertake and debate these sorts of differences between senior law professors formerly in the public service concerning possible liability for war crimes prosecutions in connection with their lawyering. How did we end up here? How did we end up in a situation in which good bright lawyers and law professors are being described by their peers as war criminals or as complicit in war crimes or in conspiracy to violate the laws of armed conflict, and in which their colleagues are having to rebut these characterizations? How did it happen that we now have to draw distinctions of this kind among our friends and colleagues? The answer has to do with attitude,

---

[26] See, e.g. Bilder and Vagts, 'Speaking Law to Power: Lawyers and Torture.'

[27] Robert O. Keohane, 'Letter: Wrong Target Chosen over Torture Memos,' *Financial Times*, December 14, 2005, p. 14. Cf. Philippe Sands, 'Comment: America cannot circumvent the law on torture,' *Financial Times*, December 9, 2005.

[28] On the merits, I am happy to accept the accuracy of Keohane's account. See also Goldsmith, *The Terror Presidency*.

environment, and culture, and I want to end by speaking directly to those who may in the future take up the sort of legal positions I have been talking about.[29]

New lawyers, about to enter public service, ought to reflect carefully upon their relation to the Rule of Law, this ancient ideal which (as I said earlier) is the focus of our allegiance as lawyers, the key to the honor of our profession, the foundation of the dignity of the work that we do. They ought to think very carefully about the attitudes that they culti-vate among themselves so far as law, the Rule of Law, and the interna-tional order are concerned. An organization of like-minded people can be a wonderful thing, but it can also sometimes blind us to our broader responsibilities and by a sort of group-thinking lead us to treat with con-tempt or derision practices, virtues, institutions, and constraints that are in fact—when seen from a wider perspective—of deep and inestimable value.

In this connection, I would like to invite readers to reflect upon a pas-sage written by C.S. Lewis in his book *The Problem of Pain*, in the chap-ter devoted to human wickedness.

[M]any of us have had the experience of living in some local pocket of human society—some particular school, college, regiment, or profession where the tone was bad. And inside that pocket certain actions were regarded as merely normal ('Everyone does it') and certain others as impracticably virtuous and Quixotic. But when we emerged from that bad society we made the horrible discovery that in the world our 'normal' was the kind of thing that no decent person ever dreamed of doing, and our 'Quixotic' was taken for granted as the minimum standard of decency.[30]

It is a chilling thought. And it seems particularly applicable to settings where people move in a closed world, intoxicated by power and rein-forcing one another in their contempt for what many regard as the sim-plistic standards and ideals of international legality. Sure even in that situation, everyone has some scruples—and C.S. Lewis suggests that when you emerge from such a milieu, you may well find that '[w]hat had seemed to us morbid and fantastic [Kantian] scruples so long as we were in the "pocket" of this organization now turned out to be the only moments of sanity we there enjoyed.'[31] Think about that. So long as one was in the administration, it might have seemed that international law

---

[29] The material in this chapter was presented originally at a Federalist Society student conference held at Columbia Law School.
[30] Lewis, *The Problem of Pain*, p. 56.　　　[31] Idem.

was something to be derided. So long as one remained in that environment, one could afford to laugh at one's own legalistic scruples about torture, rendition, indefinite detention, and the violation of the Geneva Conventions as unwelcome leftovers of your liberal legal education. But when one comes out into the world, one sees the country's reputation reeling from the damage that has been done and one hears one's friends and family saying, 'What could you have been *thinking* of, to have been a party to all this?' I do not want to anticipate the answer to any of the hard legal questions that have to be faced, in relation to the war on terror and other issues. But I do want to say that we may all have reason to regret what we say or write on these issues, if we lose our bearings so far as the Rule of Law is concerned.

Whether I am right or wrong in the particular analysis I have given, the Rule of Law is an important scruple to hang onto in a situation like that, a key not only to moral health but also professional honor. Our self-esteem may initially be bound up with the skills and clever opinions that we pledge to our unscrupulous bosses, like the Robert Duvall character in the movie, *The Godfather*. But our honor—as legal professionals—is bound up with something beyond that. It is bound up with the ethos of the Rule of Law and what I have wanted to argue—in what I am afraid is more in the nature of a sermon than a lecture on international law—is that that intimate connection between the Rule of Law and good lawyering in government service applies equally in the international realm as it does in constitutional law or administrative law or anywhere else.

Bibliography

ALFORD, C. FRED, 'Levinas and Political Theory,' *Political Theory*, 32 (2004), 146.

ALSTON, PHILIP, *Report of the Special Rapporteur on Extrajudicial, Summary or Arbitrary Executions: Mission to Israel and Lebanon* (2 October 2006).

AMAR, AKHIL REED, 'Some New World Lessons for the Old World,' *University of Chicago Law Review*, 58 (1991), 483.

AN-NA'IM, ABDULLAHI A., 'Toward a Cross-Cultural Approach to Defining International Standards of Human Rights: The Meaning of Cruel, Inhuman, or Degrading Treatment or Punishment' in An-Na'im (ed.), *Human Rights in Cross-Cultural Perspectives* 19.

——(ed.), *Human Rights in Cross-Cultural Perspectives: A Quest for Consensus* (University of Pennsylvania Press, 1992).

ANGELL, JULIE, 'Ethics, Torture, and Marginal Memoranda at the DOJ Office of Legal Counsel,' *Georgetown Journal of Legal Ethics*, 18 (2005), 557.

ANONYMOUS, 'The Suspension of Habeas Corpus during the War of the Rebellion,' *Political Science Quarterly*, 3 (1888), 454.

ARAI-TAKAHASHI, YUTAKA, 'Grading Scale of Degradation: Identifying the Threshold of Degrading Treatment or Punishment under Article 3 ECHR,' *Netherlands Quarterly of Human Rights*, 21 (2003), 385.

ARENDT, HANNAH, *The Origins of Totalitarianism*, New edition (Harcourt Brace Jovanovich, 1973).

——, *The Life of the Mind* (Harcourt Brace Jovanovich, 1978).

ASAD, TALAL, 'On Torture, or Cruel, Inhuman, and Degrading Treatment', in Wilson (ed.), *Human Rights, Culture and Context*, 111.

AUSTIN, J.L., 'A Plea for Excuses,' [1956–7] *Proceedings of the Aristotelian Society*, 1.

BALKIN, JACK M., 'Brown as Icon,' in Balkin (ed.), *What* Brown v. Board of Education *Should Have Said*, 3.

——(ed.), *What* Brown v. Board of Education *Should Have Said: The Nation's Top Legal Experts Rewrite America's Landmark Civil Rights Decision* (New York University Press, 2001).

BANNER, STUART, 'The Second Amendment, So Far,' *Harvard Law Review*, 117 (2004), 898.

BASSIOUNI, M. CHERIF, *Crimes against Humanity in International Criminal Law* (Springer, 1992).

BENTHAM, JEREMY, 'Principles of the Civil Code,' in Bentham, *The Theory of Legislation*, 109.

——, *The Theory of Legislation*, C.K. Ogden (ed.), (Routledge and Kegan Paul, 1931).

——, *An Introduction to the Principles of Morals and Legislation*, J.H. Burns and H.L.A. Hart (eds), (Athlone Press, 1970).

——, 'Anarchical Fallacies' (excerpted in Waldron, *Nonsense Upon Stilts*, 53).

BERLIN, ISAIAH, *Four Essays on Liberty* (Oxford University Press, 1969).

BERNDT, THOMAS F., 'Ghost Detainees: Does the Isolation and Interrogation of Detainees Violate Common Article 3 of the Geneva Conventions?' *William Mitchell Law Review*, 33 (2007), 1717.

BETTS, RICHARD K., 'Systems for Peace or Causes of War? Collective Security, Arms Control, and the New Europe,' *International Security*, 17 (1992), 5.

BILDER, RICHARD B. and VAGTS, DETLEV F., 'Speaking Law to Power: Lawyers and Torture,' *American Journal International Law*, 98 (2004), 689.

BLACKSTONE, WILLIAM, *Commentaries on the Laws of England* (University of Chicago Press, 1979).

BOULLE, PIERRE, *The Bridge Over The River Kwai* (Random House, 2007).

BOWDEN, MARK, 'The Dark Art of Interrogation,' *Atlantic Monthly*, October 2003, 51.

BROWNLIE, IAN, *Principles of Public International Law*, 6th edition (Oxford University Press, 2003).

BURKE, EDMUND 'Speech in General Reply (on the impeachment of Warren Hastings, Esq.),' May 28, 1794), in Burke, *The Works of the Right Honorable Edmund Burke*, Vol. 11, 157.

——, *The Works of the Right Honorable Edmund Burke,* Revised edition (Little, Brown and Co., 1867).

BUTLER, JOSEPH, *Fifteen Sermons Preached at the Rolls Chapel,* 4th edition (John and Paul Knapton, 1749).

BYBEE, JAY, 'Standards of Conduct for Interrogation under 18 U.S.C. 2340–2340A,' Memorandum from the Justice Department's Office of Legal Counsel for Alberto R. Gonzales, counsel to President Bush. August 1, 2002 (also in Greenberg and Dratel (eds), *The Torture Papers*, 172).

CHAYES, ABRAM, 'A Common Lawyer Looks at International Law,' *Harvard Law Review*, 78 (1965), 1396.

COADY, C.A.J., 'Terrorism and Innocence,' *The Journal of Ethics*, 8 (2004), 37.

COHEN, JAMES A., 'Lawyer Role, Agency Law, and the Characterization "Officer of the Court"' *Buffalo Law Review*, 48 (2000), 349.

COHEN, MARSHALL (ed.), *Ronald Dworkin and Contemporary Jurisprudence* (Duckworth, 1983).

COLE, DAVID, 'Enemy Aliens,' *Stanford Law Review,* 54 (2002), 953.

——, 'Their Liberties, Our Security,' *Boston Review*, December 2002/January 2003.

COMEY, JAMES B., 'Fighting Terrorism and Preserving Civil Liberties,' *University of Richmond Law Review*, 40 (2006) 403.

CONNOLLY, W.E., *The Terms of Political Discourse*, 3rd edition (Princeton University Press, 1993).

COUNCIL OF EUROPE, *Collected Edition of the 'Travaux Préparatoires' of the European Convention on Human Rights*, Vol. II (August–November 1949) (The Hague: Martinus Nijhoff, 1975).

COVER, ROBERT, *Justice Accused: Antislavery and the Judicial Process* (Yale University Press, 1975).

——, 'Violence and the Word,' *Yale Law Journal*, 95 (1986), 160.

CRANSTON, MAURICE, 'Human Rights, Real and Supposed,' in Raphael (ed.), *Political Theory and the Rights of Man*, 43.

DANNER, MARK, *Torture and Truth: America, Abu Ghraib, and the War on Terror* (New York Review Books, 2004).

DAYAN, COLIN, *The Story of Cruel and Unusual* (Boston Review, 2007).

DERSHOWITZ, ALAN, *Shouting Fire: Civil Liberties in a Turbulent Age* (Little Brown, 2002).

——, *Why Terrorism Works: Understanding the Threat, Responding to the Challenge* (Yale University Press, 2002).

——, 'When Torture Is The Least Evil Of Terrible Options,' *The Times Higher Education Supplement*, June 11, 2004, p. 20.

——, 'Tortured Reasoning,' in Levinson (ed.), *Torture: A Collection*, 257.

DICEY, A.V., *Introduction to the Study of the Law of the Constitution* (Liberty Classics edition, 1982).

DUGARD, JOHN, 'International Terrorism: Some Problems of Definition,' *International Affairs*, 50 (1974), 67.

DUXBURY, NEIL, *Patterns of American Jurisprudence* (Oxford University Press, 1995).

DWORKIN, RONALD, *Taking Rights Seriously*, Revised edition (Harvard University Press, 1977).

——, 'Principle, Policy, Procedure,' in Dworkin, *A Matter of Principle* (Harvard University Press, 1985).

——, *A Matter of Principle* (Cambridge: Harvard University Press, 1985), 87.

——, *Law's Empire* (Harvard University Press, 1986).

——, *Life's Dominion: An Argument about Abortion, Euthanasia, and Individual Freedom* (Alfred A. Knopf, 1993).

——, *Freedom's Law: The Moral Reading of the American Constitution* (Harvard University Press, 1996).

——, 'Comment' in Scalia, *A Matter of Interpretation*, 115.

——, *Sovereign Virtue: The Theory and Practice of Equality* (Harvard University Press, 2000).

——, 'The Threat to Patriotism,' *New York Review of Books*, February 28, 2002.

D'ZURILLA, WILLIAM T., 'Individual Responsibility for Torture under International Law,' *Tulane Law Review*, 56 (1981), 186.

ELKINS, CAROLINE, *Imperial Reckoning: The Untold Story of Britain's Gulag in Kenya* (Henry Holt, 2005).

ELSHTAIN, JEAN BETHKE, 'Reflection on the Problem of "Dirty Hands,"' in Levinson (ed.), *Torture: A Collection*, 77.

ELSTER, JON, *Alchemies of the Mind: Rationality and the Emotions* (Cambridge University Press, 1999).

——, 'Fear, Terror, and Liberty: A Conceptual Framework,' paper prepared for the seminar on 'Terrorism and Civil Liberties,' at Columbia University, Spring 2006 (unpublished manuscript on file with author).

EVANS, MALCOLM and MORGAN, RODNEY, *Preventing Torture: A Study of the European Convention for the Prevention of Torture and Inhuman or Degrading Treatment or Punishment* (Oxford University Press, 1998).

FALLON, RICHARD H., 'Reflections on the Hart and Wechsler Paradigm,' *Vanderbilt Law Review*, 47 (1994) 953.

FANON, FRANTZ, *The Wretched of the Earth* (Grove Press, 1966).

FEIGENSON, NEIL et al., 'Perceptions of Terrorism and Disease Risk: A Cross-National Comparison,' *Missouri Law Review*, 69 (2004), 991.

FINNIS, JOHN, *Natural Law and Natural Rights* (Clarendon Press, Oxford, 1980).

FOOT, PHILIPPA, 'Moral Arguments' in Foot, *Virtues and Vices*, 96.

——, 'Moral Beliefs' in Foot, *Virtues and Vices*, 110.

——, *Virtues and Vices, and Other Essays in Moral Philosophy* (Oxford University Press, 2002).

FORCESE, CRAIG, 'A New Geography of Abuse,' *Berkeley Journal of International Law*, 24 (2006), 908.

FRANK, JEROME, *Law and the Modern Mind* (Peter Smith, 1970).

FRANKENA, W.K., 'The Naturalistic Fallacy,' *Mind*, 48 (1939), 464.

FREY, RAY and MORRIS, CHRISTOPHER (eds), *Violence, Terrorism, and Justice* (Cambridge: Cambridge University Press, 1991).

FULLER, LON L., *The Morality of Law*, Revised edition (Yale University Press, 1969).

FYFE, JAMES and SKOLNICK, JEROME, *Above the Law: Police and the Excessive Use of Force* (Free Press, 1993).

GAETKE, EUGENE R. 'Lawyers as Officers of the Court,' *Vanderbilt Law Review*, 42 (1989) 39.

GENTILI, ALBERICO, *On the Law of War* (Carew translation, Hein Online, last accessed January 5, 2010).

GEORGE, ROBERT P. (ed.), *The Autonomy of Law: Essays on Legal Positivism* (Oxford University Press, 1996).

GIGERENZER, G., 'Dread Risk, September 11, and Fatal Traffic Accidents,' *Psychological Science*, 15 (2004), 286.

GOLDSMITH, JACK, *The Terror Presidency: Law and Judgment Inside the Bush Administration* (W.W. Norton & Company, 2007).

GOLDSMITH, JACK and POSNER, ERIC A., *The Limits of International Law* (Oxford University Press, 2005).

GOMIEN, DONNA, HARRIS, DAVID, and ZWAAK, LEO, *Law and Practice of the European Convention on Human Rights and the European Social Charter* (Council of Europe, 1996).

GOODIN, ROBERT, *Political Theory and Public Policy* (University of Chicago Press, 1982).

GRANT, W.W., 'Suspension of the Habeas Corpus in Strikes,' *Virginia Law Review*, 3 (1916), 249.

GRANUCCI, ANTHONY F., 'Nor Cruel and Unusual Punishment Inflicted: The Original Meaning,' *California Law Review*, 57 (1969), 839.

GREENBERG, KAREN (ed.), *The Torture Debate in America* (Cambridge University Press, 2006).

GREENBERG, KAREN J. and DRATEL, JOSHUA L. (eds), *The Torture Papers: The Road to Abu Ghraib* (Cambridge University Press, 2005).

GREY, THOMAS, 'Langdell's Orthodoxy,' *University of Pittsburgh Law Review*, 45 (1989), 1.

GRICE, PAUL, *Studies in the Way of Words* (Harvard University Press, 1989).

GRIFFITHS, A. PHILIPS (ed.), *Of Liberty* (Cambridge University Press, 1983).

GRISWOLD, ERWIN, *The Fifth Amendment Today: Three Speeches* (Harvard University Press, 1955).

GROSS, OREN, 'Are Torture Warrants Warranted? Pragmatic Absolutism and Official Disobedience,' *Minnesota Law Review*, 88 (2004), 1481.

GROTIUS, HUGO, *The Rights of War and Peace*, Richard Tuck (ed.), (Liberty Press, 2005).

HALBERT, SHERRILL, 'The Suspension of the Writ of Habeas Corpus by President Lincoln,' *American Journal of Legal History*, 2 (1958), 95.

HAMILTON, ALEXANDER, MADISON, JAMES, and JAY, JOHN, *The Federalist Papers*, Isaac Kramnick (ed.), (Penguin Books, 1987).

HAMPTON, JEAN, *Hobbes and the Social Contract Tradition* (Cambridge University Press, 1988).

HANDL, GUNTHER F. et al., 'A Hard Look at Soft Law,' *American Society of International Law Proceedings*, 82 (1988), 371.

HARE, R.M., *Moral Thinking: Its Levels, Method, and Point* (Oxford University Press, 1982).

HARLOW, CAROL and RAWLINGS, RICHARD, *Law and Administration* (Butterworths, 1984).

HARRIS, BRUCE, 'The Third Source of Authority for Government Action,' *Law Quarterly Review*, 109 (1992), 626.

HARRIS, D.J., O'BOYLE, M., and WARBRICK, C., *Law of the European Convention on Human Rights* (Oxford University Press, 1995).

HARSANYI, JOHN C., 'Can the Maximin Principle Serve as a Basis for Morality? A Critique of John Rawls's Theory,' *American Political Science Review*, 69 (1975), 594.

HART, HENRY M. and SACKS, ALBERT, *The Legal Process: Basic Problems in the Making and Application of Law*, William N. Eskridge and Philip P. Frickey (eds), (Foundation Press, 1994).

HART, H.L.A., 'Positivism and the Separation of Law and Morals,' *Harvard Law Review*, 71 (1958), 593.

——, *Punishment and Responsibility: Essays in the Philosophy of Law* (Oxford University Press, 1963).

——, 'Rawls on Liberty and its Priority,' *University Of Chicago Law Review*, 40 (1972–73), 534.

——, *The Concept of Law*, Revised edition, Joseph Raz and Penelope Bulloch (eds), (Clarendon Press, 1994).

HAYEK, F.A., *The Constitution of Liberty* (University of Chicago Press, 1960).

HAYNES, WILLIAM J., 'Action memo: Counter-Resistance Techniques' (for Secretary of Defense, from General Counsel of the Department of Defense), November 27, 2002.

HELD, VIRGINIA, 'Terrorism and War,' *Journal of Ethics*, 8 (2004), 59.

HENKIN, LOUIS et al., *International Law: Cases and Materials*, 3rd edition (West Publishing, 1993).

HEYMAN, PHILIP B., *Terrorism, Freedom and Security: Winning without War* (MIT Press, 2003).

HILL, THOMAS, 'Making Exceptions without Abandoning the Principle: or How a Kantian Might Think About Terrorism,' in Frey and Morris (eds), *Violence, Terrorism, and Justice*.

HO, JAMES C., Memorandum to John C. Yoo, Deputy Assistant Attorney-General, 'Possible Interpretations of Common Article 3 of the 1949 Geneva Convention Relative to the Treatment of Prisoners of War' (Feb. 1, 2002).

HOBBES, THOMAS, *The Elements of Law, Natural And Politic*, J.C.A. Gaskin, (ed.), (Oxford University Press, 1994).

——, *Leviathan*, Revised student edition, Richard Tuck (ed.), (Cambridge University Press, 1996).

——, *On the Citizen*, Richard Tuck and Michael Silverthorne (eds), (Cambridge University Press, 1998).

HOGG, PETER and BUSHELL, ALLISON, 'The Charter Dialogue between Courts and Legislatures, Or Maybe the Charter of Rights Isn't Such a Bad Thing After All,' *Osgoode Hall Law Journal*, 35 (1997), 75.

HOLMES, OLIVER WENDELL, 'The Path of the Law,' *Boston University Law Review*, 78 (1998), 699.

HOLMES, STEPHEN, *The Matador's Cape: America's Reckless Response to Terror* (Harvard University Press, 2006).

HONDERICH, TED, *Violence for Equality: Inquiries in Political Philosophy* (Routledge, 1989).

——, *After the Terror*, Revised edition (Edinburgh University Press, 2003).

HORTON, SCOTT, 'Through a Mirror, Darkly,' in Greenberg (ed.), *The Torture Debate in America*.

HOWE, MARK DEWOLFE (ed.), *Holmes-Laski Letters: The Correspondence of Mr. Justice Holmes and Harold J. Laski 1916–1935*.

HOYT, EDWIN, *Inferno: The Fire-Bombing of Japan* (Madison Books, 2000).

HUME, DAVID, *A Treatise of Human Nature*, L.A. Selby-Bigge and P. H. Nidditch (eds), 2nd edition (Clarendon Press, 1978).

——, *An Enquiry Concerning the Principles Of Morals* in Hume, *Enquiries*, 167.

——, *Enquiries Concerning the Human Understanding and Concerning the Principles of Morals*, L.A. Selby Bigge (ed.), (Oxford University Press, 1902).

HUTCHINSON, MARTHA CRENSHAW, 'The Concept of Revolutionary Terrorism,' *Journal of Conflict Resolution*, 16 (1972), 385.

ISSACHAROFF, SAMUEL and PILDES, RICHARD H., 'Emergency Contexts without Emergency Powers: The United States' Constitutional Approach to Rights during Wartime,' *International Journal of Constitutional Law*, 2 (2004), 296.

JACKSON, FRANK and SMITH, MICHAEL (eds), *Oxford Handbook of Contemporary Philosophy* (Oxford University Press, 2005).

JUNG, CARL, *Memories, Dreams, Reflections*, Aniela Jaffe (ed.), Richard Winston and Clara Winston (trans.), (Vintage, 1961).

KADISH, SANFORD H., 'Torture, the State and the Individual,' *Israel Law Review*, 23 (1989), 345.

KAHANA, TSVI, 'The Notwithstanding Mechanism and Public Discussion: Lessons from the Ignored Practice of Section 33 of the Charter,' *Canadian Public Administration*, 44 (2001), 255.

KAMM, F.M., 'Conflicts of Rights: Typology, Methodology and Non-consequentialism,' *Legal Theory*, 7 (2001), 239.

KANT, IMMANUEL, *Perpetual Peace*, Lewis White Beck (ed.), (Bobbs Merrill, 1957).

——, *The Metaphysics of Morals*, Mary Gregor (trans.), (Cambridge University Press, 1991).

——, *Groundwork of the Metaphysics of Morals*, Mary Gregor (ed.), (Cambridge University Press, 1998).

KELSEN, HANS, 'Collective Security and Collective Self-Defense under the Charter of the United Nations,' *American Journal of International Law*, 42 (1948), 783.

——, *Introduction to the Problems of Legal Theory*, Bonnie Litschewski Paulson and Stanley Paulson (trans.), (Oxford University Press, 1992).

KENNEDY, DUNCAN, 'Form and Substance in Private Law Adjudication,' *Harvard Law Review*, 89 (1976), 1685.

KIRKLAND, KARL, 'Efficacy of Post-divorce Mediation and Evaluation Services,' *Alabama Lawyer*, 65 (2004), 187.

KRAUT, RICHARD, *Socrates and the State* (Princeton University Press, 1987).

KRAUTHAMMER, CHARLES, 'The Truth about Torture: It's Time to be Honest about Doing Terrible Things,' *The Weekly Standard*, December 5, 2005.

KREIMER, SETH, 'Too Close to the Rack and the Screw: Constitutional Constraints on Torture in the War on Terror,' *University of Pennsylvania Journal of Constitutional Law*, 6 (2003), 278.

KROPOTKIN, PETR ALEKSEEVICH, *Paroles d'un Révolte* (C. Marpon et E. Flammarion, 1885).

KYMLICKA, WILL, *Liberalism, Community, and Culture* (Clarendon Press, 1989).

——, *Contemporary Political Philosophy: An Introduction* (Oxford University Press, 1991).

LANDAU COMMISSION, 'Report of Commission of Inquiry into the Methods of Investigation of the General Security Service Regarding Hostile Terrorist Activity (1987),' *Israel Law Review*, 23 (1989), 146.

LANGBEIN, JOHN H., *Torture and the Law of Proof: Europe and England in the Ancien Régime* (University of Chicago Press, 1977).

LASLETT, PETER et al. (eds), *Philosophy, Politics and Society*, 4th series (Basil Blackwell, 1972).

LAZREG, MARINA, *Torture and the Twilight of Empire: From Algiers to Baghdad* (Princeton University Press, 2008).

LEVINAS, EMMANUEL, 'Sur l'esprit de Genève,' in Levinas, *Les imprévus de l'histoire*, 159.

——, *Les imprévus de l'histoire* (Fata Morgana, 1994).

LEVINSON, SANFORD, ' "Precommitment" and "Postcommitment": The Ban on Torture in the Wake of September 11,' *Texas Law Review*, 81 (2003), 2013.

——, 'In Quest of a "Common Conscience": Reflections on the Current Debate about Torture,' *Journal of National Security Law and Policy*, 1 (2005), 231.

——(ed.), *Torture: A Collection* (Oxford University Press, 2006).

LEWIS, C.S., *The Problem of Pain* (Harper, 1940).

LEWIS, DAVID, *Convention* (Wiley-Blackwell, 1986).

LOADER, IAN and WALKER, NEIL, 'Policing as a Public Good: Reconstituting the Connections between Policing and the State,' *Theoretical Criminology*, 5 (2001), 9.

——, *Civilizing Security* (Cambridge University Press, 2007).

LOCKE, JOHN, *An Essay Concerning Human Understanding*, Peter H. Nidditch (ed.), (Oxford University Press, 1975).

——, *Two Treatises of Government,* Peter Laslett (ed.), (Cambridge University Press, 1988).

LODE, ERIC, 'Slippery Slope Arguments and Legal Reasoning,' *California Law Review*, 87 (1999), 1469.

LOEWENSTEIN, GEORGE, 'Out of Control: Visceral Influences on Behavior,' *Organizational Behavior and Human Decision-Processes*, 65 (1996), 272.

LUBAN, DAVID, 'Liberalism, Torture, and the Ticking Bomb,' *Virginia Law Review*, 91 (2005), 1425.

LUTHER, MARTIN, *Lectures on Deuteronomy* in Luther, *Luther's Works*, Vol. 9.

——, *Luther's Works*, Jaroslav Pelikan (ed.), and Richard R. Caemmerer (trans.), (Concordia, 1994).

MCCARTHY, ANDREW, 'The International-Law Trap: What Europe Thinks is "Cruel, Inhuman, and Degrading" doesn't Govern us,' *National Review*, December 12, 2005.

MCGINNIS, JOHN and SOMAN, ILYA, 'Should International Law be Part of our Law?' *Stanford Law Review*, 59 (2007), 1175.

MCMAHAN, JEFFREY, 'The Ethics of Killing in War,' *Ethics*, 114 (2004), 693.

MCMAHON, CHRISTOPHER, 'The Paradox of Deontology,' *Philosophy and Public Affairs*, 20 (1991), 350.

MARCUSE, HERBERT, *One-Dimensional Man: Studies in the Ideology of Advanced Industrial Society* (Beacon Press, 1964).

MARGALIT, AVISHAI, *The Decent Society* (Harvard University Press, 1996).

—— and WALZER, MICHAEL, 'Israel: Civilians and Combatants,' *New York Review of Books*, May 14, 2009.

MARMOR, ANDREI, 'Deep Conventions,' *Philosophy and Phenomenological Research*, 74 (2007), 586.

MAVRODES, GEORGE, 'Conventions and the Morality of War,' *Philosophy and Public Affairs*, 4 (1975), 117.

MAYER, JANE, *The Dark Side: The Inside Story of how the War on Terror Turned into a War on American Ideals* (Doubleday, 2008).

MEISELS, TAMAR, 'Torture and the Problem of Dirty Hands,' *Canadian Journal of Law and Jurisprudence*, 21 (2008) 149.

——, *The Trouble with Terror: Liberty, Security, and the Response to Terrorism* (Cambridge University Press, 2008).

MENARD, RICHARD H., 'Ten Reasonable Men,' *American Criminal Law Review*, 38 (2001), 179.

MEYERFIELD, JAMIE, 'Playing by our own Rules: How U.S. Marginalization of International Human Rights Law Led to Torture,' *Harvard Human Rights Journal*, 20 (2007), 89.

MICKOLUS, EDWARD F., 'Terrorists, Governments, and Numbers,' *Journal of Conflict Resolution*, 31 (1987), 56.

MILLER, DAVID (ed.), *Liberty* (Oxford University Press, 1991).

MONTESQUIEU, CHARLES LOUIS SECONDAT DE, *The Spirit of the Laws*, Anne Cohler et al. (eds), (Cambridge University Press, 1989).

MOORE, G.E., *Principia Ethica* (Cambridge University Press, 1903).

MORGAN, GLYN, *The Idea of a European Superstate: Public Justification and European Integration* (Princeton University Press, 2005).

MOWBRAY, ALASTAIR, *Cases and Materials on the European Convention on Human Rights*, 2nd edition (Oxford University Press, 2007).

MURPHY, JOHN F., *The United States and the Rule of Law in International Affairs* (Cambridge University Press, 2004).

NAGEL, THOMAS, 'Autonomy and Deontology,' in Scheffler (ed.), *Consequentialism and its Critics*, 142.

NANDA, VED P., 'Preemptive and Preventive Use of Force, Collective Security, and Human Security,' *Denver Journal of International Law and Policy*, 33 (2004), 7.

NEUMAN, GERALD, 'Human Rights and Constitutional Rights: Harmony and Dissonance,' *Stanford Law Review*, 55 (2003), 1863.

NICHOLS, MARY P., 'Rousseau's Novel Education in the *Émile*,' *Political Theory*, 13 (1985), 539.

NICKEL, JAMES and HASSE, LIZBETH, 'Review of *Basic Rights* by Henry Shue,' *California Law Review*, 69 (1981), 1569.

NOLTE, GEORGE (ed.), *European and US Constitutionalism* (Cambridge University Press, 2005).

NOVOTNE, ALFRED H., 'Random Bombing of Public Places: Extradition and Punishment of Indiscriminate Violence against Innocent Parties,' *Boston University International Law Journal*, 6 (1988), 219.

NOZICK, ROBERT, 'Coercion' in Laslett et al. (eds), *Philosophy, Politics and Society*, 101.

——, *Anarchy, State, and Utopia* (Basil Blackwell, 1974).

O'CONNELL, MARY ELLEN, *The Power and Purpose of International Law* (Oxford University Press, 2008).

O'DONOVAN, OLIVER, *The Ways of Judgment* (Eerdmans, 2005).

OLSON, MANCUR, *The Logic of Collective Action: Public Goods and the Theory of Groups* (Harvard University Press, 1971).

OPPENHEIM, L., *International Law: A Treatise*, 7th edition (Lawbook Exchange, 1948).

OVEY, CLAIRE and WHITE, ROBIN, *European Convention on Human Rights*, 3rd edition (Oxford University Press, 2002).

PARFIT, DEREK, *Reason and Persons* (Oxford University Press, 1984).

PARKS, W. HAYS, 'Teaching the Law of War,' *Army Lawyer*, Department of the Army Pamphlet 27-50-174 (1987).

PETERS, EDWARD, *Torture*, Expanded edition (University of Pennsylvania Press, 1996).

PLATO, *The Crito* in Plato, *The Last Days of Socrates*, 71.

——, *The Last Days of Socrates* (Penguin Books, 1954).

POLLAK, LOUIS H., 'Proposals to Curtail Federal Habeas Corpus for State Prisoners: Collateral Attack on the Great Writ,' *Yale Law Journal*, 66 (1956), 50.

POSNER, ERIC and VERMEULE, ADRIAN, *Terror in the Balance: Security, Liberty, and the Courts* (Oxford University Press, 2007).

POWERS, THOMAS, 'Can we be Secure and Free?' *The Public Interest*, issue 151 (Spring 2003), 3.

POZEN, DAVID E., 'The Mosaic Theory, National Security, and the Freedom of Information Act,' *Yale Law Journal*, 115 (2005), 628.

PRESIDENT'S COMMISSION ON LAW ENFORCEMENT AND ADMINISTRATION OF JUSTICE, *The Challenge of Crime in a Free Society* (1967).

PUBLIC COMMITTEE AGAINST TORTURE IN ISRAEL, *Torture in Israel/Palestine: The Black Book* (Pluto Press, 2002).

RAPACZYNSKI, ANDRZEJ, *Nature and Politics: Liberalism in the Philosophies of Hobbes, Locke, and Rousseau* (Cornell University Press, 1987).

RAPHAEL, D.D. (ed.), *Political Theory and the Rights of Man* (Macmillan, 1967).

——, *Problems of Political Philosophy*, Revised edition (Humanities Press International, 1976).

RAPOPORT, DAVID C., 'Fear and Trembling: Terrorism in Three Religious Traditions,' *American Political Science Review*, 77 (1983), 658.

RAWLS, JOHN, *Political Liberalism* (Columbia University Press, 1986).

——, *A Theory of Justice*, Revised edition (Harvard University Press, 1999).

RAZ, JOSEPH, 'The Rule of Law and its Virtue,' in Raz, *The Authority Of Law*, 210.

——, *The Authority Of Law: Essays On Law And Morality* (Clarendon Press, 1979).

——, *The Morality of Freedom* (Clarendon Press, 1986).

——, *Practical Reason and Norms,* New edition (Clarendon Press, 1999).

——, 'Intention in Interpretation,' in George (ed.), *The Autonomy of Law*, 249.

——, 'Legal Principles and the Limits of Law,' in Cohen (ed.), *Ronald Dworkin and Contemporary Jurisprudence*, 73.

RÉAUME, DENISE, 'Individuals, Groups, and Rights to Public Goods,' *University of Toronto Law Journal*, 38 (1988), 1.

RIZZO, MARIO J. and WHITMAN, DOUGLAS GLEN, 'The Camel's Nose is in the Tent: Rules, Theories, and Slippery Slopes,' *UCLA Law Review*, 51 (2003), 539.

ROSENBLUM, NANCY (ed.), *Liberalism and the Moral Life* (Harvard University Press, 1989).

ROSS, JEFFREY IAN and GURR, TED ROBERT, 'Why Terrorism Subsides: A Comparative Study of Canada and the United States,' *Comparative Politics*, 21 (1989), 405.

ROTH, BRAD, *Governmental Illegitimacy in International Law* (Oxford University Press, 1999).

ROUSSEAU, JEAN-JACQUES, *A Discourse on Inequality*, Maurice Cranston (trans.), (Penguin Books, 1984).

——, *Émile*, Allan Bloom (trans.), (Basic Books, 1979).

RUBIN, EDWARD and FEELEY, MALCOLM, 'Judicial Policy Making and Litigation against the Government,' *University of Pennsylvania Journal of Constitutional Law*, 5 (2003), 617.

SAAR, ERIK and NOVAK, VIVECA, *Inside the Wire: A Military Intelligence Soldier's Eyewitness Account of Life at Guantanamo* (The Penguin Press, 2005).

SARAT, AUSTIN and KEARNS, THOMAS, 'A Journey through Forgetting: Toward a Jurisprudence of Violence,' in Sarat and Kearns (eds), *The Fate Of Law*.

——(eds), *The Fate Of Law* (University of Michigan Press, 1993).

SAUL, BEN, 'Defending "Terrorism": Justifications and Excuses for Terrorism in International Criminal Law,' University of Sydney Law School, Legal Studies Research Paper 08/122 (October 2008), available at <http://ssrn.com/abstract=1291584>.

SCALIA, ANTONIN, *A Matter of Interpretation: Federal Courts and the Law* (Princeton University Press, 1997).

SCHAUER, FREDERICK, 'Slippery Slopes,' *Harvard Law Review*, 99 (1985), 361.

SCHEFFLER, SAMUEL, 'Agent-Centered Restrictions, Rationality, and the Virtues,' *Mind*, 94 (1985), 409.

——(ed.), *Consequentialism and its Critics* (Oxford University Press, 1988).

——, 'Is Terrorism Morally Distinctive?' *Journal of Political Philosophy*, 14 (2006), 1.

SCHEPPELE, KIM, 'Hypothetical Torture in the War on Terrorism,' *Journal of National Security Law and Policy*, 1 (2005), 285.

SCHLINK, BERNHARD, 'The Problem with "Torture Lite",' *Cardozo Law Review*, 29 (2007), 85.

SCHMID, ALEX P., *Political Terrorism: a Research Guide to Concepts, Theories, Databases, and Literature* (Transaction Books, 1983).

SCHMIDT, CHRISTOPHER J., 'Could a CIA or FBI Agent Be Quartered in Your House During a War on Terrorism, Iraq or North Korea?' *St Louis University Law Journal*, 48 (2004), 587.

SCHMUCK, RUDOLF, 'The European Committee for the Prevention of Torture and Inhuman or Degrading Treatment or Punishment (CPT)— Fundamentals, Structure, Objectives, Potentialities, Limits,' *Journal of the Institute of Justice and International Studies*, 1 (2002), 69.

SEBALD, W.G., *On the Natural History of Destruction* (Random House, 2003).

SEN, AMARTYA, 'Rights and Agency' in Scheffler (ed.), *Consequentialism and its Critics*, 186.

SHKLAR, JUDITH, 'The Liberalism of Fear,' in Rosenblum (ed.), *Liberalism and the Moral Life*, 21.

SHUE, HENRY, 'Torture,' *Philosophy and Public Affairs*, 7 (1978), 124.

——, *Basic Rights: Subsistence, Affluence, and U.S. Foreign Policy* (Princeton University Press, 1980).

SHUE, HENRY, *Basic Rights*, 2nd edition (Princeton University Press, 1999).

——, 'Preemption, Prevention, and Predation: Why the Bush Strategy Is Dangerous,' *Philosophic Exchange* (2005).

SLAUGHTER, ANNE-MARIE, 'Security, Solidarity, and Sovereignty: The Grand Themes of UN Reform,' *American Journal of International Law*, 99 (2005), 619.

SMITH, TARA, 'On Deriving Rights to Goods from Rights to Freedom,' *Law and Philosophy*, 11 (1992), 217.

STATMAN, DANIEL, 'Targeted Killing,' *Theoretical Inquiries in Law*, 5 (2004), 179.

STEINER, HILLEL, 'The Structure of a Set of Compossible Rights,' *Journal of Philosophy*, 74 (1977), 767.

——, 'How Free? Computing Personal Liberty,' in Griffiths (ed.), *Of Liberty*.

——, An Essay on Rights (Basil Blackwell, 1994).

STEPHEN, JAMES FITZJAMES, *A History of the Criminal Law of England* (Routledge, 1996).

STEPHEN, LESLIE, *The Science of Ethics* (G.P. Putnam's sons, 1907).

STEVENSON, C.L., 'Persuasive Definitions,' *Mind*, 47 (1938), 331.

STRAUSS, MARCY, 'Torture,' *New York Law School Law Review*, 48 (2003/2004), 203.

SULLIVAN, KATHLEEN M., 'The Supreme Court, 1991 Term—Foreword: The Justices of Rules and Standards,' *Harvard Law Review*, 106 (1992), 22.

SUSSMAN, DAVID, 'What's Wrong with Torture?' *Philosophy and Public Affairs*, 33 (2005), 1.

TOMKINS, ADAM, 'Legislating against Terror: the Anti-terrorism, Crime, and Security Act 2001,' *Public Law* [2002], 106

TRAYNOR, MICHAEL, 'Citizenship in a Time of Repression,' *Wisconsin Law Review*, 3 (2005), 1.

TRIBE, LAWRENCE, 'Trial by Fury: Why Congress must Curb Bush's Military Courts,' *The New Republic*, December 10, 2001.

TVERSKY, AMOS, 'Assessing Uncertainty,' *Journal of the Royal Statistical Society, Series B (Methodological)*, 36 (1974), 148.

TWINING, WILLIAM, 'Bentham on Torture,' *Northern Ireland Legal Quarterly*, 24 (1973), 305.

——, 'Torture and Philosophy,' *Proceedings of the Aristotelian Society, Supplement*, 52 (1978), 143.

VAN DER VYVER, JOHAN D., 'Torture as a Crime under International Law,' *Albany Law Review*, 67 (2003), 427.

VILLA, DANA, *Politics, Philosophy, Terror: Essays on the Thought of Hannah Arendt* (Princeton University Press, 1999).

VLASTOS, GREGORY, 'Justice and Equality,' in Waldron (ed.), *Theories of Rights*, 41.

VOLOKH, EUGENE, 'Aside: *N* Guilty Men,' *University of Pennsylvania Law Review*, 146 (1997), 173.

——, 'The Mechanisms of the Slippery Slope,' *Harvard Law Review*, 16 (2003), 1026.

WALDRON, JEREMY (ed.), *Theories of Rights* (Oxford University Press, 1984).

——, *Nonsense Upon Stilts: Bentham, Burke and Marx on the Rights of Man* (Methuen, 1987).

——, 'Rights in Conflict,' *Ethics*, 99 (1989), 503, reprinted in Waldron, *Liberal Rights*.

——, *The Law* (Routledge, 1990).

——, *Liberal Rights: Collected Papers 1981–1991* (Cambridge University Press, 1993).

——, 'Can Communal Goods be Human Rights?' in Waldron, *Liberal Rights*, 339.

——, 'Vagueness in Law and Language—Some Philosophical Perspectives,' *California Law Review*, 82 (1994), 509.

——, 'Transcendental Nonsense and System in the Law,' *Columbia Law Review*, 100 (2000) 16.

——, 'Does Law Promise Justice?' *Georgia State University Law Review*, 17 (2001), 59.

——, 'Is the Rule of Law an Essentially Contested Concept (in Florida)?' *Law and Philosophy*, 21 (2002), 137.

——, *God, Locke and Equality: Christian Foundations of John Locke's Political Thought* (Cambridge University Press, 2002).

——, 'Law' in Jackson and Smith (eds), *Oxford Handbook of Contemporary Philosophy*, 181.

——, 'Dignity and Rank,' *Archives Européennes de Sociologie*, 48 (2007), 201.

——, 'Is this Torture Necessary?' (reviewing David Cole and Jules Lobel, *Less Safe, Less Free: Why America Is Losing the War on Terror*), *New York Review of Books*, October 25, 2007.

——, 'Public Reason and "Justification" in the Courtroom,' *Journal of Law, Philosophy and Culture*, 1 (2007), 107.

——, 'The Image of God: Rights, Reason, and Order,' forthcoming in Witte and Alexander (eds), *Cambridge Companion to Christianity and Human Rights*.

——, 'Ius Gentium: A Defense of Gentili's Equation of the Law of Nations and the Law of Nature,' available at <http://ssrn.com/abstract=1280897>.

——, 'Review Article: Clean Torture by Modern Democracies,' *International History Review*, 31 (2009), 584.

WALKER, CLIVE, 'Cyber-Terrorism: Legal Principle and Law in the United Kingdom,' *Penn State Law Review*, 110 (2006), 625.

WALTERS, RON, 'The Black Experience with Terrorism,' *Howard Scroll: The Social Justice Law Review*, 6 (2003), 77.

WALZER, MICHAEL, *Spheres of Justice: A Defense of Pluralism and Equality* (Basic Books, 1983).

WEBER, MAX, *Economy and Society*, Guenther Roth and Claus Wittich (eds), (University of California Press, 1978).

WEDGWOOD, RUTH, 'International Criminal Law and Augusto Pinochet,' *Virginia Journal of International Law*, 40 (2000), 829.

WEINRIB, ERNEST J., 'Understanding Tort Law,' *Valparaiso University Law Review*, 23 (1989), 485.

——, *The Idea of Private Law* (Harvard University Press, 1995).

WEISBERG, RICHARD H., 'Loose Professionalism, or Why Lawyers Take the Lead on Torture,' in Levinson (ed.), *Torture*, 299.

WHITEHEAD, JOHN C., 'Terrorism—the Challenge and the Response,' *Journal of Palestine Studies*, 16 (1987), 215.

WHITMAN, JAMES Q., '"Human Dignity" in Europe and the United States: The Social Foundations,' in Nolte (ed.), *European and US Constitutionalism*, 108.

WILLIAMS, BERNARD, *In the Beginning was the Deed: Realism and Moralism in Political Argument* (Cambridge University Press, 2005).

WILLIAMS, DAVID C., *The Mythic Meanings of the Second Amendment: Taming Political Violence in a Constitutional Republic* (Yale University Press, 2003).

WILSON, RICHARD (ed.), *Human Rights, Culture and Context: Anthropological Perspectives* (Pluto Press, 1997).

WITTE, JOHN and ALEXANDER, FRANK (eds), *The Cambridge Companion to Christianity and Human Rights* (Cambridge University Press, forthcoming 2010).

WOLFERS, ARNOLD, '"National Security" as an Ambiguous Symbol,' *Political Science Quarterly*, 67 (1952), 481.

YOO, JOHN and DELAHUNTY, ROBERT, 'Application of Treaties and Laws to Al Qaeda and Taliban Detainees,' Memorandum for William J. Haynes, General Counsel, Department of Defense, January 9, 2002—also in Greenberg and Dratel (eds), *The Torture Papers*, 38.

Index

Note: note numbers in brackets are used to indicate the whereabouts on the page of sources quoted, but not named, in the text.